NEW ORLEANS
AFTER THE CIVIL WAR

NEW ORLEANS
AFTER THE CIVIL WAR

RACE, POLITICS, AND A NEW BIRTH
OF FREEDOM

JUSTIN A. NYSTROM

Johns Hopkins University Press

Baltimore

For the Virginia Tech Class of 2007 . . . ut prosim

Johns Hopkins Paperback edition, 2015
2   4   6   8   9   7   5   3   1

Johns Hopkins University Press
2715 North Charles Street
Baltimore, Maryland 21218-4363
www.press.jhu.edu

The Library of Congress has cataloged the hardcover edition
of this book as follows:

Nystrom, Justin A., 1970–
New Orleans after the Civil War : race, politics, and a new birth of
freedom / Justin A. Nystrom.
p. cm.
Includes bibliographical references and index.
ISBN-13: 978-0-8018-9434-3 (hardcover : acid-free paper)
ISBN-10: 0-8018-9434-4 (hardcover : acid-free paper)
1. New Orleans (La.)—History—19th century.   2. New Orleans
(La.)—Social conditions—19th century.   3. Reconstruction
(U.S. history, 1865–1877)—Louisiana—New Orleans.   I. Title.
F379.N557N97   2010
976.3′3506—dc22   2009028859

A catalog record for this book is available from the British Library.

ISBN-13: 978-1-4214-1697-7
ISBN-10: 1-4214-1697-2

Special discounts are available for bulk purchases of this book.
For more information, please contact Special Sales
at 410-516-6936 or specialsales@press.jhu.edu.

Johns Hopkins University Press uses environmentally friendly
book materials, including recycled text paper that is composed of
at least 30 percent post-consumer waste, whenever possible.

CONTENTS

Illustrations follow page 114.

ACKNOWLEDGMENTS

This project's humble beginnings came in a graduate seminar in 1999 taught by John Inscoe at the University of Georgia. Since then, many people have helped me transform it into the book you see today. Jim Cobb, my dissertation director and mentor in so many ways, gave sage counsel all along the way and held my feet to the fire long afterward so that I might finish that "damn manuscript." The support of my parents, Charles and Elsa Nystrom, did much to sustain my effort. So, too, did the generous credit terms of MasterCard and American Express, my primary sources of financial support for research activity. And, of course, my Jessica's telling me how brilliant my ideas were (and believing it) did much to bring this endeavor to its completion.

Many people from both inside and outside the historical profession have aided me at critical junctures. In 1999, while I was writing my master's thesis, Dennis Rousey of Arkansas State generously sent me copies of his research from his excellent work on the New Orleans police. That same year, David Villarrubia, of the Degas House, put a roof over my head while I did research. Moreover, through David I met Carl Lezak, plasterer, wedding celebrant, and tour guide, the O.F.W.G.F.C. ("Old Fat White Guy from Chicago") as Carl's business card described him. Through Carl I met many people, including my good friend Peter Massony, who has been enormously gracious and generous with his time, hospitality, and insight over the past eight years. Other New Orleanians have made important contributions to my understanding of the city and its history and social dynamics, including John McEnery Robertson, Adelaide Wisdom Benjamin, and Steve Ellis. New Orleans (and now San Francisco) artist Marsha Ercegovic hosted my German Shorthair Pointer and me for several extended research stays, during which I probably learned more about the city while enjoying alcoholic beverages in her courtyard than any abstemious rationalist would find plausible. Tulane University's Judith Kelleher Schafer, who continues to make brilliant contributions to the study of nineteenth-century New Orleans, guided me along with friendship, great advice, and informed critique. Peter Wallenstein, my friend and colleague at Virginia Tech, read several drafts and gave them a much-appreciated bleeding with a sharpened editor's pen. I also a debt of gratitude to Patrick Little of the University of North Carolina at Greensboro for volunteering to find typographical and grammatical errors. Their contributions came in advance of the judicious and thorough copyediting performed by Lois R. Crum, who saved me from untold embarrassments. Likewise, there can be no question that this would be far less of a work without the sage and patient guidance of Robert J. Brugger, senior acquisitions editor at the Johns Hopkins University Press. Indeed, had he not had such faith in the project, there might well not have been any book at all.

No work of this kind could exist apart from the active help of numerous archivists and librarians. The archives staff at the Historic New Orleans Collection, Tulane University, the University of New Orleans, the Diocesan archives of New Orleans, Louisiana State University, and the University of Georgia all deserve praise. The majority of my research, however, took place at the City Archives at the New Orleans Public Library. My findings would not have been possible without the knowledgeable assistance of Wayne Everard, Irene Wainwright, and especially Greg Osborn.

The events that I and those around me have witnessed have also had a tremendous impact upon what appears in the following pages. Although different in many of their particulars, the uncertainty and change that Katrina brought to New Orleans created an atmosphere in the city not unlike the one rendered by the Civil War and Reconstruction nearly a century and a half ago. Watching this drama unfold firsthand forced me to cast aside the worn-out assumptions of graduate-school days and reconsider the drama of the postbellum era on the terms of those who lived through it. The difficult times that I witnessed at Virginia Tech two years later helped me realize in a small way what the Civil War generation endured. After these singular events, I resolved to rewrite my entire manuscript so that I might incorporate this sensibility and devote greater attention to the human element. The following spring, my future wife and I spent every weekend driving the three hours from Greensboro, North Carolina, to rural upstate South Carolina, where her father was bravely dying of esophageal cancer. Whenever time allowed, I stole away to an attic bedroom to finish writing about the tragic deaths of Sauvinet, Ellis, and Ogden. The fact that events in my own life often left me identifying with the challenges faced by one figure or another certainly falls short of the historian's objective ideal. Yet such a tendency is probably inescapable for anyone who sees the humanity in history and is inclined to write from the heart. For this reason, I credit whatever merits this book may have to those family members and friends whose fellowship and shared experiences allowed me to achieve what I set out to accomplish in this work.

INTRODUCTION

EMBRACING THE AMBIGUITIES OF
AN UNCERTAIN AGE

Lies, unmitigated lies, notorious and malicious lies, have been
printed and broadcast, and willing and eager readers have been
glad to believe them.

— Henry Clay Warmoth

In 1930, Henry Clay Warmoth explained in the foreword to his classic memoir
that he had undertaken the task of writing to counter the "many false and vicious statements" being made by contemporary historians about his reign as governor of Louisiana. Eighty-eight years old when the Macmillan Company finally
published his work, Warmoth lived to be one of the last of the Civil War generation to record his thoughts about life in the turbulent postbellum South. "It seems
appropriate," he noted, "that one of the remaining chief actors should give a full
and truthful narrative of the history of that exciting era." Despite its pervasively
self-serving tone, *War, Politics, and Reconstruction* expressed a type of truth about
Reconstruction that few subsequent historians have fully appreciated. Although
he probably did not mean to do so, Warmoth constantly reminded his reader of
the moral ambiguity that so often characterized the postbellum struggle.[1]

The histories that motivated Warmoth to take up the pen had depicted the
overthrow of Reconstruction as a moral crusade whose ideals bordered on the sacred. Known collectively as the Dunning School after its leading disciple, Columbia University historian William Archibald Dunning, these narratives drew their
inspiration from Lost Cause rhetoric and the political imperative of white supremacy. The Dunningites cast the so-called Republican carpetbaggers as tyrants
who, in the wake of the federal bayonets, subjected the white South to a humiliating epoch of misrule. In contrast, the "Redeemers"—those white Southerners
who overthrew Republican rule—were lauded as the saviors of the Anglo-Saxon

race. According to such logic, the venality of men such as Warmoth justified the extralegal means by which the valiant Redeemers restored the Democracy. That the Dunningite narrative was largely nonsense did not prevent it from remaining the dominant version of Reconstruction history until well into the 1950s.[2]

With the advent of the civil rights movement in the 1950s and 1960s, however, a new dominant narrative emerged from a group of self-proclaimed "revisionist" historians, who inverted many of their predecessors' basic assumptions. The Republicans, countered the revisionists, were the true heroes of the age because they had valiantly attempted to make tangible the progressive intent of the Fourteenth and Fifteenth Amendments—not only for an untold number of former slaves, but also for poor whites who had been politically marginalized under the slaveholders' regime. For all the newness of the revisionists' message, however, like the Dunningites before them, they kept the concepts of ideological struggle and moral crusade at the center of their narrative. Even when scholars in the late 1960s and early 1970s began suggesting that the Republicans could have done far more in the name of liberty during Reconstruction, their assumptions flowed from the idea that freedom and the "emancipationist legacy" of the Civil War was the central aim of the conflict's victors. While a small measure of ambiguity crept into the "postrevisionist" writings of the late 1980s, the core message of Reconstruction as an "unfinished [political] revolution" remained essentially intact. Since then, studies of the postbellum South have undergone an atomization of sorts, analyzing the era through a broad range of interpretive frameworks, ranging from race, class, and gender, to economics, law, and violence. In one form or another, though, these works assume that in the ideological and moral sense, Reconstruction had a clearly defined purpose and destination—it was an intentional revolution left unfinished.[3]

My narrative, in contrast, steps out of the shadow of certitude and inevitability by embracing the murkiness and moral ambiguity that Henry Clay Warmoth described as a hallmark of life in postbellum Louisiana. A first step in such a methodological approach must be to temper the teleological model that lends grand design and idealistic purpose to the politics of Reconstruction by acknowledging the darker and less exalted dimensions of life after the Civil War. Ideology and moral vision may have shaped the deeds of the Civil War generation, but an aggregate of personal considerations also proved deeply influential. Ambition, fear, masculine honor, anxiety, pride, jealousy, duty, loyalty—all human impulses—played important roles in shaping outcomes. Without question, many revolutionary and often progressive changes took place during the postbellum era, but such "radical" alternatives blossomed not so much because they were morally or ideologically just but because they satisfied a broad range of the Civil War generation's societal and political needs. Though no doubt unintentionally, the "unfinished revolution" thesis has played strangely to notions of American triumphalism and, as a consequence, has influenced many observers to see grand purpose in such a crucial chapter of our nation's history. While this work does not distill the events of the postbellum era into an alternative thesis of cynical moral relativism, it strives to understand the Civil War generation on its own terms, focusing on the human rather than the moral dimension of the era. Warmoth, in his own flawed way, tried in vain to tell us that life after the war was far more complicated than most historians were willing to admit. It is time to heed his admonition by embracing the ambiguities and uncertainty that dominated postbellum life, time to begin asking new questions about the generation of Americans who lived through that difficult era.

This book employs two main structural themes. It first offers a community study of New Orleans from the moment of secession through the segregation and disfranchisement struggles of the 1890s. On a more analytical level, it supplies a generational study of those New Orleanians who came of age on the eve of the Civil War and who became the city's primary actors in the postbellum era. Its arguments grow out of the deeds of the individuals whose lives form the core of the narrative and the reaction of the wider community to those deeds. As a blend of political, social, urban, and cultural history, this work does not aim to serve as an exhaustive recounting of events in New Orleans between 1861 and 1898, nor does it focus upon the economic development of the city in the second half of the nineteenth century. It does, however, try to explain how New Orleanians "reincarnated" both the community and their private lives in the decades that followed the city's disastrous experiment with secession. Reconstruction in the Crescent City was largely defined by the Civil War generation's quest to find stability— socially, politically, and personally—during the tumultuous postbellum era. For better or for worse, many never realized this goal.

New Orleans is an excellent location for a study of the postbellum South because it contained so many of the elements that made the region tumultuous. Critics miss the point when distracted by the presence of Catholicism or Creole culture or when they suggest that, as the region's largest city, New Orleans was anomalous in the overwhelmingly rural South. It was the most valuable jewel in the crown of the former Confederacy. This fact alone guaranteed that the struggle over its control would be particularly intense. What happened in New Orleans also mattered both regionally and nationally. Key events, such as the Riot of 1866, the White League rebellion of 1874, and Homer Plessy's challenge to "separate but equal" unfolded in its streets. The large and prosperous free black community in New Orleans played a pivotal role in the debate over race and place in nineteenth-century America. The city was also home to many veterans, both black and white, Union and Confederate. Furthermore, as the agricultural locus and, in many ways, the cultural center of the vast Mississippi Valley, New Orleans represented the surrounding countryside as much as it did the urban core.

By extending to 1898, this narrative engages a broader timeline than what historians traditionally apply to Reconstruction. My generational approach has much to do with this chronology. But the choice also reflects an intentional effort to downgrade the importance of the passage and the implementation of federal Reconstruction policy and instead to emphasize the enduring legacies of the war and the postbellum struggle in Southern society. The study follows members of the Civil War generation through what Oliver Wendell Holmes Jr. termed the "incommunicable experience of war." What these individuals endured not only defined their worldview but also established the bases from which they began rebuilding their postwar lives. The following chapters chronicle the emergence, triumph, and defeat of the Republican era in Louisiana as witnessed by New Orleanians; it was a period in which factionalism and self-interest often overshadowed ideological purpose. Extending beyond 1877, this book considers the longer-term legacies created by both war and the sweeping political and social changes of the postbellum years. It explores how white factionalism and enduring Republican activism undermined the Redeemers' ability to deliver upon their promises of a return to peace and prosperity. The book concludes with the battles for segregation and disfranchisement in Louisiana, when the Civil War generation gave way to a younger group of men who set about eliminating the politically and socially destabilizing effects of laws passed during the Republican era.

Social instability, personal uncertainty, and paradox also serve as recurrent themes in this story of postbellum New Orleans. Like most other Americans living in the region, the individuals who appear in this work simply did not take anything in their future for granted. Histories of Reconstruction that are guided, as they often are, by the "crusade" narrative carry the flavor of teleological inevitability and rely heavily upon group identities. It is clear, however, that those who lived through the period did not always fit neatly into predictable categories. The unfamiliar social terrain of postbellum New Orleans forced many individuals to consider options that would have been inconceivable before the war. They include the Bourbon Democrat who fought segregation, the stalwart Republican who was universally admired by the White League, the black activist who passed his children into white society, the valiant soldier abandoned by those who had benefited most from his heroics, the aging antebellum political titan who fought for the rights of a poor mixed-race woman, and the Redeemer who became the chief antagonist of the Democratic Party. Because we have too often painted broad areas of our understanding of the postbellum era with generalizations, the deeds of such persons might surprise us. These New Orleanians, however, reflected the complexities of their generation. They were the people whom Warmoth knew.

CHAPTER ONE

POOR NEW ORLEANS!

1861–1862

> It is the custom here to keep up a continual firing of guns, pistols,
> all night long on the demise of the old year. Long after we retired,
> shot after shot echoed thro' the still moonlight. . . . Long may we
> be unused to, ought save the mimicry of war, and its stern realities
> forever averted from this eminently peaceful soil.
> —Thomas K. Wharton, December 31, 1854

E zekiel John Ellis looked on with dismay at the chaotic scene unfolding around him. Telegrams carrying news of Louisiana's secession had reached New Orleans from Baton Rouge early that January afternoon, and word of the ordinance's passage quickly spread throughout the city. Boisterous crowds spilled into the streets in noisy celebration, while the roar of cannons firing salutes echoed from Jackson and Lafayette squares. Through the tendrils of smoke and amid the wild cheering of those around him, Ellis had "a strangely throbbing heart" as he watched the U.S. flag being pulled down from Armory Hall. When Louisiana's pelican flag unfurled in its place, the crowd broke out in a stirring rendition of the *Marseillaise*. "That song of revolution and civil strife," recalled Ellis, "made me think of the convulsive struggles of the French capitol, and the exclamation of Mme. Roland while on her way to the guillotine."[1]

Time eventually revealed the merit of Ellis's analogy to the French Revolution. The passage of Louisiana's ordinance of secession on January 26, 1861, marked a point of departure from which there was no true return. Like the French revolutionaries before them and the Leninists, who came later, the secessionists placed into motion a set of uncontrollable forces that revolutionized the society in which they lived. It took a costly war and decades of political turmoil to restore a facsimile of the hard-handed stability that the slaveholding regime had once imposed upon Southern society. In the meantime, New Orleans served as a battleground on which the advocates of competing visions for a reincarnated South-

ern society vied for supremacy. Ellis thought the artillery salutes fired in honor of
secession had "sounded like the 'sod falling upon the coffin lid' of pride." Indeed,
this most pernicious of the seven deadly sins had engendered in Southern slaveholders feelings of both self-righteousness and invulnerability. It did not take
long, however, to discover just how wrong their assumptions had been.[2]

At the moment of secession, New Orleans stood at the apex of its wealth and
strength relative to the rest of the nation. The Crescent City was not just the
economic locus of the vast Mississippi Valley; it was the financial capital of the
entire South. With nearly 170,000 residents in 1860, it was more than four times
the size of Charleston or Richmond. New Orleans's strategic location on the
Mississippi River, combined with westward expansion and the advent of steam-
powered river transportation, had transformed it from its status as a colonial port
at the time of the Louisiana Purchase into the unrivaled economic capitol of
the antebellum South. It grew by a staggering 45 percent during the decade of the
1850s alone, outpacing both Boston and Cincinnati and nearly matching the
population growth of the bustling port of New York City. Louisiana's antebellum
per-capita income was second in the nation and first in the South. It was New
Orleans's role as the primary commercial gateway for the nation's booming midsection that made the accumulation of such wealth possible. More than 659,000
tons of imported goods arrived at the city's wharves in 1859, making the city third
in the nation in this respect, behind only Boston and New York. With these wares
lashed to their decks, steamboats traveled upriver from New Orleans to waiting
markets in countless towns and plantation landings, and then the boats returned
loaded to the gunwales with the enormous agricultural bounty of the West. All
along New Orleans's waterfront, an army of stevedores transferred this valuable
cargo to warehouses and eventually to the holds of oceangoing vessels. Such commercial activity also required a corresponding army of merchants, lawyers, and
bankers capable of handling the thousands of financial transactions that took
place in the city every day. On the eve of war, New Orleans was one of the nation's
few great international cities.[3]

Secessionism had been far from a majority position in New Orleans before the
election of 1860, but as elsewhere in the South, the elevation of Lincoln to the
presidency led to an emotionally charged reversal of sentiments. John C. Breckenridge, the "states rights" Democrat, received only 25 percent of the vote in November, but by the time the city sent delegates to the secession convention in January, the overwhelming majority among them approved of severing Louisiana's
ties to the Union. Although it was apparent that New Orleans had much to lose
when Louisiana threw its support behind the Confederate cause, those arguing

for secession believed incorrectly not only that separation from the Union might protect the city's lucrative slave markets but also that the port would quickly become the new Southern nation's equivalent to New York City. Men like Louisiana senator Judah P. Benjamin thought New Orleans's international ties would mitigate its loss of national commerce with the North; furthermore, they were convinced that any attempt by the Union to impose a blockade upon the city's shipping would also result inevitably in foreign intervention at sea on behalf of the slaveholding republic.[4]

Secession's most immediate burdens fell not on the shoulders of those flawed statesmen who severed Louisiana's ties with the Union, however, but disproportionately upon a generation of young men who answered their leaders' call to arms. Louisiana ultimately contributed more than its share of souls to the Confederate experiment, and conspicuous among the first wave of enlistees were the sons of the Crescent City's most elite families. In Peter Carmichael's words, these young men represented "the last generation" of the Southern slaveholding plutocracy, and nowhere had they prospered more than along the Mississippi Valley's cotton frontier. No group of men possessed a greater vested interest in the maintenance of slavery or had so much to lose in an unsuccessful war fought to preserve the institution. Like E. John Ellis, this "last generation" of elite New Orleanians were forever haunted by their memories of antebellum prosperity. The lofty heights to which they had once aspired only amplified the magnitude of their own spectacular fall to earth.[5]

Often volunteering for reasons far more personal than the grand political notions that had driven the nation into war, these men were fated to become the conflict's primary actors. The stories of the New Orleanians who appear in the following pages resemble those of thousands of other men who embarked upon the deadly enterprise of war bound by an aggregate of communal, familial, and personal expectations concerning their manhood and honor. Although they did not all come from the same racial or cultural backgrounds and did not all approach the pending conflict with the same sense of purpose, they shared key traits that increased their likelihood of acting out important roles both during the war and in the postbellum struggle for mastery. Born between 1830 and 1842, the men featured in this book, members of the rising generation, had professional or familial bonds that made them also part of elite New Orleans society. Most importantly, each harbored a romantic and unswerving sense of civic duty that, in the long run, not only linked their fates but also exacted an enormous price.

Personal relationships and blood ties played a crucial role in developing both the character and the worldview of these men and, as a consequence, influenced their reaction to the crisis of 1861. As Bertram Wyatt-Brown has shown, nineteenth-century conceptualizations of masculinity and honor crystallized in a familial as well as a class and communal context. When they volunteered for the army, these men made a critical addition to their circle of peers. For this reason, my narrative considers, in addition to the generation and the class of New Orleanians who entered military life as junior officers in 1861, the wider dialogue of words, deeds, and experiences they shared with friends, lovers, extended kin networks, comrades, business associates, and rivals. The reflection that they beheld in the eyes of others served as a constant reminder of the inviolate nature of one's obligations to family, friends, and community and also often dictated the outcome of the most important decisions made by these young men. And they found that their own actions, in turn, had the power to inspire others. Thrust into the role of military officers, these youthful soldiers discovered that effective leadership strongly paralleled their own mastery of the nineteenth century's prevailing standards of manhood and honor. Indeed, leadership may have been the only necessary military skill that antebellum civilian life had supplied to them.[6]

Making sense of this "last generation's" experience with Louisiana's Confederate catastrophe is important because it both shaped who they were as men and informed the decisions that they later made in their bid to reconstruct postbellum New Orleans. Witnesses to the Crescent City's apogee, they also watched as its prosperity crumbled, within the course of one year, under the weight of enthusiasm, hubris, corruption, and incompetence. In time, these men came to realize that this unparalleled cataclysm also marked the dawning of a new reality, one that they did not uniformly embrace.

Perhaps no member of this generation better embodied conflicted emotions of Louisianians in the spring of 1861 than E. John Ellis, the young man who had grown so melancholy while New Orleanians celebrated secession. Just twenty years old, sandy-haired, blue-eyed, intensely earnest and religious, Ellis had come to New Orleans in early November of 1860 along with his best friend, Bolivar Edwards, to study law at the University of Louisiana, the forerunner of Tulane University. Law had become the family business under the tutelage of his father, Ezekiel Parke Ellis, who, with a pioneer upbringing and little formal education, married a judge's daughter, became a clerk, and eventually scratched out a thriving practice back home in Louisiana's "Florida Parishes." Within the span of twenty years, the patriarch's thrift and determination had propelled the Ellis clan from the ranks of middling yeomen into the world of the slaveholding planter elite, a position from which he could provide his own gifted and hardworking

E. John Ellis

sons with the benefits of the college education he had never known. E. John's older brother Thomas, to whom he was thoroughly devoted, had preceded him to New Orleans to earn a law degree and was now active in political circles back home. Blessed with a sharp mind and natural eloquence, E. John came to the city not just to study law but to live up to the lofty standards established by the most influential men in his life.[7]

Ellis not only had inherited a professional calling from his father; familial influence also shaped his political ideology. Having been raised in the Whig tradition, he had pinned his hope for the Union's salvation upon the candidacy of John Bell's Constitutional Union ticket during the election of 1860. That summer, his brother Thomas was key in the creation of the Bell and Everett Union Club in their hometown of Amite, and it was under this tent that John made his first political speech, an oration apparently so odious in its delivery that it was "a relief" to his audience when he finally sat down. E. John Ellis was in New Orleans attending law lectures by the time news of Lincoln's victory in the fall election had reached the city. Although Bell had carried Orleans Parish and had run well elsewhere in Louisiana, overall the Southern Democrats led by Kentuckian John C. Breckenridge managed to secure the state's electoral votes with a mere 45 percent of Louisiana's popular vote. Even though he was only twenty years old, the magnitude of the impending disaster was not lost on Ellis. Presciently observing that the nation had set a course for a "long bloody war," he wrote his father to express his hope "that those who have brought this calamity upon us, who have misrepresented & wronged the respective sections may have the brunt of the shock to bear & meet the fate they so richly deserve."[8]

In time, the experience of war radically altered Ellis's devotion to the Southern cause, but in the spring and summer of 1861 he was an undeniably half-hearted Confederate. Graduation from law school finally occurred on the last day of March, with his friend Bolivar Edwards emerging as the class valedictorian. Ellis had enjoyed his time in New Orleans and had made many friends, but it was now time to return home to Amite. When he arrived there, he found the "military spirit" every bit as fervent as in New Orleans. In succession, news of the capture of Fort Sumter, the Confederate victory at Bull Run, and Lincoln's call for volunteers reached the hamlet and extinguished Ellis's remaining hope that the Union might yet be preserved. By June, feeling the pressure of the community upon his shoulders, he had enlisted in a local unit of St. Helena Parish volunteers; he spent the remainder of the summer drilling with other young men from his hometown at an old Methodist campground. An ardent Christian, Ellis later reflected, "Could a more appropriate place be found? Is the cause of country not next to the cause of God?" Most of the men did not yet have weapons, and some grew bored, but otherwise it was an agreeable way to spend a war, he thought. By late September, Ellis's unit had been absorbed into the service of the Confederate States of America as Company F of the Sixteenth Louisiana, and the twenty-year-old was honored by his peers in an election that made him the company's assistant first lieutenant. Accompanied by Stewart, his slave and manservant, Ellis and his company spent the remainder of fall training at Camp Moore in Tangipahoa Parish.[9]

The first of December 1861 found the men of the Sixteenth Louisiana thundering down the New Orleans, Jackson, and Great Northern Railroad bound for the Crescent City. It was a holiday atmosphere, with every passing house and station attended by handkerchief-waving well-wishers, a scene repeated on a far greater scale when the train reached its destination. Rumors of an attack on New Orleans had prompted authorities to position reinforcements twelve miles away by land at the historic old battlefield of Chalmette, the scene of Andrew Jackson's stunning victory in 1815. From camp, Ellis could see the distant "towers and minarets" of New Orleans and hear the relentless grinding of the sugar mills that dotted the surrounding countryside. Such proximity to civilization pleased him, and he spent much of his free time that December attending operas, church, and the "hospitable firesides" of friends. In early January, he even expressed in a letter to his father his hope that the war would soon end.[10]

Other young men were far more eager than Ellis to enter the fray. Just three days after the April 12, 1861, firing on Fort Sumter, twenty-six-year-old Frederick Nash Ogden walked into a recruiting office and enlisted in Colonel Charles Dreux's First Louisiana Battalion. At the time, Ogden was working in the commodities sector of the city, clerking in a cotton house, a job he had performed since he was fifteen. The details of such an ordinary existence are noteworthy only because Ogden came from a very well-connected and socially prominent family in New Orleans. That fact may even have been a primary motivator behind his decision to enlist. It would be unfair to characterize the burly red-headed bachelor as the black sheep of the family, but by any measure, his accomplishments in life thus far stood in the shadows of the other Ogden men and the family's prominent forebearers.

In a culture and an age in which genealogy trumped money as a dividing line between the elite and the masses, the Ogden family's claim to blueblood status would be difficult to challenge. The recipient of a royal land grant, the first of the Ogden line in America came to New Jersey in the late seventeenth century. Several generations later, Robert Ogden married Elizabeth Spaight Nash, the daughter of the Revolutionary War governor of North Carolina and the genesis of the

"Nash-Ogden" legacy. With four sons of his own in tow, Robert Ogden's eldest
son left North Carolina for Louisiana in the 1810s, settling first in Baton Rouge
and later in New Orleans. The four sons he brought with him, Robert, Abner,
Octavius, and Frederick Nash Ogden, became the foundational generation of a
dynasty that lives to this day in the people and place names of New Orleans. Like
their father, Robert, Abner, and Octavius Nash Ogden all became powerful lawyers and judges. By 1850, Octavius Nash Ogden also owned a sprawling Rapides
Parish cotton plantation with thirty-three slaves. Fred Ogden's father and namesake, however, had instead become a physician in Baton Rouge. This third of the
four Ogden brothers also seems to have had a bold romantic streak, a trait that
emerged later in his only son. As family legend has it, Frederick Nash Ogden Sr.
virtually abducted a teen-aged Carmelite Lopez from a Baton Rouge convent and
made her his wife. Their only son entered the world almost precisely nine months
after their marriage.[11]

The death of Fred Ogden's dashing father when he was three years old certainly made life much more difficult for him, but the blow was softened by the
enormous wealth and influence of his uncles. It also had a profound impact upon
the environment in which he reached adulthood. At fifteen, he came to live at the
New Orleans home of the eldest of these uncles, Robert Nash Ogden. Although
he soon secured a job clerking with a cotton factor, it is likely that at this time,
had he exhibited aptitude for such things, Ogden would have been given the opportunity to enter college and immediately afterward study law in the offices of
one of his prominent uncles. This was the career path taken by virtually all the
other Ogden men of his generation, including his first cousins Abner, Robert, and
John. Yet Fred Ogden's talents did not seem to lie that way. He did, however, have
an interest in politics. While still in his teens, Ogden took part in the street fighting in behalf of the Democratic Party against Know-Nothing vigilante gangs. Yet
such activism had not brought with it financial success. Now in his mid-twenties,
he was still a bachelor and a cotton clerk, rooming in a boardinghouse with other
cotton clerks. Though he was part of a legendary family, Fred Ogden's road to
fame seemed full of obstacles—that is, until Louisiana seceded from the Union.[12]

By late May 1861, Dreux's First Louisiana Battalion was already in Northern
Virginia, and Private Ogden was part of one of the first Louisiana organizations
to enter the field of battle. Here the men skirmished with Union forces as both
sides scrambled to raise armies. In one such engagement outside of Newport News,
Colonel Dreux became the first Louisiana officer to die in the Civil War. Ogden
proved far luckier. Spending that first summer of the war in Virginia gave him an
opportunity to demonstrate his enormous potential as a soldier. By mid-June, he

was promoted to battalion color sergeant, a post of honor that he held during the stunning victory at First Manassas and in the ensuing Peninsular Campaign. A major restructuring of the Confederacy's military operation in Northern Virginia soon followed, however, and this meant important changes were in store for the military career of Fred Ogden. As an early ninety-day unit, Dreux's battalion faced eventual breakup and absorption into regular Louisiana regiments of the Confederate army. Ogden was on detached service when all this organizational shuffling took place, and this status gave him an unusual amount of freedom to seek out new opportunities. Having distinguished himself on the fields of Virginia in the early months of the war, he headed home in December to New Orleans, where rumors of a pending attack had finally lit a fire under those preparing the city's defenses.[13]

In retrospect, when one considers the enormity of New Orleans's economic, industrial, and strategic importance to the Southern cause, it is almost unthinkable how comparatively few resources Confederate military planners dedicated to its protection. Its early loss might well be the single most underappreciated blunder of the entire war. Confederate civil authorities later held a court of inquiry to determine culpability for the fall of New Orleans, and the statements given by witnesses called by this panel revealed much about the state of mounting anxiety in the Crescent City as the summer of 1861 gave way to fall. Charles McGill Conrad, a former Whig senator who had been Millard Fillmore's secretary of war, a signer of the Confederate Constitution, and by the time of the inquiry the representative of a New Orleans district in the national legislature, observed with dismay the growing volume of correspondence sent by his constituents bemoaning the bumbling ineptitude of the persons preparing the city's defenses.[14]

When Conrad arrived in New Orleans that November to judge conditions for himself, he quickly discovered that such tales of woe were true and that the broader picture was even more alarming. While the Confederate army engineers charged with constructing land defenses moved at a disturbingly lethargic pace, the utter indifference with which the naval yard applied itself to the fabrication of ironclad gunboats bordered on outrage. Even though the city possessed several significant foundries and an abundant skilled labor force of mechanics, the yard worked only one shift, and that haltingly. When the irregularity of pay from the Confederate government had brought construction of the *Mississippi* to "almost . . . a dead stand," the city's civilian Committee of Safety offered the yard's owner "money without limit" and skilled hands who could work on the vessel around the clock. Yet because many of these skilled mechanics were free people of color, the government contractor not only refused the committee's offer; he rebuffed all further inducements and threats its members made aimed at speeding the gunboat's progress. Conrad laid blame directly at the feet of Stephen Mallory, the Confederate secretary of the navy, but many men participated in the incompetence and corruption that dogged the city's defenses. By early January, Conrad had come to the troubling conclusion that New Orleans's fall was inevitable. "The only question in my mind," he recalled, was whether the successful attack would come "by the gunboats from above or the fleet from the sea."[15]

Even if the city's defenders had worked with the utmost alacrity, the overall strategy for protecting New Orleans contained so many flaws that its proper execution may not have made a difference. Although they had made some token efforts in defending other approaches of attack, Confederate war planners had gambled everything on two opposing batteries downriver from New Orleans called Fort Jackson and Fort St. Philip. They were impressive on paper, but prescient military observers believed at the time that these fortifications alone would be incapable of halting the advance of modern warships. Confederate general and Louisiana native Pierre Gustave Toutant Beauregard had expressed as much to C. M. Conrad in a letter stating that "even if their armament was complete and the guns of the heaviest caliber," the forts would prove inadequate. Shortly after Jefferson Davis's inauguration, Conrad approached the Confederate president with Beauregard's letter and urged immediate action, but with little result. The problematic quality of the city's defenses was well known by the end of 1861, but even so the Confederate army soon withdrew most of the region's land forces to assist in campaigns in the Upper South. Despite Governor Thomas Overton Moore's proclamation calling for a day of celebration, anyone walking the streets of New Orleans on the first anniversary of secession was undoubtedly hard pressed to observe any of the genuine scenes of confident optimism that E. John Ellis had witnessed a year earlier.[16]

If the overall strategy and preparations for the defense of New Orleans failed to inspire confidence in its citizens, so, too, did the uneven quality of the troops remaining in the city. Some regular units, like Ellis's Sixteenth Louisiana, had arrived in late November and early December, but rumors quickly spread that they would not stay long. The size of the force detailed to remain was shockingly small, and it included many organizations of dubious value. Julia LeGrand, a young woman living in New Orleans who was a family friend of Frederick Nash Ogden's uncle Judge Abner Nash Ogden, scornfully recorded in her diary that one militia company in particular was "a sort of holiday regiment composed of the well-to-do old gentlemen of the city, who were anxious to show their patriotism on the parade ground, but who never expected to fight." Mocking them further, LeGrand noted that "on their camping-out excursions," these weekend warriors "transported comfortable bedsteads, sundry boxes, and demijohns." John Devereux, an adjutant charged with reorganizing these militia units into a more practical fighting force, had a more informed but scarcely more positive opinion of their qualities. Although a few units were both well armed and reasonably proficient in the use of their weapons, only a handful had seen any prior action. The rest, according to Devereux, "were indifferently armed, shot-guns being the prevailing weapon." Although Devereux himself was of French ancestry, he derisively noted that "two-thirds of them belonged to the French class of the population" and that they were of indifferent military character. "The better part of the fighting material," he observed, "had volunteered and been ordered elsewhere."[17]

Twenty-two-year-old Aristée Louis Tissot was the captain of one such local militia unit, the Tirailleurs d'Orleans. Like E. John Ellis, he had just finished his legal studies and was on the verge of entering his career when the war interrupted his plans. Tissot graduated in 1858 from St. Joseph's College, a prestigious Jesuit institution in Bardstown, Kentucky, and returned to New Orleans to study law under the guidance of his father, a prominent attorney. A member of the bar but not yet the head of his own household, Tissot lived with his parents at the Pitot House, a gracious dwelling located at the head of Bayou St. John. Their home, known for its beautiful gardens, was one of the oldest surviving structures in New Orleans, originally built at its idyllic setting by a Spanish colonial collector of customs in an age when trade from the American frontier regions of Mississippi came overland and across Lake Pontchartrain into the back of the city.[18]

Tissot also seems to have been filled with the military spirit that was so prevalent in New Orleans in April 1861, and he set about to play a role consistent with both his cultural heritage and his class expectations. Late that month, he ran an advertisement in *L'Abielle de la Nouvelle-Orléans* that identified him as the captain of the Tirailleurs d'Orleans and beckoned its members to meet the next day "à midi précis" at their arsenal at 112 Passage de la Bourse. Advertisements for the company's recruitment began appearing the next day, enticing "those young men who wish to become part of an elite corps" to seek out one of the distinguished members of the committee at the armory. When the Tirailleurs officially formed as a state militia unit on May 25, 1861, its members elected Tissot their captain, an honor bestowed far more for his exalted social standing than for any real notions of military leadership.[19]

For much of the summer, this jauntily named militia company performed duties of limited military value, but the increasingly perilous nature of the city's defenses eventually brought the Tirailleurs' gentleman soldiering to an end. In October the Confederate government made a call to reorganize these independent companies into the regular service so that they might more effectively defend the city against attack. Many of the militia companies that Julia LeGrand had scorned for their dilettante ways refused to yield their autonomy, but Tissot and many of his men proved more willing to sacrifice for the cause. In December, under directions from General Mansfield Lovell, Lieutenant Devereux reorganized the Tirailleurs into Company B of the Twenty-third Regiment of Louisiana Infantry and posted the renamed unit to the defenses at Fort Macomb, an aging brick and earthen embattlement overlooking one of the narrow passages between Lake Borgne and Lake Pontchartrain called Chef Menteur Pass. Here, bereft of the comforts of home and the glamour of the parade ground, Tissot and his men engaged in a crash course on the rudiments of real soldiering and the use of heavy guns.[20]

Company B definitely bore a strong Gallic cultural imprint, but only time would tell whether adjutant Devereux's generalizations about their potential as a fighting unit would prove accurate. Like more than half of the city's antebellum population, Tissot's parents were actually immigrants and, as such, were among the "foreign French" and not, in fact, Creole. Having been born in New Orleans, their son was Creole but did not belong to the legendary families who had ties to the *ancienne population*. Placide Canonge Jr., the company's first lieutenant, was the twenty-one-year-old son of a well-known French lawyer, poet, and playwright who had fled St. Domingue in the wake of Toussaint L'Ouverture's rebellion. Like Tissot, Canonge was a first-generation New Orleanian. Many of the men of the regiment belonged to this subset of New Orleans's Francophone culture and had fairly recent ties to Europe. Indeed, when Devereux noted that the militias were part of the "French class of the population," he meant just that. Such distinctions to an outside observer might seem trivial, but to New Orleanians of the nineteenth century, Creole identity was both a serious matter and a profound point of pride.[21]

A closer look at those who would have defined themselves as Creole provides a better portrait of the cultural trappings associated with the term. Edmund Arthur Toledano was, at the very least, a third-generation New Orleanian; he could trace his roots in the city to the late eighteenth century. Born in 1829, he was both an American citizen and heir to the impressive-sounding title Marquis de la Carona. His uncles Christoval, Jerome, and Raphael had fought alongside An-

[margin handwritten note: Importance of creole distinction for French class of population.]

drew Jackson at the Battle of New Orleans—an essential fragment of the city's historical lore. With dark features, thick black hair, and a full beard, he had the archetypal look of a white Creole from New Orleans. At nineteen, Toledano had exhibited some of the stereotypical Creole boldness later popularized by George Washington Cable when he boarded a steamer bound for the recently conquered California. By 1851, however, he had returned to the city of his birth and joined the rest of his extended family in the pursuit of commerce.[22]

Complex kinship ties often reinforced the cohesiveness of the city's Creole community, and this was certainly true for Arthur Toledano. An important figure in his life was his uncle Louis Florange Drouet, the younger brother of Toledano's mother. Even though he lived a considerable distance away, Toledano would make daily visits to his uncle's home at the corner of Tchoupitoulas and Gaiènnie, where the two bachelors would often share a dinner prepared by Drouet's servants. As the 1850s came to a close, and as Arthur Toledano grew in stature as a merchant, he began handling an increasing amount of his uncle's business affairs. Drouet, too, was a merchant, slaveholder, and significant owner of commercial property in the city. Yet while Drouet and Toledano enjoyed a particularly close personal relationship, theirs was just one of many bonds that tied the two families together. When Louis Drouet's father died in 1847, for instance, the viewing took place at the home of his cousin, the Battle of New Orleans veteran Christoval Toledano. The sacramental registers of St. Louis Cathedral, taken in combination with the notarial acts recorded in the books of Onesiphore Drouet, reveal a multigenerational web of blood and property ties that bound these and other old Creole families together.[23]

By the start of the Civil War, Arthur Toledano had established himself as a prominent cotton factor, a key profession in a city whose economy depended heavily upon agricultural trade. In the middle of the nineteenth century, factors served as middlemen between growers marketing their crop and textile industry buyers who came to New Orleans for the precious lint. At his office at 58 Carondelet Street, known popularly in the city as "Factor's Row," Toledano engaged in extensive dealings with cotton planters whose fertile lands lined the banks of the Mississippi all the way from New Orleans to Memphis. The commencement of hostilities with the Union had an almost immediate effect upon business along Factor's Row. Businesses such as Toledano's stopped receiving shipments of cotton by August 1861, and the combination of the Confederate government's ill-conceived declaration of an embargo on the export of the staple along with the Union's prioritized blockade of the Mississippi River's four passes into the ocean doubtlessly left many mercantile men with little else to do but consider joining *embargos*

the army. Indeed, Toledano's commercial connections undoubtedly played an important role in determining his fate in the war.[24]

By fall 1861, Toledano, along with a handful of other Creoles in New Orleans's commodities sector, had joined Watson's Battery, a unit manned extensively by the sons of Louisiana and Mississippi cotton planters. Watson's Battery was the brainchild of Augustus "Gus" C. Watson, a charismatic planter from Tensas Parish who, along with his brothers, was known both for enormous wealth and for "dashing" ways at the poker table. In a flurry of patriotism, he had purchased four six-pound smoothbores and two twelve-pound howitzers, organizing them into three two-gun battery sections. At least on paper, the unit came into existence on July 1, 1861, in New Orleans, under the command of a Mexican War veteran named Daniel Beltzhoover. (Watson, for his part, seemed less interested in fighting or leading than in supplying the necessary tools of war to others.) By the middle of August, Beltzhoover had opened a recruiting and training depot near Watson's Lakewood Plantation on the shores of Lake Bruin, an oxbow-shaped body of water fifty miles below Vicksburg that had once formed part of the Mississippi River's stream. Men from the surrounding parishes and counties on both sides of the river, along with others from New Orleans, converged on the location and began learning the science of artillery.[25]

Science of artillery

Sufficiently trained, and with its benefactor tagging along as an eager observer, the unit headed upriver and took part in its first engagement at Columbus, Kentucky, in early November 1861. Although only two men from the battery were killed in this action, the loss in horseflesh was so staggering—forty-five had been killed and all but one wounded—that they ended up losing two of their precious cannons to the enemy. When a runaway caisson cruelly mauled one of the Watson Battery's young officers, it seemed to have opened up an avenue for promotion for Arthur Toledano, who from December of 1861 began to draw pay as a second lieutenant. Yet, despite the upbeat tone of its commander's battle report, this early campaign into western Kentucky and Missouri was an overall failure. In the wake of key victories by General Ulysses S. Grant's Union forces in the West, Watson's Battery withdrew southward and by February 1862 had arrived at a major Confederate encampment at Corinth, Mississippi.[26]

The widespread presence of Catholic Creoles like Toledano differentiated New Orleans from much of the rest of the South, and so did the city's racial demographics. Overall, the majority of Louisianians were black, but in New Orleans, people of African descent represented only about 25,000 of the nearly 170,000 residents, and of these more than 10,000 were free. Many of the free people of

NOLA- 3tiered racial class system

color were of mixed race and, like Toledano, Creoles. They occupied the middle
stratum of the city's three-tiered racial caste system, a position in which they may
not have enjoyed the full benefits of white society, but neither did they suffer
the degradation of slavery. Although this dynamic had taken root in other parts
of the American South, it was in New Orleans, with its large and prosperous seg-
ment of free blacks, where the middle caste came to play such a crucial role in
the larger social pyramid, its presence making a vital contribution to the overall
dialogue of race in New Orleans. Despite the value they brought to the community, however, free people of color remained second-class citizens with circum-
scribed legal rights and absolutely no political voice. The arrival of the Americans
to New Orleans in 1803 signaled the beginning of a gradual tightening of manumission laws, aimed at stemming the growth of this community—a systematic
program that proved shockingly successful in reducing the size of the city's free
black community throughout the antebellum period. The free colored population not only represented a dangerous contradiction to the philosophical underpinnings of race-based slavery; but by mingling and at times cohabitating with
slaves, free blacks blurred the boundary separating the free and the enslaved. As
in many other slave states, Nat Turner's slave rebellion in 1832 spurred Louisiana's
legislature to adopt increasingly restrictive laws governing the movement of the
free people of color. Along with the city's reconsolidation in 1852 came repressive
laws that required free blacks to be always ready to prove publicly their status as
free to any white magistrate who demanded such proof. Some Afro-Creoles with
sufficient financial means chose to leave such indignity behind forever, fleeing to
France, Haiti, Mexico, or other countries where their status as free men went un-
challenged. In 1857 Louisiana outlawed manumission entirely.[27]

The antebellum life of Charles St. Albin Sauvinet, however, stood as testimony to the fact that, while the law governing free people of color included severe restrictions, the reality of daily life for the more elite members of this caste
often exhibited a far more organic nature. Although he was not a slaveholder, as
were some "black masters" who lived predominantly in the state's sugar-growing
region, Sauvinet definitely belonged to the most elite stratum of free blacks in
Louisiana. His bachelor father, Joseph Sauvinet, a native of France and one of the
city's many émigrés from St. Domingue, was a lawyer, a banker, and an associate
of the notorious patriot-pirate Jean Laffite. A portrait of Joseph Sauvinet painted
in 1832, less than three years after Charles's birth, depicts a confident, wealthy,
lean-faced man in a stylish black coat and high neckcloth. His *placée*, or professional mistress, and the mother of Charles Sauvinet, was Rose Dazema, a free
woman of color who had also come from St. Domingue. Joseph Sauvinet had a

manumission = owners freeing slaves

↑ motivations?

cottage built for Dazema on Kelerec Street in the Faubourg Marigny, the neigh-borhood next to the French Quarter on the upriver side of Esplanade Avenue, and it was here that young Charles, his mother, and his siblings lived. By the time he reached his twenties, Charles Sauvinet had learned to speak several languages and may possibly have even furthered his education in Europe, where he spent several years traveling in the antebellum period. With a complexion so fair that an unknowing observer would never have guessed he had African ancestry, Sauvinet could enjoy many of the social privileges of a white man. Indeed, some later ex-pressed surprise at learning that he was considered a man of color at all.[28]

But the coming of the war forced to the surface the contradictions that faced Sauvinet and other prominent free people of color in New Orleans. Although many Afro-Creoles hoped to demonstrate their loyalty to the city and the state of their birth, it was difficult to ignore that the government created by secession continued to deny them the basic rights of citizenship. The Native Guards, a militia regiment manned solely by the city's free people of color, was the Confed-eracy's solution to the embarrassing problem of prosperous and loyal free blacks who sought an active role in the coming conflict. There had been a rich legacy of free black participation in the militia in New Orleans that dated back to both French and Spanish colonial periods. Free blacks had also played a pivotal role in the defense of New Orleans when Andrew Jackson defeated the British on the plain of Chalmette in 1815. As early as April 1861, prominent members of the city's Afro-Creole community called for a meeting of the *gens de couleur libre* at the Couvent School, the South's first educational institution run specifically for the purpose of educating students of color. These "defenders of the native land" quickly resolved to swear their fealty to Louisiana at this meeting, the news of which caused a sensation in the local press. In May the Native Guards assembled for the defense of Louisiana. As a reflection of his prominence in the city's Afro-Creole community, C. S. Sauvinet received a commission as a captain.[29]

Captain Sauvinet's company of Native Guards seems to have been among the most dedicated of these unusual Confederate units. Press coverage of a grand review that took place on Canal Street in November 1861 made special note of the conspicuously neat and orderly quality of the uniforms worn by Sauvinet's "fine corps" of men. These accoutrements were not supplied by the Confederacy—in fact, the Confederate and state governments had such a difficult time supplying their troops that many regular white organizations often received little help. These Afro-Creoles had almost certainly furnished themselves. In all, about seven hun-dred fifty officers and men mustered into the Native Guards, most, if not all, with Creole heritage that ran as deep as that of Arthur Toledano or Charles Sauvinet.[30]

Although concrete answers will probably never be found, the question of why these men would have cast their lot with the slaveholders' regime begs analysis. A few scholars have suggested that they enlisted out of fear, worrying that local authorities would repress free blacks who failed to demonstrate their loyalty. This argument, based entirely on retrospective statements made by individuals who were later called upon to defend the decisions of men who joined the Native Guards, seems to grow out of a need to support a thesis of Afro-Creole racial egalitarianism. The chief flaw behind such logic is that from an administrative standpoint, state authorities seemed more flummoxed by the problem of what to do with those who *wanted* to join the Confederate military effort than by concern over those who did not. The free men of color may have taken part simply to preserve the privileged if tenuous status that they had achieved in the antebellum era. Some may have been like E. John Ellis, who had been dubious of secession's wisdom but felt obligated once Louisiana had joined the Confederate experiment to rally around his homeland's banner. The vast majority of the city's free people of color also shared important blood and financial ties with the city's white population, and as a class they had often sought ways to demonstrate their fidelity to Louisiana. Most importantly, standing idly by while one's homeland faced serious injury would have smacked of cowardice, and the fear of appearing less than fully a man was a worldview that seems not to have been tempered by the color of one's skin.[31]

No sooner had E. John Ellis begun a furlough to visit his parents in Amite than he received an urgent telegram from a comrade with the terse message, "Come back immediately, we are ordered away." It was mid-February 1862, and it turned out that this was Ellis's last visit home until the war was over. Scrambling to join his unit, which had been ordered to Corinth, Mississippi, Ellis changed trains in New Orleans. He arrived there on a cold, rainy day and could hear "the piercing scream" of newsboys shouting, "Heahs yer extra-a Srender of Fort Donilsen." Despite the gloom that seemed to hang on every face in town, Ellis rationalized that surely along with victories would come the occasional defeat. Boarding a train the next day for Corinth, he arrived at 3:00 a.m. to find a singularly dreary encampment, where cold, wet weather, and disease stalked the men of the Sixteenth Louisiana. In this fashion Ellis spent the month of March, fighting off alternately illness, cold, and boredom.[32]

The pace of life at Corinth quickened considerably at the very end of March. To Ellis's surprise, his youngest brother, Stephen, just fifteen years old, had turned up in camp and, having lied about his age, enlisted. Several days later, the Sixteenth Louisiana was ordered out toward Pittsburg Landing on the Tennessee River. By the morning of April 3, E. John Ellis and those around him knew that something major was afoot, for thousands of soldiers, including Toledano and the Watson Battery, joined in a great northward advance into west Tennessee. Ellis was still so weak from a fever that he had to be carried along in an ambulance, but with his younger brother now part of the army, there was no way he would accept suggestions that he was unfit for duty and should remain behind. His example had inspired his own brother to risk his life; he had no other option but to fight.[33]

Unfortunately for Ellis, his physical weakness was so obvious that it caused a superior officer to place him in charge of an ordnance train far from the front lines, a position that left him listening anxiously to the sounds of gunfire echoing across the morning sky. He knew that somewhere out in front of him Stephen was in the middle of a heated fight and had been in the army only a scant two weeks. Soon, the wounded came streaming past his position to a nearby field hospital, offering Ellis his first glimpse of the gore of battle. Through the afternoon and evening his emotions wavered between anxiety and shame—alternately worrying about his brother and ruing the fact that he had missed out on the action. Finally, as darkness began to settle on the battlefield, Ellis ran into a doctor from his hometown of Amite, who reassured him that although the Sixteenth had been "badly cut up" in a charge against enemy artillery, Stephen had made it through the mayhem unscathed. The day's fighting had gone well for the Confederates, it seemed, but the battle of Shiloh was far from over. The next day, repulsed at every turn, Beauregard ordered his army on a demoralizing mud-soaked retreat to Corinth. "Had the enemy known how weak we were," reflected Ellis, "they could have captured the entire brigade without trouble."[34]

The ignominious fall of New Orleans later that month could be classified as comedy if people had not lost their lives in its defense. General Mansfield Lovell, the senior military officer on the scene, inherited a difficult situation when he first assumed command on October 18, 1861. His predecessors had already committed most available resources to the strategy that relied upon Fort Jackson and Fort St. Philip as the primary bulwark of defense. Well-meaning but meddlesome civilians constantly wanted to know what was being done to hasten the work of the defenders, and both superiors and subordinates reacted to Lovell's requests with an air of unconcern. Moreover, he had no authority over the Confederate naval forces in the region. By January 1862, most members of the city and state government understood that New Orleans was growing more imperiled with every passing day. Yet the state had recently passed a law reorganizing its militia, and Richmond now requested that Lovell send away even more precious manpower to go fight in Kentucky and west Tennessee. When news finally arrived on

April 18, 1862, that the U.S. Navy had begun bombarding Fort Jackson and Fort St. Philip with mortar barges, Lovell surely knew that the city's capitulation was certain—it was only a matter of time.

Several days into this bombardment, Lovell boarded a fast steam packet bound for those forts to observe the situation firsthand. Upon his arrival, at just before two o'clock in the morning, he quickly noticed that the *Louisiana*—a hastily built ironclad gunboat—had not been relocated so as to block the advance of the enemy fleet as he had ordered the day before. Moreover, an unusually high flow from the Mississippi River had not only carried away the barrier chains that might have slowed the enemy's advance past the forts; it had also begun to soak the portions of the defenses that had not already been burned to cinders by the hot shot lobbed into the forts by the Union mortars. Yet there was no time to haggle with subordinates now. Just half an hour after his arrival, the federal line of warships began making its run past the forts. Lovell scrambled back to his packet, which had to make all possible steam in its run toward New Orleans to stay out of the range of the powerful federal guns. Over the stern of his fleeing ship, Lovell could see the enemy's line of battle pass by the forts one by one; the night was lit up by the combatants' blazing away at each other in a hail of fire and smoke. Aside from a few conspicuous examples of valor, the craft in the small flotilla of defensive vessels added to the scene's ignominy by fleeing pell-mell from the much more powerful Union navy. After briefly stopping at the Chalmette defenses below the city to unload the powder he had initially hoped to deliver to Fort Jackson, Lovell continued on to New Orleans, where panic had already begun to set in.[35]

When Frederick Nash Ogden returned to New Orleans at the end of 1861, he soon discovered that men who possessed real military experience were now in great demand. By February, he had become part of a newly raised regiment, the Eighth Louisiana Battalion; only this time Ogden was a lieutenant—an officer and a gentleman—under the command of Lieutenant Colonel William Pinkney. After a few more weeks of training, Ogden received another promotion, this time to major. Such a meteoric rise in rank was not altogether uncommon in the Civil War, but it was undoubtedly welcome to this former cotton clerk. General Lovell positioned the Eighth Battalion's raw recruits along the defensive works at Chalmette, recently vacated by troops sent to Corinth. Here, as if to reenact Jackson's stunning 1815 victory, they guarded the only viable landward approach to New Orleans. Unfortunately for them, because their position had never been intended as a river defense, these men could bring only nine guns to bear upon the rapidly approaching Union squadron. Compounding such discouraging circumstances was that the bulk of their munitions had either been sent downriver to Fort

Jackson and Fort St. Philip or had been used to supply the navy's gunboats. As they watched Lovell's departing packet churn upstream toward New Orleans, surely Ogden's men knew that the only thing to be gained by their continued presence in the path of the enemy's advance was to salvage the few shreds of honor that remained in what was otherwise one of the Confederacy's most humiliating defeats.

When the *Cayuga*, the lead ship in Farragut's squadron, rounded a bend in the river and steamed within a quarter mile of their position, Pinkney's battalion leaped to its guns and poured a thundering volley at the oncoming vessel. Most of his men had never before fired a heavy gun, however, and their aim was wild in comparison with the well-served pieces on the ships that now bore down on their position. Yet it was good enough to make the *Cayuga* momentarily fall back. Indeed, between their fire and that from the five pieces on the opposite bank, this last line of Confederate defenders managed to strike the warship fourteen times. But when the *Brooklyn*, the *Pensacola*, and Farragut's flagship, the *Hartford*, hove near enough to rake their position with canister, the general commanding the works ordered a retreat. Leaving behind anything they could not physically carry, including their heavy guns, Fred Ogden and the men of the Eighth Battalion began a discouraging retreat toward New Orleans, through a heavy downpour. A large proportion of the men grew increasingly drunk with every passing mile of this disagreeable march, and by the time the battalion reached the train that would take them to Camp Moore, many had deserted.[36]

Even as Ogden and his men blazed away at the federal squadron, a telegram arrived at Fort Macomb ordering them to abandon the position. New Orleans was about to fall into the hands of the enemy, and like all other regional forces, the men stationed at Fort Macomb were now ordered to rendezvous at Camp Moore outside of Tangipahoa. Captain Capers, the senior officer at the fort, would have preferred to stay in place, but by the evening of April 25, the garrison made hasty preparations to board the steamers that waited to carry them to the north shore of Lake Pontchartrain. Among the evacuees were Captain Aristée Tissot and his Company B of the Twenty-third Louisiana Infantry. The men of the Twenty-third had volunteered to defend their home, the city of New Orleans, as part of the elite Tirailleurs, but instead General Lovell had not only converted them into a decidedly pedestrian regiment of heavy artillerists; he had stationed them in this remote, waterlogged outpost where they had not been allowed a single shot at the enemy. Their placement at a post where the greatest threat came from boredom was surely some reflection of Lovell's lack of confidence—and perhaps prejudice—regarding their soldierly qualities. It probably came as little surprise, then, to Capers or Tissot when many of these men slipped away and headed back

to New Orleans the minute they reached dry ground. Yet Tissot must have cultivated some real leadership qualities while stationed at Fort Macomb, for when
he and the scant remnants of the Twenty-third finally straggled into Camp
Moore at the beginning of May, most of Company B still remained with its
commander.[37]

Charles Sauvinet and the Native Guard's free men of color suddenly found themselves posted to defend a city that was on the verge of civil collapse. Their very
existence as a unit had been thrown into question the previous February when the
state reorganized the militia, temporarily disbanding the Native Guards. By late
March the increasingly dire situation in New Orleans had compelled Governor
Moore to call up his free black volunteers once again, but no real plan for their use
was decided upon until April 24, when news of Farragut's fleet steaming upriver
spurred a subordinate of General Lovell to hastily distribute old muskets to the
Native Guards and post them along the Esplanade side of the French Quarter.
What they were supposed to accomplish is difficult to say. Confederate authorities all around them were busily packing up whatever military stores could be
transported and carrying them either to the Jackson railroad depot or to waiting
steamers on the southern shore of Lake Pontchartrain. An observer of even the
meanest intelligence could easily deduce that Lovell was abandoning New Orleans to the enemy. Like many of the white gentleman militia who stayed behind
instead of retreating with the regular army, the soldiers of the Native Guards
quietly slipped home, where they hid their uniforms and weapons and awaited
the Union army's arrival. If Sauvinet was disappointed about being cheated out of
an opportunity to prove his manhood, however, he need not have been. He eventually got his chance, but not in a slaveholders' army.[38]

The frustration of the city's white, pro-Confederate residents left behind by
the retreating defenders was profound. "Poor New Orleans," Julia LeGrand recorded in her journal. "What has become of your promised greatness? . . . The
wretched generals, left here with our troops, ran away and left them. Lovell knew
not what to do; some say he was intoxicated, some say frightened. Of course the
greatest confusion prevailed, and every hour, indeed almost every moment, brought
its dreadful rumor. After it was known that the gunboats had actually passed, the
whole city, both camp and street was a scene of wild confusion. *The women only
did not seem afraid. They were all in favor of resistance, no matter how hopeless
that resistance might be.*" Dr. Warren Brickell, a renowned surgeon and a member of the Committee of Safety, witnessed the breakdown of civil authority that
took place in the streets of New Orleans the day the federal fleet appeared at the

riverfront. "I saw large quantities of sugar, molasses, bacon, and some corn being carried off from the town by the populace—men, women, children; black and white—all without restraint; on the contrary, with the encouragement of a man on horseback, dressed in a Confederate uniform."[39]

A scene of complete mayhem greeted Farragut's squadron by the time it finally anchored in front of the levee in New Orleans. Ships and unloaded cargoes burned furiously along the wharves, and angry mobs looted anything left unattended. With the river at its present height, the great guns from the Union flotilla could aim point-blank into the city, driving home the futility of resistance, Julia LeGrand's resolve to defend New Orleans notwithstanding. Braving a constant downpour and an unruly throng of bystanders, two naval officers came ashore and headed to city hall to negotiate the city's surrender. Unfortunately for these brave sailors, the leverage that the fleet's enormous firepower gave the Union negotiating position was undermined by fact that Northern forces did not yet have sufficient ground forces at the ready to actually hold the city of New Orleans. This meant that for three additional days, General Lovell continued to drain the city's military resources while general disorder ruled supreme. Finally, on May 1, General Benjamin Butler arrived with his infantry and took possession of New Orleans. Whether anyone at the time appreciated the fact or not, this moment signaled the beginning of Reconstruction in the South's largest city.[40]

In later investigations, Lovell became a favorite scapegoat of subordinates and superiors alike who hoped to wash their hands of responsibility for the boondoggle that was the defense of New Orleans. In reality, Lovell's quick realization that all was lost once Fort Jackson and Fort St. Philip had failed to halt Farragut's advance not only saved many lives but did much to minimize the military dimensions of the disaster. Second-guessing the Confederacy's imbecilic attitude toward defense of New Orleans, however, remained a favorite pastime of Louisianians, both during the war and for decades to come. The city that authorities in Richmond had believed untouchable fell to the Union navy in a matter of months. Yet, while the majority of the city's white occupants harbored resentment toward the Confederacy for its gross mismanagement of New Orleans's defense, they focused the lion's share of their frustrations upon the Northern invader who first stepped onto the levee on April 25, 1862—a justifiable reaction, perhaps, for a people whose sons and husbands were still on the other side of the battle lines, fighting for a cause that many Southerners were only beginning to define.

The memory of the city's cataclysmic relationship with the Confederate experiment lingered forever in the minds of its Civil War generation. In a period of fifteen months, New Orleans had plummeted from its position as one of the nation's most prosperous metropolises to a financially bankrupt municipality under military occupation. The Civil War ruthlessly altered New Orleans's course, its promise as the economic locus of the nation's midsection, and in the process assigned the city its fate as the stage upon which the nation's most fundamental questions of politics, race, and reunion unfolded.

Those young men who had been swept up by the heady days of spring in 1861 found themselves, at the end of April 1862, separated from their families and homes by the impenetrable barrier of the war's battle lines. But the powerful lessons of war were just beginning to take hold in their minds. Not only had they been witnesses to the prosperous twilight of Louisiana's antebellum era; each of them was, in one way or another, the product of that society. They had each volunteered for the defense of their native land for complex motivations. Few seem to have been solely animated by the great political questions of the day. Instead, they had joined because society expected it of them, and perhaps they expected it of themselves, as New Orleanians, as men. As the city fell, they were just beginning to learn about the nature of leadership, as well as how other men would act when faced with an ordeal by fire. They learned a great deal more in the three years before Appomattox. Yet, even as war eroded away the foundations of the society that they had hoped to inherit, it created an entirely new set of opportunities, particularly for men of their generation, class, and education who were unafraid to embrace the uncertainty of the age.

CHAPTER TWO

THE DAWNING
OF NEW REALITIES

1862–1865

≈ ≈ ≈

We confederates of New Orleans consider that Louisiana has been neglected by our Government.

—Julia Legrand, June 1862

harles St. Albin Sauvinet was clearly a man unafraid to act on instinct. The last remaining Confederate forces had barely fled the city when this former captain in the Native Guards tendered his services to the staff of General Benjamin Butler. Sauvinet's personal ties with the loyal white New Orleanians who first greeted Union authorities in April of 1862 are unclear, but both his knowledge of this network and its use yielded undeniable results. Merely four days after Butler's ascendancy, the multilingual Sauvinet had been appointed as the translator of a Union army provost court, making him the first man of color to serve in an official government capacity of any consequence in occupied New Orleans. Whether Butler or any of his subordinates knew that Sauvinet bore African ancestry was another matter.[1]

Sauvinet was unusual in many ways, and none was more significant than his ability to recognize and accept that New Orleans was on the precipice of fundamental change. It was understandable that pro-Confederate whites might don blinders, hoping that some omnipotent and providential hand might defy the cold calculus of reality and undo the cruel reverses that had befallen what they considered to be a righteous enterprise. Yet even the city's conquerors probably did not fully grasp the magnitude of the social transformation that would take place as a result of their deeds. In the coming decades, various forces conspired to turn back the hands of time on the social changes brought by the conflict, but despite whatever successes future counterrevolutionaries might someday claim, the city that had existed before the war was gone forever. In late spring 1862, most New Orleanians were only beginning to come to grips with this fact.

The collapse of Confederate New Orleans not only ushered in a new social dynamic in the city; it also had affected the worldviews of its occupants. Both Northern and Southern leaders had pitched their respective war aims in idealistic terms, and although some soldiers undoubtedly looked past such rhetoric and saw the political and economic calculus behind the conflict, many fought for what they believed were high ideals. It was ironic, therefore, that the war did so much to usher in the Gilded Age cynicism that characterized the last quarter of the nineteenth century. George Fredrickson and Louis Menand have both written of the changes that the war imposed on the worldview of Northern intellectuals such as Oliver Wendell Holmes and William James. The conflict dampened youthful "hearts of fire" and left in its wake a reductive ethos that decades later manifested itself in the philosophy of pragmatism. The hardships faced by those who witnessed the war produced a generation of Americans who afterward looked upon the romantic idealism of the earlier age as impractical and even undesirable. As historian Reid Mitchell has observed, "tough-mindedness was a legacy of the Civil War." The emergence of such sentiments had a profound impact upon the nature of the postbellum struggle for mastery.[2]

The very difficulty of the war also provided an opportunity for those who fought it to prove to themselves and to others who they were as men and, in turn, lay the foundation for who they would become in the postbellum years. The ease with which fresh recruits from both armies tossed about abstractions such as honor, duty, and courage in the festive days of April 1861 was long gone by the time the war entered its second year. By 1862, the importance of deeds quickly overshadowed the value of words, and the approbation of comrades became more important than that of folks back home. Combat forever separated these soldiers from the rest of society in important ways that probably only a survivor of a similarly bloody enterprise can fully understand. Oliver Wendell Holmes Jr. tried to explain this phenomenon in his famous "Soldier's Faith" speech delivered on Memorial Day 1895 at Harvard University. Holmes described such "faith" as "true and adorable which leads a soldier to throw away his life in obedience to a blindly accepted duty, in a cause which he little understands, in a plan of campaign of which he has little notion, under tactics of which he does not see the use." His words were an admonition from "the generation born about 1840" to his younger listeners about the evils of crass materialism, but they were also an articulation of his belief that those who came later would never fully grasp what the Civil War generation had endured. Holmes had entered the war as an ardent

abolitionist. He emerged from it skeptical about the moral authority of those political radicals who had promoted the abolitionist cause. Like the men described
in the following pages, Holmes discovered along the way that the practical man
who did his duty and stood by his comrades was the one he truly admired.[3]

Both the ill-conceived strategy for New Orleans's defense and the subsequent
abandonment by the Confederate army shattered forever the illusions of those
who had naively believed the government could deliver on its promise of guaranteeing peace and prosperity. Soon afterward came the bitter realization that the
old order had not only lost control of the city; it was not even in command of its
own future. The failure of New Orleans's Confederate experience was so devastating and universal that even the most sanguine secessionist had to admit that
the city's era of prosperity had been put into abeyance, perhaps permanently.
Such circumstances fostered resentment between the city's residents and the
Confederate government, but the white residents who had within a span of days
witnessed the discomforting phenomenon of social inversion reserved the majority of their wrath for the recently arrived representatives of Union authority. Economic distress played a prominent role in generating such antipathy. Lost forever
were the substantial resources that had gone into the Confederate effort, and the
disruption of the city's agriculturally based trade had caused a severe shortage of
food, cash, and optimism. The fact that Confederate currency was now worthless
only highlighted a simple fact; New Orleans residents were defeated *and* broke.
Yet privation did not lie at the core of civilian outrage. Unlike Atlanta or Vicksburg,
cities that later witnessed protracted struggles in the name of their defense, New
Orleans had been ceded with a comparative whimper—it had been betrayed.[4]

The chief target for civilian resentment and the most popularized villain during New Orleans's early months of occupation was unquestionably General Benjamin "Beast" Butler. An admittedly self-promoting political soldier, Butler commanded the military occupation of the city beginning in May 1862. From the
moment he stepped ashore, Butler engaged in a bitter and largely petty tit-for-
tat confrontation with the city's elite white women. When Martha Walton, whose
husband was away in Virginia commanding the elite Washington Artillery, refused to remove a Confederate flag that decorated her bonnet, Butler placed her
under house arrest. More unladylike behavior, such as spitting at and dumping
chamber pots on passing men in blue, resulted in Butler's infamous "woman order." This edict proclaimed, "When any female shall, by word, gesture, or movement, insult or show contempt for any officer or soldier of the United States, she
shall be . . . held liable to be treated as a woman of the town plying her trade."

This exchange grew partly out of the precarious situation in which some New Orleans women now found themselves. The capture of the city had placed them on the opposite side of a largely impenetrable barrier represented by the battle-front. Separated from the men upon whom they depended financially, these women tried to adjust to an economic situation with which many of them were unfamiliar. For example, Julia LeGrand confided to her journal, "If I could get outside these hateful lines, I could use my Confederate money, and Claude, poor fellow could send me some more, even if we could not get to Texas. Ah, well, some people are born for both small and large mishaps." Yet many white women remained more defiant than resigned. When soldiers came to the Waltons' fashionable Camp Street residence to search for more subversive Confederate flags, the officer in charge apologized for any pains he might cause. His contrite attitude only encouraged Emma Walton, the twenty-one-year-old daughter of James and Martha Walton, to reply, "I can only be pained by my equal and I am certainly not pained now."[5]

Unconquered Confederate women were not Butler's only target. Other infamous stunts included rather heavy-handed methods for assuring respect for the Union itself. Fidel Keller, a bookseller from Switzerland, exhibited a skeleton in his shop window under a sign that read "Chickahominy." Keller boasted that his macabre tableau depicted a dead Union soldier killed in that battle, although in reality he had purchased the bones from a financially strapped medical student. The flamboyant exhibit earned Keller a two-year stay at the army prison on Ship Island off the coast of Mississippi. William Mumford was not so lucky. In a fit of belligerence, the professional gambler tore down and shredded the Stars and Stripes that flew from the flagstaff at the Orleans Mint on Esplanade Avenue. Convicted of treason and sentenced to death at Butler's order, Mumford was hanged publicly in front of a shocked and mortified populace.[6]

Yet it was Butler's zealous enforcement of the Confiscation Act, passed by the U.S. Congress in early 1862, that led to his denouement in New Orleans. When he entered foreign legations in the city in search of hidden Confederate assets, the general precipitated a minor diplomatic crisis, engendering the wrath of Lincoln, who had never been a political ally. Another scandal, surrounding his subordinates' dealings in confiscated cotton, caused Butler to exit New Orleans dogged by a reputation for corruption and thievery. Although Butler himself was never convicted of wrongdoing, and the tales of his larceny were often inflated for propaganda purposes, individuals around him, including his brother Andrew, managed to amass considerable fortunes not commensurate with their army pay grade.[7]

Butler's tenure in New Orleans had its highlights, however. Among them was the creation of the first meaningful contingent of black soldiers in the Union army. The standard narrative of what transpired between the former Confederate Native Guards and Benjamin Butler comes originally from the classic 1911 history written by Rodolphe Desdunes, *Nos Hommes et Notre Histoire*, an account cited by most subsequent scholars. According to Desdunes, brothers Henry and Octave Rey, along with Eugène Rapp and Edgar Davis, all of whom had been officers in the Native Guards, approached Butler not long after the invasion with the purpose of turning over the arms that they had stashed away in various Afro-Creole mutual aid society buildings across the city. When queried by Butler regarding their loyalties, the delegation eventually assured the general that while they could not speak for the entire community, most of New Orleans's free people of color stood foursquare behind the Union cause. "Fifteen days later," wrote Desdunes, "Butler's order came, inviting the population of color to enlist under the banner of liberty." In reality, Butler did not immediately desire the use of colored troops and had even discouraged subordinates from enlisting such help in the field. It was not until many weeks later, that August, when faced with a threat from a Confederate force in the region and lacking a sufficient force of his own, that the general authorized a provisional regiment of colored troops.[8]

In his version of events, Desdunes appended a curious line about the involvement of Charles Sauvinet in the creation of the Union Native Guards: "Let us say further in passing that Mr. St. Albain Sauvinet acted as interpreter in General Butler's office. Mr. Sauvinet was a Creole. There is no doubt that he contributed toward facilitating this interview between General Butler and the associates of Octave Rey." Desdunes knew personally each of the four men who made up this delegation, but because their adult lives had overlapped little, it is doubtful that he would have known Sauvinet firsthand. Yet his description of him as "Creole" and not "a Creole of color," as he so often does to clarify the point in his narrative, also raises questions. Sauvinet was every bit as much an officer in the Native Guards as the Rey brothers had been, but it seems he had chosen to navigate a most treacherous path—one that carried him to both sides of the color line. Moreover, Sauvinet did more than "contribute" to this meeting: he was clearly the man on the inside, the one who could facilitate connections between white and Afro-Creole worlds. Time revealed the honorable intentions of his efforts, but to his contemporaries on both sides of the color line, Sauvinet must have been a difficult man to know.[9]

Butler's call resulted in an overwhelming response by the New Orleans black community and led directly to the raising of three colored regiments. After weeks of drilling and inspection, these eager soldiers held a formal review parade on Canal Street. It was a hopeful moment for the city's people of color and an anxious time for pro-Confederate whites. Abby Day Slocum, whose husband was serving with the elite Washington Artillery in faraway Virginia, described the development in the most derisive terms: "Butler has armed 10,000 Nigs with Enfield Rifles & knives & has taken the intelligent houseservant & made them officers to these regiments—these men walk the streets with plumed chapeaux & if any white man dares smile at them he is at once arrested." For everyone, the scene was emblematic of the dramatic changes taking place in their midst.[10]

Like so many other aspects of his life both before and after the war, Sauvinet's experience with the U.S. Colored Troops was anything but ordinary. Along with his fellow elite Creoles of color, he enlisted as a junior officer in the Union army. There was, however, an important distinction about his service. Sauvinet received an appointment as quartermaster of the Second Louisiana Native Guards, and though he was only a lieutenant, this appointment made him a member of the staff and not the line. Nearly all of the line officers during the early months of the Native Guards' existence, that is, the captains and lieutenants of individual companies, were men of color. Most of the regimental officers—chaplains, majors, colonels, adjutants, and quartermasters—were white.[11]

At the beginning of October 1862, Butler deployed Sauvinet and the Second Native Guards along a twenty-mile stretch of the New Orleans, Opelousas, and Great Western rail line, starting from a small depot near the Algiers bank and extending all the way to Raceland. Like most colored troops during the war, the Second soon got a taste of the kinds of mean-spirited discrimination the army was capable of inflicting upon its own. White officers who resented either their commands or their superiors complained incessantly about the performance of black soldiers, white enlisted men either ignored or defied outright soldiers of color who outranked them, and all the while the regiment could expect the most demeaning, labor-intensive, and ultimately meaningless duty possible. It is remarkable that these men persisted as well as they did under such circumstances. Like soldiers in nearly any army of any age, they had yielded their individualism upon enlistment, and some men deserted rather than submit to such servitude. Yet the uniform of the U.S. Army also represented something much larger than military discipline: for the first time in their lives, these men existed as *men*, perhaps even as citizens in the eyes of the government. An important door had opened.[12]

The appointment of Nathaniel P. Banks, who replaced Butler in mid-December 1862, portended drastic changes for the black troops stationed across the Gulf

South. Like Butler, Banks was a political general, but unlike his Democratic pre-
decessor, he was a Republican and had powerful ties within the party. Just forty-
one years of age, the dashing, ambitious, and socially connected Banks had been
both the governor of Massachusetts and Speaker of the House. Had he performed
merely as a competent general, he might have one day become a serious con-
tender for the presidency. Unfortunately, his enormous shortcomings as a military
strategist had already been proved beyond any doubt on the battlefield. His transfer to a theater of war where the Union army had thus far met with overwhelming
success, however, must have given Banks some hope of salvaging his military
reputation. As a political administrator, he took a less stern course in dealing with
New Orleans's rebel sympathizers, rescinding many of Butler's less popular edicts
in the vain hope of winning the hearts of former Confederates. Banks was also far
less enthusiastic about black soldiers, especially black officers. Although he committed one regiment of colored troops to combat during the siege of the Confederate stronghold at Port Hudson, he remained dubious of their military value and
even less convinced of their equality as men. The arrival of Banks was not good
news for the Afro-Creole activists who had hoped to engage the cause of freedom
by joining the army.[13]

In late December 1862, Banks relieved Sauvinet's Second Regiment of the
Native Guards from duty along the New Orleans, Opelousas, and Great Western
and relocated them to Ship Island, just off of the Mississippi coastline. Assignment to this remote outpost greatly reduced the likelihood that these men would
ever see combat, and it also eliminated the perceived problems associated with
having a black military unit deep in Louisiana's sugar-producing regions at the
exact moment the Emancipation Proclamation took effect. The order, however,
gave Sauvinet a welcome opportunity to see his wife, Angela, who was at the time
eight months pregnant with their third child, and it seems that during his two-
week visit the couple may have come to a momentous decision about the future
of their children. After the birth of their daughter and Charles Sauvinet's departure for Ship Island, Angela took all three of her offspring to the recorder of
births. It was not unheard-of for nineteenth-century parents to record the births
of multiple children born in different years all at the same time, and that is what
took place in this instance. James Nelson, born in 1859, Charles Silas, born in late
1860, and the infant Marie Clothilde appear on consecutive certificates in the
birth-record books for Orleans Parish. What was unusual about this occasion was
that for all of them the racial classification was "white." Whether this designation
resulted from a conscious decision of Angela or Charles Sauvinet or from a mere

mistake by the recorder of births, it could hardly have escaped the Sauvinets' notice.[14]

Back on Ship Island, the vast majority of the regiment's duty involved the drudgery of guarding prisoners or constructing seaward fortifications, but occasionally more edifying tasks came their way. One such episode occurred in April 1863, when a contingent of the Second Native Guards took part in a daring raid on the Confederate-held town of Pascagoula. Certainly this successful expedition, which resulted in capturing a stand of enemy colors, did much to boost the morale of black soldiers everywhere. Yet an even more profound phenomenon occurred daily in camp: the men were acquiring the important skill of literacy. "Out of my regiment," observed Sauvinet, "I presume there are some 200 men that went in who were slaves before the war and who came out of the regiment knowing how to read passably." Soldiers at the garrison on Ship Island could expect to rise at dawn and be actively engaged in their duties from 7:00 in the morning until 8:30 in the evening. "As soon as they were free of their regular duties," noted their quartermaster, "they all had their books, and you could see them all day long trying to learn."[15]

As the spring of 1863 turned into summer, Nathaniel Banks intensified his efforts to rid the department of the Gulf of the problematic presence of black officers. Using a variety of tactics, including competency tests and the assignment of black units to useless fatigue duty, Banks and his immediate subordinates either goaded officers of color into resigning or removed them outright under the pretense that they were unfit for service. However, Lieutenant Sauvinet neither resigned nor was removed. In September, when Banks's purge was almost complete, the colonel in command of the Second Native Guards (now designated the Twenty-ninth Corps D'Afrique) recommended to his superiors that Sauvinet be promoted to major. "He is a man I believe in every way worthy of the position," noted Colonel Alfred Hall, "and has always performed his duties honestly and faithfully." Headquarters did not approve this request, but Sauvinet remained an officer in the U.S. Army for the duration of the war. Moreover, in 1865 he was promoted to captain, and he received an honorable discharge in July 1865, making him the longest-serving black officer in the entire army.[16]

The same critical manpower shortages that had spurred Benjamin Butler to finally give serious consideration to the fighting potential of New Orleans's loyal blacks also inspired him to raise similar units of loyal white Louisiana men. Butler's effort to recruit white Southerners to the cause of the Union was not without parallel in other Southern states, particularly Virginia, but it did have greater potential for success. The city had fallen well before Confederate authorities could conscript large numbers of New Orleans's working-class whites, many of whom were immigrants who had come to Louisiana in the 1850s. They may have had ties to the old slaveholding regime, but not particularly strong ones. When the war was over, these regiments provided the nucleus of a white, blue-collar Republican voting base in New Orleans, something unknown in most other Southern cities following Appomattox. In the meantime, they helped address a manpower shortage that had been created by the Union's own success at conquering enemy ground.[17]

Butler also needed veteran officers to lead these new loyal regiments; thus were created opportunities for men who had come to New Orleans with his army and who were willing to take a chance on the unknown. It was a situation tailor-made for a man like Algernon Sydney Badger, a twenty-two-year-old shop clerk from Milton, Massachusetts, who, like Fred Ogden, had joined a regiment of volunteers as a private just four days after the firing on Fort Sumter. When his ninety-day enlistment was over, Badger secured a lieutenant's commission in the Twenty-sixth Massachusetts, one of the army regiments destined for the invasion of New Orleans. He saw relatively little action in the war until he transferred into the First Louisiana Cavalry in November 1862. Badger's precipitous rise in rank began shortly thereafter, starting in February of 1863, when he received a promotion to captain and company commander. Across the summer, his unit participated in the small Battle of Bisland and the much larger siege of the Confederate garrison at Port Hudson, a place where Badger and his dismounted troopers joined an ill-fated attack made by the First Native Guards. Less than a year after transferring into the First Louisiana, Badger received yet another promotion, this time to major. He had just turned twenty-four and was now in command of the entire regiment. Thus far, both the war and Louisiana had been good to him.[18]

The difficult work began in earnest for Badger's Unionist Louisianians in the spring of 1864, when General Banks began his ill-fated Red River campaign. From March until late June of that year, the First Louisiana saw nearly continuous campaigning, skirmishing, and battle, all stretched over hundreds of miles ranging from Alexandria, Louisiana, to the Texas border. At the Battle of Sabine Crossroads in early April, Confederate general and Louisiana native Richard Taylor surprised the Union column with his impetuosity and delivered the federal forces their most stinging defeat in the region. Badger's men, fighting dismounted at this engagement, took heavy casualties. Yet despite all of the bloodletting that took place throughout the spring, Badger himself managed to escape unharmed. His luck continued to hold until June 5, 1864, when his regiment fought a skirmish near the False River in Pointe Coupee Parish. Here Badger was shot in the leg, and the bullet broke his left tibia. The surgeons at the hospital in New Orleans that treated him were particularly concerned about his wound and thought it likely that he would lose the leg, because the projectile had passed through the horse's belly before lodging in its rider's calf. Badger proved resilient to infection, however, and kept all of his limbs. Moreover, by the time he returned to his command, now stationed at Morganza, Louisiana, he had been promoted to lieutenant colonel.[19]

Badger's regiment spent the last months of the war crisscrossing southern Alabama and Mississippi and northern Florida in search of the Confederacy's last holdouts. During this time, at an engagement near the Escambia River, he witnessed a poignant scene of the futility and waste brought about by the war's needless prolongation and, in addition, the cost in life that men like himself were willing to pay to prove their manly honor. While traveling northward to participate in the siege of Mobile, Badger's men encountered the tattered remnants of two dismounted Alabama cavalry regiments who had somehow hoped to halt the advance of his well-supplied veteran troopers. Shortly after Badger ordered his men to charge, though, the Alabamians broke in panic and confusion. "The enemy was demoralized to such a degree that arms, clothing, and in fact everything that could impede their flight was thrown away, and scattered along the road and through the woods," Badger recorded in his report. What he observed next, however, moved him deeply. With the bridge over the Escambia burned and their route of escape barred, some of the fleeing rebels rode their mounts off the bluff and into the water, where both horse and rider drowned in the swift springtime current. Badger's men captured scores of Confederates that day, including a general, and one of his men received the Medal of Honor for wrestling a stand of colors from the hands of a rebel soldier, but it was not without cost. Badger recorded in his official report, "I deem it justice to pay a tribute to Lieutenant Shaffer, who was killed at the extreme advance." Flush with the excitement of victory and the prospect of valor, the young officer became one of only two men in the regiment who were slain that day by a broken enemy. Civil War historians have often written of masculine honor in regionally constructed terms, but accounts of men like Badger and his mortally wounded subordinate, as well as of the fleeing Confederates who would rather drown than submit to defeat, reveal that Northern and Southern citizen-soldiers often hewed to a similar standard of masculinity.

For Badger, as for Oliver Wendell Holmes Jr., what had begun as a war for union had become a study in comradeship and duty.[20]

Frederick Nash Ogden and Aristée Louis Tissot were among the thousands of officers and men who converged at Camp Moore in the last week of April 1862 following the disaster at New Orleans. With conditions at the training depot teetering on the edge of chaos, the days that followed doubtlessly challenged their leadership abilities. Most units arrived with only a fraction of their normal contingent, the rest of their number having either remained in New Orleans or deserted along the line of retreat. The inglorious fall of their hometown had been their first taste of combat for most of these men, and the fact that many had never intended to leave southern Louisiana for the sake of Southern nationhood fueled discontent in the ranks. Nor were they in the clear. General Mansfield Lovell, already aware that authorities in Richmond would likely blame him for the loss of New Orleans, began to exhibit some of the first signs of a man bordering on psychological breakdown. He did, however, retain enough of his wits to send reinforcements upriver to Vicksburg just as soon as the first available units had sufficiently regrouped. Nobody in the Confederate command structure possessed reliable intelligence about the enemy's intentions, but it was clear that they could not afford to sit idly by while the Union navy seized the entire Mississippi River. Meanwhile, mountains of supplies that had been hastily pulled out of New Orleans now had to be transferred to locations where they might do the most good. The responsibility for transforming this broken army into a force capable of carrying out the orders that might ensure its own immediate survival fell on the shoulders of a group of young field and staff officers like Ogden and Tissot. It was an enormous task.[21]

Fred Ogden and his men were among the first of thousands of Confederate defenders who poured into Vicksburg in May 1862. Less than two weeks after the men of the Eighth Louisiana had abandoned their position at Chalmette, they found themselves preparing entrenchments at another critical point along the Mississippi River. The geography of Vicksburg placed its defenders at much greater advantage than they had encountered in New Orleans. High bluffs along the city's riverfront offered a commanding panorama of any approaching enemy ships, and furthermore, the series of waterline and lower-town batteries that were capable of firing point-blank into enemy ships offered great discomfort to any vessel that hoped to pass unscathed. Ogden had been placed in command of the Whig Office Battery, two heavy guns that lay in the absolute center of these works.[22]

It had taken a bit more time at Camp Moore for Tissot's Twenty-third Louisiana to reach a minimum standard of readiness. Having been stationed at Fort Macomb during the fall of New Orleans, none of this unit had yet seen any combat, and desertion had reduced its strength to merely three companies. Finally, on May 25, what was left of the reorganized unit elected Aristée Tissot as lieutenant colonel, but for some reason—because this group of fighting men hardly constituted a regiment, because of their suspected Gallic liabilities, or because Mansfield Lovell's son was the current lieutenant colonel of the company—the commanding general, Mansfield Lovell, set aside Tissot's promotion. Thus the seeds of a growing antagonism between Tissot and his Anglo-Confederate superiors were sown. This insult to his honor still lingering in the air, Tissot and his men boarded the train to Vicksburg, where they joined Frederick Nash Ogden and the Eighth Battalion along the waterfront batteries.[23]

They arrived just in time for the first round of fighting in the Union's protracted campaign to take the city. Admiral Farragut had first anchored his Gulf Blockading Squadron below Vicksburg as early as May 18, but it was not until some hours before first light on June 28 that he formed his squadron into a line of battle and braved the batteries along the waterfront. The Confederate guns and the Federal fleet blazed away at each other in the bonfire-lit darkness, but in the end, Farragut proved that he could pass the citadel if he chose, though he would have to choose his moment very carefully. Manning the guns at Gibbs's upper battery, Tissot and his men also engaged the Federal ironclad *Essex* and the ram *Queen of the West* as they made an unsuccessful attempt to sink the ugly but formidable Confederate ironclad *Arkansas*, which was moored below the city's bluffs. By the end of July, the seasonal drop in the Mississippi River's level and the military conclusions of Farragut and his subordinates that Vicksburg could be taken only by a landward approach brought a temporary calm to the Confederate lines. Tissot and Ogden, however, had other tasks at hand.[24]

By the beginning of August, Tissot was not only festering under the insult of having his promotion set aside; he was also suffering from what two different army surgeons termed "Hepatitis Chronica." He tendered his resignation on the back of one surgeon's certificate, stating that he had "used every means for the recovery of my health," but that "it becomes every day more impaired." Unimpressed with Tissot's plight, Colonel Fuller, the acting commander at headquarters, responded, "Capt. Tissot is a French Creole and is anxious to return to his home within the enemy's lines. He evidently has the '*maladie du pays.*'" Not only was it a strong accusation to make against a brother officer, but it was the second grave insult he had received at the hands of his superiors within the space of six months. Nevertheless, somehow Tissot's request made it past Fuller's authority, and in September, in the midst of his failed invasion of Kentucky, Braxton Bragg approved Tissot's resignation. Tissot was not yet done with the army, though. Eventually, the secretary of war approved his promotion to lieutenant colonel, and by November, with such vindication fueling his recovery, Tissot reported back as "unresigned" to Fort Hill, the northernmost riverfront anchor of Vicksburg's now sprawling landward defenses. He remained in this general vicinity until the city fell.[25]

At the beginning of February 1863, Julia LeGrand sat with her diary in New Orleans, scribbling away on a particularly long-winded passage of unconfirmed gossip: "Fred Ogden, too, the young captain of a gun or two at Vicksburg," gushed LeGrand, "is engaged to somebody, whose name I can not learn." The young lady in question was Laura Bryson Jackson, and if the blueblood LeGrand had had any idea of her commonplace heritage, she probably would have appended a few characteristically petty remarks. Laura Jackson was strong, however, and undoubtedly had to be to survive the environment in which she lived. Just seventeen years old when she accepted Ogden's proposal of marriage, Jackson was the second-youngest of five parentless children who had once taken up residence in the house of a local planter. Her oldest brother, C. L. Jackson, had accompanied William Walker on his 1858 filibustering expedition to Nicaragua; he went on to become a Confederate colonel known popularly in the region as "the rider of the gray horse." Even though she may have lacked the social rank of the other women typically taken as wives by Ogden men, Laura Jackson was an undeniably good match for the dashing Fred Ogden, who himself had never quite fit the family mold.[26]

When Vicksburg finally fell to Union forces on July 4, 1863, Tissot and Ogden were among its starved defenders who marched out of the city to a parole camp at Enterprise, Mississippi. By December, both men had made their way back to friendly lines, but in completely opposite directions. Ogden, cited for "gallant conduct" at Vicksburg, had found something he was good at—perhaps even enjoyed. Tissot, however, had returned to New Orleans and made his separate peace. Within a matter of weeks he once again bid adieu to his parents' home on Bayou St. John, only this time to board a steamer bound for France, where he spent the rest of the war advancing his legal training at the University of Paris. Tissot did not return to New Orleans until 1866.[27]

In contrast, Fred Ogden spent the rest of the war proving his considerable abilities as a leader of men. In March 1864, he was placed in temporary command of the Ninth Battalion of Partisan Rangers, a cavalry unit that roved southern Louisiana and Mississippi in search of targets of opportunity. Ogden received a chilly welcome from his new command, however. Many of these men believed that there were officers in their own ranks more worthy of promotion than this artillerist who had surrendered at Vicksburg. Yet in spite of this rocky start, Ogden eventually earned their trust and admiration. In fighting near St. Francisville, Louisiana, some staff officers observed the unit charging madly toward camp in a cloud of dust and feared the worst. Coolly observing the movements through his field glasses, the commanding general reassured his men, "No, they are not retreating, Ogden comes in front." When the Ninth Battalion's regular commander later returned, this same general decided that Ogden should remain in control of the unit. In three short months, he noted, Ogden had taken a body of men who "had just emerged from a turmoil of discontent and insubordination, and had . . . brought . . . [them] . . . into a highly disciplined state." The following month, Ogden was promoted to lieutenant colonel, and a month later to full colonel.[28]

Only two weeks after fighting at the battle of Jackson, Mississippi, on July 5–7, 1864, Fred Ogden reunited with Laura Bryson Jackson. The two were married in Rankin County, Mississippi—a romantic and chivalric moment in an uncertain era full of upheaval and destruction. Ogden was soon back at work, spending much of his time intercepting and destroying cotton that planters across the region had hoped to transport to Union lines in defiance of crumbling Confederate authority. It was a curious task for a man who had once worked in the commodities trades, and perhaps it was an unwise one for someone who was going to reenter the business later. A dishonest man placed in such a position could certainly have made a fortune. Ogden was not one to put profit in front of principle, though, and this trait made him an ideal commander in a region that had grown increasingly marked by corruption on both sides of the conflict. Down the road, men in New Orleans openly praised the honesty and courage of Frederick Nash Ogden, even while they quietly lent support to his dishonest rivals. One cannot help but wonder if the seeds of their duplicity and resentment had been planted on the violent cotton frontier of the Trans-Mississippi. In any case, his demonstration of character had earned the genuine admiration of one of his company commanders, Thomas C. W. Ellis, E. John Ellis's older brother and closest confidant. Thomas, a planter and a prominent lawyer, had avoided service, but by the end of 1863, his enlistment was inevitable. John had once urged his brother to join a capable unit lest he be conscripted into a regiment of green cannon fodder, advice that Thomas seems to have heeded. It was the first tie between the Ellis brothers and Fred Ogden—the beginning of a lifelong bond between men who shared the "soldier's faith."[29]

The war was barely a year old when Arthur Toledano suddenly found himself in command of the entire Watson Battery. Because some officers had been killed or wounded and others had proved unfit for duty, promotion became likely for junior officers who, like Toledano, had managed to both survive and acquit themselves well during the Shiloh campaign. The war had ceased being a gentleman's outing, and both the Confederate and the Union armies started to recognize the wisdom of promoting veteran officers who had proved their mettle in battle rather than merely allowing soldiers to elect their commanders. By the end of April 1862, the Watson Battery's senior officers had left for Vicksburg to assume even greater responsibilities, leaving Toledano in charge and making possible the promotion of several of the unit's capable noncommissioned officers to the rank of lieutenant. The result was a well-trained and capably led battery of artillery. Unfortunately for Toledano and his men, the selection process for high command in the Confederate army remained a popularity contest. The veteran soldier Jefferson Davis should have known better. Instead, as he was beset by considerations of personality and politics, the logic behind his choice of generals differed little from the rationale employed by green recruits when they had elected their captains in April 1861. Saddled with charismatic but incompetent leadership, the Watson Battery was in for a disagreeable year of campaigning and defeat.

A good example of the problems encountered by Toledano and the Watson Battery was those that occurred during General Earl Van Dorn's ill-conceived campaign to recapture Corinth in early October 1862. On the night after the first day of the battle, Van Dorn had given Toledano's brigade commander, Brigadier General John S. Bowen, a crude and wholly inaccurate sketch of some enemy emplacements and ordered him storm them at first light. When Bowen attempted to carry out his orders the next morning, it became obvious to all that the intelligence received from Van Dorn was terribly wrong. Bowen brought four guns of Toledano's battery forward and ordered them to test the enemy works with spherical case shot. Immediately, the Union lines lit up with more than twenty heavy guns, killing or wounding fifty-five men. Bowen ordered his brigade to retreat and find cover, but it was only the beginning of the day's retrograde movement. Nightfall found the Watson Battery in the midst of a heated rear-guard action, using canister to mow down a determined Union counterattack. On the same day that his retreating brigade reached Holly Springs, Mississippi, the disgusted Bowen promptly requested a court of inquiry to investigate Van Dorn's actions.[30]

It was at Port Hudson in the summer of 1863, however, where the Watson Battery faced its most difficult duty. Just upriver of Baton Rouge, Port Hudson was a final Confederate stronghold on the Mississippi that ultimately earned the dubious distinction of the site of the most protracted siege in American military history. Between the bluffs that fronted the river and the swampy topography that defined many of the landward approaches to the town, taking Port Hudson presented any attacker with a formidable challenge. Its defense depended not only upon the large water batteries that threatened river traffic, but also upon field artillerists like Toledano whose shot, grape, and canister mowed down repeated ground assaults. It was here in late June 1863 that the Second Regiment of Louisiana Native Guards made a valiant but doomed attack against the citadel, a case of Creoles killing other Creoles. The assault resulted in many deaths, including that of the Second Regiment's brave commander, André Cailloux, a man who had once called himself "the blackest man in New Orleans" and had encouraged his soldiers forward with commands in both French and English. Amid this bloodbath, seventy-five hundred Confederates held firm against forty thousand Union soldiers for forty-eight days, despite a determined siege and literally no receipt of reinforcements or supplies. Reduced to eating mules, cats, and any other creature unwise enough to pass within musket shot, Toledano and his men endured a miserable time.[31]

"Yesterday we were shocked by the firing of 100 guns to celebrate the fall of Port Hudson," Emma Walton wrote from New Orleans to her father serving in faraway Virginia. "All things considered," she added, "we have not yet become depressed." The surrender of Vicksburg on the Fourth of July had sealed the fate of those who had so tenaciously defended the Confederacy's last citadel on the Mississippi at Port Hudson. In negotiating the terms of capitulation, the Union generals agreed to parole the Confederate enlisted men, but not the majority of their officers. Four days after the Federals' triumphant salvo deafened the Crescent City, Toledano boarded the steamer Suffolk at Port Hudson with the rest of the Confederate prisoners and began the brief downriver journey to the city of his birth.[32]

The occupying Union forces had turned the upper floors of the massive U.S. Custom House on Canal Street into a prisoner detention facility, and it was here that Arthur Toledano spent the remainder of the summer. From the windows of the Custom House, he could have seen the office on Carondelet Street where only two years before he had traded in cotton. As passers-by taunted them for having eaten mules and cats while in the garrison at Port Hudson, one prisoner shouted out, "Confederate mules and Confederate cats are a damned sight better than Yankee pork!" Despite the obvious discomfort of Toledano and his comrades, however, the general opinion among them was that they would soon be exchanged. The luckier officers even obtained three-hour passes under the order of General Banks, much to the delight of many pro-Confederate young women. Writing to her father in October, Emma Walton declared that their visits were "the first *Carnival* in N.O. since the War." In early September, one of E. John Ellis's former law professors, the noted German-American jurist and Union loyalist Christian Roselius, petitioned General Banks on Toledano's behalf. He vouched for the Creole officer's character and guaranteed that he would not violate the parole. Banks approved this request, and for three consecutive days Toledano enjoyed a brief period of freedom. A cruel reversal of fortune was in store for him, however. Unlike Tissot and Ogden, who after surrendering at Vicksburg received their parole at Enterprise, Mississippi, Toledano and the other officers captured at Port Hudson were shipped by Union authorities to the Johnson's Island prisoner-of-war camp, the inhospitable island in Lake Erie's Sandusky Bay. Although rumors of a pending exchange provided daily fodder for conversation among the inmates at Johnson's Island, the Creole officer did not leave until he finally took the oath of allegiance on June 11, 1865.[33]

For E. John Ellis, even the simple goal of returning home seemed uncertain, and he must have felt quite homesick in February 1864 as he sat down to write a letter to his sister Mary back in Amite City. Ellis was a long way from his father's plantation in St. Helena Parish, Louisiana. When he gazed out the window, he could see sleighs crackling their way across the frozen expanse of Lake Erie's Sandusky Bay. Recently turned twenty-four years of age, Captain E. John Ellis, like Arthur Toledano, was now an inmate at the Johnson's Island prison for Confederate officers. That such a cold and inhospitable place even existed might not have crossed his mind before the war. Now it was his home until the fighting was over.[34]

As Ellis had led other young men from his home town of Amite, the war had supplied him an education in duty, politics, and character that no other academy on earth could have furnished. He had come to admire the dash of P. G. T. Beauregard, respect the fury and discipline of Braxton Bragg, and despise the petty tyrants who used their rank to make the life of the average soldier a living hell. Two years of military campaigning had also seared images into Ellis's memory that surely lasted a lifetime: the bloody days of Shiloh; a rowdy furlough in Mobile—"Oh, the whisky and noise of that night"; a shell burst showering the skull and brains of a fellow officer all over his men; a charge into canister. After an engagement at Murfreesboro, Ellis walked out through the dead lying on the darkened battlefield. In the moonlight he examined the bloody, motionless faces of the Union soldiers, the dew already beading on their bodies, and convinced himself that these poor farm boys and immigrants had been swindled by their government. A swaying figure on the edge of his vision interrupted these thoughts and Ellis went to investigate. He discovered a Union soldier, one hand clutching a sapling, the other a vine, swinging to and fro in a deep state of delirium. Getting no response from his call, Ellis grabbed the man's arm, at which point the soldier "turned and broke into a loud vacant laugh and at the same moment the moon-light shone on his face and half lit up his fierce restless eyes." The man had a lead ball lodged in his forehead and was smeared thoroughly with blood and mud. "I never saw a more hideous sight," Ellis wrote later. His days of combat ended at the battle of Missionary Ridge, when Union troops surrounded the young officer and what was left of his unit. As he ashamedly recounted the scene, "A Yankee captain demanded my surrender. I threw my sword down the ridge and with very bad grace, submitted." He arrived at Johnson's Island in early Decem-ber, right in time for a brutal Great Lakes winter.[35]

Although many defining moments had long since transformed E. John Ellis from a doubting Confederate into an ardent supporter of the cause, perhaps the most poignant of these was the ordeal and fate of his young friend Oliver Evans. Ellis first met the boy while attending law school in New Orleans, when both Ellis and Bolivar Edwards roomed at the home of Evans's father. A year later, al-though he was slight of stature and barely old enough to serve, Evans clamored to join Ellis's regiment while it bivouacked outside New Orleans. Determined in his course, the boy successfully volunteered despite the protests of both his father and his officer friend.

Oliver Evans managed to make it through the war mostly unscathed until Murfreesboro, Tennessee, in late December 1862, the same battle after which Ellis walked through the night contemplating the living and the dead scattered across the battlefield. On the last day of the engagement, amid a furious attack led by Ellis's Louisianians, Evans was wounded in the leg. Unable to retreat with Bragg's army, the young soldier was left behind and taken prisoner. As fate would have it, Evans was sent to a military hospital in Cincinnati, the home of his uncle Caleb Evans. Upon hearing of his nephew's condition, Caleb Evans came to the hospital to offer every possible human comfort and the best medical attention that could be obtained, but such charity came with an important stipulation: his nephew must take the oath of allegiance to the Union. Cherishing his honor more than life, Oliver Evans refused, and he festered in prison some months until he finally received exchange the following spring.

E. John Ellis finally reunited with his friend on the field of battle near Chicka-
mauga late in the summer of 1863, only to discover that Evans had once again
been wounded, this time much more seriously. As Ellis gazed down upon Evans,
"whose body was too weak for the activity and energy of his mind and spirit," he
felt sadness and admiration for the boy "who had bled for his country and was
ready to bleed more and to die if it was God's will for her honor and independence." Ellis left his manservant Stewart to look after Evans in the field hospital,
but no amount of attention could halt the advance of the fever that was quickly
extracting the life out of its host. Ellis visited Evans's grave a week later. At his side,
Stewart relayed the dead soldier's final words and handed Ellis the last bundle of
letters he had written. "This blow," recalled Ellis, "though not unexpected, fell
heavy." Oliver Evans had joined not just out of love for his country but to live up to
the honorable example of his friend and captain. It was a heavy blow indeed.[36]

One can only speculate as to the significance of Ellis's captivity as a formative
experience. One thing is certain: prison changed his life dramatically while he
was there. Although he made time pass with books, letter-writing, and association
with other captives from his home state, there could be no escape from the ever-
present reminder of his condition. When a valise full of much-needed clothing
arrived at the prison in May 1864, John searched vainly for an accompanying letter. Surmising the identity of his benefactor, he wrote, "The articles coinciding
so perfectly with those that I asked for and marked so beautifully with a woman's
care, by woman's hand need not the information of an accompanying letter to
lead me to whose generosity I am indebted." The silence of the woman who sent
the clothing fueled Ellis's palpable anguish, her mute charity at turns aiding and
torturing him. Mustering a vain effort to maintain his manly honor in absentia,
Ellis continued, "Please accept the enclosed blank due bill, fill up the blank with
the proper figures, and if you go to Amite my father will honor it." His days of
combat may have lain behind him, but the young captive's psychological trauma
persisted.[37]

Confinement also left Ellis plenty of time for reflection. In one angry and
candid letter, he revealed doubts about the Confederate leadership, opining that
if he could endure prison, Jeff Davis should also stand firm. Yet, by the time he
began his second winter at Johnson's Island, he started thinking of the future.
Writing to his mother, Ellis prophesied, "There will be many changes in the
Country in its people and its institutions. Slavery I think will be abolished and I
for one won't care a particle—Indeed I think it will be advantageous in many
respects—and I think also that the government will recommend such a course to
the states before the close of the next year." Ever the paternalist, Ellis had even

concluded that Southern blacks would willingly serve as the Confederacy's great resource. "If the worst comes to worst," he wrote, "they will see lines of black soldiers, slaves of yesterday, freedmen of that day, trained and disciplined and under the lead of southern officers, their former masters; men who used to command them and whom they love and trust and will follow." Ellis could no more conceptualize that black people wanted to be free than he could envision them as his social equals; yet even from his position of remote isolation, he astutely recognized that the nation could never return to the antebellum status quo.[38]

Even as Ellis dreamed of returning to his native Louisiana, newcomers were making their way to New Orleans to seek their fortunes. Not many of these individuals could match Henry Clay Warmoth's blinding ambition and social aplomb, and even fewer could hope ever to as effectively employ such qualities. His character combined the earnestness, if not the honesty, of a man like E. John Ellis with the personal courage of men like Algernon Sydney Badger and Frederick Nash Ogden. Becoming a lieutenant colonel of a Unionist Missouri militia regiment at age nineteen, Warmoth was far more precocious than any of those men. He never missed a party and never passed up opportunities to meet influential men or to flirt with their wives and daughters. And he had an uncanny knack for being at the right place at the right time, seemingly everywhere when important things happened.[39]

Warmoth had been seriously wounded in May 1863 during a failed Union assault at Vicksburg. Had he known then just how much trouble his leave of absence would cause, he probably would have stayed to recover near the front lines. Instead, by nightfall, he was headed north aboard a steamboat full of wounded soldiers and was sharing tales of his service with a "jackass correspondent" from the *Cincinnati Commercial Bulletin*. Along the journey to St. Louis, and beyond to his home in Rolla, Missouri, Warmoth met with friends and became acquainted with influential men and pretty women. He attended a benefit for the orphans of St. Louis, politicked for friends in Illinois and Missouri, and even took in a performance of *Richard III* starring John Wilkes Booth. As a wounded war hero fresh from the front, the young lieutenant colonel basked in his newfound notoriety. Yet when Warmoth returned to his command two months later, he received disconcerting news. General Grant, now safely in possession of Vicksburg, had turned his attention to the unflattering reports the young Missourian had circulated in the press about Grant's tactics during the city's siege. Not one to shy from comment, Warmoth admitted that he had indeed given interviews while at home, in fact from the moment he stepped aboard his outbound steamer, but he protested Grant's accusations of wrongdoing. These denials did the young colonel little good, and Grant cashiered him from the service under the pretense of being absent without leave. This was a terrible blow to Warmoth's ego and put his promising future in jeopardy. Yet it also served as a useful experience in dealing with high-level conflict, something Warmoth learned to do while he set about to clear his name.[40]

After spending tireless days soliciting letters of support from any influential source available to him, Warmoth began a long trek to Washington to meet in person with President Lincoln. On August 30, carrying his bundle of supporting evidence, the tall, handsome, rail-thin former farm boy left the Willard Hotel and set out for the White House. He arrived at the appointed hour only to see a long line of petitioners in front of him, some of whom were other officers seeking reinstatement. Warmoth fought back his inner dejection, but his heart sank when he overheard Lincoln deferring one soldier's hearing until after the war. His sense of alarm grew by the minute as, one by one, the callers filtered out until there was only Lincoln and himself. Warmoth's emotions boiled over from the excruciating wait. He burst out, "Mr. President, I cannot wait until the war is over for my vindication, I must have justice now." Lincoln listened earnestly to his case and read over the multitude of letters presented by Warmoth. He sympathized with his fellow westerner and, although he made no concrete promises, endorsed his plea for reinstatement with the judge-advocate. It was enough. Two weeks later, on September 14, 1863, Henry Clay Warmoth left Washington with a clean record and renewed optimism.[41]

In October he took command of a Missouri regiment at Corinth, Mississippi, leading his men through the rugged countryside of northern Alabama and middle Tennessee. In November, Warmoth's Missourians fought at the battle of Lookout Mountain. As E. John Ellis became a prisoner of war less than a mile away on the same battlefield, Warmoth reveled in the "brilliant performance" of his unit as it fought its way across Missionary Ridge. And within a week of Ellis's departure from Nashville for the misery of Sandusky Bay, Warmoth left the Tennessee capitol to spend the holidays at home with his family in Rolla.[42]

In February 1864, Warmoth saw the Crescent City for the first time. As the boat approached New Orleans, it began passing through some of the richest plantation country in the entire region. The scene inspired Warmoth to record private ambitions in his diary: "I see today a chain of Plantations on both sides of the river. The finest houses & manors that I have ever seen. It is perfectly lordly to live down here with such improvements." Warmoth's first stop in New Orleans was brief. He quickly left for the coast of South Texas, a remote outpost far from the scene of glory. Events on distant battlefields, however, rescued him from this backwater. General Banks's woes with the forces of Kirby Smith and Richard Taylor prompted a massive transfer of all available Union forces to shore up the wobbling Red River campaign. This move returned Warmoth to Louisiana and the scene of opportunity.[43]

Back in New Orleans, Warmoth made a favorable impression on many influential men. General Banks's wife particularly doted on the twenty-two-year-old soldier, saying he reminded her of her husband of twenty years ago. Some of this fondness undoubtedly rubbed off on the general, because by June he had appointed Warmoth as a judge in the provost court. At first, Warmoth was unsure whether he wanted the job, but it did not take long for him to realize what a golden opportunity it represented. He soon began associating with influential Union men like E. John Ellis's old law professor Christian Roselius. J. Q. A. Fellows, one of the few Unionist members of the influential Pickwick Club, also became a friend. In the courtroom, Warmoth frequently dealt with cases involving large sums of confiscated cotton. He also punished disloyal New Orleanians such as the two "respectable ladies" he sent to Ship Island for sixty days for "shouting for Jeff Davis." In fall 1864, Warmoth made a triumphant return to Washington to network with important people. He had big plans for his return to New Orleans, and it did not hurt to make friends in high places.[44]

As the war drew to a close, many Northerners could look forward with satisfaction that the war for the Union was nearly won. Yet for most New Orleanians, whether black or white, Union or Confederate, the difficulties and drama were really only beginning. The war may have forever ended the system of slavery and pushed the slaveholding oligarchy to the margins of power, but on balance it produced more unanswered questions than solutions. Supporters of the Union in New Orleans could hope that the era of slavery and John Slidell Democracy were forever dead. For the city's free Afro-Creole population, war brought a new sense of optimism, but it remained unclear whether the peace would finally deliver on the dream of full citizenship that they had once been promised under the terms of the Louisiana Purchase. Certainly the halting progress that the elite Afro-Creoles had made as officers in the army must have given them pause. The freedmen had escaped bondage, but their status as Americans remained ambiguous. For Union men of both Northern and Southern persuasion, occupied New Orleans seemed like a place of tremendous political and economic opportunity. It was a plum waiting for those with enough sense to pick it. Yet the very diversity of the group of people who drooled over the demise of the Confederacy should have served as some sort of warning to the aspiring architects of the new order. The whole of the spoils did not equal the sum of these individuals' divergent ambitions, and once the pie had been divided, someone was going to have to leave the table hungry. The question of who might ultimately reap the benefits of the Union victory created friction between both friends and enemies in postwar New Orleans.

There was one important shift that most observers likely perceived, however: aging statesmen and generals were no longer going to dictate the course of events in New Orleans. Having paid their dues, the young officers, of both North and South, who had led the men of their generation during the war now claimed their place. Military expediency had allowed men like Badger, Ogden, Warmoth, and even Tissot to reach staff-grade rank with all its awesome responsibilities. Ogden was the oldest of these four, and he was only twenty-eight years old when the war ended. Warmoth was barely twenty-three. Reconstruction, much like the war itself, was thus destined to be guided by youth and its attendant ambition.

The war experience also redefined the lives those young officers who had shouldered the war's greatest burdens. At the war's beginning, E. John Ellis had harbored serious doubts about the South's bid for nationhood. In defeat, he became an ardent Southern nationalist. Despite the undeniable hardships endured by Ogden, the war had given him an opportunity to embody the chivalric warrior ideal, a role that could have been penned by Sir Walter Scott. Algernon Badger, a man with whom Ogden was going to have a long and symbiotic relationship, also found a level of accomplishment in war that peacetime could have never provided. Warmoth, in combining an earlier ethos of masculinity with an emerging modernistic and morally ambiguous code of honor, set about to create an empire on the ruins of Louisiana's slaveholding past. Charles Sauvinet had not only carved out a new role in the army; he challenged the very identity that antebellum society had once placed upon him. Both Aristée Tissot and E. A. Toledano, in contrast, had promising careers interrupted only to endure great hardship that was due in large measure to the incompetence of others. Without question, the youthful enthusiasm that had attracted these men to war in 1861 failed to survive the conflict intact.

The war had supplied this generation with a unique sort of education. It is doubtful that any of the individuals described in this chapter could have emerged from the war not knowing who they were as men. They had participated in a war of unprecedented scope and unspeakable violence and doubtlessly harbored traumas for the rest of their lives. As Oliver Wendell Holmes Jr. declared in 1895, they had "shared the incommunicable experience of war." Political ideology had played an important role in bringing about the war, and as Civil War scholars

fewer and fewer inmates, and many of the holdouts were fellow Louisianians who had voluntarily entered a pact not to take the oath until the Trans-Mississippi's army surrendered. In a prison that once held twenty-eight hundred soldiers, there were, by his estimates, only about one hundred thirty-five men left. Writing to his father back in Louisiana, Ellis proclaimed: "There is no blood on my hands. Had the war terminated favorably to the South I would have always thought that we were right in opposing secession." Satisfied that he had maintained his honor to the end, he took the "hated and accursed" oath on June 13, 1865. Less than three weeks later, on the Fourth of July, he arrived home at Amite, where he expected "to stay a white man."[2]

The inner-directed and personal nature of Ellis's concerns contrasts sharply with the manner in which historians of Reconstruction have often portrayed the postbellum era's political and social chaos. Although interpretations of the period have changed dramatically in the past century, from the vitriolic diatribes of the "Dunning School," to the apologia of the revisionists, to the more nuanced approach of the postrevisionists, most narratives still condense Reconstruction down to a struggle waged by competing group identities. Drawing upon a fund of familiar stereotypes, they recount how unreconstructed rebels brought about a white supremacist millennium by overthrowing Republican state governments run by flawed but usually well-meaning carpetbaggers and their scalawag and freedmen allies. Even more recent biographical works, usually of prominent Republicans, add little personal dimension beyond their immediate subject. To arrive at a deeper understanding of Reconstruction, we need to take a closer look at the private challenges that the Civil War generation faced during the tumultuous postbellum period, a line of inquiry that the historical field has only begun to engage. Partisan allegiance and regional identity often merely lent shape to the inner struggle faced by Reconstruction's actors.[3]

The unprecedented nature of the postbellum era's political challenges had an important parallel in the private lives of countless men and women who had just endured four years of an "unhappy war," and nowhere was this task more burdensome than among the South's pro-Confederate whites. Many of the region's long-established social institutions wilted in the face of the war's carnival of destruction, leaving these defeated Southerners facing personal challenges greater than any of their forebearers had ever known. Even in the absence of a costly war, emancipation would have been a colossal shock to the region's economic and social underpinnings. The shame of defeat, added to the destruction, the dislocation, and the lives wasted by the war, must have made it a truly difficult time for those who, like Ellis, had dedicated the previous four years to the false promises of the Confederacy. When one inventories the hardship endured by these people, it is not surprising that some would lash out violently against the persons they held most responsible for their misfortunes. Having conceded much to mutability's invasive presence during the war, white Southerners were loath to let it remain their constant companion in postbellum life. Indeed, veterans like Ellis probably did not yet grasp the potential for far-reaching social change that the war had unleashed. Antagonism toward the Northern foe reemerged in the postbellum era, therefore, not only from a partisan impulse but from the desire of Southerners to stem the advance of change in their personal lives.

Black Southerners also faced profound uncertainties after the war. The unpredictability of the age forced all people of color, whether part of the free antebellum population or ex-slave, to navigate an unfamiliar terrain littered with pitfalls and obstacles. On the surface, it appeared that the blacks who were emancipated gained the most out of the conflict, but freedom itself did not bring Southerners of color—even those who had always been free—much closer to citizenship than they had been in antebellum times. Save for their unequal pay, black men who had bravely fought for the Union had yet to receive any meaningful civic compensation for their devotion. Even a highly educated veteran officer such as Charles Sauvinet still could not vote. Emancipation might have been an enormous change, but it did not take long for blacks to discover what a limited victory it represented. Yet, despite a deep and abiding national racism, black Southerners were hopeful over the prospect for tangible progress after the war. Becoming involved in the Radical politics of the Northern conqueror, however, remained a hazardous business. Not just a political abstraction for black Southerners at war's end, the quest for meaningful freedom was a personal journey.

Even as black and white native New Orleanians struggled to redefine their lives, another group of relative newcomers sought to build more lasting foundations in a place that most had never even visited before 1862. As both a river town and a seaport, New Orleans had always attracted fugitives, adventurers, and wandering souls. Newly arrived Union army veterans like Henry Clay Warmoth and Algernon Sydney Badger merely continued a trend that had begun with the city's founding. In the previous sixty years alone, New Orleans had greeted the arrival of American migrants from both Northern and Southern states, thousands of black and white émigrés from the Caribbean, Germanic liberals fleeing the chaos of the 1848 revolutions, and an even larger wave of impoverished Irish potato famine victims. In time, each of these groups left its mark on the city, building civic associations and political coalitions and, when the war came, playing a key role in it. Yet, compared to the young Union army veterans, none of these newcomers had ever laid such a sweeping and immediate claim to the city; nor had they arrived as an invading force. Both factors colored the reception that awaited newly arrived Northern men. When the competing aspirations of the postwar generation finally collided in New Orleans, the outcome carried national implications.[4]

Blessed with hindsight, we now know that the combined forces of war, westward expansion, and modernizing transportation networks had already placed the city on a path of relative decline, but to most Americans of the Civil War generation, New Orleans was the South's greatest city. They did not look at its Creole culture or its Catholicism and dismiss the city as a regional anomaly. Instead they saw a metropolis that dwarfed Charleston and Mobile and, unlike Richmond, stood unscathed by the physical destruction of war. It was also one of the nation's greatest ports, an important feature in an era when the federal government received most of its revenue in the form of duties. Outside the city limits stood the most fertile and potentially profitable agricultural basin in the nation. And perhaps most importantly, not only did the city have an enormous head start over other Southern cities in the process of reconstruction, with its large population of educated people of color and Louisiana's historical support of a protectionist tariff; the state held out the greatest promise for Republican success in the South. Americans correctly identified New Orleans and, by extension, Louisiana, as a bellwether for both the Republican Party's aspirations in the postbellum South and the ultimate success or failure of its Reconstruction policies. These factors destined the city to become the main stage upon which the nation would act out its most defining moments of race and politics in the nineteenth century.

Yet, while New Orleans might have seemed like potentially fertile ground for the growth of Southern Republicanism, the city's unique wartime experience had also left it an incredibly volatile place. Starting with secession, its people had witnessed one social convulsion after another. The Confederacy's usurpation of federal authority, the city's ignominious surrender just fourteen months later, the advent of military rule, the establishment of a provisional Unionist civilian government, and, by the end of 1865, the growing resurgence of the former slaveholding class had undermined confidence and respect for civil authority. In the course of three years, Louisiana had seen no fewer than five claimants to the office of governor. Meanwhile, a social revolution promulgated by the black military experience, emancipation, and the rising political expectations of freedmen threatened to fundamentally alter the city's racial dynamics. At the same time, a steady stream of newcomers—immigrants, Northerners, freedmen—swelled New Orleans's population and changed its demographics. No matter where people stood on the key social and political questions of the era, the uncertainty and anxiety that such convulsions produced left few of them unaffected. It is not surprising, then, that the actors in this narrative resorted to both revolutionary and reactionary deeds to secure a tenuous foothold in society. Nor is it surprising that, after they had been schooled for four years in the political efficacy of might, their deeds often took the form of organized violence. The effort by one historian to cleverly invert Carl Von Clausewitz's famous maxim and assert that "Reconstruction politics became the continuation of civil war by other means" not only misses the point that Von Clausewitz was trying to make, but it obscures the applicability of its genius. As scholars such as Bertram Wyatt-Brown and John Hope Franklin have shown, a variety of societal forces, including patriarchy and slavery, fed a culture of violence in the South. The Civil War upped the ante considerably, however, and made *organized* violence integral to the region's political culture; it was a legacy that lasted well into the twentieth century.[5]

Because New Orleans fell so early in the war, Lee's surrender brought fewer immediate changes to the city than to other Southern communities. Whitelaw Reid, then a twenty-six-year-old war correspondent, described his immediate reaction when he arrived there in June 1865: "Crossing from Mobile to New Orleans was going from the past of the South to its present. Till within a few weeks, Mobile had been among the latest strongholds of the rebellion; for some years New Orleans had been held by the national authorities, and had been changing under the operation of Northern influences." Returning Confederates must have had a very similar reaction, though few would have described what they now beheld in such ebullient terms. Observing Carondelet Street late that month, Reid noted that "sometimes it was impossible to approach within a couple of squares of the Provost-Marshall's office, so great was the throng of returning rebel soldiers, applying for their paroles. It was a jolly, handshaking, noisy, chattering crowd. Pushing about among them could be seen women, sometimes evidently of wealth and position, seeking for their brothers or husbands." Those men who had left New Orleans to fight for the Confederacy were surely grateful to see their loved ones again, but with the somber task of adjusting to postwar realities ahead of them, few could have described their mood as "jolly."[6]

Like E. John Ellis, Arthur Toledano had waited at Johnson's Island until the second week in June before taking the oath of allegiance. When he finally returned home to New Orleans in October 1865, he found that not only had the city changed; so had the makeup of his uncle's household. Someone he had never seen before was now living there: his mixed-race first cousin, Louise Marie Drouet. The dramatic chain of events that had brought Louise Marie under her father's roof had begun a month earlier when Louis Drouet's personal servant discovered him lying unconscious in the yard. Frightened, she cried frantically for help. Henry Schwartz, a Bavarian-born tailor who for the past fifteen years had been a tenant on the ground floor of Drouet's house, heard the commotion outside his window and quickly came to the scene. With some difficulty, the pair managed to get the sickly old Creole up the stairs to his bedroom, where Schwartz kept a watch over him. By eleven o'clock that evening, Drouet regained consciousness. Perhaps because of his ill health or the trauma of his day, the normally reserved old gentleman began to speak freely. "I am going to tell you something I have never told you," Drouet said to his tenant. "I have a daughter, she is in a convent." Schwartz may have recalled then the little girl who frequently visited at the house with her quadroon mother years ago. Yet this uncharacteristic forthrightness on the part of his normally reticent landlord stunned him. "Why do you not take her with you?" quizzed Schwartz, to which Drouet opined, "Perhaps it would be better for her to remain in the convent." The tailor was incredulous. He urged Drouet to bring his daughter to the house to live. After all, Schwartz pointed out, Drouet had been terribly ill and needed someone to take care of him. "I'm afraid people will talk about that," fretted the sickly old Creole. "Let people talk," Schwartz fired back. Two weeks later, eighteen-year-old Louise Marie Drouet came to live with her father.[7]

We will never know more than a handful of tantalizing fragments about the chain of events that brought Louise Marie Drouet into this world. Sometime in 1846, Louis Florange Drouet had entered a *plaçage* relationship with a twenty-year-old Afro-Creole woman named Elizabeth Bresson. Before long, he had negotiated the rental of a cottage on Constance Street where he installed his young mistress. Found predominantly within the Creole community, *plaçage* consisted of an arranged sexual relationship outside the bounds of marriage between white men and typically freeborn mixed-race women. Brokered between a female guardian of the young *placée* and the man to whom she would become a mistress, these agreements often involved significant financial support on the part of the man, including direct monetary support and living accommodations, typically a rented house. Custom dictated that the father would also financially support any offspring resulting from the union, but such plans could and often did go awry. Often a *placée* came from a family in which for several generations the women had served as mistresses to white men.[8]

Although she was only twenty years old when she entered into a union with Louis Drouet, *plaçage* was already a way of life for Elizabeth Bresson. Two years earlier, she had begun an unsuccessful union with another man, by the name of Samuel Morgan. Not long after she became pregnant with his child, Morgan skipped town and was never heard from again. Louis Drouet's offer rescued Elizabeth from financial jeopardy and also conferred upon her, as the kept mistress of a wealthy white man, a type of status peculiar to its time and place. As long as her relationship with Drouet lasted, this young free woman of color had her own home and a certain measure of independence. While one might wonder what role genuine affection played in the relationship, for Elizabeth Bresson, it was by necessity an economic decision.[9]

There was only a distance of about ten blocks between the home of Louis Drouet and the cottage where he kept Bresson, but the difference was quite literally between night and day. As 1846 turned into 1847, neighbors observed Drouet's carriage tied in front of the Constance Street cottage "every night and sometimes during the day." Soon, Elizabeth became pregnant, and by July 1847, she had given birth to a daughter. Drouet visited his mistress frequently throughout the pregnancy and delighted in the birth of his child. Yet, when Elizabeth's brother William and a childhood friend carried Louise Marie Drouet to St. Louis Cathedral to be baptized, Louis Drouet was not in attendance. The intimate aspect of the relationship between Louis Drouet and Elizabeth Bresson also ended shortly after the birth of their daughter, yet mother and child remained an important part of Drouet's life. In addition to the customary financial support, Drouet often visited his daughter at the Constance Street cottage, and eventually he asked Elizabeth to start bringing Louise Marie to visit with him either at his own home on Tchoupitoulas or at his feed store across the street. Even though Elizabeth had, as her brother put it, "got [another] man to support her," she continued to bring Louise Marie for monthly visits to her father.[10]

The last antebellum decade brought important changes to Louis Drouet's life and, in turn, heavily influenced the fate of Louise Marie, his mixed-race daughter. In 1852 he decided to rent out a portion of his mostly empty two-story home to a young German immigrant couple. Henry and Mary Schwartz were sober and industrious tenants, and in time they became Drouet's closest friends outside of Arthur Toledano. The Schwartzes noticed the periodic visits of Louise Marie and her mother but were discreet enough to not ask questions about the girl. Yet, through the grapevine, they came to know the truth. When Drouet's young slave boy Sam told Mary Schwartz that Louise Marie was his master's daughter, she already had her suspicions. In a bout of uncharacteristic loquacity, Louis Drouet once commented to Henry Schwartz that Louise Marie was not as "good-looking" as her mother. At no time, however, did he ever introduce Elizabeth or the child during their visits to any of his handful of white friends.[11]

Around the same time that the Schwartzes came to live with Drouet, Arthur Toledano also began making regular visits to his uncle's home. He had recently returned from California and was now busily learning the family's mercantile ways, his uncle serving as a mentor. Toledano soon proved his skill in commerce and eventually began handling all of Drouet's financial affairs. He also become his uncle's closest confidant, and if he ever missed his daily visit to the house on the corner of Tchoupitoulas and Gaiènnie, his uncle would send for him. Despite the bond that had developed between the two men, however, or indeed perhaps because of it, Drouet kept the knowledge of his affair across the color line a secret from his nephew.[12]

Elizabeth Bresson's sudden death early in 1858 brought Louise Marie's monthly visits to an end, and for the next few years she lived with her great-aunt Fanny Porée in Jefferson Parish. Louis Drouet had not forgotten about his daughter, however. In early 1861, he sent for Fanny Porée and instructed her to carry Louise Marie to the Carmelite convent attached to the St. Augustine Catholic Church at the corner of Bayou and St. Claude in the heart of New Orleans's old Afro-Creole community of Tréme. It may actually have been Arthur Toledano's departure for the war in 1861 that had made Louise Marie's placement into the convent possible. His daily handling of his uncle's business came to a temporary halt in 1861 when he joined Watson's Battery. If Louis Drouet had wanted to keep knowledge of his illegitimate daughter from his family, Toledano's absence certainly facilitated his ability to do so. The need to keep her existence a secret from his family seemingly explains why he waited three years after Elizabeth Bresson's death to place Louise Marie in the convent. It was hardly the last link between the destinies of Louise Marie Drouet and Arthur Toledano. One needs to look no further than the summer of 1863 to witness the broad irony of the war's sweeping impact upon the social fabric of New Orleans. Even as Arthur Toledano sat confined in the Custom House, less than a mile away Louise Marie Drouet remained sequestered behind the walls of the Carmelite convent, both of them acting out roles defined by fates and forces that neither controlled.[13]

A new equilibrium descended upon the Drouet house following the war. Edmund Arthur Toledano resumed his daily trips to his uncle's home, sometimes staying for dinner, where he sat at the table with his uncle and his first cousin. Toledano's new wife, Celeste, periodically accompanied him on these visits. Louise Marie now joined her father on his nightly rambles in his buggy through the streets of uptown New Orleans. They attended plays and circuses together, and the old Creole showered her with affection, which by all accounts she returned in full. When Louise Marie went out visiting or on errands, neighbors could see her father anxiously waiting at the street corner for her return. It all seemed quite normal, particularly as the turmoil of war had so altered the composition of many households in New Orleans. Such a change in living arrangements would have hardly elicited comment. To those who did not know better, Louise Marie undoubtedly passed for white.[14]

Unfortunately for everyone involved, the profound societal changes that had brought Louise under her father's roof also unleashed forces that eventually threatened the familial ties that had made it possible. The old three-tiered racial caste system that had ordered New Orleans society since its founding now faced obsolescence. Emancipation diminished the uniqueness of the city's free people of color by reducing the distance, at least in the eyes of the law, between former slaves and the Afro-Creole elite in the decades to come. Over time, the diminishing status of New Orleans's free people of color also made their white relatives grow increasingly uneasy about acknowledging blood ties across the color line, for white Creoles in particular were already anxious about their own racial identity. In 1866 these changes had only begun to take place. By the end of the nineteenth century, however, matters had become far different.

Emancipation also led to an epic identity crisis for those who belonged to the city's caste of elite free mixed-race people. There were several options available to them, and each held different risks and rewards. Some of these individuals conspicuously proffered their services as natural political leaders for the freedmen, only to confront resistance both from white Republican politicians who sought to harvest the fruit of victory for their own benefit and from the freedmen who remained skeptical of their social betters' newfound interest in the plight of freedmen. Less conspicuously, others of the elite group edged toward the single most attractive option left available to them, the option of crossing the color line. If the city's fair-skinned "black" population failed to retain their status as the black elite, and if they failed to pass into white society, then the middle caste stood to fall to the lowly status of freedmen—a situation many found disconcerting.[15]

Louise Marie Drouet may well have been completely oblivious to all of the great social changes taking place around her, but as girl on the threshold of womanhood, she undoubtedly found the stability of her father's house a welcome change. She had been born into a world where her future prospects might include becoming a *placée*, much as her mother—and her mother's mother—had been. Living with her father exposed an entirely different path, the path toward becoming not just a woman, not just a mistress, but a *lady*. Perhaps over time, she might even cross the color line, assuming the role of Louis Drouet's *legitimate* daughter. But if this was her plan, the stakes were higher than she could have known. One thing was certain: the world of the *placée* no longer existed, and there was simply no going back to the way things were before the war.[16]

On May 12, 1865, the clock had finally run out on Colonel Fred Ogden's band of cavalrymen. About fifty miles southwest of Tuscaloosa, at the small hamlet of Gainesville, Alabama, what remained of Ogden's regiment, including E. John Ellis's older brother Thomas, surrendered their military accoutrements to Union authorities and pledged allegiance to the Constitution of the United States. The war, or at least the portion of it fought in Confederate uniform, was now over for the colonel. Once back in the Crescent City, however, Fred Ogden soon took up the cudgel once again. By the end of the year, the twenty-eight-year-old soldier was the president of an organization called the Young Men's Democratic Association. On the night of October 14, 1865, Ogden's band of returning veterans packed into the St. Charles Street Opera House to attend a strategy session for the coming November elections. Before adjourning in the wee hours, the group set forth a series of resolutions. The Young Democrats had accepted the "verdict of the sword" and had pledged to uphold the federal government, but they also voiced some grievances. Paramount was the belief "that the regulation of the rights of suffrage rests exclusively with the States, and that the General Government possesses no constitutional right to abridge or modify that power." In a related resolution, the Democrats denounced the Louisiana Constitution of 1864, urging its repudiation. They also asserted that "the confiscation of private property for alleged political offences is a barbarism of the past" and that Radical Republicans' pursuit "for the blood of Jefferson Davis is unchristian and un-American." The Young Democrats admitted that they had lost the war, but in their mind, with the conflict now over, it was time for the meddlesome Yankees to go home.[17]

These diehard Confederates chafed at what had happened politically in Louisiana during their absence. The Free State constitutional convention of 1864 had produced a document that significantly altered the old antebellum code. Its foremost provision abolished slavery, but the constitution contained more socially pervasive clauses. The establishment of biracial public education and its inherent open-endedness on the issue of Negro suffrage gave conservatives pause. After several months of political jockeying, combined with the omnipresent hand of General N. P. Banks, the provisional government installed a new governor in the person of the former slaveholder and planter J. Madison Wells. The new legislature also replaced two antebellum titans of the U.S. Senate, John Slidell and Judah P. Benjamin, sending reliable Union men in their place.[18]

In retrospect, the stances taken by the returning Confederates at their October 14 strategy session were not only unrealistic but bordered on the irrational. They operated in a state of what George Schivelbusch terms "dreamland": a powerful psychological elixir that transformed the depression felt by defeated homeward-bound soldiers into a self-deluding sense of normalcy. In this frame of mind, it was completely rational that they should return to their antebellum roles as leaders within the Crescent City's political community. President Andrew Johnson's lenient plan for Reconstruction fueled this delusion, allowing most of the formerly disloyal to quickly regain the rights of honest citizens. Ironically, returning Confederates increasingly fulfilled their fantasies of political resurgence through the good graces of the allegedly Unionist governor, J. Madison Wells, a man who proved to be a chameleon. Wells had essentially been appointed by Banks, but he quickly recognized the rising influence of returning veterans and soon began currying their favor. As the tumultuous year 1865 came to a close, it seemed as though Fred Ogden's unrepentant Young Democrats were on the verge of reclaiming control over Louisiana's civil government.[19]

Thomas C. W. Ellis was one of the many former Confederates who managed to secure a seat in the state legislature in the November 1865 elections, a position from which he hoped to revive both the sagging fortunes of his family and the defeated planter aristocracy to which they belonged. Writing from his father's home in Amite, E. John Ellis penned an encouraging letter to his brother that brimmed with support from back home. "Your friends here all seem gratified at your fine prospects in New Orleans, and while they regret that you are to be away so much they are all of opinion that it is best for you. Take care of your health & *climb*. The people here think that there is no place too high for your attainment & they are right." Ellis's optimistic tone reflected the hope harbored by many white Southerners at the beginning of 1866 that President Andrew Johnson would prevail in his rolling feud with the Radical wing of the Republican Party in the nation's capitol, paving the way for a restoration of traditional patterns of political authority in Louisiana. By February of that year, there were tangible signs that gave substance to such optimism. In New Orleans, Thomas Ellis was busy courting the favor of Governor Wells, hoping to secure a judgeship for his father, Ezekiel Parke Ellis. E. John Ellis's close friend and former classmate Bolivar Edwards had gained the post of attorney general for Louisiana's Sixth District. Adding further to this sense of returning normalcy, Stephen Ellis, the youngest son, who had at fifteen years of age appeared in camp with the Sixteenth Louisiana just days before the battle of Shiloh, was now studying under Christian Roselius at the University of Louisiana's school of law. E. John Ellis, meanwhile, remained at Amite, quietly recovering in his father's house. The war and his long captivity had weakened him physically and undoubtedly had traumatized him in ways that he probably did not fully understand. Not until November 1866 did he return to the practice of law, and even then he maintained only a small caseload for local clients.[20]

In the first twelve months after Appomattox, men like Fred Ogden and the Ellis brothers not only worked toward restoring their prosperity and political influence; they also set about reestablishing their social status and cultural authority. The most conspicuous vehicle for such a restoration in New Orleans was Carnival. By the mid-nineteenth century, both Carnival culture and the city's elite private clubs that organized the celebration had become fundamental building blocks of the city's social pyramid. While exclusive establishments such as the Boston and Pickwick clubs were hardly unique to New Orleans, the way in which these clubs controlled both the private and the public celebration of Mardi Gras made them far more culturally significant than their counterparts in New York or Charleston. Carnival season had for some decades offered the city's elite club society its raison d'être, staging exclusive masked balls; but not until 1857 did the clubs make a bid to redefine the holiday's public street celebrations. In 1856 a group of up-and-coming professional men affiliated with the Pickwick Club had formed the Mistick Krewe of Comus, the first and most prestigious Mardi Gras parading society. Their invention both instituted "modern Carnival" and became the first step in the holiday's transformation from a democratic, and at times cabalistic, street celebration into an ordered display of wealth and culture controlled by the elite. Their procession proved so wildly successful that by the time the war came along, the men of Comus stood as the undisputed apex of Carnival culture. With the majority of the group's members fighting in northern Virginia, Comus did not made an appearance in the streets of New Orleans during the war, but when it was finally over, the members who had survived the conflict yearned for a revival of the Mistick Krewe.[21]

When Comus returned to the streets on Mardi Gras Night, 1866, its theatrical displays reflected the aspirations of a generation of defeated white Southerners. Anxious spectators first spotted the procession heading down Royal Street toward the Henry Clay statue at Canal. Passing below the Great Compromiser's impassive gaze, led by a "splendid brass band" and illuminated by a team of "freedmen" flambeaux bearers, Comus paraded onward to the Varieties Theater, where it counseled observers on the lessons of past, present, and future. The tableau of "The Past," noted one witness, "was most appropriate, but most melancholy. Strife, Destruction, Want, Grief, Terror, were represented." "The Present" advocated "Peace, Industry, Commerce, Science, Agriculture, Mechanism, and the Arts." "The Future," attended by representations of "Peace" and "Plenty," concluded the tableaux on an optimistic note.[22]

Yet despite such constructive and cheerful sentiments, these returning white veterans overwhelmingly pursued a course that reflected their inability to grasp the fundamental national power shift that the war had accomplished. The faith that many white Southerners had invested in Northern racism, combined with the leniency of the federal government in the months immediately following the war, made it difficult for these men to accept that their misdeeds could engender the wrath of the victorious North, which, except for a few conspicuous individuals, had demonstrated only limited compassion for the millions of slaves that their armies had freed. At best, the white Southerners assumed that emancipation represented some sort of forced modernization of an obsolete labor system but at its root did not fundamentally alter the relationship between black and white Southerners. With the fighting over, and if they could force labor back into the fields, perhaps peace and plenty were within reach. Had they truly apprehended the precariousness of their own political position, maybe they would not have allowed the most hard-fisted and reactionary among them to emerge as their party's spokesmen. Instead, these postwar governments pursued such an unrepentant course that they sowed the seeds of their own destruction and empowered those in Congress who yearned for a broader reordering of the South's political landscape.

Shortly after his discharge from the army, Charles Sauvinet once again embraced the cause of the Northern invader by accepting the position of head cashier at the New Orleans branch of the newly established Freedmen's Bank, a much more important job than its title implies today. In fact, Sauvinet had been hired to act as something of a branch president of this bank in New Orleans. On October 17, 1865, he boarded the *Republic*, a fast commercial steamer set to leave New York City the following day on its regular run between there and New Orleans, where he would set about establishing an office. The *Republic*'s cargo reflected the aspirations of its chiefly mercantile passengers, men who saw unbounded opportunity in the postbellum South. Everything from patent medicines and religious icons to expensive lamps and personal luxuries crowded the ship's hold, destined for Southern markets where the war had pent up demand for such things. The ship also contained an astounding four hundred thousand dollars in gold and silver specie—money that might purchase an empire at depressed postwar prices.

Sauvinet and the twenty-odd other passengers aboard the *Republic* could not have known that their attempted passage to New Orleans was going to be anything but routine. The growing swell off the Carolina coast was the first sign of trouble, and by the time the *Republic* had reached the latitude of Savannah, the rising wind and sea and the falling barometer were proof enough of the vessel's misfortune: it had sailed directly into a hurricane. In a matter of hours, those on board experienced the awful realization that a collection of iron fittings and six inches of oak were all that stood between them and the ocean's floor. The vessel began to take on water almost immediately after entering the storm. Then its walking-beam steam propulsion system failed, leaving the ship dead in the water. Throughout the night and into the next morning, all hands waged a losing battle against the sea with pumps and buckets, but by the following afternoon, the captain, seeing that his craft would soon founder, ordered the boats away. An hour later, as survivors paddled furiously away from the wallowing craft, the *Republic* split in two and went straight to the bottom. Daybreak the following morning found Sauvinet and ten others crowded into the captain's gig, completely alone; all the other boats had drifted away in the night. Three days and four miserable nights later, without food or a drop of drinkable water and at the edge of mental and physical collapse, they spied the sail of their rescuers on the horizon.[23]

Perhaps the fate of the *Republic* should have served as an omen for all those who believed that the defeated South would soon return to peace and prosperity. By the time Sauvinet finally reached New Orleans in early 1866, he noticed a growing air of hostility between former Confederates and Union men. Immediately after the war, Sauvinet believed that white Southerners had come to accept defeat; he considered their stance "perfectly tame." But in a matter of months, he saw a new belligerence emerge. "It shows itself by words, by cross looks, as though they were trying to cow down parties," he explained. One day while Sauvinet was riding on a streetcar, a former rebel "began to curse and damn the Yankees," exclaiming that "he had fought against them four years, and God damn them, he would kill several others before he got through." Sauvinet noticed that these white Southerners reserved their greatest hatred for Southerners who had fought for the Union during the war. "Northern men they can get along with better than with those who were born here and who remained loyal and fought against them," noted Sauvinet. "These they cannot bear."[24]

Sauvinet was behind his desk at the Carondelet Street office that he had rented for the Freedmen's Bank on July 30, 1866, when he saw the police force of the first and the fourth districts charge past en masse outside his windows. A few moments later he heard the sound of gunfire coming from the street. A porter then burst into his office with a panicked look on his face, bearing news of the fighting taking place outside the radical political meeting over on Dryades Street. Sauvinet had attended the convention earlier in the week but, with a quorum lacking, had felt his time better spent at the bank. He now looked out his windows and saw frightened men and women running down the street, "and almost immediately I heard the alarm, and I saw an engine pass by my place." The firemen, under the guise of duty, were on their way to participate in the melee.[25]

The failure of Union men to firmly establish total victory in New Orleans was perhaps the paramount political mistake made anywhere in the nation during the first twelve months following the war's end, and it was this failure that mushroomed into the violence that Sauvinet witnessed that witheringly hot summer afternoon. Encouraged by Andrew Johnson's lenient policies, many white Southerners came to believe that the federal government might abide an even more aggressive seizure of power. Governor Wells had substantiated his claim to office in 1865 with the help of such men, but he soon discovered what a Faustian bargain he had made when the 1866 legislative session began. In a vain effort to rein in the authority of these former rebels, Wells vetoed several heavy-handed bills passed by the statehouse, which was now dominated by ex-Confederates. Among the vetoes included some, but not all, of the newly crafted Black Codes—laws designed to restrict the movements of freedmen. By February 1866, the legislature retaliated against Wells by successfully moving for new municipal elections in New Orleans, which ultimately returned to power the antebellum mayor, John T. Monroe, as well as the prewar chief of police, Thomas E. Adams. Although Adams personally did not subscribe to the excessive behavior of unrepentant rebels, many who served as officers under his command by 1866 thirsted for the blood of their Republican opponents. Mayor Monroe had a reputation for tolerating political vigilantism, having intimate links to the bands of violent gangs hired by the Know-Nothings in the 1850s; they served as "political mercenaries who could be counted on to intimidate, beat, or even murder a man to keep him from voting." Other members of the force were simply Confederate veterans in desperate need of work who were disinclined to interfere with violence directed at the Radicals. These developments paved the way for a bloody massacre known euphemistically as the Riot of 1866.[26]

The clash finally came when Governor Wells moved to slay the monster he had done so much to create. Recognizing that Negro suffrage remained the only salvation for Union men in Louisiana, he reconvened the 1864 constitutional convention to extend the franchise to the freedmen. The Radical-dominated assembly met at the Mechanics' Institute on Dryades Street amid an explosive atmosphere of racial tension. When Mayor Monroe ordered the city police force to break up the "illegal" convention on July 30, all hell broke loose. The police shot at, clubbed, and stabbed a largely black crowd that had gathered outside the institute in support of the convention's proceedings. Regrouping, and reloading their revolvers, the police then stormed the building itself in an orgy of unmitigated violence. In the end, three white and thirty-four black supporters of the convention lay dead, and scores of others were wounded, some seriously. There was one fatality among the police. By the time federal troops arrived on the scene, there was not much left to do but count bodies.[27]

In December of 1866, a special U.S. House of Representatives panel came to New Orleans to hear testimony in relation to the riot. Among the witnesses was Charles Sauvinet. When asked about the ability of Louisiana's "colored people" to understand the federal government's responsibility for their freedom, Sauvinet gave an unequivocal answer: "There is not a colored man who does not understand what he owes to the government of the United States. There is not one but would do everything for the government. I presume the black man here in Louisiana could wield the ballot as well as the musket." Sauvinet went on to describe the dynamics that, in his mind, would ensure Louisiana's loyalty to Union principles in the future and also pave the way for an elite black political ascendancy. "As soon as the colored population possess[es] the right of suffrage," assured Sauvinet, "there are enough of very intelligent colored people in all the large centers of population and in some of the parishes who would canvass the city and parishes, and every place in fact. The colored men here in New Orleans," he continued, "as well as in Boston, as soon as they have the right of suffrage, would put forward men of wealth and education, men highly respectable, who might carry some of the offices."[28]

Throughout his testimony, Sauvinet referred to people of color as "they" instead of "we," and he even made the incredible and untrue statement that he had been with the U.S. Army at the time of Butler's arrival. Perhaps his word choice was merely a reflection of rhetorical style, but it differed greatly from the language employed by Afro-Creole activists who, even as Sauvinet testified, stressed the commonality of all people of color in the pages of their newspaper, the *Tribune*.

Yet if Sauvinet was trying to pass himself off as white, he was employing a most singular strategy. Perhaps he thought posing as a white man would bolster his credibility with the committee. But in the course of his testimony, he took the radical and dangerous step of becoming a warm advocate of universal suffrage. As a witness to the riot at the Mechanics' Institute, he surely knew the potential price of his actions.[29]

Henry Clay Warmoth had described the 1866 riot on Dryades Street as "a dark day for the City of New Orleans," yet the blundering intemperance of the Monroe administration and the duplicity of Wells ultimately paved the way for the ascent of men like himself and other "carpetbaggers." The outrage at the Mechanics' Institute, combined with other violent reprisals against Republicans and freed-men across the South, motivated Northern voters to send a Radical super-majority to Washington in the fall elections of 1866. This new Congress attempted in the following year to right the badly listing Reconstruction effort in the South before it sank completely. The first of four Reconstruction Acts passed in March 1867, serving as an unambiguous clarion call of Radical ascendancy. Warmoth had actually planned on being at the Mechanics' Institute for the constitutional con-vention on that hot day in July. In fact, he had been there earlier in the day but, like Sauvinet, had left when the assembly recessed without the quorum of dele-gates necessary to conduct the day's business. As he walked back to the Institute, Warmoth grew alarmed at the growing throng of hostile whites and armed police-men milling about in the vicinity of the convention. He stopped at a friend's resi-dence on Canal Street to share his concerns when the sound of gunfire rang out in the humid summer air. Stepping out onto the balcony, the young lawyer saw the police kill two fleeing black men. Fearing for his safety, his friends persuaded Warmoth to return inside, lest any of the mob recognize him.[30]

Warmoth's companions had good reason to hustle him indoors. Even before the war was over, his duties as a judge of the provost court had engendered hatred among Confederate sympathizers within the city. His financial success also prob-ably helped to foster such enmity, for Warmoth had managed to fulfill the post-bellum dream of riches that many had harbored but few ever realized. At the age of twenty-three, Warmoth walked away from both his judgeship and the army, perhaps realizing that the surprising amount of influence that he had been able to amass in the course of two years would allow him to make a fortune representing the very planters who had until now come into his courtroom to plead for the return of their precious cotton. But Warmoth had bigger aims than financial suc-cess, and it was his political ambition that would have made him a dead man had he been present at the Mechanics' Institute. Since the end of the war, he had become conspicuous in Radical politics, both in Washington, DC, and in New Orleans, and had been active in the formation of Louisiana's new state Republican Party. As the historian Richard Nelson Current observed, the ambitious young man made himself "a kind of Radical pet."[31]

Although competition for the control of political office in New Orleans was intense, it was a task particularly suited to the young smooth-talking Missourian. Warmoth noted the process on display at a social gathering not long after he had set foot in the city. "A goodly number of sharp gentlemen were working their cards for certain specific objects," he noted in his diary. In stark contrast to the "innocence of the ladies," thought Warmoth, stood "the rascality and duplicity of the men." A year later, he found himself elbow-deep in such "rascality," jockeying for position among the state's Radical politicians. Warmoth blended old notions of masculinity with a newer, more modern, worldview and sense of obligation. Undeniably courageous, but with a troublingly elastic concept of honesty, he was the embodiment of the late-nineteenth-century man on the make, a prototypical adherent of the nascent Gilded Age. In 1866 Warmoth had no wife, children, or familial ties to New Orleans, nor had he become a holder of property yet. It is not surprising that his critics would characterize him as a vulture, but Warmoth also possessed an undeniable quality that set him apart from other so-called carpetbaggers. On one hand, no figure of Reconstruction-era Louisiana, no matter how unpopular, could engender so much individualized rage. On the other hand, despite his modern acquisitive ways, Warmoth exuded a visceral quality that garnered a begrudging respect from his adversaries that few of his peers could match. Whether he was betting on a steamboat race, running for office, or facing down a mortal threat, Warmoth was always willing to risk it all. Southern men recognized and often respected this trait.[32]

Warmoth posed the greatest threat not to conservative whites, however, but to the elite Creoles of color who recognized that if white Republican outsiders emerged as the leadership of the party, their own bid for political relevance would be foreclosed. For this reason, the Afro-Creole leadership in New Orleans trusted most "carpetbaggers" such as Warmoth scarcely more than native rebel-sympathizing whites did. They were enraged that Warmoth and others should position themselves as the spokesmen for the mass of newly freed black Louisianans; it was a role to which New Orleans's Afro-Creole elite, having long demonstrated their attachment to the city, believed they had a truer claim. The very soil of Louisiana had been soaked with the blood of generations of Afro-Creoles, and the Union's victory, in which they had played a role, seemed to hold out the promise that their community might finally receive its long-delayed justice. As

early as 1862, the Afro-Creole community, through the French-language newspaper *L'Union*, espoused its desire to lead all people of color toward freedom and
political equality. This weekly newspaper enjoyed widespread support from the
close-knit francophone community that lived in Faubourg Tréme.

A faction of the Afro-Creole elite eventually coalesced into active opposition
against white Union men in general and Henry Clay Warmoth in particular. By
the time the war ended, this rivalry showed its first serious signs of strain. In an
effort to counter the increasingly reactionary edicts of Andrew Johnson and the
complicity of Governor Wells, Republicans in Louisiana worked to rally supporters around the issue of universal male suffrage, a cause broadly supported by
Afro-Creole activists. At first the two factions appeared to find common ground
in their struggle, but both jealously guarded their power even as they worked in
concert. As it turned out, the Afro-Creoles had good reason for skepticism. In late
1865, knowing that the emboldened Democrats would continue to consolidate
their power at the polls in November, the Republicans opted instead to hold an
unofficial plebiscite for the territorial delegate to Congress. Although the election
held no real constitutional authority, it provided the first-ever opportunity for
Louisiana's black population to vote. Thomas J. Durant, a prominent white lawyer and Unionist who had lived in New Orleans for more than thirty years, was
the favored leader of this movement. Yet Durant declined the nomination as delegate, and the ambitious Henry Clay Warmoth insinuated himself as a suitable
replacement. His Afro-Creole opponents now powerless to stop him, Warmoth
easily won his first elected office.[33]

All of the shameless networking Warmoth had done during previous trips to
Washington paid dividends when he arrived in the nation's capitol as Louisiana's
territorial delegate. In 1866, both legislative chambers refused to seat representatives elected by recalcitrant Southern states. These included men like Alexander
Stephens, the former vice president of the Confederacy, who had the gall to expect to return to Washington as the newly elected senator from Georgia. Warmoth, however, as a mere territorial delegate, managed to secure a spot on the
floor of the House. It was a perch from which he learned much about the dynamics of the national political struggle between the president and Congress. When
he saw the violence in the streets of New Orleans that day in 1866, Warmoth must
have understood that it would provide the necessary ammunition that the Radicals needed to make their move.[34]

The Reconstruction Acts, which paved the way for Warmoth's ascendancy,
also put Charles Sauvinet into his first post of civil authority. As part of a military
district that included Texas and portions of "Indian country," Louisiana now fell

under the command of General Phil Sheridan. As a bold cavalry commander, Sheridan had so devastated the farms of the Shenandoah Valley during the Civil War that he allegedly boasted that a crow would have to carry its own provisions should it desire to fly across its breadth. Sheridan relished the opportunity to wreak vengeance upon those he held responsible for the Riot of 1866. On August 1, 1867, the general selected Sauvinet to serve as one of the replacement members of the New Orleans city council. He was one of the few men of color who was appointed to the council, but again, the organization's biracial composition hardly singled him out. Other members were the Afro-Creole activist B. F. Joubert, a supporter of the *Tribune* and a member of the universal-suffrage committee, and Oscar J. Dunn, an African American and a rising star in Republican political circles. Sheridan's appointments also included Edward Flood, a white man who later proved far more conservative than his new position would seem to indicate. The appointment of men like Sauvinet, Joubert, and Dunn to the city council might seem trivial, but it was anything but for New Orleanians. No matter the angle from which one viewed this turn of events, these appointments not only were radical; they held out the promise for even greater change.[35]

Black participation in the new order was not confined to elite Creoles like Sauvinet, however. Probably no single factor determined the actions of common folk more heavily than military experience during the Civil War. Recruitment for the U.S. Colored Troops had been extensive in New Orleans, and when these men later returned, they possessed a much greater understanding of the social movements taking place in their midst. The experiences of one such soldier, Peter Joseph, were emblematic of the social changes taking place in New Orleans in the 1860s and of their life-altering nature. Joseph had been born a slave sometime around 1845, but by his own account he received his de facto freedom at the age of ten, having been purchased by his white father. By the time the city fell to the Union, he was "nothing but a young fellow working at odd jobs in the city of New Orleans"; by 1864 he had married a sixteen-year-old girl named Cora Laine. Unlike many other free men of color, however, Joseph had not chosen to seek his destiny by volunteering for the army. Perhaps it is ironic, then, that in May 1865, with the war all but over, he received a draft notice. At the time he had been working as a grocery wagon driver, and his skills as a teamster attracted the attention of a quartermaster officer who needed a reliable man to work at the Touro building, then serving as a warehouse for army supplies. Although his military experience lasted scarcely more than six months, it had a profound impact upon the rest of Peter Joseph's life. As a teamster on detached service to a staff officer, he worked under the direct command of Captain Frank Morey, who later became a Republican member of the Louisiana Legislature and a U.S. congressman from the state's Third District. Yet as important as these new political ties were to Joseph, they were matched in significance by his learning to read and write during his brief stay in the army. In May 1865, Joseph had signed his enlistment papers with an *x*, but when he walked into Charles Sauvinet's Freedmen's Bank one October day in 1866, he signed his own name in a clean, clear hand.[36]

E. John Ellis could hardly believe how badly and in how short a period of time the political situation had soured. In the course of a year, the state legislature, composed of men from his own class and persuasion, faced removal from office by the Reconstruction Acts. Even worse, Louisiana was now being run by General Sheridan, a military commander who had neither the inclination nor the obligation to accede to the wishes of men such as himself. Admittedly, the most intemperate among Ellis's class had provoked outrages both in New Orleans and elsewhere and as a result had spurred the U.S. Congress into action. Yet the fact remained that all conservative white Louisianians would now pay the price for such misdeeds. A new, sterner policy toward former Confederates took the form of a new Radical canvass that registered the masses of freedmen as voters and put into place a new state constitution that codified their rights as citizens. The new state government was virtually guaranteed to be both unquestionably radical and inimical to white property owners. Despite such discouraging prospects, however, Ellis was not ready to accept that measures of this kind would enjoy broad national acceptance. Recovered from the war at least physically, he now committed himself to engage in an all-out struggle against the Republican ascendancy.

The beginning of 1867 also found Ellis extremely busy in his personal affairs and professional career. On January 28, he married Josephine Chamberlain, or "Josie" as he affectionately called her. Balancing his anxieties over politics and the stress of introducing his new bride to the family back home in Amite, Ellis wrote his father while honeymooning in New Orleans in early February, explaining that Josie "sends love & kisses to you all and is prepared to claim the place of daughter & sister and occupy it with love and constancy," but, he went on, "Dan W. Voorhees of Indiana the great Northern Copperhead orator speaks tonight at the Mechanics Institute and Josie & I want to hear him and hence we remain here until Thursday morning." In the summer he argued his first case before the state supreme court, after going up in May against his old law professor, Christian Roselius, in the courtroom. "I felt like a calf among elephants," Ellis wrote his mother of the event. Ellis's growing stake in society probably only heightened his anxiety over what the Radical ascendancy meant for his political future. Like many men of his generation and class, Ellis did not believe that illiterate, recently freed slaves possessed sufficiently sound judgment to be good voters, but he had to admit that he felt the same way about less-educated whites. Yet, although he harbored a passionate hatred for the Reconstruction Acts, Ellis remained relatively passive as the state constitutional convention met in New Orleans during the winter of 1867–68. All of that changed in the following year.[37]

At the age of twenty-seven, Ellis was representative of a new generation of political leaders in Louisiana. He had been a dedicated Whig and Unionist before the war, but now he canvassed New Orleans as well as four rural parishes north of the city for the Democratic Party. From this vantage point, he watched with growing alarm as his Republican counterparts, almost universally men who had recently come from Northern states, moved from village to village recruiting and registering the newly enfranchised freedmen. White Southerners across the South used mock paternalistic rhetoric when explaining their feelings about the loyalties and interests of black voters, but a private letter Ellis wrote to his brother Thomas in August of 1867 suggested that such sentiments could be more than simply partisan posturing. In disgust, Ellis angrily noted that the Republican leaders had "assembled the Negroes under pretense of the treating them to dinner, assembled about 13,000 of them marched them nearly to death and then charged them 50 cents for dinner, 10 cents for a glass of ice water and 25 cents for a bit of blue ribbon and a ticket with the cabalistic word 'Loyal League' upon it. It is estimated that not less than eight thousand dollars were thus stolen from the poor Negroes by their pretended friends." Although Ellis's belief that white Democratic elites such as himself had the best interests of the freedmen at heart may have been self-deluding, that does not necessarily mean that his cynical attitude toward Republican efforts was misplaced. With little native leadership of their own, the freedmen of St. Helena and Washington parishes seemed to be merely trading masters, seeking refuge with individuals who were not likely to ever deliver upon their attractive promises. The greatest tragedy may have been that neither Ellis, who in his impaired way believed he understood the black man, nor the Republican newcomers who aspired to represent him in Congress ever truly apprehended the freedmen's most basic needs. As W. E. B. Du Bois noted in 1935, and as the "postrevisionist" historians of the 1970s echoed, the freedmen desperately needed the economic independence that came with land ownership. Yet that would not have been enough. They also needed advocates whose interests were their interests, not politically ambitious outsiders or local patricians who pined for a docile workforce.[38]

Even as twenty-six-year-old Henry Clay Warmoth became the state's new governor in April 1868, Ellis, like many other men of his class and political persuasion, did not necessarily see the Radical ascendancy as a fait accompli. Instead he looked with eager anticipation toward the November elections, when the nation would elect both a new president and a new Congress who might reverse the edicts of their Radical predecessors. Fueled by apocalyptic visions of the future, Ellis both organized and took part in a desperate effort to elect as many Democrats as possible. For a legally minded man who throughout his life demonstrated an abiding faith in procedure, his actions in fall 1868 navigated a fine line between activism and the fulfillment of the vow he had made as a prisoner of war to fight on as a guerilla. Among other things, Ellis decided to swear fealty to a secret order known as the Knights of the White Camellia. Most likely started in Acadiana by the Cajun firebrand Alciabade DeBlanc, the organization made its way to New Orleans and from there, eventually, to Ellis's St. Helena Parish. The Knights have been compared to the Ku Klux Klan of the same era, although in reality they probably had just as much in common with traditional nineteenth-century political associations. Few of the Knights, unlike members of the secretive Klan, ever denied having belonged to the order, nor were they concerned with concealing their identity. By Ellis's own admission, its objectives were "to protect our race from amalgamation and miscegenation and other degradations as we thought and believed, and as we still believe, were sought to be forced upon us by the dominant radical party."[39]

Based on a tip from black men whom he characterized as "loyal," Ellis claimed secret knowledge of a plot orchestrated by Republican operatives in St. Helena Parish that was designed to provoke an incident like the 1866 Mechanics' Institute riot in New Orleans. Referring to the Riot of 1866 and the subsequent enactment of the Reconstruction Acts, Ellis rationalized that white Southerners "had suffered at the hands of the federal Congress and of the military power, and so much from the alleged outrages, and from riots, &c., that it was our constant desire to keep the peace at all hazards." Ellis was not just a member but the "chief of circle" of his local contingent of the Knights of the White Camellia, and he organized a troop of his men to patrol the roads of the parish in anticipation of trouble. "I was on horseback more than half a dozen nights, all night," explained Ellis, commanding men armed with "pistols, shot-guns, and sometimes hickory sticks." He later scoffed at any notion that these men wore the pointy hoods or robes of the

Klan or tormented freedmen. Yet despite Ellis's claim that his circle of Knights had rejected participating in the physical intimidation of Republicans and his own sincere abhorrence of political violence, several bloody outrages took place in St. Helena and surrounding parishes. John Kemp, a black Republican, was dragged out of his home one night in October 1868 and riddled with bullets on a dirt road by a band of thugs Ellis characterized as "parties who are a disgrace to civilization." Undoubtedly some individuals took advantage of the political instability to settle old personal scores, while others engaged in political violence on an ad hoc basis. One incident in particular should have convinced Ellis of the futility of trying to contain political violence. One night he entered a tavern in Amite City and came across three "excited, noisy, and boisterous" drunks who proposed that they all go hang the Republican registrars in town. On this occasion, "after a good deal of persuasion," he was able to get these men to go home. But as the fate of John Kemp plainly illustrated, the voice of reason sometimes went unheard.[40]

E. John Ellis embraced other strategies, which had an undeniable effect on Republican election turnout. William McKenna, a Republican registrar who had come to Louisiana with a Massachusetts regiment during the war and now canvassed the black population of St. Helena Parish, had already been witness to several incidents of voter intimidation by the time the November election arrived. "On the day of the election," noted McKenna, "I saw, at the poll in Amite, a young man named Ellis giving certificates to colored men who had voted the democratic ticket, stating that they had done so." His deeds just inside the boundaries of the law, Ellis explained that the purpose of the certificates was so that white Democrats could "be friendly to those who befriended us."[41]

The violence and intimidation that took place in St. Helena Parish during the fall canvass paled in comparison with events in New Orleans, the hub of Republican activity in the state. Governor Warmoth had anticipated trouble from the start. There is no doubt that as he recalled watching his unarmed political constituency get shot down like dogs on Canal Street during the Riot of 1866, Warmoth was reminded of his new administration's vulnerability to political violence. In July 1868, the twenty-six-year-old chief executive moved quickly to establish a reliable armed force that, unlike the army, was answerable directly to him. Federal troops retained a presence in Reconstruction New Orleans, but the slaughter at the Mechanics' Institute stood as a stark testimony to their inability to maintain order. At least on paper, his newly created Metropolitan Police would act as the primary law enforcement agency in Orleans, Jefferson, and St. Bernard parishes, replacing the heavily Democratic and all-white police forces that operated independently in the three metro parishes. Of course, Warmoth also hoped to build the Metropolitan Police into a powerful state-run paramilitary brigade that could reliably support the aims of the Republican Party. Unfortunately for those involved, the Metropolitans had not yet coalesced into an effective force by the time the fall political canvass in New Orleans began.

In the early twentieth century, writers wallowing in Lost Cause mythology heaped derision upon the memory of the Metropolitan Police. One characterized the organization as being "mostly negroes," while another asserted that it "was composed of the scum of the earth and was officered by outcasts of all nationalities." Working-class men were the backbone of the Metropolitan Police force, and the census reveals that they lived among people who made their living through toil: draymen, laborers, washerwomen, and seamstresses. Most rented rather than owned their homes. Like the party itself, the force was diverse but dominated by white men. Blacks who joined the Metropolitan Police tended to come from the former caste of free people of color, possibly because some minimum standard of literacy was necessary to hold the job. A little more than one-fourth of the force was of mixed race, a proportion roughly reflecting that in the overall population of New Orleans at the time. Immigrants, who were overwhelmingly Irish, were the other dominant group in the Metropolitan Police. Like the Afro-Creoles on the force, many of these men were also veterans. It mattered little to conservative white New Orleanians, however, that the majority of Metropolitan policemen were white. The presence of black officers on the force, combined with their mission of protecting Republican interests in the city, quickly made them a target for the bands of Democratic toughs who increasingly roamed the streets.[42]

For Algernon Sydney Badger, who had yet to find a career that suited him as much as being an officer in the U.S. Army, the creation of the Metropolitan Police came as a welcome opportunity. He had returned with his regiment to garrison duty in Shreveport after the Confederacy's collapse, but by December 1865 Badger had joined the tens of thousands of other soldiers who had mustered out of the service. Instead of returning to Massachusetts, however, the newly unemployed officer came to New Orleans. Here Badger worked both his army and his Republican Party connections to secure a modest federal patronage job with the Custom House. Spending the first two years after the war as a port warden along the city's docks no doubt paled in comparison with the excitement of commanding an entire regiment of well-trained cavalry, but it did have the benefit of familiarizing him with the tougher part of town that thrived along the river's edge. That knowledge, along with his enormous fund of combat experience, probably made Badger as well suited as any man for his new occupation as a captain in the fledgling Metropolitan Police. He was going to need all the help he could get.[43]

Badger's new career also placed him for the first time on a collision course with Frederick Nash Ogden, who was now serving as the president of the Crescent City Democratic Club. Ward clubs were a fixture of nineteenth-century American urban politics, and they had a particularly colorful and sometimes violent history in New Orleans. In the weeks leading up to the November 1868 election, however, they established new standards for political violence in their undeclared war against the Republican Party. Unlike the Riot of 1866, Democratic violence during the fall political season could hardly be blamed on a handful of uncontrollable malcontents. Ogden's Crescent City Democratic Club unleashed a campaign of violence, carefully synchronized with broader political objectives, against the most conspicuous representatives of the Warmoth regime. Throughout the night, Republicans waited in terror, fearing that they would be dragged from their beds, beaten in the street, and have their homes ransacked. At the same time, unaffiliated bands of thugs, some undoubtedly taking advantage of the civil chaos, robbed, terrorized, and even killed working-class black men who had dared to register to vote.

The blood ties between Frederick Nash Ogden and his two cousins Robert and Horatio mirrored the symbiotic relationship between politics and violence in postbellum New Orleans. Unlike many of his peers, who were ejected from office with the Reconstruction Acts, Robert Nash Ogden not only managed to retain his seat in the Louisiana Senate; he also actively bargained with the more conservative members of the U.S. Army in New Orleans so that they would ignore the campaign of terror unleashed by the city's Democratic clubs. On one occasion, Robert Ogden, accompanied by a high-ranking army officer, suggested to Warmoth that he appoint Fred Ogden as chief of the Metropolitan Police, a move that they promised would restore order in the city. At the same time, Horatio Nash Ogden waged a legalistic war over the constitutionality of Warmoth's Metropolitan Police. While his lawyer cousins played conspicuous diplomatic roles, Fred Ogden, the soldier, organized the shadowy bands of armed men who waged political warfare in the streets. Publicly, conservative whites blamed street thugs or Sicilian immigrants for all of the outrages that took place during the fall election, but violent resistance to Republican rule had by this time already become part of official policy. From this moment forward until the final capitulation of the Republican regime in 1877, conservative political violence in New Orleans operated not as an unpredictable agent of popular sentiment, but instead with the sanction of powerful men who shared intimate bonds of blood, class, and experience.[44]

Robert Ray, a black Metropolitan policeman serving under Algernon Badger, later described the nature of the multipronged attack made by the Ogdens and their followers during the fall canvass. According to Ray, Senator Robert Ogden approached a prominent black minister who had gotten into serious legal trouble and offered "to settle his lawsuit and pay all the costs of court" if he would only give a speech that the senator had written at a black Democratic ward club. When Ray went to hear the minister's speech and spy on the club, Robert Ogden told the policeman to sign the rolls with all the other black men present that night. When Ray refused, Ogden replied that "if [he] wanted to live here in the city [he] had better join them." It was a credible threat. Three days earlier, Ray had seen two armed Democratic ward clubs, the Broom Rangers and the Democratic Workingmen's Club, sack his own Republican ward room, smashing its furniture into kindling. On another occasion, while he was on his beat near the corner of Eighth and Chestnut Streets, a "respectable" white man walked up to him and threatened his life: "All at once he drew one of those seven-shooting carbines from under his overcoat and put it to my breast, and said, 'We are agoing to do police duty. We will not recognize you, or any other police appointed by those who appointed you. We are citizens, and we are agoing to do our own police duty, and we are agoing to clean out all the damned scalawags and carpetbaggers; and all you negroes who won't turn in with us, we shall clean you out too.'" During several of its parades, the Crescent City Democratic Club carried a coffin through the streets as a warning to Republicans. It was not an idle threat.[45]

Matters got worse for Ray and the other black Metropolitan policemen in the days leading up to the election. On the night of October 26, as he rode a streetcar down Dauphine Street, Ray saw several black men running full tilt down Orleans Avenue toward Congo Square with a band of armed Sicilians hot on their heels. When these attackers spotted Ray, the only black man on the car, they refocused their attention in his direction. With a small crowd running after him and yelling "kill the son of a bitch," Ray sprinted across Canal Street to the police station, where Algernon Badger awaited the arrival of officers working the night shift. Anticipating a night of violence, Badger feared for the lives of his black policemen and ordered them to take off their uniform coats and seek refuge in their homes. In a borrowed civilian coat, Ray left the station and headed back down Dauphine in the street car, only to find at the corner of Burgundy and Esplanade a large contingent of armed Democratic clubmen carrying flags illuminated by flickering torchlight that read "Show No Quarter." In the full view of members of the U.S. Cavalry who stood on the Faubourg Marigny side of Esplanade, the mob dragged Ray from the car and searched him for weapons. "They had a good opinion to hang me to a lamp post," he recalled.[46]

It would be difficult to overstate the sense of anxiety that permeated life not just in New Orleans, but in the rest of the South as well, in the three years that immediately followed the war. The political turmoil and social dislocation of Reconstruction were so pervasive that they informed both the public and private decisions of nearly everyone who lived through the era. Some, like Henry Clay Warmoth, recognized that they were in the midst of epic change and were able to capitalize on postbellum instability. When the war began, he was an unknown, self-taught, self-proclaimed lawyer not yet out of his teens. Through an alchemist's recipe of luck, skill, and ambition, he became the governor of a state that he had never even visited before 1864. During his meteoric rise to power, Warmoth may have parroted the same rhetoric used by other Northern Republicans that lent the party's deeds the veneer of social activism, but both his actions and his personal correspondence belong to a man who, above all else, burned for individual glory. Men like Charles Sauvinet and the young conscript Peter Joseph also translated the era's instability into a rare opportunity. Neither had even been citizens in the eyes of the law before the war, but their military service in the occupier's army caused these men to see possibilities in Louisiana that would have been unthinkable in their childhood, possibilities that transcended politics. One did not have to look any further than the Riot of 1866, however, to appreciate the price one could pay for trying to change a society in unpopular ways. Luck was really all that separated both Sauvinet and Warmoth from meeting their deaths at the Mechanics' Institute. Meanwhile, Arthur Toledano and his first cousin Louise Marie Drouet broke bread together, even as the city came to grips with the collapse of the antebellum racial caste system. It would be difficult to conjure up a scene more emblematic of postbellum life's surreal nature than what unfolded during meals at the frame house on the corner of Tchoupitoulas and Gaiènnie. Yet for every heart that beat an optimistic and hopeful note in New Orleans, others resisted the changes taking place in their midst. When E. John Ellis and Frederick Nash Ogden finally returned to Louisiana under a cloud of defeat, perhaps they believed that the worst was behind them. But with the passage of the Reconstruction Acts, it was as though someone had undertaken to renegotiate the terms of surrender, except that instead of stacking weapons, they had been forced to yield their political future. During the elections of 1868, these men had not yet come to accept the presence of mutability in their own lives. The war may have been over, but it was a deeply unsettled peace.

All the violence and general discord fostered by the recalcitrant in Louisiana after the war had actually brought about the very outcome that they feared most. Former Confederates could accept military defeat in war and perhaps even some element of white Republican presence in Louisiana. The adoption of universal male suffrage as enacted by the new state constitution so taxed their credulity, though, that they actually believed the rest of the nation would soon come to its senses and, in the elections of 1868, reverse what could only have been a great misunderstanding perpetrated upon the nation by a few vindictive malcontents. For this reason they pursued a course of unrestrained violence and intimidation in an effort to carry the state for the Democratic Party. Such violence was also remarkably successful on the local level, for Democrats carried Louisiana for Seymour by an eight-to-three ratio.

Historians of Reconstruction-era Louisiana often give cursory attention to the violence that took place in the fall of 1868, perhaps in part because its only apparent long-term effect was that it empowered the Radicals to enact the Fifteenth Amendment and the Enforcement Acts. Yet one should not overlook the uncertainty that surely prevailed in the months between the rise of Warmoth and the November elections. None of these actors knew that in the national contest Northern voters would lead a Republican landslide for Ulysses S. Grant. Had it instead gone badly for the Northern Republicans, or if other states had been carried in the same fashion as Louisiana, "radical" Reconstruction might have simply become a footnote in American history. Republicans like Warmoth and other white carpetbaggers could have moved to new fields of opportunity. Men like Sauvinet, however, had staked everything on the future of the Republican Party. Indeed, the personal exposure of those Louisiana-born Afro-Creoles who had emerged as advocates of racial equality was enormous, and we should not underestimate the risks they took in their quest for civil rights.

Ironically, the embrace of organized political violence by conservative whites in New Orleans and elsewhere in the South was both a bizarre acknowledgment of the completeness of Union victory and an indication that the war had not undermined the region's essential devotion to the political process. As indefensible as we might judge such actions today, the Civil War was largely responsible for making violence a *legitimate* extension of political discourse. The Union, after all, had sustained its views on secession's constitutionality by waging a bloody struggle against the rebellious South. While a host of complex motivations animated white Southern men in their attempt to carry the election of 1868 for Seymour and Blair, they certainly viewed their brutal deeds in the streets of New Orleans as consistent with prevailing notions of civic duty.

To men like E. John Ellis and Fred Ogden, only emancipation—not black enfranchisement and the consequent handicapping of the Southern political landscape in favor of the Republican Party—had been included in the Confederacy's terms of surrender. And in some respects, the Radical ascendancy had not become a Northern war aim until *after* Appomattox. Yet in the consciousness of the Northern electorate, the political alienation of former Confederates had become an intrinsic element of any meaningful victory, and white Southerners were either unwilling or unable to see this. Many former Confederates, like Ogden and Ellis, were willing to accept the "verdict of the sword" but believed that the social and political revolution that swept the region in the wake of defeat was a matter entirely separate from the fundamental questions answered by the war. By the end of 1868, however, Ellis, Ogden, and their former comrades-in-arms had finally come to understand the magnitude of their defeat.[47]

CHAPTER FOUR

CARPETBAGGER PRINCE

1869–1872

> Would you be greatly surprised, Mr. Greeley, to be informed that
> in the judgment of the good people of this state, irrespective of
> party, the young man who now occupies the executive chair of
> Louisiana, whose crimes against his party and his people you
> charitably ignore, and whose championship you so boldly assume,
> is preeminently the prototype and prince of the tribe of carpetbag-
> gers, who seem to be your pet aversion.
>
> —Oscar J. Dunn

John F. Claiborne had been active in the Republican Party in the New Orleans suburb of Carrollton for about two years and a mounted patrolman in the Metropolitan Police for nearly as long when in July 1871 he received an order to meet in person with Governor Warmoth. According to Claiborne, he had been sent there because a superior had accused him of "not working hard enough" to ensure that Carrollton's delegates to the party convention were loyal to the governor. When the two finally met, Warmoth promised to promote Claiborne to corporal in return for his earnest support, but the policeman would have none of it, replying; "Governor, you have made me a heap of promises for my people in my portion of my district; I will not help to send any but good delegates, whom my people, the colored men will approve." Angered by such intractability, Warmoth replied, "I'll be God damned if any man shall have a place that don't support my administration." Leaving in disgust, Claiborne retorted, "It appears to me, you are making a tool of me, governor, and I can't serve you any longer."[1]

Claiborne's account of his interview with Warmoth is just one of many fragments in the documentary record that foster an image of the young governor as an unscrupulous villain, a portrayal that has enjoyed wide acceptance by a surprisingly diverse group of historians. Among the many lines written about the administration of Henry Clay Warmoth, certainly few, if any, match the self-congratulatory tone of his autobiography. Dunning-school historians writing in the first quarter of the twentieth century painted the young governor as the epitome of "Carpet-bag misrule," a scheming and rapacious interloper who built a fortune on the backs of prostrate, defeated Southerners and gullible freedmen. The verdict rendered by W. E. B. Du Bois, in his 1935 classic *Black Reconstruction*, differing little from the opinion of the white supremacist authors of the Dunning school, described the young governor as an "unmoral buccaneer . . . whose business it was to manipulate the labor vote, black and white." Instead of cleansing Warmoth's tarnished reputation, the "revisionists" and "postrevisionists" of the late twentieth century usually depicted him as the embodiment of the type of self-serving politician that had made the Reconstruction experiment fail. Eric Foner's landmark work *Unfinished Revolution*, for instance, refers to Warmoth's ascent as "unpropitious." With a few exceptions, most notably Richard Nelson Current's nuanced group biography of "those terrible carpetbaggers," recent works still cast Warmoth as a swashbuckling but opportunistic minor tyrant who placed personal ambition over the common good.[2]

Yet, while these historians may offer an accurate characterization of Warmoth's morals, they almost universally overlook the greater importance of his political career. Understanding that everything else was secondary to the creation of the long-term stability of the state's Republican Party—*his* Republican Party—explains much about the man and his actions. Without question, Warmoth was willing to compromise his commitment (if he ever had any) to high-minded ideals such as racial equality. Equally undeniable was his adherence to a cloudy code of Gilded Age political ethics. Distracted by these considerable character flaws, and guided by an understandable desire to judge Warmoth by the standards of the "second reconstruction," historians have largely missed the relevance of his plan to create a viable political coalition in postbellum Louisiana.

Warmoth was a political pragmatist, not an ideologue. He understood that Louisiana, and New Orleans even more, stood in the political balance; they were there for the taking by anyone with the sense to promise a stable regime that was neither too radical nor too reactionary. He also knew that the far right embodied by Bourbon Democrats and the egalitarian Radicalism characterized by the Roudanez brothers would always alienate voters and that both were minority positions in 1869.[3] Between these extremes lay a substantial mass of black and white voters who yearned for stability as they went about reconstructing their private lives. The familiar "morality play" of Reconstruction historiography portrays a polarized society where, presumably, Southerners of both races allied themselves with either the Republican or the Democratic Party, basing their decision largely upon self-interest, racial fear, or in the case of some Republicans, high-minded ideals. In tracing a teleological line between Reconstruction and the creation of a solidly Democratic South, however, historians often miss that the very essence of postbellum political culture was *fragmentation* and not unity. If anything, the later political career of Henry Clay Warmoth should remind us that it took an additional twenty years *after* the Compromise of 1877 for Louisiana to finally emerge out of the political chaos that began with the Civil War. When the much older Warmoth ran for governor in 1888, his Democratic opponents were so frightened that they resorted to a campaign of unbounded fraud and white-supremacist fearmongering to preserve their power. Even so, an additional decade passed before the Democrats could unite a clear majority of whites behind their standard. Not until the disfranchisement crusade of 1898 did they finally stamp out the dissent that had characterized Louisiana politics since 1865. When viewed in this light, Warmoth's ambition to create a centrist coalition in 1869 appears much less far-fetched. Whether sheer genius or sheer folly, it was well ahead of its time.[4]

In depicting Warmoth as an unusually unscrupulous historical figure, revisionist historians have in effect set him up as a "straw man," an asterisk easily explained and dismissed in their overall narrative of Reconstruction. Yet the essence of Warmoth was not, in fact, his undeniable charisma, cloudy ethics, or precocious rise to power. It was his ability to place his finger on the pulse of postbellum politics in Louisiana and astutely draw others into his schemes. Warmoth's success did not result from his buccaneering ways but came about *in spite of them*. Moreover, the ire of his rivals, whether within his own party or among conservative Democrats, arose not from moral indignation but from envy. The Dunningites and the revisionists alike spared no expense to tell their readers of the fundamental differences between Republicans and Democrats, and in some respects, they were right. Yet far from being the regrettable anomaly so often portrayed by his detractors on both sides of the political spectrum, Warmoth's aspirations were, to some extent, the aspirations of most men, both black and white, Republican and Democratic, of his generation.

The rise and fall of Henry Clay Warmoth therefore offers us an opportunity to ask new questions not only about the men who belonged to the Republican Party in Louisiana during the postbellum era, but about the very essence of the Reconstruction political contest as witnessed by those who engaged in it. For more than a century, historians of the era have placed great stock in the notion that the politics of Reconstruction were, at their heart, an *ideological* struggle, whose central issue was the fate of white political and social supremacy. But this interpretation has hinged more on the contemporary ideological needs of those historians who wrote about life in the postbellum South than on fresh examinations of Reconstruction's political actors. Needing a historical basis for segregation and disfranchisement, the generation of Claude Bowers penned a version of Reconstruction that grossly exaggerated the racial dimensions of the Republican threat to Democratic rule. Several generations later, revisionist historians such as Kenneth Stampp and Hans Trefousse found in the Radicals a historical model for the Civil Rights activists of the 1960s. Moral judgments aside, both groups used the history of Reconstruction in the same fashion, and in the process they removed nuance and ambiguity from their narrative in the name of contemporary political utility. Although the field has been greatly enriched with interpretive complexity in the half century since the *Brown* decision, the notion of ideological struggle remains a standard assumption of Reconstruction historiography. While ideology surely mattered in the nineteenth century, so, too, did far less exalted impulses. The question we need to revisit, therefore, is, To what degree were Reconstruction politics a struggle between freedom and white supremacy as opposed to being merely a bare-knuckle struggle for power?[5]

The tactics of intimidation and violence used by competing factions of the Republican Party during their 1871–72 feuds differed somewhat from the brutality of the Democratic campaigns that took place in the fall of 1868, but the motivations that animated such deeds did not. White Republicans, operating in the prevailing postbellum zeitgeist, looked at Louisiana far more as a spoilsman's paradise than as a progressive experiment in biracial governance. Conservative white Southerners living through the era of Reconstruction seldom missed an opportunity to express their views that black men had been enfranchised only to serve as the tool of scheming white Republicans, a charge later repeated by Dunning-school historians. Although partisan bias and racist beliefs often informed such notions, even the most impartial recounting of the actions of those Republicans who gathered in the statehouse during Warmoth's turbulent reign would have difficulty arriving at a wholly different conclusion. Perhaps the greatest failing of federal Reconstruction policy was that the racially egalitarian rhetoric employed by some white Radicals was, as their bitterest critics have charged, a cheap ploy for controlling the votes of freedmen. It is the same conclusion at which the cynical W. E. B. Du Bois arrived in 1935. "The carpetbaggers flattered Negroes, bribed those whom they could and gave them some recognition," noted Du Bois, "but always at some crucial point because they knew the Negro had no choice."[6]

Yet, had white supremacy endured as a dominant philosophy of our nation's collective beliefs, we would have to ask equally pointed questions of those Conservative counterrevolutionaries who sought to topple Warmoth's regime. That they would make bargains with so-called Radicals in the Custom House, ally with black political figures, and even stand foursquare in violent opposition to fellow Confederate veterans to seize power should undermine any notion that they could claim a "noble" devotion to racial purity. New Orleans and the state of Louisiana were terribly unstable, both socially and politically, in the late nineteenth century. The backgrounds and intentions of the individuals who sought to capitalize upon this instability covered a broad spectrum and were hardly confined to Republican opportunists.

Lost in the seedy murk of the New Orleans political infighting, however, were the deeds of persons who acted not because they hoped for position or profit, or even necessarily because they were "better" men, but instead because they had faith in ideology and because their ideological vision was inseparable from daily life. Although men like Charles Sauvinet and E. John Ellis came from opposite political poles, both were guided by principles that had crystallized during their military service. For them, Reconstruction was not an abstract partisan struggle—it touched something fundamental about their very identity. Sauvinet and Ellis saw a direct correlation between the outcome of the political contest during the Warmoth era and their own standing as men, and as a result they forged ahead in the postbellum era informed by an inflexible standard of personal behavior. Individuals such as these remind us that while pragmatists such as Warmoth often drove the era's political agenda, periodically the outcome of events hinged on the deeds of those who were driven by firm ideological convictions. Indeed, if there was ever a true revolution, it came about as a result of individual actions instead of a political movement. One day, both Ellis and Sauvinet were going to arrive at the disheartening realization that the future of their native land hinged not upon ideology or the dedicated virtue of true believers such as themselves, but largely upon the actions of men who exhibited far more elastic notions of honesty. But it is doubtful that they would have acted any differently had they known from the start the futility of dealing with men who operated under Gilded Age assumptions. To have done so would have meant denying their very essences.

At some level, all of the decisions made by the Civil War generation were informed by the profound social and political uncertainty that had emerged in postbellum New Orleans. Just as conservative whites could not conceive that the nation would embrace the Radical cause in 1868, Louisianians, whether black or white, had no clear sense of the state's direction as Warmoth's regime began. Perhaps most troubling for some was that their destinies were beyond their own control. Fate had chosen them to become participants in a drama of which few of them wanted any part. The manner in which they reacted to such uncertainty revealed much about their priorities and aspirations.

Although he had ridden the Radical wave into office, having been an early supporter of universal suffrage, Warmoth began building a much broader-based coalition not long after he ascended to the governor's office in 1868. His strategy was actually quite simple: to draw supporters away from his rivals in sufficient numbers that he would emerge with a ruling majority. Since the Republican Party was almost the only option for black voters in 1868, this meant poaching on Democratic turf. His courting of conservative whites began with executive appointments to the many public offices under his control, both in New Orleans and in rural parishes. He always maintained a certain following among the state's black voters, but Warmoth hurt his image among them by appointing some former Democrats and Confederates to important posts. He also quickly distanced himself from pure Radicalism when he stood in opposition to public accommodation laws making their way through the Louisiana legislature in 1869. For the time being, however, he hoped to placate black supporters with a share in patronage. Yet nowhere was Warmoth's goal for fashioning a centrist political coalition out of "carpetbaggers," moderate former Confederates, and black elites more fully demonstrated than with his revamping of the Metropolitan Police and creation of the Louisiana State Militia. With luck, these institutions might not only weld their members' loyalty to his new regime but also serve as a powerful force for its defense. It was a good plan, at least in theory.[7]

Unfortunately for Warmoth, the uncanny luck that had accompanied him throughout the war and early postbellum years abandoned him as governor; further, the ruthless and often morally base tactics he employed in amassing his power served to alienate those he needed most in his bid to forge a lasting coalition. Endowed with undeniable charm, Warmoth never doubted his ability to control or win over those equally ambitious white "carpetbaggers" within his own party whom he could not crush. Nor did he comprehend that he lived in the midst of a social revolution where members of an oppressed class would reject his rhetoric of pragmatic patience in their quest for long-denied rights. The eventual collapse of Warmoth's nascent political empire provided the first real break for the resuscitation of the defeated, divided, but by no means moribund Democratic Party.

The important role political violence played during the November 1868 election was not lost on Warmoth, nor was the vulnerability of his fledgling administration. Although federal troops were from time to time a factor in the political wrangling that took place in New Orleans, more often than not, their presence was incidental to the outcome of events. Certainly they were unreliable protectors of the Republican government. Not only did Warmoth lack any direct control over their use, but any general officer in charge of the troops at Jackson Barracks, no matter how willing to help, was loath to jump into a fray without consent from Washington. Even with a cooperative commander, however, it seemed as though many of the white soldiers stationed in New Orleans were sympathetic to the administration's enemies, a fact made all too plain to black Metropolitan policemen during the violence of 1868. For its part, the Metropolitan Police had demonstrated its own woeful inadequacy to curb the violent actions of Democratic ward clubs, a situation that demanded immediate correction if Warmoth's regime was to survive. Part of the problem was that the force was relatively inexperienced, but the quality and inconsistency of the force's leadership also loomed large in its failure. Throughout the political violence, however, Captain Algernon Sydney Badger demonstrated his toughness and loyalty to the Republican Party, and for this reason Warmoth promoted the veteran to the post of police superintendent. From this office, Badger saw that the Metropolitans were not only properly trained and equipped but also steadfastly loyal to the governor.

On paper, the Metropolitan Police was actually part of a nationwide trend toward modernization in urban law enforcement agencies. To join the Metropolitans, potential officers underwent screening for both physical and mental fitness. They were a uniformed force with badges—something relatively new in law enforcement. Some of the police served as sanitary officers whose primary responsibility was to ensure compliance with quality-of-life ordinances such as the proper disposal of trash. The Metropolitans also provided public welfare to the city's burgeoning population of destitute people by operating soup kitchens and shelters. They also acted as a first line of defense against the panoply of vagrants, cheats, and roughs that had always been a permanent fixture in New Orleans. An examination of the Metropolitans' arrest record indicates that intoxicated Irish immigrants took up a great deal of their energy. Yet under Badger's direction, the Metropolitans were also armed to the teeth, far better than most nineteenth-century police departments. In addition to sidearms, their arsenal included a stand of .44 caliber Model 1866 Winchester lever-action rifles with bayonets, a few small cannons, two Gatling guns, and the *Ozark*, a small steam-powered gunboat. All of this hardware was clearly not required to subdue alcohol-inspired malefactors from the Emerald Isle; it spoke instead to the Metropolitan's role as the strong arm of the Warmoth regime.[8]

While Warmoth had always intended for the Metropolitan Police to serve as the primary instrument of state authority, he also pursued the creation of a state militia modeled upon his vision of a new political coalition. In early 1870, the Louisiana legislature complied with Warmoth's request and authorized a force of five thousand men. Unlike the Metropolitan Police, this force would be segregated by race. Warmoth had hoped that by inviting prominent members of both black and white New Orleans society to accept commands in the militia, the force might convert political adversaries into friends and lend legitimacy to his regime. By definition, such a plan required the enrollment of former Confederates into the service. Many years after Reconstruction, Warmoth boasted in his memoirs that he had raised "twenty-five hundred young Rebels into the State Militia." Even the annual adjutant general's report for 1870 had to admit, "About one half of our force is composed of officers and soldiers who were in the military service of the Southern States during the late civil conflict." At a time when the U.S. Congress debated the passage of the Enforcement Acts as a measure to counter Klan violence, Warmoth, sensing a degree of ambivalence toward the Democratic Party among white New Orleanians, boldly invited men to the table who might otherwise array against him.[9]

At first, Warmoth was enormously successful at recruiting many of the city's elites into the new militia, an auspicious sign for his fledgling administration. Some of its members, such as William J. Behan, had truly heroic war records. In May 1861, at the tender age of nineteen, Behan had enlisted in New Orleans's elite Washington Artillery as a sergeant. By the time he surrendered at Appomattox, Behan had fought in most of the engagements in the Eastern Theater and had risen to the rank of brevet colonel. When he enlisted in the Republican militia in 1870, he was twenty-nine and had reestablished himself as a prosperous commercial grocer. Behan's comrades James B. Walton and William Miller Owen, both prominent merchants and Washington Artillery officers, also joined Warmoth's army. Their experiences in the Eastern Theater had not left these men clinging to the Lost Cause. On the contrary, Walton, whose wife had been arrested by Benjamin Butler in 1862 for displaying a Confederate flag, had resigned his command in 1864 out of disgust with the favoritism shown to others by Robert E. Lee and Jefferson Davis. Down the road, these men might don a gray uniform and parade with other Confederate veterans through streets decked with St. Andrew's Crosses, but for now, their wartime past was not as important as their political present.[10]

Another one of Warmoth's former Confederate militia officers was the young white Creole Aristée Louis Tissot. After studying law in Paris, Tissot finally returned to New Orleans in the fall of 1866 and soon thereafter began practicing law alongside his father. He married Jennie Bozonier later that same year, and the two took up residence in a Creole cottage next door to his parents on Bayou

St. John. By all accounts, the aristocratic lawyer was building a thriving legal practice, in part because his legal education was one of the best in the city, but also because he was an extremely popular and affable man. The image of affability, however, does not necessarily square with his participation in the Broom Rangers, a notoriously violent Democratic ward club that was conspicuous during the elections of 1868. Tissot, who later proved deeply sympathetic to the plight of both people of color and illiterate working-class men, obviously felt the strains of the era and joined a political club whose basic purpose was to violently overturn the Radical ascendancy. What he found appealing in Warmoth's regime is difficult to say, but it is incontrovertible that he signed on as a captain in the Republican state militia in 1870 despite "never wavering in devotion" to his Democratic principles.[11] Tissot's attitudes on race, despite his involvement with the Broom Rangers, also reflected the everyday realities and ambiguities of interracial interaction in mid-nineteenth-century New Orleans. In 1870 Tissot and his wife kept a residence next door to the Afro-Creole cigar manufacturer and philanthropist Georges Alcès and could hardly have been unaware of the activist circles in which Alcès moved. Alcès probably knew Sauvinet, and like Sauvinet, he appeared as "white" on the census recorder's sheet.

Tissot was also probably influential in the enlistment of others. John Reinecke and Alfred Meilleur, both militia lieutenants, had served as enlisted men in Tissot's company during the Civil War, and both had fairly dismal records. Reinecke, at age sixteen, managed to get captured in late 1862 in occupied New Orleans, likely after having deserted his unit following the retreat to Camp Moore. A prisoner exchange reunited him with Meilleur and the rest of the company at the siege of Vicksburg. After their parole at Enterprise, Mississippi, Reinecke and Meilleur both spent the majority of the war's remaining years malingering in hospitals, Meilleur receiving three demotions in the process. When these friends received commissions as lieutenants in the militia in 1870, both were working as cotton clerks and lived under the same roof in the city's Fifth Ward. Along with Tissot, they may have seen in their militia service an opportunity to correct whatever shortcomings they had exhibited during the war.[12]

Warmoth was also quite successful at attracting the service of New Orleans's elite Creoles of color. Charles Sauvinet, widowed not long after Warmoth took office, signed on as a colonel. So, too, did Joseph Raynal, a former slaveholder and a commission board member of the Metropolitan Police (and, coincidentally, also a recent widower). Many of the line officers in the black militia companies had been among the officers who were cashiered by Nathaniel Banks in 1863 and

1864. Among them were men like Octave Rey and J. O. Lainez, both of whom were intimate friends with Warmoth's bitter enemies the Roudanez brothers. Others did not have as impressive résumés, however. Peter Joseph, who had been a mere private in the army, and that for only a brief period of time, had managed to fall in with men who had important connections in the Republican Party. Through these ties, he became an officer in the state militia and also secured a position as a sergeant in the Metropolitan Police. It was remarkable mobility for a man who could not even read in 1864. It was also emblematic of the diversity of the adherents that Warmoth managed to attract, at least temporarily, to his new regime.

To lead his militia force, Warmoth called upon General James Longstreet of Georgia, Robert E. Lee's old "war horse." Longstreet had moved to the city not long after the war ended to start a factorage with fellow veteran and Washington Artillery officer William Miller Owen. In 1869, Ulysses S. Grant, a longtime friend, appointed Longstreet to the post of U.S. surveyor of the port of New Orleans, a sinecure that most Southerners saw as quid pro quo for Longstreet's early support of the Northern victors. As much as Longstreet's Republicanism may have disconcerted some, however, his political ideology differed little from that of the elite white New Orleanians who now served under him in the newly formed militia. He personally disdained the concept of social equality for blacks but conceded that acceptance of freedmen's political rights was both inevitable and honorable. In Longstreet's view, violent resistance to federal authority could only lead to prolonged Northern occupation, an opinion with which E. John Ellis would likely have concurred. Unlike Ellis, however, Longstreet believed the biggest obstacle to the political resurgence of conservative white Southern men was the Democratic Party itself.

Ironically, both the success and the failure of Warmoth's appointment of Longstreet hinged not on politics but on the personal relationships that the general had forged during the Civil War. Many of the important officers in the Washington Artillery shared close ties with Longstreet and ultimately joined the unit not because of any devotion to Warmoth but because they admired their former commander. Certainly men like James B. Walton, who had been a friend and subordinate of Longstreet, identified with his commander's political stance. With effort, white Southerners might even be able to abide Longstreet's Republicanism. They could not, however, countenance his alleged criticisms of the recently deceased and sainted Robert E. Lee. The festering resentment toward Longstreet harbored by other Lee subordinates soon blossomed into direct character assassination by men like Jubal Early, who portrayed Longstreet as a heartless scalawag hell-bent on blaming his own failures as a soldier on the marble man. From that point forward, Longstreet's reputation with most white Southerners was as irretrievable as a bullet fired from a gun.[13]

Finally ready to leave his father's home in Amite, on New Year's Day 1869, E. John Ellis, accompanied by his wife Josie, moved to New Orleans. At 16 Carondelet Street, not far from Sauvinet's Freedmen's Bank office and just a short block from E. A. Toledano's cotton factorage, John and Thomas Ellis formed a law partnership. Optimistic about their prospects in the city, John predicted that they would soon have an abundance of business. "Even if it takes us two or three years, the prize is worth troubling for even suffering for as I know full well we shall take no step backward and sustain whatever position we attain," he wrote to Thomas in late January. Yet such enthusiasm could not mask the deep and abiding anxiety that clouded Ellis's soul during the first six months of 1869. On one occasion in early March, when rumors of a pending attack on the statehouse caused Warmoth to rush 150 men of the Metropolitan Police to protect the building, Ellis bitterly observed that "nothing of the kind was ever contemplated [but] the apprehension was alive in the guilty consciences of these men who know they deserve only the hatred of these people and the mercy of the knife in the hands of that terrible nemesis, a popular outbreak." His hostility toward those parties whom he believed responsible for bringing about this state of affairs boiled over two months later when a congressional committee subpoenaed him and Thomas to testify about their actions during the previous fall's elections. Ellis's combative testimony that May revealed the sense of outrage that burned in the hearts of conservative white Southerners.[14]

One of Ellis's inquisitors was Job Evans Stevenson, a freshman member of Congress from a district that incorporated the city of Cincinnati, Ohio. Stevenson's inquiry, asking if Ellis had been "in the rebel army," provoked the following heated exchange:

> ELLIS: I was in the Confederate army.
> STEVENSON: You still deny that it was a rebellion?
> ELLIS: That perhaps would involve a political discussion.
> STEVENSON: Do you admit that it was a rebellion?
> ELLIS: If a man from Ohio, in the person of yourself, states himself to be better
>   than a man from Louisiana, in the person of myself, I rebel against you, but
>   I know no master.

Stevenson let the matter drop, but tensions soon reemerged when his colleague Jacob Hale Sypher took his turn questioning Ellis. Sypher, born in Pennsylvania, had first come to Louisiana as a member of an Ohio regiment during Butler's occupation. By the war's end, he was a colonel in the U.S. Colored Troops. After leaving the army he purchased a plantation, studied law, and became involved in Louisiana Republican politics. Like Stevenson, he had won his position in the fall elections of 1868, though the Democratic candidate continued to challenge his seat. Sypher embodied everything that Ellis believed was wrong with the war's outcome, and his hatred of the Northern transplant was palpable. When Sypher asked whether all Northerners on official business were called carpet-baggers, Ellis replied that no, "the gentlemen whom we call carpet-baggers are the men who leave their country for their country's good and for our bad; who come up there, and a day after their arrival are candidates for governors, and judges and congressmen, and who want to fill our offices." When Sypher asked, "Are not my interests in Louisiana," Ellis retorted, "I do not think so." A third congressman, Samuel Swinfin Burdett of Missouri, angrily cut in, asking whether it was "not true that one reason of the fact that so many persons from other States are sent to Congress from Louisiana is, that the people in Louisiana, who might be capable of representing the State in Congress, were almost universally, for four years, try-ing to cut the throat of the government?" "We wanted to let you live," replied Ellis, "but we wanted to live too." It was a far cry from the days when he had an-guished over secession.[15]

The Ellis brothers also conducted a steady dialogue with Charles Kennon, a longtime friend back home in Tangipahoa Parish. Kennon was the same age as E. John Ellis and shared his passion for political theory. The two had spent a year together at the Johnson's Island prison, and when Kennon returned, he began a medical practice in Amite. He felt that the Democratic Party had handled things badly since the close of the war, and by 1870 Kennon was furious over the state of political affairs. He railed against the deep divisions among the white population, heaping much of the blame on men who had crossed over to the Republican Party. Equally to blame, thought Kennon, were the old "party hacks" like the antebellum politician Thomas Green Davidson, once an advocate of secession and now a prominent "scalawag" who wanted to "divide the white men of the South on dead issues." In exasperation, Kennon suggested that as a last resort, white men should organize a Conservative Republican Party to defeat the political enemy from within—something of a "Trojan horse" strategy. He mused that "if a large portion of the white people act with the Republican Party and show them that the neces-sity no longer exists for exalting the negro, then 'Cuffy,' his vote being no longer a matter of paramount importance will no longer be the sable hero of elections." Thomas Ellis noted at the top of this letter, "read & return to me."[16]

Following the elections in November 1870, Kennon fired off another impassioned letter to the Ellis brothers. "The money and patronage of the dominant party and our confidence in the whites who failed to do their duty conspired to disappoint us in the result," noted Kennon. He complained further that the acceptance of the Fifteenth Amendment "broke down the prejudice which stimulated many of the ignorant class to vote against Radicalism." Kennon saw little difference between the Democrats and the Republicans now that the former had endorsed the black franchise. "We can never control the negro vote for the simple reason that it involves social equality which we can never accept." He included invective against fellow residents of Tangipahoa who had aligned with Warmoth for the sake of patronage appointments. Such patronage and the steady salary that went with it were quite invasive. "It is rumored here that Wm Perrin, the perjured wretch, supported Brady under promise of getting his support for District Judge at next election. Meaning, I presume, Radical support." Closing his political comments, Kennon declared, "The demoralization in our white ranks is incredible."[17]

As 1870 drew to a close, Warmoth was at the height of his power and had no notion that he had built his political coalition on a foundation of sand. The Metropolitan Police, to some degree, and the militia, to a much greater degree, reflected what the young governor was doing with many aspects of his power. Appointments to state offices went to both Republicans and supportive Democrats, particularly those who had had Whiggish tendencies in the past. There was grumbling from within his own party, but at the moment it was something Warmoth believed he could contain. Yet as 1870 passed into 1871, the seeds of Warmoth's downfall had already been sown. Growing disillusionment with the governor from within his own party was largely to blame; in the coming year, the coalition he had crafted with such care came apart at the seams. In part, it was bad luck, but the union's inherent contradictions also played a role.

Two great spectacles that consumed the first few months of every calendar year in postbellum New Orleans were the annual legislative session and the social spectacle of Carnival season. Mardi Gras 1871 fell on February 21, and the weeks leading up to that Tuesday were a time of conviviality, dancing, and taking stock of where one sat in the social spectrum. If the menus from such affairs are any indication, those who attended these balls came prepared to marinade themselves in alcohol and feast from a sumptuous spread of French cuisine. Yet despite the festive atmosphere of Carnival season, other events conspired to draw and quarter Warmoth's coalition. The actions of old Confederates whom Warmoth had successfully courted worried his black supporters. In turn, the growing activism of the governor's black supporters left some on his conservative flank second-guessing their own support of Republicanism. Indeed, the larger question of exactly where black New Orleanians fit into the social spectrum had placed much of the town on edge. Within the Republican Party itself, a conspiracy formed among jealous rivals. And of course, the Democrats hated Warmoth's guts. It was a lot for one man to keep track of.

Two weeks before Shrove Tuesday, Henry Clay Warmoth attended a splendid party at the St. Charles Hotel hosted by Louisiana Lottery president John Howard. It was the reception for the governor's doomed political marriage. Special guests included prominent Democrats and Republicans, judges, generals, and other dignitaries from New Orleans and elsewhere. Warmoth occupied the place of honor, and to his right sat George Carter, Speaker of the Louisiana House of Representatives. Carter had been the colonel of a Confederate cavalry regiment from Texas and was also lawyer of some reputation. The two had gained acquaintance when Carter defended Warmoth against an embezzlement charge in a Texas courtroom. When the Louisiana legislature authorized the creation of Cameron Parish in the far southwest corner of the state, Warmoth rewarded Carter with an appointment as parish judge. From there, Carter solidified his position as the district's representative and then strong-armed his way into the speakership. One wonders whether, as those assembled dined on *salmis de bocassines à la Richelieu* and drank *punch romaine*, Warmoth knew already that he had created a monster.[18]

One week after Warmoth's fete at the St. Charles Hotel, a surreal scene descended upon the Odd Fellow's Hall on Lafayette Square, where in 1861 had occurred a lavish benefit to raise money for New Orleans's Confederates bound for Virginia. It was the night of the Military and Mask Ball, with Colonel William Miller Owen's Fifth Regiment of the Louisiana State Militia. The *Picayune* recounted the 1871 spectacle: "The uniforms of the regiment are made after the model of the French Chasseur uniforms. They are gray, trimmed with blue, look very neat, and bear a striking resemblance to the uniforms worn by the gallant boys who fought so well during the four years' conflict and many of whom are now enrolled in the militia service of our state." Striking resemblance indeed— to some, it looked as if the Washington Artillery itself had come back to life and that it was 1861 all over again.[19]

Yet it was not 1861, and no quantity of alcohol could make it truly appear that way. Who better to gently remind the educated public of this fact than the Mistick Krewe? Beginning with Carnival of 1871, subtle political commentary increasingly crept into the rolling tableaux of Comus. This year's festival celebrated Edmund Spenser's *Faerie Queen*. On the surface, it was as playful as the clever *Feast of Epicurus*, which had so delighted audiences during Mardi Gras of 1867. Yet observers with some degree of nineteenth-century classical education, which many of the city's social elite possessed, would have been aware of the witty sarcasm the Mistick Krewe found in Spenser's epic poem. The *Faerie Queen*, ostensibly a work praising Queen Elizabeth, was actually full of political criticism, both in the abstract and in the setting of Elizabethan England. It did not take much imagination to draw parallels with contemporary Louisiana or the Warmoth administration. The allegory derided misrule of all kinds, but particularly misrule practiced by persons with glaring character flaws. The message was undoubtedly above the heads of the masses, but in metaphorical terms, the men of Comus were expressing their growing resentment against Warmoth's Machiavellian regime.[20]

While these scenes of public spectacle pulled at Warmoth's coalition, a seemingly small incident involving Charles St. Albin Sauvinet illustrated the essential conundrum of the governor's desire to simultaneously court white conservatives and ostensibly represent the interests of black Louisianians. A few short weeks before the Democratic men of the Pickwick Club staged their parade, Charles Sauvinet had become the first man of color to serve as the civil sheriff of Orleans Parish, a job he won in the fall 1870 elections. He quickly discovered the challenges faced by a black civil servant. Late in January 1871, Sauvinet and two white business associates left his French Quarter office in search of a noontime drink. When Sauvinet suggested a frequent haunt, one of his companions, a native New Orleanian by the name of Finnegan, commented that it was "in the French part of town and you can't get good liquor there." Ignoring this thoughtless insult to Sauvinet's Gallic heritage, the trio gamely continued down Bienville Street to Royal. Here they passed over the famous Sazerac because of similar objections. When the party stopped in front of number six Royal Street, home of "The Bank," Finnegan was finally satisfied. "Here is where a man can get a first class drink," he proclaimed. It was a place Sauvinet knew well.[21]

Sauvinet had taken a drink at the Bank Coffeehouse many times, even at the invitation of the proprietor, Joseph Walker. Yet something out of the ordinary had happened on his most recent visit to the bar. That trip had been to carry out his official duties as sheriff, to collect the Bank's rent from Walker because the landlord was in receivership. In the privacy of his upstairs office, Walker offered the sheriff a drink and proceeded to pay the rent. All was amicable as the two sat drinking cognac, when the bar owner turned to serious conversation. "I have a favor to ask of you," he said. Walker explained that it had been recently called to his attention that Sauvinet was considered a colored man. He asked that Sauvinet stop visiting the Bank's barroom because serving him in the house would injure his business. Taken aback, Sauvinet replied, "I have always drunk in all houses, and it is too late now for me to go back." No doubt this exchange with Joseph Walker was fresh in Sauvinet's mind as the three men stepped into the barroom and sat at a table. Walker was nowhere around, but when the bartender on duty spotted the sheriff in the midday crowd, he began to turn pale and act panicky. After some minutes, the boisterous Finnegan grew restive and directly requested service, to which the bartender nervously shook his head and chattered the incoherent phrase, "Never mind, it is all right." Finnegan became combative, but Sauvinet grabbed him by the sleeve and ushered his two companions outside. On the banquette, Sauvinet uttered in a restrained fury, "I know the reason why we were refused."[22]

Six days later, Sauvinet sent his attorney to Henry Dibble's Sixth District courtroom to serve a petition. The sheriff sought five thousand dollars in damages from the Bank Coffeehouse—a considerable sum. More importantly, Sauvinet threw down the gauntlet with the regard to the state's civil rights legislation. As a Republican, a militia officer, a civil sheriff, and now a man of color, C. S. Sauvinet had taken a stand that was going to threaten Warmoth's shaky coalition. The district court received the case quickly, and by mid-March, lawyers for the two sides were actively engaged in verbal combat. Walker's attorneys suggested that Sauvinet might actually be white after all and that he had made a conscious decision to identify himself as black for the purpose of political gain. When the defense's counsel asked point-blank if he was a colored man, Sauvinet responded, "Whether I am or not I do not know myself—but I am, and was legally for this reason; that prior to the war and before the Congress of the United States had passed laws granting and giving citizenship to men born on the soil whether colored or not, you had always refused me." Others had defined him as black, according to Sauvinet. Such a temporizing reply only encouraged further cross-examination. When asked, "Have you not stated that you are as much a white man and of white blood as any man in the community?" Sauvinet retorted, "I have stated so.—Ain't I?"[23]

The jury, which had taken a long time to seat, could not reach a verdict. Dismissing them, Judge Henry Dibble ruled for Sauvinet but reduced his reward to one thousand dollars. In May the Louisiana Supreme Court heard Walker's appeal but came to the same conclusions as Dibble. The decision there was not unanimous, however, with Justice William Gillespie Wyly writing in dissent: "I think the penalty wholly disproportionate to the offense. If, instead of refusing the plaintiff a drink merely, the defendant had seized a chair and beaten him half to death with it, the damages would probably not have exceeded $250. Yet, is the right to enjoy the entertainment of a drinking saloon of greater moment or more sacred than the right of personal security from violence?"[24] To those most hostile to the ruling, Sauvinet's victory meant that the state civil rights legislation was tantamount to social equality. The *Weekly Louisianian*, a black daily paper, also commented on the case. "The absurdity of endeavoring to connect either one of these acts with 'social equality' is so transparent that we regard it a waste of time to dwell on it here." These new laws were abstractions until Sauvinet became a flesh-and-blood example of the changes Reconstruction legislation promised.[25]

Sauvinet v. Walker also demonstrated that resistance to civil rights and social change needed to be enforced among whites. Many who might be opposed to integration in principle might turn a blind eye when it came to daily human interaction. Certainly, Sauvinet was a man of means, cultured, and very fair-skinned, but it is doubtful that Walker discovered overnight that society considered the sheriff to be a colored man. Sensitive to his bottom line and those who might force the issue, Walker denied service to a man he had once invited to drink on equal terms. Perhaps the five men who posted Walker's bond were behind it. Two of these men, Charles Cavaroc and John Rareshide, were members of the Pickwick Club, the organization that orchestrated the Mistick Krewe of Comus's satirical performance during Mardi Gras. At the same time, Sauvinet did not help matters by seeking an enormous, highly punitive award. Those who might otherwise support Sauvinet's rights, such as the two dissenting state supreme court justices, blanched at his aggressiveness. Yet the amount sought by Sauvinet was probably a measure of the intense outrage felt by a man who had for the first time in his life felt the direct sting of Jim Crow hypocrisy. This case and others that followed contributed to the racial polarization of society and drove those who had once stood by in ambivalence toward action.[26]

While the *Sauvinet* case played out in state court, smaller incidents occurred in New Orleans that cumulatively had a similar effect on public opinion. Arthur Toledano, the white Creole Confederate veteran, ultimately had a front-row seat to such a confrontation. From a financial standpoint, Toledano had done well during Reconstruction. Yet, if he previously had no particular animosity for the Republicans who now ruled Louisiana, an experience that he had on a city streetcar in March 1871 probably changed his mind. The history of Jim Crow acrimony on New Orleans's "omnibus" streetcars dated back to the "star car" incidents during the federal occupation, when black military officers refused to abide by the city's segregation laws. From that moment forward, the horse-drawn cars became a potent symbol of Reconstruction's most tangible aspects—in New Orleans and elsewhere. The Louisiana Constitution of 1868 included provisions for ending segregation on public conveyances, and additional laws passed in 1869 strengthened the letter of the law, if not its enforcement. Although many blacks simply chose not to force the issue, it did on occasion bring them into direct confrontation with whites who took it upon themselves to resist the new order. News of such incidents in schools, barrooms, trains, and elsewhere had periodically appeared in the papers by the time Arthur Toledano and his wife returned home from a visit to Carrollton.[27]

It was about six o'clock in the evening when the inbound streetcar pulled up to the Carrollton depot. This route was called the Carrollton Railroad. Arthur Toledano and his wife Celeste waited for the driver to open the door, then climbed up the steps into the wooden trolley car. As Toledano paid the fare, Celeste anxiously looked up and down the aisles for an empty seat but did not find any. Just then, a man waved her over and graciously relinquished his own seat to her. Thanking the man, Celeste sat down and waited for the car to begin moving. In the seat next to her sat Jane Price, a twenty-nine-year-old mixed-race domestic servant on her way home to the Lower Garden District. After lurching several blocks down St. Charles Avenue, the already crowded car stopped once more to take on additional passengers. One of these was a friend of Celeste's seatmate, and the two women waved to each other. Trouble began almost as soon as the car started moving again. Perhaps Jane Price was incensed that no gentleman yielded his seat to her friend, or maybe she was just reacting against years of second-class citizenship. Whatever the case, Price crossed her arms high on her chest and began purposely elbowing Celeste Toledano in the face in the hope that she might force the white Creole lady to give up her seat.[28]

Outraged by Price's actions, Toledano sternly warned her that he would give her five seconds to put her arms down. When Price replied that she "was as good as anybody having paid fare, she would do so as she pleased and sit as she saw proper," the enraged Toledano grabbed the woman's hand and jerked her elbow away from Celeste's face. Price promptly resumed her offending pose a second time and Toledano again pulled her away, this time threatening to throw her out the window if she tried it again. Price remained undeterred and resumed elbowing Toledano's wife. When Arthur Toledano grabbed her by the wrist a third time, Price sprang up, struck him across the face, and ripped his collar loose from his shirt, all the while cursing him repeatedly. This torrent of oaths sent the other passengers into a fury and they angrily called for the driver to halt the vehicle. When it finally came to a stop, several passengers ejected Price and her friend.[29]

As if the ride that evening had not upset Toledano enough, a few days later a Metropolitan policeman served a warrant for his arrest. Jane Price had filed assault charges against Toledano for striking her without provocation. Fortunately for him, the witnesses who came forward on his behalf offered far more corroborative and detailed accounts of the affair than had Price and her friend. The Recorder's Court quickly dismissed the charges, but the whole experience must have been rather unsettling. Price's actions had struck at the most central fear held by white Southerners, the sanctity of white womanhood. Unable to protect his wife from such insults, Toledano had failed to fulfill his honorable duty as a white Southern man.[30]

One wonders what must have gone through Arthur Toledano's mind when he next visited his Uncle Louis's house and saw his mixed-race cousin, Louise Marie Drouet. Maybe he wondered how far removed this blood relation of his was in principle from Jane Price, the woman who had so humiliated him on the streetcar. She too aspired to social equality—in fact, to a much greater extent than Price because Louise Marie had begun to think of herself not only as a lady but as one of the family. Perhaps he wondered if by virtue of blood ties and wealth Louise Marie might someday become Celeste's social equal. If so, he was hardly the only white man in New Orleans who contemplated at what point, if ever, society might place a boundary on all of this creeping racial egalitarianism. Moreover, Louise Marie's now openly acknowledged relationship with his uncle might throw the entire family's racial purity into question. The incident aboard the Carrollton Railroad undoubtedly reminded Toledano of many troubling possibilities.

There were important differences between the *Sauvinet* case and Toledano's confrontation with Jane Price, and these differences exposed the societal fault lines along which not just Warmoth's regime, but also subsequent Republican regimes, would founder. No matter how just the February 1869 act was, the one passed by the Louisiana legislature to "provide for carrying into effect the one-hundred thirty-second article of the Constitution of the State," the fact that Joseph A. Walker lost his right to bar whomever he saw fit from his private property was not lost on the general public. Indeed, this "private property rights" logic supplied the core of the argument against the passage of the Civil Rights Act of 1964 nearly a century later. In contrast, none of the Carrollton Railroad's riders protested that Jane Price boarded the streetcar, even though, like Walker's barroom, it was covered under the hated public accommodations laws. Only when Price ran afoul of deeper social conventions did a confrontation ensue.

Public transportation was a potent symbol, but it did not come close to generating the same explosive reaction among conservative whites as when the law forced a much more privileged space like Walker's barroom to admit patrons freely. Elites could separate themselves from the rest of society with relative ease when it came to public transport or even schools, just as they continue to do today. Yet the sweeping interpretation of public accommodations laws rendered by the judiciary in the *Sauvinet* case threatened the protective barrier of social rank. This danger is undoubtedly why elite men associated with the Pickwick Club posted Joseph Walker's bond. Since emancipation, white Southerners had endured, if not embraced, a great deal of change, including black political enfranchisement and integration on the city's streetcars. If there was a breaking point for Warmoth's coalition or any other centrist effort at postbellum governance, it was when legal changes threatened, at least in concept, the preserve of elite white privilege.

Warmoth had sought political cover on the race issue by allying himself with a black politician who was every bit his equal when it came to parliamentary maneuvering and a willingness to go for the jugular when necessary. Unlike the elite Creoles of color who dominated black political activity in the city, Pinkney Benton Stewart Pinchback was African American and not from New Orleans. Born in 1837 to a manumitted slave woman and a white Mississippi planter, Pinchback had endured a tumultuous youth, particularly after the death of his protective father in 1849. He had worked as a riverboat steward and part-time gambler on both the Ohio and the Mississippi rivers and for a while fell in with the notorious cardsharp George Devol. By the time he reached adulthood, this free man of color had proved himself to be a tough survivor. When news of New Orleans's fall to the Union in 1862 reached him, Pinchback made his way through enemy lines to the Crescent City. Using money he had saved from his wages and money that had come by way of a faro table, the adventurer opened a recruiting office at the corner of Bienville and Villere streets. Soon he had enough men to fill out Company A of the Second Regiment of the Native Guards with himself as captain. It was the same regiment that Charles Sauvinet served in as quartermaster, but unlike the quiet, businesslike Creole, Pinchback was not cut out for the unrewarding duty at Ship Island. By September 1863, he had had enough of such futility. In tendering his resignation to General Nathaniel Banks, Pinchback explained, "I can foresee nothing but dissatisfaction and discontent which will make my position very disagreeable indeed."[31]

Pinchback returned to New Orleans in early 1867 after an unsuccessful stint attempting to rally black political support in Alabama; he bought a two-story frame house on Derbingy Street, not far from Canal. To look at the man, most in the city might have taken him for one of the mixed-race Afro-Creole elite. His impeccable dress, light skin, and straight hair seemed to point to a wealthy French ancestor. But such observers could not have been more wrong. In fact, Pinchback grew increasingly disenchanted with the men with whom he seemed to have common cause. He believed that the much more radical Afro-Creoles made unrealistic demands of society. Always a pragmatist, Pinchback voiced a thinly veiled reference to the Afro-Creole radicals in a bold speech to the Republican convention in June, 1867: "Colored men of Louisiana, I caution you to be aware how you listen to this hissing of the serpent, lest in an unguarded moment you will have planted in your heart a damnable Jealousy and Prejudice that will cause you to turn and bite the hand that fed you."[32] It is unclear when Warmoth and Pinchback first met, but it probably occurred not long after the latter had opened a Republican Party office in New Orleans's Fourth Ward, if not earlier. One was an ambitious, dashing, yet strangely pious, tall, thin Midwesterner with expansive visions of political glory. The other was a handsome mixed-race man of equally impressive height and bolder proportions who had often chafed at the notion that his mother's race kept him from attaining the heights to which he knew his keen intellect could take him. The historian, no matter the wealth of sources at his disposal, can never truly peer into the soul of his subjects, but at least on the surface, these two men appear to have been cut from the same cloth. Like Warmoth, Pinchback was daring but also morally ambiguous. He may not have been enamored with Warmoth, but again and again, he sided with his fellow outsider. The two adventurers needed each other and in time both proved to be remarkable political survivors. Warmoth commanded respect within the larger Republican world and had made a mind-boggling number of connections in a few short years. Pinchback brought credibility among the freedmen to the emergent Warmoth machine. It seemed like an ideal Louisiana political marriage.

Pinchback had certainly done much to cultivate his reputation as a champion of black people in the Pelican State. He had been one of the key proponents behind Article Thirteen of Louisiana's state constitution of 1868, which had in theory outlawed segregation in all places of public resort. The following year, he championed a civil rights bill that put some enforcement behind Article Thirteen. In 1870 Pinchback again backed a measure that gave civil rights cases preference in court, and Warmoth signed this bill into law. The new law was a primary reason why the *Sauvinet* case made it so quickly to the state supreme court. By 1871 his reputation with black voters was substantial. Pinchback knew exactly how much power that gave him.[33]

Like Warmoth, Pinchback also found ways to prosper financially during these early years of congressional Reconstruction. In 1869 he began a factorage with a man he ultimately came to despise, Caesar Carpentier Antoine, a member of New Orleans's antebellum free Afro-Creole elite. At 114 Carondelet Street, Pinchback & Antoine Commission Merchants lay nestled amid the factorage houses of the city's most established firms. Pinchback's founding of the *Weekly Louisianian* newspaper in late 1870 reflected the blurry lines between commerce, journalism, and politics drawn by many of his contemporaries in Louisiana. Indeed, Pinchback grew increasingly wealthy because of his political connections. Among other schemes, he had a hand in the great City Park swindle and used his influence to become a primary shareholder in an "official" state river packet company.[34]

Despite having lukewarm feelings toward the governor, Pinchback allied himself with Warmoth for perhaps no greater reason than to counterbalance the presence of Lieutenant Governor Oscar J. Dunn, Pinchback's main political rival as the leading black politician in Louisiana. The son of a free black woman, Dunn was a native of New Orleans and one of the earliest and most prominent members of the black leadership class that emerged during Reconstruction. He was an able politician and enjoyed a reputation for honesty—something neither Warmoth nor Pinchback could ever claim. Alienating Dunn may have been Warmoth's most deadly political mistake. Dunn grew increasingly disillusioned with the young governor's ambivalence toward the political and social rights of the freedmen. When serious opposition to Warmoth within the Republican Party surfaced among ambitious federal patronage employees in the U.S. Custom House, Dunn openly broke with his boss and joined this opposing faction. Until O. J. Dunn went over to the Custom House, these rivals presented more of a nuisance than a threat to Warmoth. Now that the lieutenant governor had taken his considerable clout with black voters across Canal Street, the Custom House could make a realistic bid to unseat the governor.[35]

The Custom House ring, as Warmoth's rivals came to be known in New Orleans, had for months jealously eyed all the power the young governor had accumulated. Some of these men felt they had been wronged by Warmoth. Others, who could scarcely be characterized as less grasping than Warmoth, harbored grandiose dreams of themselves in the governor's chair. Such was the case with the brains of the Custom House operation, Stephen B. Packard. A Union veteran from Maine, Packard had served with little distinction during the war and, like Warmoth, had come to New Orleans in 1864 with the army, practicing law and seeking a position within the Republican Party. Packard's persistent pursuit of spoils paid off when he received an appointment as the U.S. marshal for Louisiana in 1869. From his office in the Custom House, Packard successfully bid for the party's chairmanship in 1870. Although he owed Warmoth no loyalty, others openly betrayed the young governor when they joined the Custom House ring. Speaker Carter, who owed his political career to Warmoth, bolted to the Custom House not long after the Carnival season of 1871. William Pitt Kellogg, a man Warmoth had done much to make a U.S. senator from Louisiana in 1868, now also sided with Packard. The defection with the most political consequences, however, was that of James F. Casey, the collector of customs and a brother-in-law of President Ulysses S. Grant. Most people believed, correctly, that having Casey in their corner would bring the Custom House ring the support of the president and the national party.[36]

Warmoth perceived with growing alarm that the Custom House faction had the potential to deliver a mortal blow not only to his political coalition, but to his very future as the head of Louisiana's Republican Party. His vulnerability had much to do with the political geography of New Orleans, which in the Radical political context was always more important than the rural parishes. As in any American city of that era, power in the Crescent City hinged on one's ability to control a majority of the various ward clubs scattered throughout the city. The defection of Oscar J. Dunn to the Custom House precipitated a sea change in the allegiance of many of these Republican ward clubs, particularly where African Americans, and not Afro-Creoles, dominated the membership. Despite lingering antagonisms between Warmoth and certain members of the Afro-Creole elite—a rift that has been greatly overstated by historians—a significant portion of this caste actually remained loyal to Warmoth's coalition. Men like Octave Rey and Eugene Ràpp, for instance, had once been among the delegation of four who approached Benjamin Butler in 1862 to swear the allegiance of the city's elite Afro-Creoles to the Union. By 1871 they were captains in Badger's Metropolitan Police, and their deeds spoke to their dedication to Warmoth's faction.[37]

Urban ward politics had often been tough business in New Orleans, and so they were in the summer of 1871 as Warmoth moved to neutralize the threat presented by the Custom House faction. Scholars who have written about this period in the city's history have paid scant attention to the low-grade battle that took place between the two Republican factions in the weeks leading up to the August 9 convention, yet the struggle for spoils and power that raged between Republicans that summer raises important questions about the legitimacy of the party's claim to democratic principle and the cause of racial solidarity. In many important ways, Republican tactics seem to have differed little from those pursued by their conservative opponents during the fall of 1868. Perhaps the greatest irony of all was that Warmoth ended up using the Metropolitan Police not to fend off Democratic ward gangs but to intimidate Republican opponents into submission.[38]

Warmoth's political adversaries later painted a portrait of Algernon Sydney Badger as a tyrannical janissary who used the Metropolitan Police force not to preserve the peace but as a well-armed and organized partisan street gang. Among his primary accusers were policemen who claimed to have lost their positions because they had refused to obey orders to break up Custom House–friendly ward meetings. The probity of their statements is far from pure, and the same can be said for the accusations of U.S. Marshal Stephen B. Packard, a man who enjoyed little reputation for honesty and who clearly committed perjury at several junctures in his testimony. Yet the corroborative statements of Oscar J. Dunn and others who were known for candor command our attention. So do the consistencies with the later, well-documented actions of the Metropolitans as they played a vital role in allowing Warmoth to stave off a determined and equally brazen attack by a mob led by his Custom House rivals. It is quite possible, even probable, that the work of Algernon Sydney Badger's Metropolitans was just this ugly.

The testimony of Badger's accusers was replete with tales of the harassment and intimidation that Custom House–friendly members of the force suffered at the hands of the superintendent's trusted captains and sergeants. One dissenting sergeant, Thomas H. Wynne, testified that "the police force of my precinct, some times in part, and sometimes in the whole, were taken from their beats at night to mass upon clubs in different wards of the city, where they were invariably joined by the day force of my precinct." James Riley, another sergeant, described the violent breakup of the Third Ward Republican Club by a band of Metropolitans wearing civilian clothes: "The police force immediately rushed inside and filled the hall. . . . Superintendent Badger and Captain Schreiber were present within twenty feet of the doors when they were burst open, but did not interfere to prevent it. As soon as the possession was taken of the hall, the violence became great, and repeated shouts were given for Warmoth." Several former policemen claimed to have seen the familiar faces of notorious street toughs among the crowds that burst in upon these ward meetings and presumed they had been hired for that purpose by the Warmoth faction. According to another witness, when Oscar Dunn tried to bring the club back to order, Badger personally broke up the assembly, shouting "Police, do your duty!" Badger's command inspired Lieutenant Governor Dunn to flee out a rear exit. "I was seized by the back of the neck and the lapel of my coat by Police Officer Mooney," described a member of the ward club, "and dragged through the side door of the club to the side yard where

I was kicked down by Mooney. I jumped up as fast as possible, and retreated in fear of my life." Robert Magee, another former Metropolitan, recounted a scene at the precinct station that occurred on the morning of the day his ward club was to elect delegates to the Republican convention: "Sergeant Van Kirk, standing at the head of the line, held a ticket up in his hand and said, 'This is the ticket you all must vote: these men are our friends, and we must stand by them; see that you poll this ticket and vote as often as you can.'" When Magee asked about voting in a ward in which he did not live, another sergeant replied, "There'll be no question where you live. Hold this ticket in your hand so that the commissioners can see it is the right ticket."[39]

Sergeant Peter Joseph had clearly become a particularly trusted subordinate of Superintendent Badger, and if the testimony given by fellow officers and Custom House Republicans is to be believed, he was waist-deep in the political ruckus that took place during the summer of 1871. Members of the Tenth Ward Mother Republican Club testified repeatedly to the prominent role played by Peter Joseph during the breakup of their club one late July evening. Oscar J. Dunn and George Carter had been invited to give speeches that night in favor of the Custom House faction, and it was the last meeting of the ward club before it selected its delegates for the August convention. A band of Metropolitans in civilian clothing led by Joseph arrived at the hall early and occupied as many seats as possible to prevent regular members from participating in the proceedings. More ominously, they were accompanied by "Red" Bill McMickle, a man characterized by witnesses as a "desperate thug," as well as Lucien Adams, who was known to have participated in the Riot of 1866. A scuffle soon broke out and rapidly mushroomed into a full-scale riot. "Sixteen lighted transparencies hanging in the club-room were torn down by the mob, and a portrait of General Grant repeatedly groaned," noted one observer. "Police Sergeant Peter Joseph was conspicuous by his violent threats against all that were not Warmoth men," testified another. The Metropolitans arrested Battle Payne, the president of the club, along with others who played leadership roles. When Peter Joseph dragged a prominent white scalawag named Frank Reitmeyer out of a gutter to arrest him, the bleeding club member asked in despair, "So this is how you treat Republicans?"[40]

The conservative *New Orleans Times* looked down upon Warmoth's ruthless efforts to maintain power with smug satisfaction. Referring to the supposed orders given to the Metropolitans, the editorial observed that there seemed to be special instructions to break up meetings "in which the colored element prevails." Continuing, the paper noted that "the poor negro, having at last acquired the rights of American citizenship, learns that the conditions of the concession is as his chief directs: even the sacred precincts of the meeting houses are invaded and taken possession of, and their 'societies' voted down by intruders, mostly policemen in citizens' garb." Certainly this was true of events in the Third and Tenth Ward Republican clubs, both organizations that had African American leadership and strong ties to Oscar J. Dunn. The participation of Metropolitans such as Peter Joseph and Octave Rey in their breakup also begs analysis. Both men were fair-skinned Creoles, and Joseph in particular seems to have been light enough to pass for white. Were their decisions informed by the same racial consciousness that seemed to permeate all of New Orleans society? Should we interpret their actions as some indication of the importance of caste within the broader political question of black enfranchisement? At a minimum, these men had placed political loyalty ahead of racial solidarity. Their actions also serve as evidence of the systemic nature of Reconstruction-era placemanship.[41]

Warmoth believed that he had both outsmarted and outfought his rivals in the Custom House, only to learn just days before the Republican convention that he had come up short on both counts. Having rented out every available meeting hall in the city, the governor thought he had all but forced the convention to meet at a venue that he and the Metropolitan Police controlled. He did not consider that the Custom House faction might hold the event in the Custom House itself, nor did he anticipate that Stephen B. Packard would arrange for federal soldiers to occupy the facility on the day of the convention. Having a few days to survey his options, Warmoth made a variety of contingency plans to deal with Packard's clever parry. Arriving at the Custom House on the appointed day, with P. B. S. Pinchback, Algernon Sydney Badger, and about thirty supporters in tow, Warmoth entered the building's grand foyer and gazed directly into the yawning muzzle of a Gatling gun served by U.S. troops. Realizing that Packard was much too well-prepared to allow him or any of his supporters to enter the convention, Warmoth made a token protest against his foes in the Custom House and quickly retreated to a backup plan. Before the throng departed, however, Warmoth paused in front of the Custom House steps to make a boisterous speech castigating his opponents within. About Grant's brother-in-law, Warmoth said, "My friend Jim Casey is a clever fellow. He hasn't enough sense to be a bad fellow. [Laughter.] A man to be a bad fellow must have some character—he hasn't any. [Much laughter.]" When these comments reached Washington, Grant was not as appreciative as Warmoth's original audience.[42]

No blood was shed on the day of the convention, but events that day might well have turned out quite differently. Not realizing that he would encounter federal troops, Warmoth had ordered Algernon Sydney Badger to prepare plans for an all-out assault on the Custom House by the Metropolitan Police in the event that Packard barred the pro-Warmoth delegation. Badger plotted strategy with his captains late into the night before the convention and ordered them to be ready for action by first light. At the Third Precinct station at nine the following morning, patrolman John Claiborne found the place packed with policemen. "The roll was called of both night and day force; our pistols were inspected by Captain Rey and Sergeant Hussey." An hour later, the men filed off in twos along a prearranged route to the Custom House. When they arrived, they saw about three hundred Metropolitans massing along the approaches to Canal Street, and they were not alone. "As Governor Warmoth approached the court-house [*sic*] building entrance," noted one Metropolitan, "I saw Lucien Adams standing by the post office corner of the building, and about forty men, known to me for many years as thugs in New Orleans." Anticipating trouble, Sergeant Hussey called out, "Well boys, we must keep together, and if any fighting goes on here, we must rush up the stairs and seize the soldiers' muskets." The Metropolitans waited in the August heat for Badger's signal, but it never came, and by noon they were headed back to their station houses. In a few short years, many of these same men again found themselves bearing arms on Canal Street, but under very different circumstances and with very different results.[43]

Having for the first time outfoxed Warmoth, the Custom House faction, through the help of Speaker Carter, tried to engineer a quorum in the Louisiana legislature to impeach the governor and seat Lieutenant Governor Dunn in his stead. But Dunn's unexpected death that November foiled Packard's plans before the vote on impeachment could take place. Some Republicans, and not a few Democrats, speculated that Dunn had met with foul play, perhaps poisoning. Pinchback's *Weekly Louisianian* quickly rebuked such rumors, but considering the depths to which the Republican feud had sunk, the suspicions were understandable. Officially, Dunn died of "congestion of the brain." Before the mortar on Dunn's burial vault had cured, however, the two Republican factions had begun warring over his replacement. The Custom House ring had not given up their fantasies of impeaching Warmoth, so they considered it crucial to put one of their own into the position of heir-apparent. Nobody understood this more than Warmoth. Blending several parts old-fashioned deal-making, one part bribery, and a dash of treachery, the governor guaranteed that the post of lieutenant governor would go to his sometimes political ally P. B. S. Pinchback.[44]

The potential for political violence between the warring Republican factions grew precipitously once the legislative session of 1872 began in early January.

Even though Pinchback was now lieutenant governor, the Custom House faction, aided by some Democrats, persisted in their effort to impeach Warmoth, or at the very least suspend him. When Speaker Carter called the House to order, he was certainly aware that Warmoth would make an effort to prevent this from happening. Indeed, Warmoth had decided that the time was right to take the offensive against the Custom House faction, and he once again turned to the Metropolitan Police to carry out his plans. Algernon Sydney Badger had ordered a detail of fifteen men under the command of Sergeant Peter Joseph to the statehouse on the opening day of the legislative session, no doubt in anticipation of trouble. Toward the end of the day's session, a Warmoth-friendly legislator motioned to declare the Speaker's chair vacant, and a throng of Warmoth supporters rushed the podium. Carter was ready, however, and a group of "fighting men" emerged from a room behind the dais to defend him. The next day, he was not so successful. Badger had augmented his contingent at the statehouse by another "fifty or one-hundred men," and he, along with Joseph and "certain turbulent men in the community," managed to expel Carter from the House.[45]

Marshal Stephen B. Packard retaliated against Warmoth the following day by swearing in deputy federal marshals and issuing warrants for the arrest of the governor, Pinchback, Badger, roughly a dozen pro-Warmoth legislators, and numerous policemen including Octave Rey and Peter Joseph. The move backfired on Packard, however, when one of his deputies ended up killing a member of the legislature. Warmoth and his followers soon bailed out of jail, and that same afternoon the governor called a special session of the House to seat a new Speaker. With the statehouse now teeming with armed Metropolitans and the order having gone out to mobilize the state militia, Carter, Packard, Casey, and the rest of the Custom House faction retreated to the "Cosmopolitan Club Room" in the old Gem Saloon at the corner of Royal and Canal streets. Here they organized a rival legislature and rallied an armed mob to their standard. Carter's speeches to the crowd were undeniably incendiary, but with Warmoth so heavily protected by his militia and police, the Speaker's vision of storming the Mechanics' Institute appeared increasingly quixotic, particularly since Packard was unable to persuade the new general in charge of federal troops, William H. Emory, to intervene on the Custom House's behalf.[46]

Some Democrats had at varying junctures cooperated with the Custom House faction, if for no other reason because of their burning personal hatred for Warmoth. Once Carter was reduced to organizing a putsch at the Gem Saloon, these Democrats began to worry that their opportunity to remove Warmoth, their sole reason for allying with Carter, was beginning to slip away. To rally their troops, the Democratic Parish Committee held a mass meeting in Lafayette Square, attended by a bizarre menagerie of conservative white Democrats, carpetbaggers, and black Republicans. The only factor that nominally united them was that they all had been left out of Warmoth's coalition. The *Picayune* printed a list of several hundred men who signed on as "vice-presidents" of the meeting. Among the rally's supporters was Aristide Mary, an Afro-Creole activist who later became intimately involved in the struggles of Homer Plessy, as well as Collector Casey and P. B. S. Pinchback's erstwhile business partner C. C. Antoine. Arthur Toledano, having undergone something of a political awakening after his confrontation with Jane Price on the Carrollton Railroad, signed on as a vice president. A few officers from Warmoth's militia companies, both black and white, also appeared, including C. C. Antoine's younger brother Felix. Speakers included a conservative Democrat from Caddo Parish by the name of J. C. Moncure and a black carpetbagger from New York, J. Henri Burch. Under normal circumstances, Burch would have been considered the embodiment of everything white conservatives hated, and Moncure the symbol of Bourbonism's grossest evils. It would have been difficult to concoct a scene more emblematic of the uncertainty and chaos to which politics had descended in New Orleans.[47]

The Custom House leaders also surveyed their dwindling options. With an eye toward provoking federal military intervention in Louisiana, Carter, Packard, and Casey approached key Democratic-leaning officers of the Louisiana State Militia, hoping that they might induce them to betray Warmoth and attack the protective cordon of Metropolitan policemen and loyal militiamen that ringed the statehouse. In return, they promised these officers that the national Republican Party would support their actions and demonstrate its gratitude for the militia's deposing of Warmoth by sharing power with conservative Democrats. It was a farcical plan, but the real objective of Casey and Packard was probably to instigate such an enormous level of violence in the streets that the federal government would have no option but to intervene on their behalf.

One of the militia officers invited to the Custom House was Eugene Waggaman. Like James B. Walton and William Miller Owen, Waggaman was a distinguished Washington Artillery veteran; he was now a disgruntled commander in Warmoth's militia. He was also a good friend of E. John Ellis, and the two men had a heartfelt talk before Waggaman headed to the Custom House to hear what the Republicans had to offer. Ellis had smoked out the plans of Packard and Casey from the start, and he urged caution. Beyond the distinct chance that the Republicans might double-cross them, Ellis argued, the idea of uniting with the Custom House gang seemed like a deeply dishonorable act. Despite his growing personal disdain for Warmoth, Waggaman listened closely to what the earnest young lawyer from Amite City had to say.

As Ellis later recounted the scene to his brother Thomas, Waggaman lectured Packard and Casey when they refused to assure him of federal support. "What guarantee have we that while you are reaping the fruits of victory won by us over one enemy, you will not get rid of your remaining enemy by marching me and my co-laborers away under the Ku Klux law and saddling the responsibility of another riot upon a people who have already suffered so much for riots and disturbances real and fancied?" Packard stood mute, hands in his pockets, as Casey impishly promised that there was no such danger. Refusing the deal, Waggaman stomped out of the meeting and averted needless bloodshed. He would not collaborate with one enemy to get rid of another. E. John Ellis expressed satisfaction that he had "worked fruitfully for what I regarded to be right." Reflecting on the events of the previous several months, Ellis made this assessment: "Thus far, Warmoth is the master of the situation. The corrupt men of our party . . and the equally corrupt men of the Carter faction couldn't withstand the influence of Warmoth money." As early as 1867, Ellis had allied himself with the Democratic Party, but he actively worked to undermine the actions of some of his party's members when they worked in combination with Custom House Republicans to overthrow Warmoth. In closing his letter, Ellis noted, "I am glad my friends approve of my course." He had good reason for such sentiments. The *Picayune*, in its denunciations of Warmoth, glossed over the fact that many white native Louisianans remained by his side, including Washington Artillery veteran Colonel Charles W. Squires and his regiment of the Louisiana Volunteer Field Artillery. Had Packard persuaded Waggaman to attack the statehouse, it would have been partly a contest between two groups of Confederate veterans— Washington Artillery veterans—acting under the banners of competing Republican factions. And of course it would have been a complete fiasco for conservatives in the state.[48]

With his loyal militia and Metropolitan policemen standing guard, Warmoth was eventually able to regain control of the statehouse. Except for three members, the legislators who had once met at the Gem Saloon trickled back to the Mechanics' Institute, and by the end of the month, Warmoth was able to order Badger and a contingent of Metropolitans to break up the remaining followers of Carter. He had survived a determined effort by his rivals to unseat him, but the struggle had squandered whatever political capital he once possessed. Nor had he been able to completely vanquish the Custom House faction. More importantly, his government, the Metropolitan Police, and the Republican Party in general had severely diminished whatever legitimacy they might have otherwise cultivated among the very people that Warmoth had once hoped to court.

By the time Warmoth's opponents in the Custom House made their move against his administration, the militarization of politics had taken firm root in New Orleans. While the struggle for power in the antebellum city featured parades and even occasional street violence on the part of ward clubs, the Civil War had upped the ante considerably. Both Union and Confederate veterans now fused the tactics that they had mastered during the conflict with broader political objectives. The violent acts committed by Democratic clubs during the 1868 elections and the Republican infighting during the intraparty feud of 1871–72 were fundamentally different, however, from the bloodshed caused by the Riot of 1866. Such dirty deeds could no longer be dismissed as the random work of malcontents. Instead, violence organized on a military basis had become a fully integrated component of the larger political process, and Warmoth's embrace of such methods only served to legitimate its use. It was a game, however, that the Republican Party ultimately proved ill-equipped to play.

An odd event took place that served as a postscript to the political drama of January 1872. Accompanied by a group of supporters, former Speaker Carter took a train to Bay St. Louis, Mississippi, just over the border from Louisiana. In another car on that same train rode Algernon S. Badger with his corresponding cadre of well-wishers. A carnival-like atmosphere took over the procession as the engine chugged toward the sleepy Gulf Coast town and the pending duel between Carter and Badger. Outside the depot, after the train stopped, two shots rang out over the murmur of voices and the sound of a hissing, stationary locomotive. Armed with rifles at sixty paces, neither man drew blood, much to the disappointment of the *Picayune's* correspondent. Afterward, the entourage of legislators, police officials, and other spectators headed to Bordage's grocery for a "sumptuous lunch of crackers, cheese, and whiskey." It was a quintessential example of the uncertain and, at times, surreal lives led by people in postbellum New Orleans.[49]

The manner in which each of the individuals in this narrative went about establishing his position in the unstable postbellum environment explains much about the era's complexities. Charles Sauvinet, in confronting those who would deny him the honor of manhood, revealed that his reputation and personal dignity came first. Whether he saw himself as a crusader for civil rights is difficult to say, but without question he was deeply affronted on a personal level. After his term as sheriff expired in 1872, Sauvinet retreated from both public life and political associations. Like Sauvinet, Arthur Toledano did not seek out racial confronta-

tion; it came to him unbidden. His altercation with Jane Price was the first indication that his uncle's interracial household would not be able to withstand the
pressures of a society in turmoil. In contrast, Peter Joseph seemed to accord more
value to partisan loyalty and the potential for position than he did to racial solidarity. Comradeship and unit cohesion bound Joseph to men like his superior
officers Octave Rey and Algernon Sydney Badger. And these bonds endured well
beyond the era of Republican rule in Louisiana. Ironically, among these men it
was E. John Ellis, a man who held undeniably reactionary views, who anguished
the most about ideological purity.

The years of Henry Clay Warmoth's reign also highlight the complexity and
ambiguity of the individuals engaged in Reconstruction-era politics. Had it not
been for the Radical ascendancy, the Fourteenth and Fifteenth amendments
probably would never have become part of the Constitution, and so the nation
owes a continuing debt of gratitude to those responsible for this "unfinished revolution." It is also clear that some individuals championed ideals during this uncertain time that, had they been embraced, would have furthered the cause of
liberty. A human-scale inventory of postbellum politics in New Orleans also reveals that personal ambition and partisan gamesmanship, practiced in abundance by a wide range of individuals, often triumphed over ideological principles.
Yet, is it fair to wring our hands about what we judge as absence of character and
a lack of racially egalitarian vision among Reconstruction's actors? A broad spectrum of historians have scorned Warmoth as the sort of carpetbagger who substantiated the bad reputation of his kind and as a latent white supremacist who
stood in opposition to black civil rights. However, expecting men such as Warmoth to be the predecessors of twentieth-century civil rights activists and judging
them by the standards of the "second Reconstruction" not only obscure the unique
challenges that they faced but also diminish their real accomplishments. These
actors were not informed by a teleological interpretive model that couched their
deeds as the first steps toward the civil rights revolution of the 1950s and 1960s.
Instead, they were reacting to the unstable political environment that emerged in
the wake of a civil war and the equally unpredictable social chaos that followed
emancipation. Unlike some of their black allies, they did not hope to engender a
social revolution. Yet by disrupting traditional political patterns and fighting for
place and position, they set in motion an "unwitting revolution." Indeed, for all
of his moral ambiguity, Warmoth accomplished quite a lot, according to the
standards of his day. His schemes undermined conservative white devotion to the
Democracy, while supplying the military apparatus that might have made Republicanism and a meaningful black franchise viable in Louisiana. It is difficult to

say how much more he might have changed the political trajectory of Louisiana had it not been rent by ambitious rivals. One thing is certain: his Republican successors were not nearly so successful.

Ironically, the ideological ambiguity exhibited by Republicans during the reign of Warmoth paled in comparison with the utter lack of principle demonstrated by their conservative counterparts. Revisionist historians of the 1960s and 1970s expended great energy chronicling the lies the Dunning School told about Republicans but focused little attention on the equally large number of lies that the Dunningites told about their heroes, the Redeemers. Far from being the ideologically pure advocates of white supremacy as depicted in the literary fantasies of Thomas Dixon, the white conservatives who plotted Warmoth's downfall demonstrated just how morally flexible they could be to obtain power. In their failed effort to unseat the governor, they made alliances with corrupt scalawags such as George Carter and equally corrupt Custom House Republicans such as James Casey and Stephen Packard. At the same time they made common cause with black Radicals such as C. C. Antoine and J. Henri Burch. These so-called conservatives even threatened to shed the blood of fellow Confederate veterans, men with whom some had fought side-by-side from Manassas to Appomattox. Their deeds were less about restoring "home rule" than they were a shameless attempt to destroy the man who exposed the fundamental weaknesses of the Democratic Party. Their failure also revealed just how fragmented Democratic and Conservative forces were in New Orleans as 1872 began.

Ezekiel John Ellis, 1861. This jaunty daguerreotype depicts a
youthful Ellis before his travails as a soldier and a prisoner of war.
Courtesy Steven Ellis, Downsville, Louisiana.

Victor Pierson and Paul Poincy, *Volunteer Fireman's Parade on Canal Street* (1872). Before the city organized a regular force in 1891, New Orleans depended upon the Volunteer Fireman's Association, a civic group headed by community leaders. The parade depicted here is emblematic of the urban civic and political street theater commonly found in nineteenth-century New Orleans. The Henry Clay Statue, which was then located at the intersection of Royal–St. Charles and Canal streets, was the city's most important public rallying point. On the morning of September 14, 1874, representatives of the White League stepped onto the balcony of the Musson Building (depicted on the corner of Royal and Canal) to address the crowd that had been called to assemble at this location. Courtesy Louisiana State Museum, New Orleans, Louisiana.

1873 Comus parody of Badger. The Mystick Krewe of Comus poked fun at Charles Darwin's *Origin of the Species*, but they did so by way of political satire. Their parade included effigies that depicted prominent Republicans, including Benjamin Butler, Henry Clay Warmoth, and President U. S. Grant, in animalistic forms. Algernon Sydney Badger appeared as a sleuthing bloodhound with the police superintendent's signature mustache. Courtesy Carnival Collection, Manuscripts Department, Tulane University Libraries.

Henry Clay Warmoth, 1875. Although he was only thirty-three years old when he posed for this portrait, Warmoth had already been a colonel in the army, a provost court judge, and governor of Louisiana. He remained a powerful figure in the Republican Party well into the twentieth century. Courtesy Southern Historical Collection, Wilson Library, University of North Carolina at Chapel Hill.

Cotton Levee, Canal Street, circa 1890. The heaviest fighting during the battle between the White League and the Metropolitan Police took place near the levee at the foot of Canal Street. The long, low building on the right was the passenger depot for the New Orleans and Mobile Railroad. Directly in front of the depot, in the center of Canal Street, stood the "Iron building," where Metropolitan commander Algernon Sydney Badger fell wounded while leading his men. Companies of the White League attacked from the left, the present-day Central Business District, and made their way along the levee using cotton bales (like the ones pictured here) for cover. The Metropolitans either fled to the right, into the French Quarter, or found sanctuary in the Custom House, the tallest building to the right of Canal Street in this photo. The Harrah's Casino occupies the battle site today. George François Mugnier Photograph Collection, courtesy Louisiana Division/City Archives, New Orleans Public Library.

The Combine against the Democracy, *New Orleans Daily States*, January 4, 1896. Fear that a fusion campaign might topple the Democratic party caused conservatives to revive the old ghosts of "Communism," "Bounty," "Negro Domination," and "Carpet-Baggery."

CHAPTER FIVE

LESSONS OF THE STREET

1872–1873

Political parties are becoming so inextricably mixed—or so
strangely unmixed that it is hard to tell which is which. . . . The
GREAT Republican party has split into two parties—a large piece
and a small one. The GREAT Democratic Party is splitting into two
pieces, a small piece and a large one. And the perplexity among
our patriots (all our political leaders are patriots) is how to splice
the splitted pieces.—and what pieces ought to be spliced—or can
any of the pieces be spliced at all. Some desire more splits—some
do not want any splitting—and some do not know what they want.
—From *Morning Star and Catholic Messenger*, June 1872

A week before Carnival in 1872, Royal Edict No. 1 appeared in the *Picayune*, commanding Louisiana State Militia colonel Charles W. Squires "to hold himself in readiness with a battery of artillery at the foot of Canal Street, on Mardi Gras, February 13th . . . then and there to fire such salutes as may be deemed by his Royal Highness, the 'King of Carnival,' necessary to the proper maintenance of his state and dignity." This missive came from "Carnival Palace" under the hand and seal of the holiday's newly self-proclaimed sovereign, Rex. Only three weeks before, Squires's artillerists, many of whom were veterans of the Confederate Washington Artillery, had been emplaced around the statehouse, standing ready to fend off any attempt by the Custom House faction's mob to overthrow Governor Warmoth. Now they were going to salute the arrival of a new cultural monarch. From the headquarters of the Louisiana Volunteer Field Artillery, Squires replied that he recognized Rex's "supreme power" and that he would "respectfully submit to its mandate."[1]

The publication of Rex's "royal pronouncements" in the local papers in the days leading up to his promised debut left few unaware of his plan for the parade to assemble at the Henry Clay Statue at the intersection of Royal Street, Canal

Street, and St. Charles Avenue on Mardi Gras Day. By three o'clock in the afternoon, throngs of spectators and aspiring maskers choked the thoroughfares of the French Quarter and the present-day Central Business District, some even clambering up to the Great Compromiser's shoulders for a better look. Amid this crush of humanity, the first Rex procession formed, led by Metropolitan Police superintendent Algernon Sydney Badger and a phalanx of his captains, including Octave Rey and the recently promoted Peter Joseph. Rex—a young Jewish businessman, Lewis J. Salomon—followed immediately behind this escort, and after him came an odd procession of maskers: they ranged from Klansmen to the ubiquitous black-faced whites, Basin Street prostitutes, and a smattering of ad lib satirical effigies of political figures. Among them were "bitter representations of President Grant, Abraham Lincoln, even of the governor and the mayor." One wag dressed as Horace Greeley, carrying a placard that displayed the phrase "what I know about farming." The procession then turned down St. Charles Street toward a throng of waiting spectators in Lafayette Square. Reaching City Hall, Rex pulled up his mount and gazed across a viewing platform occupied by an interesting collection of dignitaries, including the Grand Duke Alexis of Russia, General George Armstrong Custer, Henry Clay Warmoth, and General James Longstreet. After sharing a champagne toast with these men, Rex continued down St. Charles Avenue, followed by his eccentric train of maskers. In their wake came a group of prominent businessmen dressed as playing cards. They called themselves "the pack," and as they approached the viewing platform, they handed each of the honored guests a deck of cards. Their costumes displayed a series of suggestive phrases: "Here is the Pack," "Our Carnival Game," "May the Best Hand Win," "This is Our Little Game," "Euchre us if you can."[2]

The memory of Rex's debut during the afternoon of Mardi Gras 1872 has long overshadowed the spectacle staged by the Mistick Krewe of Comus later that night, but Rex was only half of the dialogue that took place in the streets of New Orleans that year. Unlike the procession of Rex, which had paid homage to the governor in front of city hall, the Mistick Krewe's performance of the "Dreams of Homer" took aim against those white Southerners who had supported Warmoth's regime. With this allegory, more explicit than the previous year's portrayal of Spenser's *Faerie Queen*, Comus hoped to drive home its sharp criticism of white men of its members' class. Drawing analogies to the elite white New Orleanians who had sought allegiance with Warmoth, and bemoaning the absence of white political unity, an editorial in the *Picayune* explained the meaning behind the Mistick Krewe's procession this way: "We are ravished like Paris with the beauty of Helen. . . . We are familiar with each bloody turn in the tragic drama of the

Trojan war. We understand the very motives of Achilles' wrath, the dire effects of dissention. We have experienced our own *Iliad* of disasters and woes." The night parade of Comus began with the siege of Troy and, "more especially," the wrath of Achilles. In alluding to the *Iliad*, the tale of how the Greeks finally broke the siege of Troy through the ingenious use of the Trojan Horse, perhaps the Mistick Krewe was making a vague reference to the strategy that some had suggested conservative Louisianans pursue in order to defeat the Republican Party from within. It was a plan neither fully tested nor entirely discarded as 1872 began. Comus's final tableaux depicted "The Battle of the Frogs and the Mice," a poem sometimes attributed to Homer but likely not written by him. This mock battle reenacted in the streets of New Orleans and again at the Grand Ball of Comus for the benefit of the Grand Duke Alexis clearly parodied the intraparty feud between Warmoth and the Custom House faction. Yet it remained unclear who, in real political life, was going to fulfill the role of the giant crabs—the peace-makers who, in the end, scatter the warring mice and frogs.[3]

Although the processions of both Rex and Comus were the products of elite white New Orleans society, there were subtle yet important differences between the two groups from the start. The most obvious difference was that the Mistick Krewe of Comus was associated with the Pickwick Club, whereas Rex was the creation of the much more established Boston Club. Historians have differed over the reasons for Rex's genesis, a moment that overnight redefined Carnival. Popular legend suggests that the more youthful members of the Boston Club sought to commemorate the approaching visit of the Grand Duke Alexis, and it became the justification they needed to form a rival parading society of their own. Recent scholars have also persuasively argued that these elite Bostonians wanted to impose order on the raucous and extemporaneous masking of the streets during the daylight hours of Shrove Tuesday, much as Comus had done for Mardi Gras night. Yet this theory ignores the fact Rex, in the beginning, was much more inclusive than Comus had ever been. While the hoi polloi might not be part of the king's court, Rex originally welcomed maskers to "second line" behind their procession. Whatever the origins of Carnival's new king, certainly many New Orleanians could appreciate the utility of a benevolent monarch in the midst of Louisiana's social and political turmoil. Few bore this sentiment more than the men of substance in Rex who suffered financially from the uncertainty in the statehouse.[4]

The emergence of Rex also stemmed from the strained relationships that Warmoth's regime had created among elite white conservatives in New Orleans. If the planners of Rex sought merely to impose order on street maskers during the day, they hardly needed an absolute monarch to accomplish that task. The Mistick

Krewe of Comus and, by extension, the many conservative Democratic members of the Pickwick Club, had been the true royalty of Carnival since 1857. In 1872 Rex assertively crowned himself "King of Carnival" and challenged Comus as the marquee event of Mardi Gras. From one perspective, the men of Reconstruction-era Rex and Comus seem nearly indistinguishable. They tended to come from the same economic class, had a generally conservative outlook in terms of race, and were more or less antagonistic to the Radical wing of the Republican Party. But the differences between the two organizations were, quite literally, day and night. The key factors that divided Comus and Rex—the Pickwick and the Boston clubs—all revolved around their diverging opinions as to the best route for restoring "home rule." Although there were notable instances of overlap between the two exclusive social orders, when Rex first appeared, the Bostonians were, as a group, much more likely to accept key political changes that had occurred as a result of the Radical ascendancy. The most crucial of these was the Fifteenth Amendment. Generally speaking, the men of Comus were less compromising, at least outwardly. As the *Picayune* reporter astutely observed, conservative elements had felt "the dire effects of dissension" over the proper course for overturning Radical rule and for the Democratic Party. Much like the rift between the conservative whites, the differences between Rex and Comus diminished years later. When Rex first appeared, however, elite white society stood divided.

Because it was an election year on both the gubernatorial and the presidential levels, the political stakes were extraordinarily high in 1872. Several Southern states, including North Carolina, Virginia, and Georgia, had already been "redeemed" by the Democratic Party, and conservative elements believed optimistically that Louisiana might soon join their ranks. In the presidential contest, Ulysses S. Grant remained widely popular with the vast Northern electorate, but the increasing din of accusations of corruption against his administration made the hero of Appomattox appear vulnerable. Henry Clay Warmoth was now weakened considerably within his own party at both the local and the national level, and his Republican rivals seemed not nearly as capably led. Yet as promising as these events appeared to conservative elements within Louisiana, there were major obstacles to bringing a Democratic revival to the Pelican State. The divisions among conservatives in the state prevented them from capitalizing on the recent feud between Warmoth and Packard, as the split between Rex and Comus illustrated; and furthermore, the gulf between opposing sides seemed to be widening.

In the thirteen months between the Carnival seasons of 1872 and 1873, most of the emotional and contradictory impulses that had fueled the postbellum era's political and social instability were on display in the streets of New Orleans. By the late nineteenth century, spectacle and the claiming of public space was a long-established aspect of urban political culture in the Crescent City. Yet, as Mary P. Ryan has observed, the pageantry of public politics diminished in its democratic essence after the Civil War, yielding to "military force, governmental bureaucracies, and corporate franchise." Through the ritualistic parades staged by both Carnival societies and political ward clubs, elite white New Orleanians of the Civil War generation converted the politics of the street from its individualistic antebellum form into a carefully orchestrated tool of instruction. Whether this change was democratic in spirit or not, the personal trials of war and the turbulent politics of the postbellum had influenced conservative white leaders to recast both the use and the message of this cultural form. Moreover, the period's mass rallies, torchlight processions, Carnival parades, and organized violence spoke of something more fundamental than mere partisan impulse; they reflected the Civil War generation's spasmodic quest for order amid the social chaos of the South's postbellum landscape. Blending emotionalism with reason, these men hoped to rally New Orleanians around a unifying vision of the future. They quickly discovered, however, that their audience was wary of the conservative message and unconvinced of its ultimate success.[5]

The competing parades of Rex and Comus in the spring of 1872 served as a prelude to several renewed efforts by elite white merchants in New Orleans to forge a centrist political movement capable of seizing control of Louisiana from the Republican Party. The first group to organize was the Committee of Fifty-One, which four days after the end of Carnival season called for a mass meeting on the steps of City Hall. The list of the meeting's 162 vice presidents included prominent New Orleanians such as former Confederate general Richard Taylor, Leeds Foundry president Charles Leeds, noted attorney Charles Conrad Jr., and the famous physicians Drs. Samuel Choppin and Warren Brickell. A sampling of the meeting's attendees reveals that most were quite wealthy (see appendix A). And although young men were involved, older, more experienced men were more common. A handful of Afro-Creoles took part, including former Native Guards officer Emile Detiege and educator Adolph Duhart. Staunch Democrats, like Frederick Nash Ogden and Robert Hardin Marr, also signed on to the meeting, but the gathering was dominated by the moderate members of the Boston Club who were responsible for the creation of Rex. Thirty-nine Bostonians were among the meeting's vice presidents, including a future chief justice of the U.S. Supreme Court, Edward Douglas White. The selection of Isaac Newton Marks as the committee's chair reflected the influence of the Bostonians at the meeting.

Marks, who had come to New Orleans as a young man in 1836, was widely re-spected by his peers for both his sagacity and his devotion to civic causes. Al-though a former Whig and an economic elite, he had ties to the city's ethnic working class as the president of a volunteer fireman's company. And, like many of the men gathered in Lafayette Square, Marks had suffered from the war, hav-ing lost one of his two sons to the Confederate experiment. Yet, as the president of the New Orleans, Florida, and Havana Steamship Company, he was also a modernizer who feared that continued political instability would forever dim what had once been the city's bright economic future.[6]

The resolutions passed by the Committee of Fifty-One bore little resemblance to "straight-out" Democracy and reflected the wishes of wealthy merchants who prioritized the restoration of New Orleans's prosperity over slavish devotion to the Lost Cause. They called for the creation of a new political party—the Reform Party—and scheduled a convention for the selection of candidates for the coming election, open to men "regardless of color and previous political associations," so long as they favored reform of the state's political institutions. By early March, the Reform Party issued a more detailed platform from its headquarters at 27 Caron-delet Street. The platform was an effort to appeal to a broad spectrum of Louisi-anans who remained wary of both the Republicans and the Democrats, although its rhetoric definitely exhibited a conservative flavor. "The want of political sym-pathy between the black and white races of Louisiana," read the platform, "has for several years rendered her a victim to the most frightful spoliation and rob-bery." Brimming with antagonism toward Warmoth's regime, it blamed the lion's share of the state's woes on his "treachery, duplicity, and tyranny." The Reformers promised that there "shall be no distinction, political or civil," because of race, but they fell conspicuously short of endorsing the public accommodation legisla-tion passed by the Republican statehouse. Moreover, amid such rhetorical flour-ish, the Reformers failed to acknowledge that many men of their race and class remained within the Warmoth camp. Nor did they clearly articulate why the Democratic Party could not fulfill the objectives that the Reformers sought. The creation of the Reform Party stood as a testimony both to the polarizing nature of Warmoth's presence and to the serious doubts among the city's elite about the viability of the Democratic Party in New Orleans. Its creation was also a tacit ac-knowledgment of how popular Warmoth's ideas had been in the city, because the Reformers hoped to forge a party nearly identical to the one the young governor had engineered. That is, without Warmoth.[7]

Despite the moderate tone of the Reformers' rhetoric, many blacks, especially those with a stake in the Republican Party, spoke out forcefully against what they characterized as the new party's siren's song. With Charles Sauvinet's barroom incident no doubt in mind, P. B. S. Pinchback's *Louisianian* pointed out what it saw as "Democratic hypocrisy" in the Reformers' overtures toward blacks and suggested the following test to determine their sincerity: "Let a colored man ask one of them to take a 'smile' in one of the fashionable bar rooms. If you don't see that Reformer wilt and say he 'don't feel like drinking' we are no prophet. Yes, the colored men are good to support a candidate, but not good enough to travel on the same steamboat, ride in the same train or sleep under the same roof as 'us Democrats.'" There were limits to the Reformers' liberalism, much as there were to Henry Clay Warmoth's. Yet the Reform Party also marked an important departure for conservative whites with respect to their attitude toward black ballots. Although the Democratic Party had conceded that the Fifteenth Amendment was now the law of the land, few took seriously their efforts to court black voters. As limited as the Reform Party's overture to black voters might seem, it represented a fundamental philosophical shift toward accepting, however begrudgingly, the permanence of black political agency.[8]

The emergence of a reformist coalition was not an entirely new idea among white Southern conservatives and was certainly not unique to Louisiana. Across the unredeemed states of the South, "New Departure" Democrats emerged in the early 1870s as a response to the failure of the traditional Democratic Party to restore so-called home rule. These movements often advocated a solution that incorporated some degree of compromise with the Radical social agenda, and all, in one form or another, hoped to court black votes. Almost universally, these splinter groups fought an uphill battle, opposed by both the Radicals and the conservatives.[9]

Like the Democrats, the Republicans faced their own factional crisis as the 1872 political season began. The intraparty feud between Warmoth and the Custom House faction not only endured beyond its dramatic climax in January; it presaged the emergence of profound fissures within the national party. In Louisiana, Collector Casey's familial relationship with Grant, combined with the president's longstanding animosity toward Warmoth, had allowed the Custom House faction to both survive and retain the support of the national party. With the backing of Washington, they used federal patronage and influence to either win over Warmoth-friendly adversaries or replace them with reliable men. Despite his failure to remove the governor from office, Warmoth's bitter rival Stephen B. Packard remained the chair of the official state party, although his control was at times tenuous. Faced with such discouraging circumstances, Warmoth concluded that while bolting the national Republican Party carried with it severe liabilities, greater futility lay in trying to wrest control of Louisiana's central committee away from Casey and Packard. For this reason, he led a powerful coalition of mostly white Republicans out of the party's state convention held in July 1872 and into a larger national movement of disaffected members known as Liberal Republicanism. Led by prominent Northern Republicans who were unhappy with both Grant and the course of Southern Reconstruction, this splinter movement supplied a natural refuge for Warmoth supporters who could not resolve their differences with the Custom House. With the colorful New York newspaperman Horace Greeley as its candidate for president, the party vowed to wage a campaign that would remove the Radical wing from its position of power in Congress and deny President Grant a second term.

Although he might have won renomination as the regular party's candidate for governor, Warmoth's abandonment of the state Republican convention and defection to the Liberal Republican movement was a better fit with his own vision of centrist rule. Much as Warmoth had done as governor of Louisiana, the liberal movement's national leadership preached the virtue of reconciliation with the white South and criticized the vices of what they considered excessive racial egalitarianism. In many ways, their message anticipated what became, in less than a decade, a consensus in national policy; but the splinter movement's embrace of the mercurial Greeley probably diminished whatever chances it might have had to make a serious bid for the presidency. Liberal Republicanism posed a much more credible threat at the state level, particularly in Louisiana. With the young governor at its head, it was only natural that the party's membership would resemble the centrist coalition that Warmoth had always hoped to forge. Indeed, the Liberal Republicans were in many ways indistinguishable from the Reform Party, with the exception that they had a good relationship with the governor. Some Liberal Republican adherents belonged to the white militia units created by the governor in 1870, while others were part of the wide-reaching network of supporters in rural parishes who owed the governor for one favor or another. In New Orleans, a core of wealthy businessmen nearly identical to those who had created the Reform Party also emerged as supporters of Liberal Republicanism. Davidson Bradfute Penn, a man who belonged to this moneyed element, ultimately emerged as the party's candidate for governor.[10]

The D. B. Penn everyone knew was a popular and respectable man, even outside the boundaries of New Orleans. The son of one of the largest real estate holders in the city, Penn as a young man attended Virginia Military Institute and studied law at the University of Virginia. After coming home to New Orleans in 1858, he began a cotton press, and at age twenty-five he recruited a regiment for the Confederacy from the ranks of his employees. By all accounts, Penn fought valiantly throughout the war, serving at Gettysburg and in many other major encounters in the Eastern Theater. In November of 1863, he was captured at Rappahannock, Virginia, and ended up at Johnson's Island, where he probably first crossed paths with fellow lawyer E. John Ellis. Penn's parole documents indicate that the young colonel was about six feet tall and had black hair, dark eyes, and a dark complexion. After coming home from war, D. B. Penn resumed his business at the cotton press but largely stayed out of politics. His father had been an early member of the Boston Club, and D. B. Penn carried on the tradition. Thus, he was a likely participant in the creation of Rex. Penn was also clearly in search of some alternative to the Democratic Party as the year began, for his name appeared on the list of prominent men who supported the Reform movement's "meeting of the people" in February 1872. At some point he must have met Warmoth and developed a friendship, for it was the governor's support that enabled Penn to secure the Liberal Republican Party's nomination for governor.[11]

Probably few of Penn's associates were aware that he had a mixed-race child. In 1858, shortly after his return to New Orleans from law school, he had a liaison with a quadroon girl by the name of Josephine Keating. In January of the following year, Blanche Penn entered the world, just twelve days before her mother's sixteenth birthday. The young mother and child went off to stay with Josephine's father, a brick mason living in the Third Ward. In 1868 Josephine Keating died at age twenty-five and Blanche went to live at her Aunt Olivia's boardinghouse. When census workers visited the residence in 1870, Blanche was still just a girl, yet old enough to know that there was some advantage to identifying herself as white. There is no way to know whether D. B. Penn supported his daughter financially, but it certainly would have been within the realm of possibility—from the standpoint both of societal expectations and his own personal code of ethics. Perhaps it was this personal experience that shaped his outlook on race and encouraged him to eschew the hard-edged racial rhetoric of the Democratic Party's Bourbon wing.[12]

The emergence of the very similar Reform and Liberal factions among conservative whites in New Orleans promised to spell disaster for Democrats in the fall elections, and few observers could have been unaware that both splinter movements were attributable in some measure to the disruptive political legacy of Henry Clay Warmoth. Although the governor had personally repudiated the regular Republican Party in Louisiana, he had so thoroughly altered assumptions about the state's political landscape that his removal from power remained an all-consuming obsession for many Democrats. This obsession led inevitably to deep divisions within Democratic ranks. When the party's convention finally met in April 1872, a significant contingent of its membership arrived with no other plan than to express its "holy hatred" of the governor. The animosity that these discontented Democrats felt also extended to the moderates of their party who had worked with Warmoth throughout the young carpetbagger's term and who now promoted an alliance of all anti-Grant factions. What transpired at the Democratic convention was yet one more manifestation of what Charlie Kennon had identified as the "incredible" demoralization that white political divisions had created within the party's ranks. Almost immediately, the most ardently anti-Warmoth delegates proffered a motion condemning the governor. Many of these men had been among the Democrats who had collaborated with the Custom House faction a few months earlier, including emerging political titans and future Gilded Age senators J. B. Eustis and B. F. Jonas. One delegate even added some harsh words for the men of the Boston Club for promoting the Reform and Liberal Republican abandonment of the Democracy. The scene on the convention floor grew ugly, with both sides taking the podium and pointedly arguing their case. During one pro-Warmoth speech, a voice interrupted from the balcony, "I want to save Louisiana—I am willing to cohabit with the Devil—I am willing to cohabit with the Republican Party—I am willing to cohabit with the naygur, but I am d—d if I will cohabit with Governor Warmoth!" The assembly burst into cheers, laughter, and recriminations.[13]

A warm advocate for the union of all anti-Grant forces, E. John Ellis looked upon the convention's proceedings with dismay. He certainly harbored no love for Warmoth, but he was also too much of a political realist to suggest that the Reformers and Liberal Republicans were not needed as allies. Even worse was the bravado of one delegate who suggested that if "the old banner is to go down, let it sink like the flag of the *Alabama*, untarnished and leading the hosts in a fight we believe right." Ellis had no intention of letting the Democracy slip beneath the waves like the fabled Confederate raider, nor did he intend to make the author of such foolhardy bombast its captain. In response to the speeches condemning Warmoth, Ellis took the floor and pointed out that the problem was Grant: "All of the evils coming from Governor Warmoth were due to the agency of General Grant. Unless the stream is purified at the source, it is useless to purify it at the bottom. All the evils that have afflicted Louisiana have flowed from Washington sources of Reconstruction."[14]

When the Ellis brothers' longtime friend Charles Kennon reported on events in Tangipahoa Parish in late May, he urged the Democratic Party to accept the

Liberal Republican presidential ticket as its own: "Democratic nomination under present circumstances is defeat," he concluded. John expressed his agreement as he wrote his brother Thomas: "A compact or organization of all conservative or anti-Grant elements.—This is what I have labored for, what I am still laboring for. Now that the Radical Party has repudiated Warmoth, it is easy to control him and his money." In spite of the moderate appeals of the Liberal Republicans and the Reformers, Ellis predicted that politics in the state would eventually come down to racial divisions, and ultimately white voters would view the Democratic Party as their refuge. Until that time, Democrats needed to work with what was available to them. In closing, he noted, "It may well be that the long night is about ended. God grant it be so."[15]

Other episodes that summer must have cast a shadow of doubt on Ellis's optimism. Bolivar Edwards, one of his closest friends and a companion during the dark days at Johnson's Island, was now planning to run against John's father for parish judge on the Radical ticket. This decision must have been particularly discouraging to Ellis. In 1864 he had described Edwards as "a friend of earlier days, one tried by years of association and intercourse, my class and room mate at college, my bosom friend since 1854, one whom I trusted and who never faltered in that trust and whom I love and still cherish scarcely less than a brother." Charlie Kennon, a mutual friend, tried to soften the blow by explaining that "these are uncertain times and office seekers may commit themselves not thinking that they are departing from principle in the chaos that surrounds us." As Ellis soon discovered, Edwards's lack of popular support in the parish ended the candidacy almost before it began. Yet, the whole experience had to be disheartening. "Forgive him yes I do, but I pity & commiserate the weakness of the man," wrote E. John to his brother Thomas. If someone as close to the family as Edwards could flirt with Radicalism for the sake of a small parish office, it did not bode well for the reliability of others.[16]

As August 1872 began, there were three competing slates among the various conservative camps. The Liberal Republicans had chosen Penn and a host of other moderates, including the Afro-Creole Francis E. Dumas, for offices. A former slaveholder, Dumas had been the candidate put forth against Warmoth by the Roudanez brothers in 1868. The Reform Party selected an attorney, George Williamson, for the head of their ticket. When the Democrats met in April, they nominated John McEnery of Ouachita Parish for governor and, for the remaining posts, a host of other "last-ditch" Democrats, many of whom had been in alliance with the Custom House ring in their effort to remove Warmoth the preceding winter. Several months of wrangling had yet to iron out the serious obstacles to their union, and time was running out.

The fact that both the Reformers and the Democrats generally despised Warmoth meant that their union proved the easiest to effect. By the second week in August, such a merger was already in the works, although not without some significant grumbling. The Reformers simply had little influence outside of New Orleans and had failed to attract the black support upon which they had originally counted. The more difficult task was going to be performing a "shotgun wedding" between the seemingly unreconcilable Democratic-Reform and Liberal Republican factions. The most divisive, but by no means the only, issue was what Warmoth's expectations might be out of such a merger. Despite advertisements that proclaimed the miraculous effects of "Demphill's Patent Wind-Mill," which supposedly forced "10,000 cubic feet of cool and pure air through the auditorium every sixty seconds," one can only imagine the heat building inside the grand theater of David Bidwell's Academy of Music as the Liberal Republicans convened there in the second week of August. At two in the afternoon on the ninth, the delegates returned to the chamber following a recess to hear a speech from their true leader, Governor Warmoth, who had just turned thirty. Under normal circumstances, this would be just a footnote, but those in attendance were fully aware that the young governor was now eligible to sit in the U.S. Senate. Many Democrats believed that the price of union with the Liberal Republicans would be a promise to send Warmoth to that most exclusive club. Thus, when Warmoth mounted the dais and announced that he would not accept any office stemming from such a merger, it surprised the opposition and paved the way for the fusion of white conservative political factions.[17]

On September 7 the Democratic Central Committee released a bulletin announcing the "honorable and hearty fusion" between themselves and the Reformers and the Liberal Republicans. "Before agreeing upon this ticket," the resolution continued, "each party was called upon, to a certain extent, to sacrifice party pride and the claims of personal attachment or friendship to the paramount object of uniting our efforts to redeem the state from impending ruin." The Democrats had in fact given up quite a lot in the combination, but the one point on which they would not yield was the head of the ticket. John McEnery, their candidate, was a thirty-nine-year-old lawyer from Monroe. He had been involved in party politics since the late antebellum period; during the war he rose to the rank of lieutenant colonel and was twice wounded in action. After his return to Louisiana, McEnery served in the state legislature until he lost his rural seat to a

Republican during the April 1868 election. He was not the skilled orator that Warmoth was and had a reputation for making blunt statements in public debate. Even the sympathetic *Jewell's Crescent City Illustrated* had to describe his style euphemistically as "equally marked with strength and terseness" without "fondness for rhetorical ornament."[18]

While the resulting Fusion ticket placed McEnery at its head, most of the other Democratic nominees were replaced by either Liberal Republicans or Reformers—testimony to the relative strength of each faction, particularly in New Orleans. Some of the Democrats punted by the realignment were so bitter that they ultimately worked against the Fusion ticket. This reaction spoke volumes about the power of personal political ambition in the supposed holy Democratic crusade of Redemption. Davidson B. Penn became the Fusion ticket's candidate for lieutenant governor. Warmoth believed that placing Penn at the ticket's head and enticing P. B. S. Pinchback to run for the post of congressman-at-large would have all but assured victory; yet like most shotgun weddings, the Fusion ticket exhibited the inauspicious circumstances of its genesis. Warmoth's astute suggestions went unheeded.[19]

Horatio Nash Ogden, Fred Ogden's cousin, was another of the few Democrats who remained on the Fusion ticket, filling the slot of attorney general. This choice was likely made because Ogden had also been involved substantially with the Reform movement. On September 12, he showed up at the club meeting of the "Melpomene Ditchers" to deliver a lengthy oration in support of the coalition. He articulated in the bluntest terms what many white Louisianians no doubt believed about black voters and, even more revealingly, what most black Louisianians correctly identified as the true nature of Fusion's attitudes on race. "Take the colored man away and where is the National Republican party of the State of Louisiana?" asked Ogden. "Where is the Grant party of the State of Louisiana to-day if you take the colored man out of it? I answer, and without fear of contradiction, nowhere." In spite of their reliance upon black ballots, Ogden pointed out, when it came to the formation of the Republican ticket, "two colored men, one for the office of lieutenant governor—and I understood from the first that they were anxious to get him out of that position—and the other filling some subordinate position" were the only nonwhite candidates to be found.[20]

But lest his listeners confuse his rhetoric as a call to political egalitarianism, Horatio Nash Ogden clarified his main point: "The white people of this state are anxious to make a reconciliation with the colored people because they think that that large vote ought to be controlled in the best interests of the State, and not by carpet-baggers and corruptionists." Referring to the presence of Antoine Dubuclet, a man of color and a former slaveholder from Pointe Coupee Parish who was the Fusion ticket's choice for state treasurer, Ogden went on: "There is already a colored incumbent, who, so far as I know, has discharged his duties of that office with more fidelity than any other officer who has been charged with the interests of the State during the past four years." While Ogden's accusations against the Republicans were not entirely accurate, his observation that they increasingly relied upon black ballots for survival was difficult to deny. Yet many whites also remained with the national party or quickly returned to its ranks after fusion with the Democrats had taken place—primarily because John McEnery emerged as the Fusion candidate for governor, and with every passing day, Fusionism came to look more and more like Democracy in disguise. Among the discontented were many of the white Republicans who had at first followed Warmoth out of the party, only to again cross lines and with mixed feelings support the Custom House faction. Among them were James Longstreet and Algernon Sydney Badger, men who had been essential to the maintenance of Warmoth's regime.[21]

Aristée Louis Tissot also emerged as a favored candidate on the Fusion ticket, filling the slate's spot for the Second District Court for the Parish of Orleans, which was one of the most important local-level benches in the state. The Second District was the main civil court for the city and as such had an enormous amount of power over the lives of New Orleanians who brought cases before it. In the nominating process, Tissot had beaten out older, more experienced men—a mark of the esteem he had built both as a lawyer and as a valued Democrat. If Tissot won in the fall election, he would, at age thirty-three, become the youngest person to ever sit on the bench in Orleans Parish. Without question, Tissot had been an active participant in civic affairs since his return to the city in 1866. Not only had he founded the charitable Pelican Benevolent Association; he had been an officer in the Warmoth militia and, rather contradictorily, the president of the Democratic Broom Rangers. Association with these three very different organizations might seem unusual, but his membership in each was emblematic of the political ambiguity that characterized the city's professional and commercial classes.[22]

While the state's prominent conservatives hammered out the details of their political coalition, a dramatic campaign to rally the city's white voters behind the cause of Fusionism took place in the streets of New Orleans. During Warmoth's reign, conservatives had discovered to their dismay that the need for racial political unity was not self-evident among white voters. Victory in 1872 therefore hinged upon their ability to both bring about white unity and encourage ambivalent whites to turn out for the election in large numbers. The difficulties they faced, however, were enormous. The Enforcement Acts and the belief among conservatives that intimidation would fuel increased federal intervention on the behalf of Republicans had temporarily removed violence as weapon from the Fusionists' arsenal. Moreover, the Fusionists believed they could not afford to alienate the small amount of black support that they had attracted through employing themes of racial moderation. Instead, they crafted a strategy that tapped into a deep emotional reservoir of anxieties that had built among white New Orleanians since the heady days of April 1861.

As leaders of the city's influential political ward clubs, young veterans like Tissot were going to play an important role in attracting a new generation of white Southerners to the banner of Democracy. These clubs staged torchlight parades in late summer and early autumn 1872 that drew for the first time broad parallels between the Lost Cause imagery of heroic sons who had answered the call of the Confederacy in 1861 and a rising generation of white Southern men who through their political devotion might bring about a restoration of the South's golden age. Democratic ward clubs that, like Tissot's Broom Rangers, had emerged out of the violent campaigns of 1868 now spawned cadet or auxiliary groups of young men "about to assume that great boon of American freedom—citizenship," so that they, too, "may assist in the great work of regenerating this our beloved State of Louisiana." Young veterans like Tissot hoped to reenact the dramatic mobilization that they had witnessed during the turbulent months that followed Louisiana's secession from the Union. Through the use of ceremonial uniforms, flags, and parades, as well as an overt appeal to the rising generation's sense of masculinity and honor, the Fusionists hoped to inculcate in New Orleans youth the sort of pride in race and region that had propelled the Confederacy forward through four years of bitter struggle.[23]

In September, the "Swan Cadets" were among the first to hold a "grand torchlight procession . . . to celebrate the reception of their marks of approbation from their lady friends." The cadets, "a handsome set of young fellows . . . clad in their neat white uniforms with red collars and cuffs," rendezvoused at the head of Marigny Street in the Third District and proceeded toward their first destination accompanied "by especial invitation" by the "McEnery Cadets, Jonas Cadets, and Broom Rangers." They arrived at a residence on Spain Street where a young lady presented them with a banner. "The campaign is open," she proclaimed, "and you are called to the front to battle for the liberty and honor of your country." Of the banner, the *Picayune* noted, "[It] is of red silk on one side, which bears an excellent portrait of Mr. Swan in gilt; on the other, which is white satin, is inscribed (also in gilt) 'Swan Club, inaugurated August 12, 1872.'" A second young lady came forward to present the cadets with the American flag, and a third brought forth "a

magnificent wreath about two feet in diameter, of red and white flowers resting
on gilt leaves." As she made her address, the wreath's bearer reminded the cadets
that "no more can be said to encourage you to do your duty; no more can be done
to assure you of our confidence." In gratitude, a young man speaking for the cadets replied, "Take this, Mr. Standard Bearer, and carry it aloft, that the eyes of
its recipients may look on it with pride and admiration, and that no act of ours
may ever tarnish its spotless purity." Such pageantry differed little from the days
of 1861 when Tissot's Tirailleurs beckoned young men to join their regiment for
the defense of Louisiana.[24]

Lest the cadets fail to make the connection between their duty to protect their
women and the need to vote for the Fusion ticket, speeches made during the procession of the "Broom Rangers, Jr.," clarified the matter. Drawing parallels between New Orleans's white women and those Spartan mothers "who were wont
to accompany their husbands and sons to the threshold of their cities and there
bid them to return on or with their shields," one speaker alluded to the indignities
that white women had endured at the hands of Benjamin Butler for their devotion
to Southern nationhood. "Women of all ages have in the hour of their country's
peril endeavored to rouse the energy and courage of their fellow countrymen,"
he reminded his audience, "as was the case during the period of our lost cause."
Other speeches played more directly to white fears of intimate interracial contact.
A young woman named Annie Stevenson addressed the topic in particularly strong
terms during a mass torchlight procession of the "Wiltz Guards": "Formerly men's
minds were shocked with that which they now see passing before them and which
shall always be unless the people rally and stand together, and elect men of whom
we have no doubt as to their honesty and integrity, who would not be guilty of
such practices which in former times were accounted crimes of the blackest
kind, crimes which called for all the severity of public justice—no petitioning for
mercy—no pardon was allowed. That such is our present state of affairs, you your-
selves are witnesses, and you need not any testimony from me." The rhetoric that
energized the parades of the Democratic "cadet" ward clubs in 1872 reemerged
in the White League campaign of 1874 and 1877 remained a staple of political dialogue for the rest of the century.[25]

Securing an alliance with P. B. S. Pinchback would undoubtedly have brightened
the prospects of the Fusion campaign, but the inherent political incompatibilities
prevented such a union. Pinchback had actually considered becoming a Liberal
Republican in the early weeks of the movement, but he was a Grant man through
and through, and the nomination of Horace Greeley for president was a non-

starter. The placement of McEnery at the head of the Fusion ticket ended almost all remaining speculation there might have been that Pinchback would throw his support behind the effort. He was already well on his way to taking his influence back to the regular Republican Party, now dominated by the Custom House. In his own words, he did not want to "swallow" the Custom House ticket, but given the alternative, he would "sugar coat it and swallow it whole."[26]

The ticket resting on Pinchback's dinner plate included at its head William Pitt Kellogg, Warmoth's former friend and the sitting U.S. senator from Louisiana. Caesar C. Antoine, Pinchback's former business partner—with whom there was no love lost—was the nominee for lieutenant governor. It was bitter fare indeed. The rest of the Republican ticket demonstrated what a transformation had taken place in the wake of Warmoth's temporary fall from grace. It contained two white carpet-baggers and, contrary to Horatio Nash Ogden's charges, five black politicians. For all practical purposes, it fulfilled the old Lost Cause prophecy of Yankees hell-bent on "Africanizing" state politics, and as such it probably only increased the weight of Ogden's accusations. When the Republican Party under the auspices of the Custom House ring repudiated Warmoth, they committed themselves to an overwhelming reliance on black ballots. The Republican ticket that emerged in 1872 represented the essential problem of Republicanism in the postbellum-era South— that the party was an untenable union between a handful of white carpetbaggers like Kellogg and Southern blacks whose only realistic hope of political survival depended upon the willingness of federal authorities to ensure that officials made a fair count in Louisiana's elections. Nowhere was the shift more devastating to Republicanism than in New Orleans, which was still roughly 70 percent white in the 1870s. By jettisoning Warmoth's centrist strategy and retreating toward its African American base, the Republicans had returned to the racial polarization that had dominated Louisiana's politics in 1866. To energize its base, the Republicans would have to increasingly promise civil rights legislation that it had no real expectation of enforcing. All the while, the party would further alienate whatever white support it had once enjoyed. It was in exactly this environment that E. John Ellis had predicted that the Democratic Party would once again thrive.[27]

Victory eluded the Fusionists in 1872, however. According to historian Joe Gray Taylor, "the election of 1872 was so shot through with fraud that no one ever had any idea of who actually won." Abundant irregularities committed that November on both sides of the contest made it virtually impossible to arrive at an objective conclusion. Violence was almost nonexistent, but certainly the old Louisiana traditions of ballot-box stuffing, ballot-box vanishing acts, secret polling places, and other trappings of corruption were widespread. Warmoth, who had spent September and October campaigning for the Fusion ticket, believed that he would be able to use "all legal means" to ensure his side's victory. Several election laws that he either signed or held in reserve would allow him to control the returning board and thus the outcome—or so he thought. Kellogg's Republicans also held some powerful cards, not the least of which was the support of Grant and the federal judiciary. When the Republicans cried foul over Warmoth's handling of voting returns, they filed an injunction against his returning board. In the end, a federal judge placed a Custom House–friendly returning board in charge of counting votes, and to no one's surprise, Kellogg's ticket claimed victory. The antagonism between Warmoth and Grant that had begun as far back as the siege of Vicksburg had finally come home to roost. Eager for revenge against Warmoth, the Custom House faction now finally possessed the muscle necessary to impeach him. Although they failed to secure a conviction in the state senate, Warmoth remained suspended for the remainder of his term. This twist of events brought P. B. S. Pinchback, the lame-duck lieutenant governor and one-time Warmoth ally, into the governor's chair. He became the first black governor of any state and the only one until Douglas Wilder won the 1988 gubernatorial contest in Virginia.[28]

Pinchback soon discovered, though, that the white militia units Warmoth had so carefully assembled during his term as governor now refused to recognize his executive authority. Fortunately for Pinchback, Algernon Sydney Badger had been unable to countenance an alliance with John McEnery, and therefore the regular Republican Party retained control of the Metropolitan Police. Pinchback ordered Badger to take a substantial force of Metropolitans to besiege the Carondelet Street Armory and force the surrender of a militia regiment under the command of colonels James B. Walton and Eugene Waggaman. Upon arriving at the armory, Badger sent a messenger to the front door with a note requesting the capitulation of the militiamen. Unimpressed by Badger's ultimatum, Walton replied to the police superintendent that he would submit only to federal soldiers, "when a force of authorized troops make, in force, the demand for such surrender." Walton had thrown his support behind the Republican Party in the first years of Warmoth's regime but had grown restive and disillusioned with his own cooperative stance. Having no desire for needless bloodshed, Badger wisely held back. If Walton would surrender only to the U.S. Army, the Metropolitan commander concluded, then so be it. Badger's decision may have saved lives that afternoon, but both he and the Metropolitan Police had been humiliated in the process.[29]

The hardened reaction of moderates like Walton reflected the 1872 election's galvanizing effect on the conservative opposition to Republican rule. That the

Republican-dominated national government could decide the election in favor of its own kind, in this case Kellogg, also undermined faith in the democratic process and validated in many minds the justifiability of resorting to other means, including violence. Whether this was a rational stance or had any basis in electoral reality is almost irrelevant. In spite of the Enforcement Acts, violence had become a legitimated part of the political process in postbellum Louisiana, and it was a form that was hardly the exclusive province of conservative whites. Fusion's loss to the Republicans also helped clarify political realities for many conservative whites. Although there must have been feelings of self-doubt among Fusionists as to the unity and commitment of those engaged in their cause, the overwhelming sense was that the Grant administration had illegally handed control of Louisiana to Kellogg and had wronged the white natives of the state. Such indignation made the selling of white unity and Redemption far easier for the Democratic Party in the future.

The disputed election of 1872 also marked a turning point in the use of racially charged rhetoric in New Orleans Carnival. It was a fact made terribly plain by a new Carnival society on January 6, 1873, the "Twelfth Night." Like Rex, the Twelfth Night Revelers were one of several new "krewes" that emerged during New Orleans's tempestuous postbellum era. Their leader was called the Lord of Misrule, in itself a not-so-subtle jab at what its organization considered misrule in their daily lives. The Twelfth Night Revelers had debuted in 1871 but quickly grew in popularity so that by 1873 many in the city had begun to view their parade as the official start of Carnival season. That year the krewe selected "The World of Audubon" as their theme. On the surface it was a celebration of one of New Orleans's native sons, the famous naturalist and artist James Audubon. When the tableaux rolled that evening, however, there could be no mistake as to the Lord of Misrule's message.

One of the more pointed displays, car six, mocked not just miscegenation but political miscegenation as it depicted "The Doves' Wedding," which showed the union between "White Dove and Ground Dove in matrimony, Cardinal Grosbeak officiating with soft satire." The boldest statement came on car fifteen, however, "The Crows in Council": "Over the float was an expansive arch, bearing the legend, 'Union—Justice—Confidence.' Inside, hung the scales of the blindfold goddess, and under these were spread the wings of the emblematic pelican. The interior revealed the assembly room of the Louisiana State Legislature, and at the rostrum stood a venerable Crow, who pounded his desk 'with a most suggestive umbrella.' Beside him a squat Raven in full canonicals unctuously was praying from a book. A Bat was seated in the role of secretary, and in the group were

Crows, and Crows, of all varieties, including the Carrion Crow with carpet-bag in hand."[30] Through the satire of Carnival, the Fusionists used public space to depict Kellogg's regime as an illegitimate government sustained by black ballots and a corrupt federal government.

The Fusionists also believed that projecting an image of popular legitimacy in the city's public spaces would bolster their chances of successfully overturning Kellogg's victory. On January 14, as William Pitt Kellogg quietly took the oath of office inside the Louisiana State House, the Fusion candidates conducted a competing inauguration ceremony a few blocks away in Lafayette Square. Here, Aristée Louis Tissot, having indisputably prevailed over his Republican opponent for the Orleans Parish Second District Court, administered the oath of office to D. B. Penn, John McEnery, and the remaining slate of Fusionist executive officers. Under the watchful eye of the Metropolitan Police, McEnery made an inaugural speech on the steps of city hall that counseled the thousands listening to present a dignified face and to avoid confrontation with their political opponents. Warmoth followed McEnery with a speech in which he defended his term and immodestly took credit for ameliorating the actions of a legislature he now characterized as ignorant and greedy. Moved deeply by the show taking place before him, E. John Ellis hoped optimistically that this symbolic inauguration would inspire the U.S. Congress to reverse the election's outcome. Telegramming his brother Thomas back in Amite City, E. John declared, "We are *Confident* and *Jubilant*." Following the ceremony, the McEnery legislature took up residence in the Odd Fellows Hall, almost directly across Lafayette Square from City Hall. As acting governor, McEnery began appointing parish officials and awarding contracts while the Fusionist legislature printed "official" documents and passed laws. With Kellogg's assembly doing the same thing a few blocks away at the Mechanics' Institute, it inevitably meant that rival claimants for office would emerge in almost every parish of the state. In time, it also led to bloodshed.[31]

With these two competing state legislatures operating as Mardi Gras approached, it was inevitable that the parades of Rex and the Mistick Krewe of Comus would make their own rhetorical contribution to the rapidly deteriorating political situation in the city. Once again, Algernon Sidney Badger led the King of Carnival's procession as it surged down St. Charles Avenue for its second annual presentation in front of City Hall. Badger must have been mortified by what happened next. Waiting for him on the platform in front of city hall was none other than Colonel James B. Walton, the man whom Badger only a month before had been sent to subdue. Stopping at the platform, Rex made a mock arrest of both the mayor and Walton and escorted the two "detainees" to a waiting carriage that stood directly behind Badger. As Walton smugly rode with Rex's royal entourage, the Metropolitan Police's superintendent endured the taunts and jeers of Rex's spectators. In this insulting gesture, Rex made clear that he was capable of performing duties of the kind that Badger could not.[32]

The editors of the *Republican* undoubtedly had no idea what was coming later that evening when they urged their readers to pull back the drapes so that their gaslights might help illuminate the nighttime production of Comus. The theme of the Mistick Krewe's parade that evening, titled "Missing Links to Darwin's Origin of Species," picked up where the Lord of Misrule had left off. Most of the creatures in the "missing link" parade were bold satirical effigies of unpopular political figures. President Grant appeared as a tobacco grub clutching a tax-collection box. The hyena embodied Benjamin "Beast" or "Spoons" Butler as he shamelessly carried a large silver spoon over his shoulder and a carpetbag in the other hand. Even though the Metropolitan Police provided a security escort for the krewe, the Pickwickians heaped additional abuse upon Badger by lampooning him as a sleuthing bloodhound with a large protruding nose. Perhaps this is why the Metropolitans at several junctures refused to clear pedestrian traffic for the procession. The Republicans' black political partners received the roughest treatment, however. A black man was "portrayed as the Missing Link himself, half-human, half gorilla, playing a banjo and wearing a pink collar, a 'simian Cupid' seeking a Psyche for his 'nobler mate.'" As Reid Mitchell points out in his history of Mardi Gras, "the krewe held up the contemporary political and social order as unnatural."[33]

🐝

On Ash Wednesday, Governor John McEnery abandoned his passive role and, using his presumed authority as commander-in-chief, called for the conservative citizens of New Orleans to take up arms in support of the Fusionist legislature. To lead this erstwhile militia, he called on the most dashing soldier he could find— Frederick Nash Ogden. Since the violent days of 1868, Fred Ogden had been working with modest success to establish a firm with business partner William Bell, selling cotton baling supplies. He had also become involved in social circles, joining the Pickwick Club, which had just staged Comus's bitterly racist "Origins of the Species" parade. Ogden had even dabbled with the Reform movement when it first emerged. Yet, unlike his politician-lawyer cousins, Fred Ogden was a doer of deeds, not a man of words or commerce. The war years had shaped who he was. In his heart, in his outlook, he was a soldier. McEnery's call was an opportunity to fulfill his destiny.[34]

Unfortunately for Ogden, he had very little time to raise and equip, or especially to train, a militia capable of confronting Algernon Badger's Metropolitan

Police. Only a week after McEnery appointed him general of the Fusionist militia, the acting governor ordered Ogden into battle. Leading between five hundred and six hundred men, and aided by Colonel Eugene Waggaman, Ogden focused his main attack on the central Metropolitan Police station, housed in the old Spanish Cabildo on Jackson Square. The attack went poorly almost from the start. By 9:30 p.m., Ogden's followers had already begun to show a worrisome lack of discipline when they broke into and plundered a gun shop on Chartres Street as well as a cigar shop and coffee store, emptying all establishments of their contents. Badger ordered a contingent of his Metropolitans to push back the attack when the mob started to fire on the Cabildo. Late into the night the two groups continued to exchange shots, but generally without much effect. The Metropolitans employed a small howitzer but wisely started by firing blanks to frighten rather than kill, a move that minimized bloodshed.[35]

With mayhem in the streets, Kellogg frantically requested help from General Emory, the commander of federal troops in the city. Although Emory was reluctant to engage in battle, he did send a detachment to negotiate with the mob. One of the officers of this group made his way to Ogden to persuade the Fusionist commander to call off the attack. A veteran soldier, Ogden undoubtedly realized the futility of continuing the fight with an unprepared and undisciplined horde and began to withdraw. By 2:15 the next morning, the Metropolitans were in complete control of the Jackson Square police station and the surrounding streets. The collision downtown injured numerous people, including Ogden himself, and resulted in about sixty-five arrests but only one fatality—an unlucky German immigrant bystander out on his wedding night. The scene proved uglier in the Carrollton precinct, however. The lightly defended police station there had fallen easily to the McEnery militia, but when the Metropolitans retook their Jefferson Parish outpost the next day, they severely injured one insurgent and fatally shot another in the stomach. In the wake of this fiasco, Fusionism also appeared to be mortally wounded.[36]

The following day, Kellogg seized his opportunity to shut down McEnery's rival legislature and sent Badger and a strong column of Metropolitans to seize Odd Fellows' Hall. In a coincidence of beautiful symmetry, one of the few McEnery legislators present was Speaker Joseph Moncure. When a sergeant from the Metropolitans ordered all those who were not members of the legislature to step toward one side of the hall, Moncure exclaimed, "What does this mean! Are we prisoners?" As the Metropolitans arrested and hauled the intemperate Democrat to the city lockup, the irony was probably not lost on some of his associates that Moncure himself had scarcely a year earlier goaded fellow conservatives to join the Custom House ring in their plan to storm and disperse Warmoth's legislature. Now, along with a handful of associates, including the future governor, Murphy J. Foster, Moncure spent the next few days in jail. Unlike those he had actively encouraged to engage in open rebellion, John McEnery had fled the city before any real street fighting began.[37]

The conservative campaign to overthrow Republican rule in the 1872–73 political season revealed both the possibilities and the limitations of using public space to promote a partisan message. In taking their message to the streets, conservatives had hoped to rally white Southerners behind their standard in the same way that war had, at least in popular memory, united a divided community in the cause of Southern independence. Although the Fusion campaign was unsuccessful, it introduced themes that resonated with white Southerners for generations. Veterans like Tissot tapped into their own angst-ridden memories of the spring of 1861 to instill a similar sense of purpose among the rising generation of young men whose own youth had denied them the war experience. In doing so, these Democratic ward clubs made explicit the connection between white female purity and the political duty of white Southern men. More importantly, this campaign also inaugurated an important relationship between the Civil War generation and the men who made up the postbellum generation. Schooled by their elders, this younger set of men achieved in the 1890s a sort of social reordering that the Civil War generation could never accomplish.

Fusionism failed not because it offered an unattractive message but because it was unable to eliminate the profound personal divisions between the men who rallied around its standard. No single issue was more divisive than the continued presence of Henry Clay Warmoth in the Fusion coalition. It was difficult to rally white voters around a campaign of reform and native white ascendancy when a Northern incumbent who was the very symbol of Republican corruption played a conspicuous role in the canvass. Fusion's failure was made all the more frustrating by the fact that conservative whites in other Southern states had managed to employ similar strategies and paper over their differences long enough to overthrow Republican rule.

The collective inability of conservative whites to bring about political unity culminated in the poor showing of Fred Ogden's "militia" in its weak attempt to violently overthrow Kellogg's state government. Ill-planned and lacking popular support, the failed raid and the subsequent breakup of the McEnery legislature marked a low point for the men who had hoped to force a regime change. Yet this debacle was not a total wash. With the exception of the few Fusionist legislators temporarily detained by Badger's Metropolitan Policemen, none of the primary advocates of violence were punished by Kellogg's government, nor were they prosecuted under the Federal Enforcement Acts. This tacit admission of the Republicans' relative weakness was an encouraging sign that if properly pursued, violence might yield more favorable results. Leading an ill-prepared mob into battle was a mistake that Frederick Nash Ogden did not make twice.

Fusion's failure in 1872 also supplied the framework around which white conservatives ultimately forged a temporary unity capable of overthrowing Republican rule. Calls for civic reform, appeals to the manhood of a rising generation, and rhetoric that played upon the racial and sexual fears of New Orleans's whites all reemerged in the much more successful White League campaign of 1874. Before that could happen, however, the architects of counterrevolution would have to reconcile the contradictory elements within their own camp. The federal government aided them tremendously in this regard when it interceded on behalf of Kellogg's Republicans in the election of 1872. Indeed, intervention was probably the greatest gift that the Grant administration could have given to Louisiana's most reactionary elements. It fostered a myth of federal tyranny that in turn fueled a protracted effort by Democrats to retake the state. The irregular means by which the Republican administration sustained its allies in Louisiana not only fostered a crisis of political legitimacy; they also weakened the position of reformers in New Orleans who had hoped to forge a new conservative political party devoid of the divisive qualities of the Democrats. Faced with such a discouraging defeat, the public message of Rex had changed from one of cooperation with civil authority to one that mimicked Comus's overt antagonism toward all Republicans. Conversely, Fusion's defeat salvaged the prospects of the Bourbons and strengthened the hand of the men whom Ellis had called "the corrupt men of our party." Many of those men had either sat on the sidelines during the fall canvass or had actively worked against Fusion's success.

Lastly, the fact that Kellogg had been sustained not just by the federal government but also by black ballots signaled the dawning of a new political reality in Louisiana. There was no longer any denying that black voters had to be taken seriously, and this realization angered conservative whites who, in their delusional and paternalistic way, believed that blacks could be cajoled or intimidated into supporting their aims. Robert Nash Ogden proclaimed, for example, that the black vote "ought to be controlled" by men such as himself. Such anger created a receptive audience for sharpened racial rhetoric, as characterized by the "World of Audubon" tableaux of the Twelfth Night Revelers and the Mistick Krewe of Comus's "Origins of the Species." Interracial political cooperation, however, was not killed completely by the ascendancy of Kellogg. Within the conservative white political tradition there remained a significant number of realists who later sought allies among New Orleans's black electorate.

As a postscript, one wonders how Louisiana's history would have been different had the Fusion ticket prevailed in the election of 1872. Such an outcome may have had little impact upon the growing racial polarization within the state, and it is doubtful that it would ever have lived up to the egalitarian rhetoric that the Fusionists occasionally employed in their campaign. Yet the Fusionists, like Warmoth, had certainly not overpromised to black voters. A Fusion coalition may have legitimated black political participation and would undoubtedly have strengthened the hand of reformers in the city. Even in defeat, the forces that had animated the Reformers and the Liberal Republicans endured in New Orleans for two more decades in a protracted struggle against Bourbonism. Perhaps at such a crucial juncture, the balance of power might have been tipped in a different direction. Moreover, it requires little imagination to believe that a Fusionist administration would have completely altered the outcome of the election of 1877 and given the presidency to the Democratic candidate, Samuel Tilden—a turn of events that would have changed the course American history in significant and unpredictable ways.

CASTE AND CONFLICT

1873–1874

The day that a single mulatto believes
That we, the Negroes, are his equal,
That day you'll turn into a horse,
And I, I'll become white, I think.
You must be dumb not to understand that!

Against us the prejudice of the mulattoes
Will never end
They despise us; so rest assured,
Mulattoes will be our Pontius Pilate:
You're not too dumb to understand that!

Equality, unification
Will create a peculiar sort of race, I think,
Since the child of such a union
Will be neither white, nor yellow, nor black.
You're not too dumb to understand that!
—From *Le Carillon*, July 1873

A dramatic event took place one afternoon in October 1872 that forever changed the relationship between Louise Marie Dronet and her white relatives. Her father's health had always been fragile, and his poor physical condition was one of the initial reasons that he had made the bold decision to bring his mixed-race daughter to live with him in 1865. Now, seven years later, Louise Marie was one of the several people standing vigil over the unconscious Louis Drouet as he lay dying. When he succumbed to his illness later that night, Louise Marie ran from the room in distress, crying "My father is dead!" As she sat sobbing in the evening air on the gallery, Arthur Toledano tried to comfort her. "Louise, you must not think all the good men are dead," he pleaded, "as long as [you] shall conduct yourself as you have been, I shall stand by you because I know you are the dutiful daughter of my uncle."[1]

Louise Marie Drouet had been "conducting herself" as someone with a mind toward crossing the color line, and there were several indications that she was well on her way to succeeding in this endeavor. Her sickly father's doctor, the grocer who lived across the street, and a young man who had lived in the house as a tenant for a little over a year in 1868 all believed she was a lawful daughter—and neither Louise Marie nor her father had made any effort to disabuse them of this notion. When a census worker came to their Faubourg St. Mary home in the summer of 1870, he inscribed a W in the column beside Louise Marie's name to denote her race. After all, this young Creole lady had an Irish domestic servant waiting on her. Not only had Louise Marie Drouet been engaged in racial passing; her father and, to a lesser degree, Arthur Toledano had been complicit in the deception, even if each had different motivations for establishing her white identity.[2]

Louise Marie Drouet may have been a marginal figure in the greater debate over race, politics, and social stability that raged in postbellum New Orleans, but her plight encapsulated not only the dilemma of racial identity faced by her caste and generation, but the role that the human condition often played in determining their fate. Just as Charles Sauvinet had wrestled with notions of his own racial identity, so, too, did countless others in New Orleans whose blood bound them to both sides of the color line. The egalitarian legal apparatus that had been constructed by the federal Reconstruction amendments and reinforced by state and national civil rights legislation held out the promise of removing, at least in law, the inequalities that mixed-race people had always faced in New Orleans. Closing the legal distance between blacks and whites, however, exposed both groups to new and unanticipated risks. As a consequence, many whites who had once shared the most intimate ties across the color line now became the leading advocates of a new binary racial order. This was certainly true for Joseph Walker, who had once been willing to drink at the Bank Coffeehouse with Charles Sauvinet, and was now going to apply to Arthur Toledano. Both Walker and Toledano faced the pressures of a community that made them feel vulnerable.

Although the New Orleans mixed-race community differed in important ways from the vast majority of the postbellum South's black population, their occupation of the racial borderland between black and white worlds placed them at the center of the debate over the meaning of race in the second half of the nineteenth century. In the antebellum era, the presence of freeborn, fair-skinned, mixed-race New Orleanians had so undermined the philosophy of race-based slavery that the white power structure had actively sought means to reduce the number of free blacks in their midst. With the war came the destruction of slavery but not its underlying philosophy that linked race to social status. Despite the emergence of black enfranchisement and the legal codification of the recent concept of "civil rights" in the postbellum era, unmistakably black freedmen did not fundamentally undermine the maintenance of the nation's white-supremacist culture. The continued presence and racial ambiguity of New Orleanians who possessed a fractional amount of African ancestry, however, posed a continual threat to a social-order philosophy that made skin color so important. Not until society had closed the door on the racial mobility of individuals like Charles Sauvinet and Louise Marie Drouet could the ambitions of those who sought the imposition of a modernized white-supremacist ideal be realized.

Yet even as late as the mid-1870s, those who championed the cause of white supremacy discovered that white New Orleanians remained divided in their attitudes toward the status of the city's substantial population of mixed-race citizens. For the Civil War generation of whites, this caste represented either "white men in dark skins" or a diabolical combination of the most venal elements of white and black culture. Blood ties across the color line could and often did feed both liberal and reactionary impulses, with bonds of kinship often mitigated by the white social stigma of racial impurity. The status that wealth and cultural attainment conferred upon mixed-race elites in New Orleans had in some significant measure endured both the destruction of war and the acrimony of postbellum politics. Missing from much of the literature on Reconstruction is the acknowledgment that even as America tried to reconcile questions of race with constitutional rights, the rest of the Western world moved in a decidedly different direction. Racial theories and the pretense of spreading moral uplift drove the imperial machinations of Europe for the rest of the nineteenth century. In the decade that had passed since Benjamin Butler first stepped ashore, this new, modernistic form of racism had also emerged in New Orleans. It was not grounded in paternalistic custom but instead found its basis in the fanatical polygenistic pseudoscience of men such as Josiah Nott and Louis Agassiz and came to be articulated locally in the pages of the French-language newspaper Le Carillon. For white elites who yearned for a return to the sort of social stability that their parents had known under slavery, these new theories held a special appeal, offering to a new generation the means by which it might justify holding blacks in an inferior social position. As the Mistick Krewe of Comus had shown, these ideas had begun to take root in popular discourse, however tongue-in-cheek their theatrics had been. One zealous writer even assumed that Comus was an attack on the theory of evolution and sent Charles Darwin copies of the 1873 program. Darwin replied, "I can't tell from the wonderful mistakes in the article whether the writer is witty, ignorant, or blunders for the sake of fun." This lighthearted tone did not last, however. By the time the postbellum generation superseded its Civil War elders in the 1890s, these theories were central to popular belief about race not only in America but in the entire Western world.[3]

An internal debate over identity and social standing had also begun within New Orleans's mixed-race community in the postbellum period. Although Louisiana's Republican government had enacted legislation that granted people of color something approaching true citizenship, it did not change fundamentally the role of racial prejudice in society. A flood of freedmen into the city following emancipation had not only increased the black presence in New Orleans; it had also prompted racial conflict. Such tensions flourished not only between whites and blacks but between the elite and middle-class mixed-race residents and the darker, generally poorer, newcomers. Moreover, the influx of German and Italian immigrants to the city after 1865 had added a new layer of ethnicity and racial complexity to the already diverse population of the city. Amid this confusion, perhaps not even fully sure of their own identity, an increasing number of New Orleanians who had a fraction of African ancestry took steps toward crossing the color line.[4]

The sharpening of racial rhetoric in New Orleanians had consequences in both the private lives of the postbellum generation and the political discourse of the city. In the months that followed Comus's racially charged "Origins of the Species" parade, a series of confrontations took place that symbolized the growing rift between black and white New Orleanians. Neither accidental nor inevitable, they reflected the conscious effort of individuals who, driven by a multitude of impulses, pinned their hopes for the future upon the promise of white racial solidarity.

The hostility that grew out of the failed Fusionism campaign of 1872 spilled out into many corners of New Orleans's society, and perhaps nobody felt its effects more acutely than the interracial Creole world. The timing of larger political and social events was particularly inauspicious for Louise Marie Drouet, who had in 1865 come to live with her white father at his home on the corner of Tchoupitoulas and Gaiènnie. The growing intensity of racial politics made it necessary for a person in Louise Marie's situation to walk an increasingly fine line should she successfully fabricate her new identity as a white Creole lady. Louise Marie was not ready, however, for the perils she was to encounter while attempting to straddle the color line, for although she yearned for the benefits of belonging to white society, she was not yet able to fully relinquish her ties to the Afro-Creole community. As the 1870s wore on, it became painfully obvious that she could not have it both ways.

Louise Marie Drouet's most problematic relationship was unquestionably the one that she maintained with the old Afro-Creole widow of Pierre Laurent. This woman had known Louise Marie's father since the early 1840s, and although she had known Elizabeth Bresson only by sight, she may well have been part of the network of women who had brokered the *plaçage* union between the two. Shortly after the death of her mother, Louise Marie began making regular visits to see the widow Laurent—trips that were interrupted only by her stay in the convent. Louis Drouet was hardly enthusiastic about his daughter's ongoing social ties with Laurent after she came to live with him. Although the widow would occasionally come to the Drouet home, it was usually in the capacity of a seamstress. When Laurent offered to alter Louise Marie's dresses for free, Louis Drouet insisted on paying for such services, because he did not wish to be beholden to this woman. The old Creole even expressed to a tenant his anxiety over his daughter's choice of friends, saying that Louise Marie had been "too good, too particular, and if she had a little more judgment, it would give him pleasure." The same tenant later observed that Drouet was "very particular as to what society she went into."[5]

If Louise Marie had an alter ego during her stay at her father's house, however, it was another regular visitor, her half sister Sylvanie Morgan. Although Sylvanie was two years older than Louise Marie, the critical difference between their lives was the character of the relationship between their mother and their respective fathers. Unlike Louis Drouet, Samuel Morgan had forsaken all responsibility to the offspring that resulted from his union with his *placée*, Elizabeth Bresson. Not only had this action placed an economic burden on Sylvanie Morgan; it also eliminated her only direct link to the white world. By the time Louise Marie came to live at her father's house, Sylvanie had married an Afro-Creole man and soon thereafter had started a family. Louise Marie's sister had not, however, completely abandoned hope of benefiting from her fair complexion. Sylvanie maintained ties with white society through her frequent visits with her half sister at the home of Louis Drouet and hoped that she might one day successfully pass her own children into white society. She did the same thing Angela Sauvinet had done in 1863: when Sylvanie Morgan registered the birth of her eldest child, she acquired a valuable asset toward her newborn daughter's new racial identity: a birth certificate that declared her child as white.[6]

Both the widow Laurent and Sylvanie Morgan had in some respect sought to share in Louise Marie's good fortune by placing themselves in the orbit of white society. To them, Louise Marie represented the potential of racial mobility in uncertain times. What they either could not or chose not to see was that while their proximity to Louise Marie's world conferred status on themselves, it had the opposite effect on Louise Marie. Her white relatives undoubtedly viewed their aspirations with alarm, and even her father, who seems to have genuinely loved Louise Marie, wished she would exercise "more judgment" in selecting her company. A special set of circumstances had opened the door to the possibility that Louise Marie might someday pass into white society, but doing so relied a great deal upon her discretion. Louise Marie's inability to turn her back on the past ultimately proved to be an essential component in her undoing.

In spite of all of Louise Marie's efforts to blend in with the family—or perhaps because of them—she had plenty of reasons to worry about her future after her father's death, for the family dynamics were now entirely different. The paternal nature of the relationship had been replaced by a lateral connection with a host of cousins who viewed her as both a rival claimant to their uncle's estate and a mixed-race woman who was making a bid to become their social equal. With the protective hand of her father removed, and despite Arthur Toledano's promises on the day of Louis Drouet's death, the relationship between Louise Marie and Toledano also began to sour. It would be impossible to decide precisely what caused the greatest conflict between the two, mostly because there were several factors that fed upon one another. Louise Marie continued to live in her deceased father's house for a while, but Arthur Toledano wasted no time in banishing the widow Laurent from further visits. Laurent bristled at this restriction, boldly claiming that Louise Marie's father had no objection to his daughter's mingling in "good society." Perhaps Laurent's assertion that she was a friend of the family reminded him of that afternoon on the streetcar when he had suffered at the hands of Jane Price. Of the seventeen nieces and nephews who stood to inherit from Louis Drouet, some were undoubtedly aghast that their uncle had ever taken Louise Marie in to live with him. One of them, Alexis Drouet, had worked as the foreman on his father's cane plantation in antebellum days and seems to have had no notion of Louise Marie's right to the estate. Unlike Arthur Toledano, some of Louise Marie Drouet's white cousins were clearly in need of cash and probably worried about her claim on the estate should the courts recognize her as a daughter and thus, under the Louisiana Constitution of 1868, a forced heir. Perhaps from his own convictions, perhaps goaded by his cousins, Arthur Toledano, as executor of his uncle's estate, moved to disinherit Louise Marie.[7]

On the face of things, one might think that Louise Marie Drouet had been dealt a poor hand in the coming struggle with her white cousins, but some surprising things happened when she decided to fight for her legacy. By far the biggest of these occurred when Louise Marie secured the legal services Charles Magill Conrad & Son. C. M. Conrad Sr. had been Millard Fillmore's secretary of war, a signer of the Confederate Constitution, a member of the rebel legislature, and lately a champion of the Reform Party. He had long been identified with the interests of Louisiana's planting elite. His son, Charles M. Conrad Jr., was the brother-in-law of Davidson Bradfute Penn, the Fusion candidate for lieutenant governor in Louisiana's disputed election of 1872 (and the father of a mixed-race daughter). Conrad & Son had decided to take Louise Marie's case pro bono when "a friend who pitied the helpless condition of the orphan" brought her plight to their attention. The identity of that "friend" of Louise Marie will forever be lost to history, but that person's deeds meant that a powerful team of white elites would represent a penniless mixed-race woman in her quest for justice against a Confederate veteran. Clearly Louise Marie had made a positive impression on people who moved in very influential circles. When direct negotiation with Toledano failed to bring about an "amicable settlement," Conrad & Son filed suit against the succession of Louis F. Drouet.[8]

The events that followed seem to have had far less to do with money than with fundamental issues of identity and community standards of fair play. Although Louis Drouet left behind a substantial estate, his only daughter did not seek a large inheritance. Instead, she prayed for fifty dollars per month in alimony, an amount that would provide sufficient income to survive but could scarcely be construed as the basis for luxurious living. More importantly, an award of alimony from her father's estate would serve as an acknowledgment of not only her paternity but also her relationship with her father's living relatives. For these heirs, the social stigma that such alimony represented far outweighed the financial consideration of Louise Marie's request. If she won her case, Louise Marie was unlikely to become her cousins' social equal, but the victory would nevertheless serve as a perpetual reminder of the Drouet clan's racial impurity. Conversely, the motivation of Louise Marie's white supporters begs analysis. Perhaps their own conception of Louise Marie was that she was, in fact, more white than black and that within the standards of the law *and* the custom of the community, she should be entitled to recognition by the estate.

Conrad was especially critical of what he characterized as the "peculiar ill grace" on the part of the defense's legal arguments. Toledano's attorneys posited that the constitution of 1825, the law in place at the time of Louise Marie's birth, dictated her claim to her father's estate. Ignoring completely the Louisiana Constitution of 1868, they asserted that because Louise Marie could not produce any

legally recognized documentation of her paternity and because she was an illegitimate person of color, she could not inherit from her father's estate. Should this
spurious legal theory fail to prevent the court from ruling in Louise Marie's favor,
Toledano's lawyers also included an exception based on a legal technicality, arguing that in this instance the law did not allow her to sue the estate's administrator
for alimony payments.[9]

In May 1873, Louise Marie Drouet, Arthur Toledano, their lawyers, and the
witnesses for both plaintiff and defendant entered the halls of the city's Second
District Court, presided over by Aristée Louis Tissot. As a judge, Tissot had quickly
cultivated a reputation for acting "firmly but courteously" toward those in his courtroom. He had also been thoroughly identified with the Fusion campaign, both as
the president of the Broom Rangers and as the man who administered the symbolic oath of office to John McEnery and Davidson Penn. His ruling in *Drouet v.
the Succession of Drouet*, however, was going to add a new layer to the complexity
of understanding his vision of justice and order in the postbellum city.[10]

In court, Arthur Toledano seemed particularly obsessed with proving the dubious assertion that Louise Marie was not the child of his uncle Louis. All of the
witnesses called by the defense were nephews and heirs to the estate of Louis
Drouet. In succession, they lamely suggested that their uncle never said anything
about having a daughter, but they had to admit that they visited him infrequently,
if ever. Toledano, who knew better, hinted that Louise Marie was more of a servant than a member of a family and denied ever having dined with her. He suggested that if Louise Marie had in fact been his uncle's daughter, Louis Drouet
would have provided her with a legal will. Toledano claimed that he had urged
his uncle to do just that, pointing out that all of his heirs were "provided for," but
that his uncle was so superstitious about death that he had refused to discuss the
matter. According to Toledano, Drouet ended one such conversation with "après
moi le déluge," an apocryphal quote attributed to Louis XV and translated literally as "after me, the flood"; it meant, in essence, that he did not care what happened to Louise Marie once he was gone. In response to the assertion that Louise
Marie's upbringing as a lady and weak constitution prevented her from making
a living, Toledano acidly replied, "She can work." Contradictory at several junctures and teeming with malice, this testimony was not a credit to his character.[11]

In contrast, the plaintiff's witnesses paraded to the stand one after another.
White men such as Henry Schwartz, Louis Drouet's longtime tenant, described
the affectionate familial bond between Louise Marie and her father, and he was
not alone. His fifteen-year-old son William directly contradicted Toledano's assertion that he and Louise Marie never dined together—as did three other witnesses.

Under cross-examination, Toledano's testimony began to reek of perjury. A steady stream of both black and white witnesses unmistakably established Louise Marie's paternity and praised her conduct as a dutiful daughter.

Conrad's able counsel brought initial results. Judge Tissot, persuaded by the testimony of the plaintiff, awarded Louise Marie the alimony she had prayed for. Yet it was not to be. Toledano successfully appealed the case to the Louisiana Supreme Court, a body that had in the *Sauvinet* case demonstrated its willingness to recognize the legal rights of minorities. Unfortunately for Louise Marie, a technicality voided the lower court's decision. In fact, Louise Marie Drouet could not, in this circumstance, sue an estate for alimony. It seems that in seeking the wrong remedy, Conrad had failed her. In spite of the many members of white society who had supported her cause, this interpretation by the Louisiana Supreme Court may also have been a manifestation of what legal scholar Virginia Dominguez has characterized as a "culture of resistance" to the rights of children born to mixed-race unions during and after Reconstruction. As the novelist Charles Chesnutt opined in his work *The House behind the Cedars*, "in these matters, custom *is* law." So the custom that allowed for Louise Marie's disinheritance proved stronger than the tempering force of compassion within the community. Conrad & Son must have recognized the futility of pursuing Louise Marie's claim any further, for no ensuing legal action took place.[12]

The trial and resulting judgment seemingly reaffirmed the notion that white Creoles became increasingly self-conscious of their interracial relatives as Reconstruction wore on. Yet the fact that such an unusual collection of defenders came to aid of this Afro-Creole woman also defies the conventions of a racist culture. Louise Marie Drouet's supporters had been moved by her character, and the weight of their testimony demonstrated that she had made her father's final years happy; they had been his happiest years. When the seventeen nieces and nephews of Louis Drouet denied Louise Marie's modest appeal for alimony, it apparently struck the community as a grossly dishonorable act. Thus, Conrad & Son took her case, and a string of white men and women joined her Afro-Creole relatives in an effort to correct such an outrage. Toledano and his white cousins may have ultimately won the suit, but in the process they lost immeasurable prestige in the eyes of their peers. Their tight-fisted disavowal of Louise Marie Drouet seemed to confirm all of the rotten things Anglo New Orleanians muttered about white Creoles behind closed doors. The case also demonstrated that racism had its limits, even in racially charged times. More importantly, the case suggests that even as late as 1873, New Orleanians remained divided over what place the mixed-race caste should occupy in society.

The courtroom drama of Louise Marie Drouet and Edmund Arthur Toledano was but a small episode in a much larger ongoing crisis in the interracial Creole world during the postbellum era. This crisis was about both cultural and racial identity, and the tangled familial web of the Toledano-Drouet clan demonstrated the inexorable link between the two. For white Creoles such as Toledano, the presence of a woman so intimately linked to both Afro-Creole society and his own bloodlines was a source of great anxiety—not so much because of her mere existence, but because the relationship had become so very public. If the case of Louise Marie Drouet is any indication, disowning loyal Afro-Creole relatives meant running the risk of censure within the larger community. Embracing them brought into question one's own racial purity, particularly amid the whispers uttered by some Anglo-Orleanians intimating that even self-identified white Creoles might not be the genuine article. As racial politics intensified, white Creoles grew increasingly sensitive about the subject of their heritage.[13]

A common aphorism used by those trying to explain the outpouring of cinematic masterpieces during the Great Depression suggests that "difficult times produce great art." Following such logic, the South's postbellum era should have produced a much greater artistic flowering than it did. New Orleans in the winter of 1872–73 did, however, inspire several important works by the legendary French impressionist Edgar Degas. The artist arrived in the Crescent City in October 1872—right in time to witness the convulsive struggles that played out in the streets between the Fusionists and their Republican rivals. He had journeyed to America to visit his uncle Michel Musson, his cousins Estelle, Desiree, and Mathilde, and his brothers René and Achille, who operated an unsuccessful trading company in New Orleans under the name of Degas Frères. Edgar Degas's mother had been born in the city, and he had hoped as part of his journey to make a connection with a land that was in some way responsible for making him who he was.[14]

The Civil War and the postbellum period had been disastrous for the Musson-Degas clan. Michel Musson, who had once been a prosperous merchant in the city, now teetered on the verge of bankruptcy. During the war, he had invested a considerable portion of his fortune in Confederate bonds, even selling a house that had once belonged to his nephew Edgar so that he might raise more capital for the Southern cause. His daughter Estelle had married a nephew of Jefferson Davis on the eve of war but was soon widowed and left to raise an infant child who had never seen her father. Estelle's second marriage to René Degas, her feckless cousin, ultimately set into motion a series of reversals that eventually broke

Musson's finances as well as his spirit. The visit of Edgar was a rare bright spot in what had otherwise been an exceedingly dismal time.[15]

Art historians have argued that the time the great impressionist spent in New Orleans had a lasting influence on his long career. Initially, plagued by eye ailments and general hypochondria, Degas languished indoors and bided his time by painting family portraits. By January, however, he had become particularly fascinated by the commercial enterprises of his brothers and especially his uncle's cotton factorage. Degas's infatuation with cotton resulted ultimately in *A Cotton Office in New Orleans*, painted during the dramatic weeks that led up to Carnival 1873. Set inside the offices of Musson, Prestidge & Company, the painting shows Michel Musson in the foreground, pensively tugging away at a cotton sample. Behind him sits René Degas, casually reading a copy of the *Daily Picayune*. A sea of cotton spills over the edges of a table in the center of the picture, with men, including Musson's son-in-law William A. Bell, standing nearby. Perhaps most fascinating is the great likelihood that the mysterious bearded man standing behind René Degas, with red hair and wearing a tan duster, is none other than William Bell's business partner Frederick Nash Ogden. New Orleans could be a very small town indeed.[16]

A Cotton Office is also a portrait of men in the midst of dramatic events. Even as Degas had picked up his brush, members of the Fusionist legislature plotted insurrection a few blocks away at the Odd Fellows Hall. As Degas scholar Christopher Benfey posits, perhaps Musson's contemplative countenance spoke to his firm's having failed, quite literally, midportrait. Certainly by March of 1873, Musson was no longer in the cotton business. René, who through the good graces of his Uncle Michel had joined the Pickwick Club, was about to take part in Comus's racially charged presentation of "The Origins of the Species." And of course, as Fred Ogden posed for the great master, he could have been contemplating the rebellion he soon after led in the streets of New Orleans.[17]

An inveterate joiner, Michel Musson dabbled in numerous conservative political movements in New Orleans after the end of the Civil War. It is possible that he had crossed paths with Fred Ogden before the Civil War, but if not, they most certainly were aware of each other by the fall of 1865 when Musson attended the first meeting of the Young Democrats, which had been called by Ogden. More recently, both had toyed with the Reform movement despite their definite Democratic leanings. In the spring of 1873, however, the two temporarily parted ways as Michel Musson experimented with a quixotic biracial scheme for Redemption— a plan that Ogden reportedly denounced as a "Covenant with Hell."[18]

The unusual campaign with which Musson became involved aimed at creating political unity, at least nominally, between black and white Louisianans.
More accurately, it was a union of Afro-Creole and white elites who hoped to
salvage some shred of the old social hierarchy that the war and the postbellum
period had largely destroyed. Shortly after the breakup of McEnery's legislature,
the *New Orleans Times*, a newspaper with strong ties to the old Reform movement, began drumming up interest in this cooperative effort, arguing that true
racial reconciliation was the only hope for ejecting the corrupt administration of
William Pitt Kellogg. Such commentary undoubtedly would have attracted the
attention of Musson, for he harbored a consuming hatred for the carpetbagger.
Supportive editorials eventually spread to competing newspapers, including the
strongly Democratic *Picayune*. While the media trumpeted the virtues of this
new organization, a committee of the movement's principals outlined a course of
action behind closed doors.

By mid-July, the secret Committee of One-Hundred revealed its master plan:
the Unification Movement. The ten resolutions put forth that day were remarkably radical propositions for an organization ostensibly championing redemption.
They endorsed all of the civil rights provisions that had been part of the state
constitution since 1868, including full accommodation in places of public resort
and transportation. The Unifiers went much further, however, advocating integration for public schools as well as for private restaurants, taverns, and hotels. They
called on factories to hire and promote employees in a "colorblind" fashion and
implored financial institutions and insurance companies to provide services without regard to race. Their manifesto bore a remarkable resemblance to the Civil
Rights Act of 1964.

The men behind the Unification Movement were every bit as extraordinary as
the document that they had produced. Many had been involved in the Reform
movement of the previous year, and as in that earlier effort, Isaac Newton Marks
played a strong leadership role. Pierre Gustave Toutant Beauregard, the old Creole Confederate general, took time out from overseeing the Louisiana Lottery
Company's official numbers racket to chair the resolutions committee. If the presence of Marks failed to surprise anyone, certainly the involvement of conservative
men such as Harry T. Hays, of the famous "Hays Brigade," would have. The black
leadership that signed onto the Unification Movement was as impressive as its
white counterpart. Afro-Creoles dominated this half of the assembly, with Aristide Mary and the Roudanez brothers leading the way. The participation of the
fair-skinned Edmund Rillieux must have been of particular interest to Michel

Musson, for he was the old Creole's first cousin. Several of these men had first entered the political arena during the Union occupation but had lost out to Warmoth and other white Republicans. In theory, Unification would allow them a renewed opportunity to gain political influence.[19]

Although great journalistic hoopla accompanied the announcement of the Unificationists' manifesto, there were signs that the movement suffered from internal conflicts and also that its base of support was relatively thin. One of the most problematic signs was the inclusion of Kellogg's lieutenant governor, Caesar C. Antoine, and the African American carpetbagger J. Henri Burch on the committee. Both had a significant stake in the future success of the Republican Party and had an even greater stake in the Custom House faction that controlled it. The motivations behind their presence aroused justifiable suspicion. More troubling was that, much like the Reform movement a year earlier, Unification drew hardly any support from outside New Orleans. Even within the city, it was not quite as popular as the newspapers had first claimed. Robert Hardin Marr, a conservative lawyer and an acquaintance of E. John Ellis, sent a letter to the *Picayune* when the newspaper printed his name as a supporter of Unification. He was in favor of any organization that made an effort to unite the citizens of Louisiana and "heartily approved" of racial harmony. Yet Marr pointed out that Unification was "in some of its details and specifications, impracticable and objectionable, and an invasion of the rights of other citizens."[20]

By July 1, Beauregard found it necessary to defend his position on Unification. The most unpopular provisions of the Unification platform involved integration of public transportation and city schools, both of which remained flashpoints of conflict in the coming century. Beauregard pragmatically argued, however, that acceptance of integrated institutions was not tantamount to social equality. Offering a bizarre analogy, he explained, "It would not be denied that, in traveling, and at places of public resort, we often share these privileges in common with thieves, prostitutes, gamblers and others who have worse sins to answer for than the accident of color; but no one ever supposed that we thereby assented to the social equality of these people with ourselves."[21]

Father Abram J. Ryan, Lost Cause poet and editor of the predominantly Irish *New Orleans Morning Star and Catholic Messenger*, was beside himself with indignation. Of Beauregard's comments, Ryan's paper exclaimed, "That address is argumentative, explanatory, and apologetic. As an argument, it is very lame. As an explanation, it is more lame. As an apology, it is most lame." The editor went on to suggest that Beauregard was both a suspect Catholic and a lousy specimen of Southern honor. Ryan characterized the Unification Movement with an analogy of his own: "The end of the movement is the moral, social, and political salva-tion of Louisiana. These gentlemen of the new movement have come to the conclusion that Louisiana is sick unto death morally, socially, materially, politi-cally. They constitute themselves the physicians of the dying patient. They are sure of their own skill and power. They have a patent medicine, which if admin-istered in huge doses will revive the dying state."[22]

When the Unification Movement first announced its resolutions in June, it called for a meeting in one month's time to officially launch its campaign. But those who gathered to celebrate the christening of Unification instead attended its funeral. Beauregard failed to show up for the meeting, and if the list of sup-porters printed in the newspaper was any indication, numerous other white con-servatives had also abandoned the cause, including Michel Musson. Isaac Marks gamely presided over a largely black assembly, but even his optimism must have withered as J. Henri Burch took the podium to sarcastically congratulate whites for finally seeing the light when it came to racial equality.[23]

The fundamental reason for the failure of the Unification movement was that racial opinion in New Orleans and the rest of Louisiana had already started moving in a decidedly different direction, particularly after the rise of Kellogg. The grim reality may be that there was never a time during the postbellum period when Unification would have not crumbled under the weight of its own contradictions. Moreover, it had promoted public accommodations without re-gard to race; this idea was what Robert Hardin Marr directly decried when he noted that Unification contained elements that were "an invasion of the rights of other citizens." By the end of July, Father Ryan crowed from the pages of the *Morning Star* that the movement was "Dead and Buried." Rodolphe Desdunes later observed of Unification: "If it did not succeed, it was because it was pre-mature. The people were not prepared to renounce their way of thinking: we could not hope to see them ratify a policy destined to reverse long-established customs."[24]

The essential question of the Unification Movement, however, was not whether it could ever have succeeded but why it took place at all. Both the Unification Movement and the much more private trials of Louise Marie Drouet suggest that even amid a growing climate of racial antagonism, not everyone was prepared to embrace the emergent rhetoric of a strictly binary form of white supremacy. Some, though believing in the prevailing nineteenth-century notions of white superiority, also believed in a gradation of merit that corresponded with the pro-portionate mixture of black and white blood. Such a philosophy may not have flown in the face of emerging Darwinian thought, but it ran counter to a growing polygenistic movement that decried "mongrelization" as the potential downfall of Western civilization.[25]

One can also analyze the Unification Movement in a more cynical way. A significant number of its early white adherents may have simply viewed it as one more in a series of bizarre and ultimately unpalatable combinations aimed at removing a political enemy. The history of otherwise unimaginable political unions in New Orleans dated back to the ill-conceived alliance forged between the Custom House faction and Bourbon Democrats in the summer of 1871. Unification also had some unlikely supporters, including Charles Cavaroc, who had financially backed Bank Coffeehouse owner Joseph Walker in his lawsuit with Charles Sauvinet and, like René Degas, had been part of the overtly racist "missing links" parade staged by the Mistick Krewe of Comus in 1873. Viewed in this light, the Unification Movement represented only another spasm of political desperation. The contradictory behavior of these men may also have been an indication that they did not know the limits and extent of their own racial beliefs. It is true that racial egalitarianism had concrete limits in New Orleans during Reconstruction, but these were also fluid and uncertain times. Unification itself underscored such uncertainty, for its very occurrence revealed that, even as late as July of 1873, some community leaders could not foresee the ultimate resurgence of the Democratic Party.

The participation of New Orleans's Afro-Creole elite in the Unification Movement also begs analysis. That they sought a return to the political stage is a distinct possibility, and without question, Unification involved far more concessions on the behalf of their white partners. Yet there was another dynamic afoot in the city's interracial Creole world. These men may have joined out of a desire to preserve their fleeting status as the masters of a small world. The same forces that might have inspired Afro-Creoles to seek a desperate union with conservative whites may also have been the inspiration behind the Drouet heirs' perjury-laden disavowal of their cousin Louise Marie. It was the threat of the ongoing campaign for white Creole racial purity spearheaded by the strident editor of *Le Carillon*.

Dr. J. W. Durel, a former Confederate surgeon, founded his newspaper in 1869 with a dual purpose: to establish the racial purity of white Creoles and to diminish the position of the Afro-Creole elite. He wanted to strip the very name "Creole" from people of color, reserving it solely for "pure" whites. Miscegenation, integration, racial passing, and black political power were a pantheon of evils to be vanquished. Such shrill rhetoric found a more receptive audience in the wake of the failed election of 1872. With the advent of the Unification Movement, the vituperative spirit of *Le Carillon*'s attacks increased. Just days before the Unification Movement's disastrous July meeting, Durel's sheet espoused an entirely different course: "The time has come to indicate what the sons of Louisiana want—that one must be either WHITE or BLACK, that each person must decide for himself. There are two races here: one superior, the other inferior. . . . Their separation is absolutely necessary. So let us separate ourselves as of today into two distinct parties—the White Party and the Black Party." *Le Carillion*'s cry for a White Party was an eerie foreshadowing of things to come.[26]

Ever since Anglo-Americans began arriving in large numbers to New Orleans in 1803, they had often projected a reputation for racial impurity upon the city's white Creoles. The passing of several generations only seemed to strengthen this general impression. The hypocrisy of Anglo Orleanians' own interracial sexual relationships did not seem to matter. Proof positive of Creole miscegenation was the endless number of Afro-Creoles who shared family names with white Creoles. As Reconstruction politics increasingly devolved along racially polarized lines, particularly after the rise of Kellogg, they raised the stakes of maintaining one's own whiteness. They also brought about the abandonment and outright denial of some long-standing folkways, including the custom of *plaçage*. Afro-Creole relatives like Louise Marie Drouet became a liability. At the same time, passing for white held a growing appeal for racially ambiguous people, while representing a danger to the reputations of white Creoles, particularly the relatives of those who attempted such passing. The racial bullying of *Le Carillion* took root in this fertile ground.[27]

The racial rhetoric in the pages of J. W. Durel's newspaper did not flourish in isolation, though. In 1866 the longtime proslavery crusader and Mobile, Alabama, physician Josiah Nott published his arguments for black inferiority in a work titled *The Negro Race: Its Ethnology and Descent*. Essays by Nott also appeared in postbellum issues of *DeBow's Review*, a popular business journal printed in New Orleans until 1867. Durel, himself a physician and an amateur racial theorist, could not have been unaware of Nott's theories. The entire medical community of the city would have been familiar with his writings. As early as 1848, Nott had delivered lectures at the University of Louisiana advancing the notion that mankind did not share, as the Christian faith had taught, a common ancestry. His theories encountered resistance in the romantic antebellum age, but with the encroaching modernity of postbellum life, he found white Southern audiences more receptive. Although at some level the Mistick Krewe of Comus had poked satirical fun at the serious scientific discourse of Darwin with its production of the "Origins of the Species," Durel's journalistic ranting revealed that some took such concepts much more seriously.[28]

When George Washington Cable's short story "Belles Demoiselles Plantation" appeared in the pages of *Scribner's* in April 1874, it touched off a violent reaction among New Orleans's white Creoles and revealed how thoroughly they had sought to distance themselves from any suspicion of African heritage. Less than a year after the death of Unification, Cable's tale scandalized white Creoles with its clear implications of racial impurity and lack of moral character. That the author's stories rang so true made it all the more horrifying. Had Cable chosen to apply his literary mastery to the personal story of Louise Marie Drouet, the resulting work would have fit right into the *Grandissimes*. White Creole anger at Cable ran so rampant that in 1880 the poet Adrien Rouquette produced an anonymous pamphlet calling the author the result of "unnatural Southern growth, a bastard sprout."[29]

Working as a clerk in a cotton office and as a reporter for the *Picayune*, George Washington Cable enjoyed the perfect vantage point from which to observe the shifting patterns of New Orleans society. Although it remained the South's largest city, it was still in many ways a small town. He probably had met Michel Musson and his nephews and unquestionably knew Frederick Nash Ogden, for his exploits as a Confederate cavalryman served as inspiration for his novel *The Cavalier*. It is quite possible that Cable had even been aware of Arthur Toledano and Louise Marie Drouet. Cable had also been a supporter of the Unification Movement, as was his good friend and literary mentor the physician J. Dickson Bruns. Like many of the white conservatives in the wake of the movement's failure, Bruns increasingly soured on the idea of racial cooperation as an avenue for retaking the state from the Republicans. Cable lamented his friend's hardening attitudes, but he was a rare exception. As his writings increasingly made him persona non grata in the city, Cable decided to leave New Orleans and live the rest of his life in the Northeast. Although he was a member of the Civil War generation and even a Confederate veteran, the city of his birth had been rendered unfamiliar by the changes of war and Reconstruction. Postbellum life had also profoundly changed Cable.[30]

One piece of legislation that had passed under Kellogg's watch during the 1873 session sought to undermine the efforts of the Unification Movement. It was another civil rights bill with stronger enforcement language than the earlier versions passed during Warmoth's tenure as governor. Outside of the *Sauvinet* case, public accommodations laws had gone largely unenforced in New Orleans. Thus, when this new legislation went into effect at the beginning of 1874, several stories appeared in the city's newspapers about blacks who set out to test the extent of their newfound rights.[31]

David Bidwell's Academy of Music was one of New Orleans's most popular places of amusement. It was where the Grand Duke Alexis had supposedly fallen in love with the burlesque actress Lydia Thompson in a production of *Bluebeard* during the Carnival season of 1872. The proprietor claimed to operate his business in accordance with the civil rights law but was quick to note that a "committee of colored citizens" had requested separate seating and that he had acceded to their wishes by furnishing a well-appointed booth in the "Family Circle" portion of the theater. It was no Jim Crow gallery, Bidwell attested—the Family Circle was just outside the Dress Circle. And besides, he added, no policy required blacks to sit there.

One Saturday evening in early March 1874, Metropolitan Police captain Peter Joseph and his friend Frank Rierdon met for dinner and afterward headed down to Bidwell's Academy of Music for an evening show. Rierdon, a white man, stepped up to the ticket booth and purchased two parquette tickets before Joseph could remove his wallet. He handed a ticket to Joseph, and the two entered the theater's vestibule and walked over to the doorman, David Owens. Just as Rierdon entered the theater, he heard the doorman tell Joseph, "You can't go in!" Captain Joseph protested, but Owens repeated, "You can't go in! . . . Look at the ticket and you will see why!" Both men raised their voices in anger as Owens shoved Joseph out the door and onto St. Charles Avenue. During the scuffle, Joseph had demanded to speak with David Bidwell, but the proprietor was unavailable. He had been bedridden with an illness for several days and did not find out what his employee had done until he read about it in the paper the following Tuesday. The story contained disconcerting news indeed. Peter Joseph was suing him for five thousand dollars in damages because he had been refused a seat at the Academy of Music.[32]

It is difficult to tell from the legal proceedings exactly what motivated Owens to bar Joseph from the theater. A disclaimer on the ticket warned that the theater's management could refuse admission to anyone they chose, refunding the one-dollar admission price. Joseph was certain it was because he was a black man, although quite possibly it was also because he was a conspicuous member of the much-despised Metropolitan Police. Like Sauvinet, Joseph was of mixed race and possessed an exceedingly fair complexion and blue eyes. Barring him on account of race would have necessarily depended on inside knowledge of Joseph's identity on the part of Owens. In delivering his opinion, Judge Bartholomew L. Lynch, an Irish immigrant and a longtime scalawag, launched into an extended philippic about the conduct of Bidwell's theater and charged that it had been the Academy of Music's policy to segregate blacks into the Family Circle. Since there had been no testimony to this effect during the trial, one might conclude that the incident had been no accident at all and that Joseph, Rierdon, and Judge Lynch had set out to make an example of David Bidwell. Just as the Louisiana Supreme Court had done in the *Sauvinet* case, Lynch ruled in favor of Captain Joseph and ordered David Bidwell to pay the policeman one thousand dollars in punitive damages for the behavior of his employee.[33]

As Peter Joseph's court case played out that May, other black New Orleanians tested the waters. When a freedman named William Smith walked into Peligrini's soda fountain and ordered a drink, the proprietor told Smith that the price of the beverage had just jumped from a nickel to a dollar. It seems that business owners were already engaging in creative ways to circumvent the intent of civil rights legislation. When Smith expressed his disapproval, another patron physically ejected the disgruntled freedman from the premises. Smith did not get a soda that day, but he did not have to eat crow either. A judge ordered Peligrini to pay William Smith thirty dollars. The conservative New Orleans press also noticed the growing tendency of white Republicans to encourage such bold behavior. In May a white member of Kellogg's government accompanied a black man into Hugo Redwitz's beer saloon on Canal Street. They left after the bartender refused them service but returned four days later to try again. The exasperated Redwitz decided to serve the black man but not the "white agitator" accompanying him.[34]

Racial confrontation in the theaters and barrooms of New Orleans became a staple of the city's newspapers, but such activity seemed like child's play in comparison to what had been going on in Louisiana's hinterland. On Easter Sunday 1873, the single most deadly incident of the Reconstruction era took place in Grant Parish. Known as the Colfax Massacre, it began as a conflict between rival claimants to local office—bitter fruit of the competing McEnery and Kellogg legislatures. It ended with a group of white men slaughtering a sizable portion of the district's black militia company. Colfax was the most dramatic of these incidents, but other parts of rural Louisiana were in a state of complete lawlessness as 1874 began.[35]

When the Colfax defendants came to trial in New Orleans in April, the event demonstrated the degree to which racial attitudes had hardened in a year's time. R. H. Marr, the associate of E. John Ellis who had so vocally opposed Unification, was their lead defense attorney. Yet even men who had supported some of the city's most adventurous political experiments stood behind the eight men on trial. When a group of leading citizens organized a theatrical benefit for the defendants, Unification's chief proponent, Isaac Marks, lent a hand in the performance. The defense of the Colfax murderers ultimately resulted in the *Cruikshank* rulings, which dramatically undercut the Fourteenth Amendment's equal protection clause.[36]

In *The Birth of a Nation*, D. W. Griffith's celluloid adaptation of Thomas Dixon's novel *The Clansman*, the most dangerous villain of all those portrayed in the film was Silas Lynch, the mulatto who, with the supposed combination of white intelligence and black cunning, envisioned the creation of a black political empire. The fact that Lynch had fair skin was no accident. In New Orleans, the mixed-race community not only undermined the precepts of white supremacy; they undermined the practical codification of social and political segregation. In short, they were far more dangerous individually to a white-supremacist vision of social order than were the far more numerous freedmen. The multitude of fears that some whites harbored about mixed-race persons were not entirely new. Educated mixed-race Afro-Creoles had once been an unsettling presence under New Orleans's slave-holding regime, a system that was propped up in no small measure by white psychological fears of "the other." The postbellum era, however, enabled mixed-race New Orleanians to achieve heights that would have been unthinkable in antebellum days. Charles Sauvinet, Louise Marie Drouet, and Peter Joseph not only blazed new paths of social mobility after the war; their success was due in no small part to their fair skin. In varying degrees, each had straddled the line between blackness and the ever more attractive privileged world of whiteness. And they did not accomplish their goals alone. Friends and relatives on both sides of the color line endorsed their actions. For this reason, mixed-race New Orleanians were dangerous to those who hoped to bring about a white-supremacist ideal. As a consequence, people like Peter Joseph and Louise Marie Drouet became the focus of white anger. Such attacks on mixed-race New Orleanians originated in many quarters. Whether it was the Toledano clan's personal anxieties over racial purity or J. W. Durel's diatribes in the pages of *Le Carillion*, Comus's "Missing Links" pageant or Peter Joseph's being thrown out of the Academy of Music, it was clear that a broad spectrum of individuals had a vested interest in establishing a bichromatic racial standard. Black should be black, and white, white. Yet in the 1870s, these forces were only partly successful; it would take another two decades for true white supremacy to become the law of the land. In the interim, there would be a great deal of turmoil over race and its place in New Orleans.[37]

CHAPTER SEVEN

THE REDEEMER'S CARNIVAL

1874–1877

You have I suppose heard of our short but decisive little fight on
Monday evening last. . . . Ask Ruff what he thinks of the blood
thirsty braves now.

—J. C. Murphy to Flora Murphy, 1874

The long series of failures that had dogged white conservative political efforts
since 1872 had, by the start of 1874, finally convinced New Orleans moderates to
once and for all abandon notions of their independence from the Democratic
Party. Nowhere was this state of affairs more evident than among the commercial
men of Rex. "Xariffa," Rex's poet laureate, kept his majesty's subjects apprised of
their sovereign's travels when he was not parading down St. Charles Avenue. She
noted that he had pared down on luggage, after observing sarcastically that "a
carpet-bag was enough to take to New Orleans." Through Xariffa, the men of Rex
bitterly recounted the electoral struggle that had enveloped Mardi Gras of 1873:

And others, whose united plans,
Were laid the King to overthrow,
Seize the throne and scepter at one blow,
Tear off the crown from Rex's head,
And plant it on Grant's brow instead.

"Well well," said Rex, "This thing is racy,"
"We see it all, Collector Casey,"
"Bribed these, my lords, last Mardi Gras,"
"To make a king of his brother-in-law."[1]

William Pitt Kellogg's greatest political accomplishment may have been that
he finally provided the Redeemers with an enemy that they almost universally

despised. Outrage over his ascendancy spilled outside of Louisiana's borders, touching off congressional investigations and nationwide editorial condemnation. President Grant's indecisive meddling on behalf of his brother-in-law's political cronies in the Custom House also undermined Kellogg's legitimacy and fanned the flames of discontent both at home and in the nation at large. Even as 1874 began, some conservatives, including E. John Ellis, still looked toward these outside forces to reverse the election's outcome—however unlikely that might be. At the same time, few could ignore the growing mayhem that swept over many of Louisiana's rural parishes in the spring of 1874. Such chaos had made possible the flowering of the White League, a political movement with wide-reaching implications.

During a late-April 1874 meeting at the Opelousas courthouse in St. Landry Parish, those present drafted resolutions that led to the formation of the first White League. When the white men of St. Landry published their racially charged manifesto in the Opelousas *Courier*, it was clear that their goal was white supremacy in its most strident form. The League quickly spread across the state, traveling through networks of commerce and kinship. When the Committee White League of Opelousas brought the movement to neighboring St. Martin Parish, for instance, it asked a leading St. Martinville resident, Alexandre De-Clouet, to speak at the inaugural rally. There, DeClouet described a sinister Republican plot to turn the black man against the white. In familiar rhetoric, he claimed, "The credulity and the ignorance of the colored man has been made an instrument of ambitious, intriguing men." Further, he asserted that "a trashy list of little tyrants," including Warmoth, Kellogg, Longstreet, and Badger, had actively helped blacks plot against white Louisianans. The militaristic White League was going to serve as a first line of defense against this imagined threat.[2]

What constituted a local chapter of the White League varied considerably from parish to parish, both in organizational structure and in ideological stance. Some groups merely renamed their old conservative political clubs White League, while others underwent a more thoroughgoing reorganization, taking on a strongly militaristic character. Although many White League chapters railed against the black franchise, others took a paternalistic stance on race. Many accepted resolutions of an entirely local character and reflected partisan divisions that rarely extended beyond the parish lines. In most instances, however, the White League harnessed the social authority of the parish's emergent conservative white elite, men who had blood ties to both the Confederate cause and the more prominent families of the region. The most common themes echoed by the various White Leagues were the belief that conservative whites had for too long been their own worst enemy and the determination that the League, through either violence or rhetoric, would bring about the unity that had for so long eluded them.

By 1874, organized armed resistance to Republican rule already had a strong tradition both in rural Louisiana and in New Orleans, and such activity was in some fashion a natural extension of commonly accepted cultural modes of nineteenth-century political discourse. Just as the Knights of the White Camellia and other militarized bodies, such as Aristée Tissot's Broom Rangers, had emerged out of ward and parish political club rooms in the summer of 1868, these same organizations gave birth to the nascent White League in the spring of 1874. Although the motives, the membership, and the tactics of the White League varied considerably depending upon its location and its leadership, the League fell conceptually within a tradition of street politics whose roots could be traced back to the American Revolution. After the Civil War, however, Republicans, and more especially Democratic conservatives in the South, transformed the public display of ward politics by fusing traditional cultural forms with the military lessons they had learned during four years of bloody warfare. This militarization of street politics by a generation of young veterans had been apparent in New Orleans as early as the Riot of 1866 and had become a mature cultural form by the time of the Republican intraparty feud of 1871. It reached its climax with the emergence of the White League in the spring of 1874. Unable to unite conservatives in their quest for regime change by the force of political rhetoric alone, influential men across Louisiana instead transformed the political canvass into the familiar language of a military-style campaign. In doing so, they not only offered veterans an opportunity to return to the field of battle, where they might correct the discomforting memories of the past, but also held out the prospect of glory to a rising generation of young men for whom the accident of birth had denied them their own participation in the most defining event of the age.

The Enforcement Acts of 1870–71 may have temporarily put the most outrageous forms of organized political violence into abeyance, but they neither crushed conservative aspirations toward armed resistance nor disrupted the organizational structures from which such strategies emerged. Moreover, as laws, they stood on shaky constitutional ground. When the verdict in the *Slaughterhouse* cases in 1873 imposed severe restrictions on the federal government's ability to enforce the equal protection clause of the Fourteenth Amendment, it greatly undermined the legal probity of the Enforcement Acts. The promise of federal military protection for Republican regimes in the South eroded further when the *Cruikshank* cases made their way through the federal court system in the spring of 1874. Although the Supreme Court of the United States did not make a final ruling on

Cruikshank until 1876, preliminary victories in lower courts in New Orleans must surely have encouraged, and perhaps even inspired, conservative whites in Louisiana to resort to militarized tactics. Yet what undoubtedly fueled the remarkable growth of this widespread and surprisingly coherent political movement was the sense of outrage, whether justified or not, felt by a growing plurality of native white Southerners. Referring to Kellogg as a "usurper" and his regime, as Alexandre DeClouet termed it, a "tyranny," the White League successfully built myths that led to a justification for organized violence. As noted Western historian Richard Slotkin has observed, the perpetrators of postbellum counterrevolutionary violence tapped into deep-seated American mythologies about unpopular government rule and made Conservative violence against Republicanism seem reasonable to the nation at large. Knowing full well that national newspapers would chronicle their counterrevolution, the leaders of the White League crafted their message to suit both a local and a national audience. If past failures at redemption had taught white conservatives anything, it was that nothing could be left to chance when it came to promoting the rightness of their cause.[3]

With the growth of the White League aided by rural chaos and abetted by conservative legal victories in the federal judiciary, many on both sides of the political fence in New Orleans expected that a chapter of the order might soon form in their city. This point was not lost on Frederick Nash Ogden, who had, in anticipation of the 1874 political season, called to order the old Crescent City Democratic Club, an organization that had emerged during the mayhem of 1868. At Eagle Hall on Prytania Street, he called together old friends such as business partner William Bell and former Warmoth militia officers William J. Behan and James B. Walton. Having observed nothing but discord among their ranks since the end of the war, these men were easily able to identify a lack of cohesion among their associates in the business community as the root cause of their own political insignificance. This time, like their rural counterparts, they were going to leave nothing to chance. In late June, Ogden and his cohorts conspired with the *Picayune*'s editors to unleash a fabricated scandal that added great urgency to the formation of the Crescent City White League.[4]

The June 30 edition of the *Picayune* ominously warned the citizens of New Orleans of a pending outbreak of black violence. On the Fourth of July, the "Black Leagues" were going to descend upon the city to assert their civil rights. Not only would these dangerous vandals demand service in the city's saloons and soda fountains, transportation on public conveyances, and accommodation at all places of business, but they also had evil designs against the white men and women of New Orleans. The *Picayune* continued, "If resisted, they were to at once fire and kill the proprietor and as many white men as possible, and then, supported by the other colored people who would rally to their support, and, as was expressed, take it for themselves, kill all the men and *keep all the women*." Such rhetoric was reminiscent of the gendered appeals that the city's Democratic ward clubs had made to their young members in the fall canvass of 1872, but it was far more overt. Recognizing the failures of the past, the architects of the White League left little to the imagination.[5]

The following day, the *Republican* accused the *Picayune* of political "bushwhacking," and Pinchback's *Louisianian* was quick to condemn the White League as the successor of the Ku Klux Klan and the Knights of the White Camellia. Despite the denials of Longstreet, Badger, and Kellogg about the presence of any such "Black Leagues," as well as the doubts voiced even by competing conservative newspapers, the *Picayune* continued the assault for several more days. Included among the more detailed information about the supposed Black League was what the paper claimed to be an intercepted copy of the organization's bylaws and a list of theatrical hailing signs that read like the script from a badly conceived minstrel show. The *Picayune*'s shameless race-baiting stories successfully fed on fears harbored by many white New Orleanians about the true motivations of civil rights legislation and the widespread perception that black people had grown far too assertive in demanding their rights.[6]

Amid this uproar, on July 1 the *Picayune* announced the formation of the Crescent City White League, with none other than Frederick Nash Ogden as president. While Ogden had always been an ardent foe of Republicanism as well as a dedicated disciple of violent resistance, many of the group's other foundational members were past Reformers, Liberal Republicans, and Unifiers who had been repeatedly burned by efforts toward political moderation. Recruits to the Crescent City White League quickly emerged in large numbers. Within weeks, more than fifteen hundred men had formed into dozens of military-style companies. Those who joined the White League in New Orleans were a diverse bunch. Tradesmen, such as carpenters, grocers, and tinsmiths belonged, as did laborers and stevedores, although more common were professional men from Factor's Row: clerks, accountants, sugar and cotton factors, weighers, and lawyers. Many of the members had strong social ties and belonged to urbane Carnival societies such as the Mistick Krewe of Comus or fraternal organizations like the Elks. That more than one hundred members of the exclusive Pickwick Club joined also lent the organization a certain amount of cachet. Undoubtedly, Fred Ogden's charismatic presence among the Pickwickians contributed to this strong enrollment. James B. Walton's beloved Washington Artillery gave its support and added both prestige and martial credibility to the League. Dozens of other military-style political parade clubs that had sprung up in every ward of the city during the election of 1872 now recast their membership as ward White Leagues, supplying an existing framework for this army of Redemption.[7]

The Crescent City White League was also overwhelmingly a youth movement, inspiring the rising generation to act like men, as Tissot had urged during the 1872 political canvass. Although the organization's leadership had a wealth of combat experience, about 30 percent of the members had been born after 1850 and would have been too young to fight in the war. Indeed, the median age of the White League, counting officers and enlisted men together, was only about twenty-eight (see appendix B). Of the sample, 44.5 percent were Confederate veterans, and among these, a significant number were born between 1845 and 1847 and were among the war's youngest combatants. These youthful Leaguers included men like Thomas Brandenburg, a twenty-six-year-old tinsmith. Brandenburg had not served during the Civil War, but his older brother had joined the Confederacy and had died in the notorious Union prison at Elmira two months before Appomattox. Eighteen-year-old George Beers, the son of a wealthy cotton broker, was clerking in a law office when he joined the White League. Beers was only six years old when New Orleans fell to the Union. Born in 1848, John Bachemin served with the Twentieth Louisiana Infantry but was dropped from its rolls, perhaps for being too young. (At the very most, he would have been seventeen at war's end.) The League offered these young men an opportunity to prove their worth to their fathers, their older brothers, and themselves. Defeat and the humiliation of federal Reconstruction policy had clouded their youth. The White League promised to supply them with an unexpected second chance at martial glory.[8]

Many of the League's adherents also hoped the movement would help to reverse the downward mobility that many of their families had witnessed since the war. James Cross Murphy, a twenty-four-year-old sugar broker, certainly felt this way. He personally had done well in the Crescent City, but he frequently sent money to relatives who lived on plantations in cane country and had felt the pinch of hard times. Late that summer his uncle offered these words of advice: "I hope there will be no bloodshed, but if Kellogg attempts any of his 'shenanigans,' give it to 'em hot and heavy." Twenty-year-old Pickwickian Mortimer Norton Wisdom harbored deep resentment for the reversal of fortune that Southern defeat had dealt his family. When he was a boy, his mother had brought him to visit Confederate prisoners held in the Custom House. Financial considerations now forced him to abandon lofty dreams of "fame and honor," prompting him instead to join "the common crowd of petty money-grubbing lawyers."⁹

The average age of a White League officer was thirty-four, and more often than not he had served with distinction in the Confederate army. Few officers were men in their twenties, and few were over forty. They were members of Oliver Wendell Holmes's "generation born about 1840," still young enough to have a long political future, yet old enough and with sufficient critical life experiences to be worthy of the respect of their employees, co-workers, and younger siblings. They were also overwhelmingly from that generation of junior officers who, during the Civil War, had shouldered the Confederacy's greatest day-to-day burdens of leadership on the battlefield. They included thirty-year-old R. C. Bond, who had enlisted in 1861 and had managed to surrender on three different occasions during his four years of service. Men like Eugene Waggaman and James B. Walton, both of whom had been senior commanders during the war and who belonged to an older generation, occupied inconspicuous roles in the White League's command structure. The White League was led by men in their late thirties, like Ellis and Ogden, who represented the political ascendancy of the rising war generation.¹⁰

For others, a host of complicated personal reasons undoubtedly contributed to their membership in the White League. Edmund Arthur Toledano seemed to be doing well financially, but his recently completed court battle with his mixed-race cousin Louise Marie Drouet may have left him grappling with questions of racial identity and community standing. Perhaps the memory of his confrontation with an assertive black domestic servant on the Carrollton Railroad still made his blood boil. If character patterns reveal anything, the incessantly glad-handing René Degas, who was the nephew of Michel Musson, joined primarily to network with important members of the community. Unlike his brothers Achille and Edgar, René had shirked military duty during the Franco-Prussian War, and perhaps he believed the White League might offer his last opportunity to prove himself a man. He may also have been heavily influenced by his uncle Michel Musson, if not by Fred Ogden himself.

Nobody was more ready for a change of government than E. John Ellis. A shortage of clients had never been a problem for the Ellis brothers' New Orleans law firm; it was more a shortage of clients who actually paid their bills. The financial panic that occurred during the fall of 1873 only exacerbated the tight money situation, and Ellis found himself increasingly robbing Peter to pay Paul. In November he sold a home, hoping to "lighten the ship enough to weather the storm." In his mind, Ellis clearly tied the Redemption of Louisiana by white conservatives to the return to prosperity. Writing his brother Thomas, he noted, "If we win politically, as I now firmly believe we shall, then the balance is easy."[11]

Ellis had also taken notice of the White Leagues cropping up all over the state. "The political pot is boiling," he told Thomas. Yet he worried at some level that racial violence would give the Republicans an excuse to request federal troops and establish martial law. Certainly, the testimony that both he and Thomas gave before the House Committee in the late spring of 1869 about his own activity in the Knights of the White Camellia lurked in the back of his mind. "Carpet-bag Gov'ts have fed on riots, slaughter, Ku Klux stories, &c, &c, and are now dying for want of such food," noted Ellis. He warned that the White Leagues "should be quiet for a while. Later in the canvass events will so shape themselves as to render White Leagues *a necessity*." Until then, to be "organizing leagues on a color basis, the government will be against us; they will seem in the defensive, we in the aggressive. Acts of violence will be hereafter laid at our door." He offered one last piece of advice: "This should be kept quiet!"[12]

The political pot boiled over that August in Coushatta, the personal Red River Parish kingdom of carpetbagger Marshall Harvey Twitchell. The Vermont native had flourished in Coushatta after arriving with the Freedmen's Bureau in 1865. He married a local girl and made a small fortune in a variety of business enterprises. Twitchell tried to follow in Warmoth's footsteps by including some Democrats in a broad-based parish coalition, but he also made a lot of enemies along the way. Local White Leaguers descended upon Coushatta in the summer of 1874, ostensibly to defend against a supposed attack by armed blacks. Not surprisingly, they also used it as the pretext for forcibly ejecting Twitchell and his cronies. The scene turned ugly as the White League escorted a handful of unarmed white Republicans outside the city and murdered them in cold blood.[13]

The wanton bloodshed at Coushatta, along with other, less spectacular, episodes of violence, caused some people in New Orleans, including Father Ryan of the *Morning Star and Catholic Messenger*, to question the wisdom of organizing the political canvass along the White League's military lines. In an editorial titled "Let Well Enough Alone," Ryan spoke pointedly of Fred Ogden and the commercially connected men of the White League:

> There is a certain fire and tow element in this State, as well as in every other community, which is more distinguished for energy than wisdom. In other words, there is a kind of madness which occasionally seizes men and makes gamblers of them. Sometimes they gamble in cotton, sometimes in money, and sometimes in blood. That is, they take the chances blindly without any definite

reason to presume on success more than failure. Now, it is well known that the Carondelet speculators generally die beggars; we know that the more undisguised gamblers of St. Charles Street are not endowed with much of the respect and confidence of their fellow citizens; and what are we to think of the other adventurers—those who gamble in revolution and blood?[14]

As the sun set on September 1, 1874, crowds converged on the Varieties Theater in New Orleans for a dramatic night political rally. The assembly numbered close to ten thousand people, including several companies of the White League. Bands played and banners illuminated by torchlight gave a festive appearance, yet a look of solemn reserve characterized the crowd as they waited for their political leaders. The White League had spent the balance of the summer purchasing weapons, drilling, and planning for warfare. Now they awaited instructions for further action. In this increasingly explosive atmosphere, the speeches that night had to accomplish the delicate task of rallying support without inciting a riot.

John McEnery was the first speaker at this out-of-season Carnival. Though feeling quite ill, he was not about to miss an opportunity to address such a large crowd of supporters. Defending the Coushatta killers, McEnery rhetorically asked what other options the people had than to free themselves from "plundering officials." His remarks were considerably softer than they had been during a rural speech where he declared whites would "wade in blood knee deep" before submitting to Kellogg, but McEnery's words remained forceful. In closing he said Louisiana had to have an "honest" and "fair election—peaceably, if we can; forcibly if we must."[15]

E. John Ellis must have held his breath as he listened to McEnery's fiery oratory. He worried that any further encouragement from above might lead to uncontrolled chaos, not only in the rural parishes but in New Orleans as well. Once Ellis took the podium, he was quick to add some disclaimers: "We must not trouble the Negro; he is but the indirect cause of our troubles. Let him vote for his candidates, whoever they may be." Ellis also warned the crowd, "There are men who need watching, men who pretend to be with us." Ever willing to point out the hypocrisy within his own party, he continued, "Kellogg raised on Carondelet Street the money that fitted out the Metropolitans." The young lawyer knew all too well how easily men in New Orleans could be bought, and he remained wary of the League's ability to forge true unity. Undoubtedly, he still felt the sting of betrayal from Bolivar Edwards's brief fling with the Republicans two years earlier.[16]

In the minds of a lot of White Leaguers, the time was ripe for revolution, and there were numerous indications that they were correct. Nationally, scandal and a weak economy had made the American voter increasingly weary of expensive federal Reconstruction policies and Ulysses S. Grant's Republican Party. The League also looked hopefully toward events that had taken place in Texas earlier in the year. Besieged by Democratic paramilitaries in Austin, the recently reelected Republican governor sent an urgent telegram to Grant for help, but the president left his pleas unanswered. Violence had redeemed Texas. In August, the "White's Man Party" in Vicksburg, Mississippi, had carried a local election by similar means. The U.S. Army had always been the greatest impediment to political violence in the South because, as a rule, armed partisans who would otherwise attack a state militia scrupulously avoided conflict with federal troops. Yet there was not much prospect of federal troops intervening in any coming conflict in New Orleans, for most of the soldiers normally garrisoned at nearby Chalmette had been sent away for fear that they might contract yellow fever. Only nineteen personnel remained on duty in the region, and they could scarcely leave the barracks without completely abandoning their post. With so few obstacles in place, all signs pointed to revolution.[17]

The militaristic activities of the White League did not go unnoticed by Algernon Sydney Badger, however, and he felt particularly heartened by the cooperation of Arthur Olivier, a gun dealer on Canal Street. Olivier had warned the Metropolitans' superintendent that several arms shipments destined for the White League were on their way, and the gun broker thoughtfully pointed out where these shipments might be best intercepted. Badger took the bait. As Olivier had hoped, the Metropolitans made a series of raids, netting a handful of obsolete Civil War surplus percussion muskets. The next day, the *Picayune* howled with mocking contempt at the seizure of private property "by a squad of valiant Metropolitans on a light spring wagon." The conservatives had once again played Badger like a fiddle, and anti-Grant newspapers in the North picked up the story and used it to ridicule Kellogg's government. Badger undoubtedly grew suspicious when Olivier again returned to his office with an invoice for a "large shipment of arms" aboard the steamer *Mississippi*, which sat docked along the waterfront in front of Jackson Square. The White League, Olivier informed Badger, intended to receive the arms through force on the afternoon of Monday, September 14.[18]

With the stage set for confrontation, a group of conservative leaders and White League officers met on September 12, a Saturday night. Davidson Bradfute Penn, the Bostonian and former Liberal Republican who had been the Fusion lieutenant governor, felt that attacking the Metropolitans was unwise. Like E. John Ellis, who had become a confidant and friend since the campaign of 1872, Penn believed that violence might once again serve as a pretense for federal intervention in Louisiana's political affairs. He suggested that instead a small group of veteran White Leaguers make a covert attack on the statehouse and abduct Kellogg and his lieutenants. The idea was an unpopular one, particularly with Ogden and McEnery. The failure of Ogden's dismal 1873 Cabildo raid probably danced through Penn's mind when he made another suggestion. He wanted the League to call a great meeting of the people. If the people came out en masse to support their cause, he would take responsibility for Kellogg's removal. Penn's satisfaction was important, because everyone present was aware that McEnery had once again planned to leave town before any fighting took place. E. John Ellis noted of McEnery, "Brave and honest and true hearted he lacks the qualities of a leader. He shrinks from responsibility." Instead the burden of leadership was going to land on the shoulders of Penn and a group of men who were all under age forty. Penn took overall command of the political leadership of the rebellion, and to avoid any confusion, he appointed Frederick Nash Ogden as the commanding general of all White League forces.[19]

The League's leadership also authorized George Washington Cable's old literary mentor J. Dickson Bruns to draft a proclamation for publication in Sunday morning's *Picayune*. The address brimmed with indignation for Kellogg's government and lamented the infringement of Second Amendment rights. In closing, Bruns melodramatically proclaimed: "*Declare that you are, of right ought to be, and mean to be free.*" For those who missed the paper, the League also blanketed the downtown with handbills announcing a mass meeting at the Clay Statue scheduled for Monday at eleven o'clock in the morning. The declaration promised speeches from a list of the city's most prominent citizens, including Michel Musson.[20]

David Bradfute Penn had a lot on his mind that Monday morning as he waited for the St. Charles Avenue streetcar. Stepping aboard, he noticed a soldierly-looking man wearing a blue Metropolitan policeman's uniform. Algernon Sydney Badger and Penn exchanged greetings then and sat in silence as the car lurched down St. Charles. It was a chance meeting between a man about to lead a rebellion and another charged with the responsibility of defeating it. When they had reached the American side of Canal Street, Penn got out. The car continued on with Badger, and Penn walked down to the Boston Club to meet with the committee members who were scheduled to speak at the mass meeting.[21]

As eleven o'clock approached, a great crowd of people gathered at the Henry Clay statue. The sweltering September heat had already risen by eleven thirty, when the doors of the Crescent City Billiard Hall's gallery opened above. Onto the balcony walked a group of distinguished citizens, including R. H. Marr, Michel

Musson, and Dr. Cornelius Beard, a man who had, in 1861, rallied Creoles to the Confederate cause by singing the *Marseillaise* on Canal Street. Musson undoubtedly looked out over the assembly with satisfaction. For the past decade he had left no stone unturned in his quest, which included the ill-fated Unification Movement of the previous summer, to force the Republican Party from office. Now he stood on a balcony looking across an energized mass of people who sought resolution through violence. Spouting fiery rhetoric, R. H. Marr worked the crowd into such a fever pitch that it descended into a shouting chant of "Hang Kellogg!" As the meeting's leaders dispatched a messenger to request Kellogg's abdication, Penn quietly made his way through the raucous assembly. He was satisfied that a sufficient number of people in New Orleans were behind the White League.[22]

Leaving the shouting throng at the Clay Statue behind, Penn turned down Camp Street and walked several blocks to the hardware store of Kursheedt & Bienvenu, where Frederick Nash Ogden waited for him with other White League commanders. As these men met to add the finishing touches to their overall strategy for attack, different companies of White Leagues had already fanned across much of the city upriver from Canal Street, using Poydras Street as a general line of defense. After reviewing his comrade's plans, Penn issued a written statement to the "People of Louisiana" outlining the White League's justification for action. He then followed it with a second notice, to "the colored people of the State of Louisiana," that he concluded with "The rights of the colored, as well as the white races, we are determined to uphold and defend." Penn knew that once the telegraph wires lit up with news of rebellion, the eyes of the nation would be on New Orleans. He left Ogden and the White League's military leadership and headed farther down Camp Street to a rallying point in Tivoli Circle (today, Lee Circle). There he joined his adjutant general and closest companion for the next three tumultuous days, E. John Ellis. With the sun now a broiling ball of fire in the sky, Penn dashed off a note to Ogden with a suggestion that he keep the men from getting bored or trigger happy by having them build additional barricades. He also queried as to whether the League had severed the telegraph wires between the train stations, ordering that it be done at once.[23]

Across town at the Jackson Square police station, James Longstreet and Badger weighed their options for confronting the pending collision. Much like John McEnery, his political counterpart who had left town well in advance of any fighting, William Pitt Kellogg had not the stomach for street violence and had just informed his subordinates that he would monitor the day's events from the sanctuary of the federal Custom House. For all practical purposes, the preservation of

Louisiana's Republican regime now rested upon the shoulders of Badger, Longstreet, and those Metropolitan policemen and state militia who remained under their command. Moreover, with the vast majority of soldiers from the army's local garrison far away, they had no hope of federal support. Around two o'clock came a report of White Leaguers rallying on Poydras Street and heading toward the river. The two veteran soldiers quickly sent their forces to hold the Custom House and the levee where it intersected Canal. At the foot of Canal Street stood the "Iron building," an ornate structure made of cast iron, built to house the city's waterworks. Despite Badger's doubts, Longstreet believed it would make a good anchor for the Metropolitan's line. By three-thirty in the afternoon, Badger had reached the location, with more than one hundred Metropolitans, artillery pieces shotted (loaded) with canister, and a Gatling gun. Clutching their Winchesters in the late afternoon heat, they awaited the enemy's advance.[24]

Earlier that same Monday morning, Edmund Arthur Toledano had grabbed his rifle and left his Garden District home. By nine o'clock, he had joined dozens of other White League volunteers at Eagle Hall, not four blocks from the house on Constance Street where his cousin Louise Marie Drouet was born.[25] Much of the morning was spent in anxious waiting and drinking coffee, but finally, around one-thirty in the afternoon, the word came from Colonel Behan to head toward Poydras Street. As he and the rest of Company A moved down Poydras, they saw the makeshift barricades at each cross street that headed toward Canal. Streetcars, iron plates, barrels, mattresses, and other assorted debris had been thrown up in a defensive position. As four o'clock approached, Toledano's company reached Delta Street. Next was the levee and combat.

When Company A wheeled left onto the levee, they saw before them an imposing line of artillery and Metropolitan policemen. Suddenly, stabs of flame and rising smoke erupted from the police's lines. As Toledano and his comrades took cover among the scattered cotton bales on the levee, they heard something that not even the veterans had heard before—the steady "pop-pop-pop" of a Gatling gun. With projectiles whizzing past their heads, Company A gathered their nerves and began returning sporadic fire at the Metropolitan line. On their right flank, Captain Reuben Pleasants's Company E countered with withering fire from their fine Remington rolling-block rifles. Colonel Behan ordered his men forward. Already, members of Company A had advanced pell-mell through the piles of freight that sat scattered on the expanse of the levee between themselves and the Metropolitans. In moments, it became a wild, disorganized charge. As Toledano and the rest of his company pressed forward, a bullet mortally wounded the popular young cotton factor Samuel Newman Jr., and some of his fellow volunteers fell wounded. Under such fire Toledano passed the head of Gravier Street and then the corner of Canal. The Iron building had probably just come into the veteran's view, when a bullet slammed into his body and jerked him to the ground. Lying amid the debris and the dung of draft animals on the earthen levee, he quickly bled to death.

Meanwhile, the situation had become quite hot for General Badger. Firing from the rooftops and windows of surrounding buildings, White League snipers had picked off most of the Metropolitan artillerists who served the Gatling gun and the howitzers. From the enemy's right came a blistering and accurate fire, and the rest of the League was in a haphazard charge toward the Metropolitan center. A bullet had already broken Badger's left arm, and another soon passed through his right hand. The commander saw the alarm growing in his men's eyes with every passing second and shouted at them to hold their position. Just as he did so, another bullet shattered his right leg. He crumbled to the ground as a fourth round passed through his body. With Badger's fall, the Metropolitans broke in panic with Leaguers in hot pursuit. They left their brave leader behind, lying critically wounded in the street in front of the Iron building.

White League captain Douglas Kilpatrick quickly came upon Badger's position. His young and inexperienced volunteers stood gaping at the Metropolitan commander as though they had not yet quite processed the dramatic scene that had just unfolded in front of them. Kilpatrick, who had fled occupied New Orleans when he was just eighteen to enlist in the Washington Artillery, watched Badger's courageous stand with admiration. He immediately ordered four of his men to fetch a mattress and to carry the badly wounded police superintendent to Charity Hospital. As the Leaguers carried Badger around the corner of Dauphine and Bourbon, a group of "loafers" shouted "Kill him! kill him!" but his escort pushed them back. Badger's valor had finally won the respect of his adversaries. He did not know yet whether he would live to enjoy such recognition.

As Frederick Ogden surveyed the action from the intersection of Common and Tchoupitoulas, a bullet struck and killed his horse. His aide quickly turned over his own mount, and the commanding general again moved coolly through the lines. René Degas found his commander's boldness in battle almost intoxicating as he watched the veteran soldier ride past his position at the corner of Camp and Canal. Soon Ogden commanded Degas's company, the Washington White League, forward to assault the enemy's position. After a mad dash across the enormous width of Canal Street, René's and his comrades turned down Charters on the far side of the Custom House. Here they collided with a reserve force of Metropolitans commanded by captains Octave Rey and Peter Joseph. The two

Afro-Creole officers had been sent to guard a post far from the main fight but soon found themselves in the midst of a smart clash guarding the distant flank of the Custom House. They held the line for a brief while, but soon it became clear that the fight was going badly for their comrades elsewhere. A stream of Metropolitans without their weapons, some hatless, others without even their uniform coats, tore past their rear in a mad panic for Jackson Square. Twenty minutes into the battle, it had turned into a White League rout.

Some brutal minutes followed as defeated Metropolitans surrendered or ran for whatever cover they could find. Some made it to the Custom House, where federal jurisdiction protected them. Others got as far as the Cabildo or the state arsenal, where they briefly rallied. The rest who did not make their way home holed up in the statehouse, which had recently been moved from the Mechanics' Institute to the old St. Louis Hotel in the French Quarter. Here they joined some three hundred members of the black state militia units who had yet to receive orders from Longstreet to fight. They had good reason to run. A grisly scene descended upon Charity Hospital, where heat, blood, and flies competed with the smell of death for primacy. Surgeons busily worked on Algernon Badger's leg but found that they could not save it. By four thirty in the afternoon, another wave of wounded and dying men began trickling in. The twenty-four-year-old laborer William Omand, only a bystander, had been shot mortally in the chest while trying to cross Tchoupitoulas Street. Charles Kitt, a homeless Chinese man, sought treatment for a gunshot wound to his arm. Fidel Keller, the old bookseller whom Benjamin Butler had once sent to Ship Island for mocking Union authority, arrived with a bullet in his leg. He never recovered. Some Metropolitans also made it safely to the hospital, including William Brown, who, like his commander, underwent an amputation that day.[26]

Although it was a brief fight, it left a shocking amount of carnage in the streets of New Orleans. In addition to Toledano, another fifteen White Leaguers were either dead or dying. Among the dead was Antoine Bozonier, Frederick Ogden's friend and antebellum boardinghouse roommate. Bozonier was also Aristée Tissot's brother-in-law. Thirteen policemen had been killed or mortally wounded, as were six bystanders. One of the noncombatants, a black man named John May, had been operating a streetcar on Magazine Street when he was shot in the head by unknown assailants. The bullet carried away the top of his skull and showered his brains about the interior of the vehicle. J. M. West, a reporter for the *New Orleans Times*, was unarmed and observing the battle from Canal Street when someone from the Custom House took advantage of the chaos and cut him down with a rifle. Bodies of several Metropolitans lay dead about the Iron building, where Badger had taken his stand, including James McManus, Michael O'Keefe, Edward Simmons, and Rudolph Zipple. If the coroner's inquest conducted later was accurate, they had been wounded in the fight but were finished off with a pistol shot to the forehead.[27]

Frederick Ogden spent the night of the fourteenth at his headquarters on Camp Street at the store of Kursheedt & Bienvenu. Throughout the overnight hours, he received dispatches from the various companies of the White League, who by now had established martial law in the city. Ogden also received telegrams from well-wishers in neighboring states. Former Confederate general Braxton Bragg cabled from Galveston, wishing the League a "speedy delivery." Another message from San Antonio inquired whether the White League needed any assistance. The chief of police of Louisville, Kentucky, offered the service of five hundred additional volunteers. Outside of the League's casualties, it had been a pretty successful day.[28]

Early the next morning, the few remaining Metropolitans and militia surrendered the Jackson Square police station and the state arsenal. The arsenal represented quite a windfall for the League, and the insurgents generously distributed the state militia's property. League volunteers who owned obsolete Civil War muzzle-loading rifles now walked off with shiny new Winchesters, Spencer carbines, and breech-loading "Trapdoor" Springfield rifles—the current arm of the U.S. Army. Drunk with enthusiasm, the victors began plundering the offices of Republican officials. One combatant who helped seize Kellogg's office dashed off a note to his wife, who was waiting at home with their infant child: "I write this sitting at the desk of Mr. H.C. Clark, ex-private sec. Of the Ex Gov Kellogg." Composing his note just before sunrise on the fifteenth, the Leaguer continued: "I never have seen so complete an uprising of the people and their faces indicated the reaction a change of government must produce. The citizen troops were received with a complete ovation."[29]

At two o'clock in the afternoon of September 15, large groups of White League members descended upon D. B. Penn's home on St. Charles Avenue. Since McEnery was still away "visiting friends" in Vicksburg, the assembly thought it appropriate to install Penn as the governor of Louisiana. Penn, Marr, and E. John Ellis entered a carriage outside the residence and made a triumphant ride to the captured statehouse. The scene must have resembled a successful coup d'état in a banana republic. Thousands crowded around the statehouse's open galleries for a look at their victorious leadership. White League companies, now dressed in captured state uniforms, formed an honor guard. Penn stepped forward to speak. He asked the people to head to church at one o'clock in the morning to give thanks to God for the day's victory and to request continued protection. E. John Ellis, mindful of the crowd's high spirits and perhaps reminded by his days in the Knights of the White Camellia of how popular violence could easily disintegrate into an uncontrolled riot, reminded them not to "let an act of oppression or intolerance dim the luster of victory."[30]

What E. John Ellis and Davidson Penn knew, as many in the crowd did not, was that federal troops were already on their way to New Orleans. When President Grant first heard of the White League's rebellion, he was so enraged that he vowed to "clean them out" even if it meant that he had to take to the field himself. He later thought better of that idea and instead delegated the task to his subordinates. This duty ultimately fell to General William H. Emory, who, with a group of army officers charged with negotiating the League's surrender, arrived in New Orleans the night of the sixteenth. When their train pulled into the station, they noticed a brass band waiting on the platform. Disembarking, they soon discovered that John McEnery had also just arrived in New Orleans—on the same train.[31]

Later that night, Emory held a conference with Penn and McEnery, informing them that the federal government intended to use force to restore Kellogg. Foreseeing no positive result of defiance, the rebel leaders assented to peaceably surrender the city, which for the past forty-eight hours had been under their control. At four in the afternoon on September 17, McEnery yielded office to Emory's subordinate, Colonel John R. Brooke. Two days later, Brooke restored Kellogg. E. John Ellis described the scene to his brother Thomas: "I was present at our surrender—It was a very sad scene. As the Adjutant General I rec'd Gen. Brooke of the USA. McEnery & his officers clustered about him all in civilian garb; Gen. Brooke and Staff brilliantly uniformed; they came with formal demand in the name of the US Govt: McEnery with husky broken voice all trembling with emotion read his reply. . . . The Soldier was then seated in the Governor's chair and we all quietly withdrew and proceeded up Royal Street to Canal. Men stood by with stern sad faces & women wept."[32]

Four days after the White League had violently taken the Crescent City, William Pitt Kellogg returned to the governor's chair. From this standpoint, the battle was a failure for the White League. Yet this was about the only aspect in which they did not benefit. When federal authorities took over New Orleans, the U.S. troops not only failed to pursue those who had just days earlier mounted coup against the lawfully recognized civil government of the city; these same soldiers cheered the victorious White League as they handed over policing duties of New Orleans to the U.S. Army. It was an unmistakable reflection of the nation's growing distaste for Republican Reconstruction policy and perhaps even black civil rights. Not a single political leader, officer, or soldier of the White League ever faced criminal prosecution for his role in the bloodshed. Much of this outcome had to do with the widespread belief—both in Louisiana and elsewhere—that Kellogg's regime was an illegitimate one. Moreover, while the League's violence had cost the lives of innocent bystanders and Metropolitan policemen, in victory they remained peaceable. Unlike Colfax or Coushatta, few of the day's victims were black, and there had been no lynching. The Crescent City White League's careful planning of this carnival of violence did much to promote the perception across the nation that their rebellion was justified.

Although the White League's action shocked Americans everywhere, the reaction it provoked was nearly the inverse of the outrage that accompanied news reports of the violence of 1866 and 1868. Overwhelmingly, white America saw the League's rebellion as the justifiable actions of a wronged people, buying unquestioningly into what proved a remarkably enduring conservative myth of Republican tyranny. When pugnacious Phil Sheridan suggested in December 1874 that the army round the Leaguers up as "banditti" and declared that, unlike William Pitt Kellogg, "he was not afraid" of the band of white Southern rebels, his comments mostly drew impatient sighs from Northern politicians and muffled guffaws from New Orleans elites. Although the situation in the city was still too hot for organized parading of Rex and the Mistick Krewe in February 1875, one waggish masker costumed himself in stolen militia garb, complete with contraband rifle and cartridge box, and marched through the streets responding to Sheridan with a placard emblazoned with "I am not afraid!" The clash, which white New Orleanians quickly dubbed "The Battle of Liberty Place," had also brought almost complete, if temporary, political unanimity to conservative whites in Louisiana. Even doubting voices such as Father Ryan's *Morning Star and Catholic Messenger* applauded the action on Canal Street. "In fact," wrote Ryan, "the contest was carried on by the citizen soldiery with all the etiquette of the duello. We are opposed to that institution, but there is a great deal of wise precaution and genuine humanity coupled with the wrong of its murderous intent."[33]

Frederick Nash Ogden quickly emerged as the great hero of the "Battle of Liberty Place," and certainly his military leadership had a lot to do with the White League's victory in the clash that took place on Canal Street. Yet from a political standpoint, conservative forces owed a much greater debt of gratitude to Davidson Penn and E. John Ellis, both of whom understood that the intemperate race-baiting conducted by some of their colleagues could easily have led to another Mechanics' Institute–style riot, thereby undermining the League's claim to political justification. If the Crescent City White League had conducted itself the way its rural counterpart in Coushatta had, Northerners would have taken Phil Sheridan's comments more seriously.

The battle had also been a transcendent moment for the city of New Orleans, surpassed in magnitude only by its fall to the Union navy in April 1862. Just as Rex and Comus had legitimated the elite's place atop the city's social ladder, the White League's Carnival of Redemption announced its arrival as an important force in the political arena. Yet more importantly, the battle had furnished succor to the damaged psyches of an entire generation of Southern white men, particularly for the great number among them who had been too young to wear Confederate gray. For the Confederate veterans who had taken part, to be able to say that one had fought the Metropolitans on September 14 provided a sense of vindication that no Lost Cause monument could ever hope to match.[34]

After Arthur Toledano's death at the "Battle of Liberty Place," the Orleans Parish probate court assigned his widow Celeste as administrator of Louis Drouet's estate, a role she did not seem particularly to want. Toledano's untimely demise undoubtedly complicated the proceedings, but there also seemed to be significant disagreement between the surviving heirs as to the proper course for selling off the assets. By 1875, several of the heirs had successfully appealed for the auctioning of the house on the corner of Tchoupitoulas and Gaiènnie as well as Drouet's other real estate holdings. In the end, legal expenses, taxes, and the passage of time served to fritter away the estate to such an extent that in the end, each of the remaining heirs received only about eight hundred dollars.[35]

When Louise Marie Drouet lost her case against the Drouet clan, she also lost all her aspirations of climbing the social ladder, and she ended up sharing the fate of many who had once belonged to the middle racial caste of antebellum days. When the tide ran out on the Republican era in Louisiana, it stranded Louise Marie in its tide pool, her rights as a citizen diminishing ever more with the passage of time. After leaving her father's home, Louise lived with her uncle William and her great-aunt Fanny Porée until 1878, when she married a politically connected Afro-Creole man and Union veteran named Edouard Phillipe Ducloslange, a plasterer by trade. The following year, Louise Marie gave birth to the first of four daughters. When her children reached their late teens, they worked as seamstresses—an occupation that Louise's white relatives had suggested that she take up to support herself instead of praying for support from her father's estate.[36]

Louise Marie Drouet's half sister, Sylvanie Morgan Duvernay, continued in her pursuit of passing her children into white society. Of her nine offspring, one certainly finally succeeded in this endeavor, but a move to Mobile, Alabama, and

then to Cleveland, Ohio, were required to finally accomplish the task. One wonders whether that son's children in the 1930s knew about the dramatic times their
great-grandmother had witnessed as a mistress in antebellum New Orleans. For
their father, Eugene Duvernay, it was a story that he undoubtedly preferred to
keep in the misty past. If his family's history had taught him anything, it was that
the stakes were simply too high to risk revealing the whole truth.[37]

The White League's stunning victory on September 14, 1874, had demonstrated
unambiguously that the Republicans in Louisiana were living on borrowed time,
and it was a story repeated across the rest of the unredeemed South. Support of
Southern Republicans through the use of federal intervention had become politically untenable for the national party. Grant's use of troops in restoring Kellogg's
regime drew extensive criticism, and in a nationwide repudiation of Republican
Reconstruction policy, American voters handed Democrats control of the U.S.
House of Representatives in the midterm elections of 1874. One of those new
Democratic members of the House was E. John Ellis, who surely felt some vindication in replacing the "carpetbagger" who had previously held the seat. Although
Kellogg remained governor of Louisiana for another year and a half, the territory
outside of New Orleans had essentially fallen into the hands of local whites under
the auspices of the White League. Within the city, the Metropolitan Police was
a broken and largely unpaid force, a mere shadow of its former self. Kellogg owed
his office to the presence of federal bayonets.

   Republican rule finally collapsed in Louisiana during the first three months
of 1877. The state's gubernatorial election had pitted the "Redeemer's" candidate,
former Confederate general Francis Tillou Nicholls, against the Custom House
Republican, U.S. marshal Stephen B. Packard. Ever since arriving in New Orleans during the waning days of the war, Packard had constantly sought political
office, and his single-minded pursuit of power had contributed mightily to the
dismal state of the Republican party he now headed. Conversely, Nicholls had
been involved neither with the White League nor even Democratic politics before he sought the executive office in 1876. Having turned just forty-two at the time
of his nomination, he was, like Ellis, a member of the new political generation
who, having passed through the threshold of war, went on to dictate the affairs of
Louisiana for the next twenty years. When election day finally arrived, however,
widespread irregularities once again prevented an accurate tally of votes. The initial count proclaimed Nicholls the victor on the state level and Democratic presidential candidate Samuel J. Tilden in the national contest. As in 1872, however,
a Republican returning board nullified the first tally and gave the election to

Packard and the Republican presidential candidate, Rutherford B. Hayes. When the national electoral landscape came into focus, it became obvious that the presidency hinged upon the results from the three unredeemed states of Louisiana, South Carolina, and Florida. With all of the "firm" state totals counted, Tilden needed only one additional electoral vote to win. But Hayes needed all twenty of the votes from the states in dispute for a Republican victory. That Hayes was in this position in the first place belied the nationwide unpopularity of Republican Reconstruction policy.[38]

Amid this electoral crisis, during the first weeks of January 1877, the White League and the Democratic Party increasingly consolidated their power in New Orleans. The Metropolitan Police had shrunk to such insignificance that they were capable only of preventing, or perhaps more accurately, slowing, a direct assault on the statehouse itself. Nor did the federal government give any indication that it intended to intervene on Packard's behalf. The crisis allowed Frederick Nash Ogden one final opportunity to lead the White League into action. On January 9, Nicholls had ordered the general to oust Packard's men from the state supreme court, then housed in the old Spanish Cabildo. The cold and rainy morning contrasted sharply with the September heat in which Ogden had last led his army. The outcome was also far less dramatic. Massing his troops in Jackson Square, Ogden dispatched a messenger to the court building's front door with an ultimatum for the building's skeleton crew of defenders. As the Metropolitans peered outside, they could see in the vanguard of Ogden's men a company of stout Leeds Foundry employees wielding heavy sledgehammers, eagerly awaiting the order to smash the doors to pieces. There was simply no use for further resistance.[39]

Once in possession of the state's judicial system, Governor Nicholls repaid a portion of his debt to the White League by appointing two of their number to the state supreme court: R. H. Marr, the man who had defended the killers from the Colfax massacre and had so successfully inflamed the crowd on September 14, 1874, and Alciabade DeBlanc, the former head of the Knights of the White Camellia and a rural White League firebrand. In a gross understatement, a centenary history of the court noted, "They were without exception leaders of the Democracy, and had taken an active part in the stirring events of Reconstruction."[40]

The Republicans' last desperate hope of maintaining power in Louisiana was to engineer a quorum in a rival state senate so as to lend a veneer of legitimacy to the partisan returning board that had awarded their candidate, Stephen B. Packard, victory in the disputed gubernatorial contest. If the state senate held session, so the logic went, then perhaps Ulysses S. Grant would use federal troops to prop up the government. The situation for Louisiana's Republicans had changed dramatically, however, since the days when similar political crises gripped New Orleans in 1871 and 1873. As a result, they had less credibility as they tried to persuade wavering Republican legislators who had won their districts with a clear majority not to cut their losses and abandon the Packard legislature for the rival Nicholls statehouse, which was going to assemble soon. Meanwhile, both William Pitt Kellogg and Henry Clay Warmoth made their rounds in the ill-fated Packard state senate chamber, each working their connections in the hope that this doomed legislative body might survive long enough to appoint them to the one open U.S. Senate seat. When P. B. S. Pinchback arrived shortly thereafter for the very same purpose, he quickly apprehended not only that had he already lost any hope of securing a U.S. Senate seat to his white Republican rivals, but that this Republican state legislature would inevitably fold in a matter of days. One of the schemes Warmoth had put into place to gain his appointment to the U.S. Senate was to sequester four Republican state legislators at various locations in the city, thereby enabling him to produce a quorum for Packard's state senate on demand. Always confident of his position, the cocky Warmoth invited Pinchback out for a drink and in the process made an uncharacteristic blunder in revealing his hand to the wily gambler. Pinchback later recalled asking Warmoth, in the course of their conversation, "By the way, Governor, what have you done with Hamlet, Wheeler, Weber, and Demas?" These were the four legislators Warmoth had hidden. Believing Pinchback posed no threat to his aspirations, Warmoth replied that two were at a boardinghouse and the others at a hotel. When the two parted company, Pinchback immediately hired a carriage and acquired amounts ranging from eight thousand to sixteen thousand dollars per state senator from the Louisiana Lottery Company to bribe them into joining the Nicholls Democratic–White League legislature. Sensing that a new political reality had descended upon Louisiana, Pinchback put in place a scheme that not only maintained his grip on black political power in the state but strengthened it considerably by offering the new Nicholls regime added legitimacy at such a critical juncture.[41]

Stephen B. Packard soon learned that Pinchback had bribed four of the legislators whom he needed for a quorum in his legislature and that Pinchback had sequestered these gentlemen in his palatial residence at the corner of Magazine and First streets. Packard immediately ordered his acting sergeant-at-arms of the senate, Algernon Sydney Badger, to bring these men to the statehouse by force. Since the battle on Canal Street in 1874, Badger had managed to recuperate from his four bullet wounds, but he was diminished in mobility by his dependence on a prosthetic leg and crutches. Despite such incapacitation, and just three days after Frederick Odgen's White Leaguers took over the supreme court and the police stations, Badger gathered a squad of his remaining Metropolitans and set out for Pinchback's residence to execute the warrant for the missing legislators' arrest. Arriving at the corner of Magazine and First Street, Badger rang the gate bell repeatedly but received no reply. Pinchback then cautiously opened the front door, allegedly with a Henry repeating rifle nearby, and greeted his longtime acquaintance. When confronted with Badger's request to turn over the Republican legislators, Pinchback replied, "I don't know anything about your authority, General, and I have nothing to say about the men you are looking for, but you might as well be warned in time that you cannot pass that gate." Badger threatened to climb the fence but reconsidered when he discovered that a substantial band of White Leaguers were detailed behind Pinchback's house with orders to hold the position. As Badger's squad retreated toward downtown, a band of White Leaguers overtook them and carried all but two of Badger's men to jail at a local police station. Badger, a hero to his Metropolitans and an adversary universally respected by his opponents, was left to return downtown alone. Except for Fred Ogden, there was probably no other individual in New Orleans who was respected more for who he was as a man.[42]

Meanwhile, in the nation's capitol, three Louisianans, Randall Gibson, E. John Ellis, and Edmund A. Burke, played a conspicuous role in the negotiations that historians later called the Compromise of 1877. Burke, a former White League associate, a future Bourbon plunderer, and a dealmaker par excellence, headed the delegation. By the middle of February 1877, negotiations were well under way toward a bargain in which Louisiana's electoral votes would go for Hayes while, rather incongruently, the state election would go to Nicholls. In a greatly simplified explanation of what historians traditionally accept as the basic narrative of the compromise, Hayes promised to withdraw federal forces from the remaining unredeemed states in the South in exchange for their electoral vote, thereby effectively ending federal Reconstruction policy where it remained in effect. There remains some debate among historians whether the so-called compromise made much difference in either the final outcome of the election or the demise of federally sponsored government in Louisiana. For his part, Ellis never put much stock in Hayes or the Republicans with whom they negotiated. Writing to his father of the situation that February, Ellis explained, "And now our struggle is for Nicholls and our Home Government—Hayes' friends are profuse in promises—*He* has promised nothing. I believe his friends are lying in order to drain and disarm the Democratic Party and particularly the men of the South. Our last hope is to defeat all army appropriations and let the army go to pieces." Arguably, federal support for Packard ended less because of any electoral bargain than because each day that turmoil endured in Louisiana, thousands of voters across the nation turned away from their support of the Republican Party. Forsaking a destructive relationship that had outlasted the attraction that had given it life, Hayes and his associates abandoned whatever hope the party had once entertained of forging a lasting and meaningful presence in the state.[43]

With the Republican era in Louisiana in an uncontrolled tailspin, the nearly victorious conservatives planned for a triumphant Mardi Gras season that would celebrate what they believed to be their long-awaited deliverance from misrule. On the Thursday night before Mardi Gras, the Knights of Momus, a rising Carnival society reared in the tradition of Comus, put on a display so outrageous that some feared it might even disrupt the ongoing negotiations to end federal Reconstruction. "Hades: A Dream of Momus," left no stone unturned in its visual assault on the Grant administration, going so far as to depict the Hero of Appomattox as Beelzebub himself. When the local general in charge of federal troops in New Orleans saw Momus's procession, he was so offended that he withdrew his offer of supplying a color guard for Rex and the Mistick Krewe for the following Tuesday. Only after broad assurances from the men of the Pickwick and Boston clubs that their parades would not take a political stance against Grant or Hayes did he eventually relent. Comus's Mardi Gras night presentation of "The Aryan Race or The Progress of Freedom," however, was hardly without political inference. "In all ages," the program declared, "the Aryans have been the devotees of luxury and from the earliest period of existence as a distinct race, they have been the dictators of fashion." Just as their Missing Links parade had suggested through satire in 1873, the men of Comus once again set forth an ideology of white supremacy and biological racial difference. In a tangible way, the twenty-four parade cars of the Mistick Krewe portrayed in cultural terms the pseudoscientific conclusions of Gilded Age racial theorists. What was far more telling, however, was that whereas Momus's political attack on Grant provoked widespread consternation, criticisms by the press or federal authorities over the racist vision promoted by Comus elicited little comment in the local or national press.[44]

The emergence of the White League a decade after Confederate defeat offered an opportunity for its adherents to correct the failures of their fathers' generation. The rebellion on Canal Street was more than just a fight for political redemption; it served as a balm to the soul of a generation of Southern white men who had festered under the shame of defeat. For the moment, the White League held together the disparate ambitions of Civil War veterans. Yet the White League experience ultimately proved far more enduring for the younger postbellum generation. For these men, it restored a sense of optimism and lived on in mythology as the moment when conservative white elites, however rightly or wrongly, reclaimed their dominion over Louisiana.

Yet, for several reasons, the defeat of the Metropolitan Police at Liberty Place was every bit as significant as the White League's victory, and perhaps even more significant. It crippled the Republican Party's ability to resist oppositional violence by substantially weakening the police force and dealing a mortal blow to the black militia, and, more importantly, it provided a powerful precedent of failure. This culture of defeat yielded a bitter harvest in the coming decades as Bourbon Democrats "bulldozed" the countryside—committing deeds that went largely unopposed. Louisiana's Republicans and independents did not need the federal government to protect them from the Bourbons because that would have been, at best, only a temporary solution. They needed to be able to protect themselves. The Metropolitan Police who met the White League threat on Canal Street in 1874 were equipped sufficiently to exact a heavy price from their adversaries. What they lacked was the resolve to do so. One can only wonder what the White League's future would have been if the Metropolitans, even in accepting defeat, had, like their leader, bravely stood their ground and fought. It is conceivable that, properly arrayed, they could have made the price of victory so high as to stall the White League's momentum, propelled as it was by the artful use of self-congratulation. Instead, the defeat at Liberty Place, as well as the massacres at Coushatta and Colfax, demoralized others who might have otherwise stood ready to fight. The defeat also reinforced old notions of Southern white dominance over people of color—a notion forged over generations of race-based slavery.

The federal government may have made only a limited commitment to garrisoning the South with soldiers who might theoretically guarantee a fair election, but the Republican Party in the state had seldom focused its energies on recording accurate vote tallies. Under Kellogg, the control of electoral procedure—returning boards and federal courts—had always proved more decisive in the party's plans for obtaining the desired outcome. Such deeds set a dangerous precedent. By employing such mechanisms to guarantee a desirable outcome rather than deploying a policing force capable of establishing the legitimacy of the democratic process, starting in 1872, the Republican regime of Kellogg had essentially established the basis for its own abandonment by the federal government. Yet even the use of federal troops to guarantee fair elections, necessarily partisan in their deployment, would have undermined faith in the state government. Training a native force capable of winning the loyalty and faith of those it hoped to protect, however, might have made a significant difference. Warmoth clearly had this vision in 1870, but for a variety of reasons he was never able to bring it to fruition.

The meaning of victory varied greatly for those who joined the White League in 1874. Some ultimately reaped its rewards. Yet, others who played such a prominent role in the League's spectacular takeover of New Orleans that September found themselves eventually cast aside by their former comrades-in-arms. In less than a decade, the factions that had come together to form the White League became bitter opponents in the struggle for dominance over Louisiana's political machinery in the last quarter of the nineteenth century.

CHAPTER EIGHT

THE SEASON OF REDEEMER DISCONTENT

1878–1886

≈≈≈

Chas E. Kennon died Oct.—1878 of Yellow Fever—Noble,
generous, constant friend, farewell until we meet in the better
land. T.C.W. Ellis

                   —Home & alone, Nov. 20, 1878, 8½ pm.

Charles St. Albin Sauvinet stared despondently at his son as the two listened to
Dr. Charles Roudanez's prognosis. Born in the midst of the secession crisis,
Charles Sauvinet Jr. had grown up enjoying many of the privileges that were
available to the mixed-race elite in New Orleans. In his early teens, however, the
boy contracted tuberculosis, and in the spring of 1878 the disease had taken a turn
for the worse. Even though he was one of the city's most eminent physicians and
held a medical degree from the University of Paris, Roudanez had little luck
convincing Sauvinet that his son was not in the last stages of life. "Doctors all say
that," the distraught father replied. "He's going to die and when that occurs, there
will be nothing left for me but to throw myself into the river." Father and son left
the doctor's office and began their somber journey back to the Faubourg Marigny. When they reached their Kelerec Street home, Sauvinet helped his son to
bed and then slowly walked to his own bedroom at the front of the house and
closed the door behind him. Once inside, he took off his coat and walked over to
the mantle, where he kept a .32 caliber Smith & Wesson revolver. Lying down
quietly on his bed, Sauvinet pressed the pistol to his right temple and pulled the
trigger. The man who had endured so much, who had fought so tenaciously, died
forty-five minutes later from a wound inflicted by his own hand.[1]

    When Sauvinet's son succumbed to his illness two weeks later, the coroner
recorded a "C" to denote his race on the death certificate. It was an ironic twist:

One's race could never matter less than in death. Yet it was also symbolic. The
son who had been declared white as an infant did not die that way in the eyes
of officialdom. Much had changed since 1861, the year of Charles Sauvinet Jr.'s
birth. During that year both optimism and trepidation existed in New Orleans's
free black community. The war had conferred upon this caste a sense of civic
standing that no amount of wealth in a slaveholder's society could ever have supplied. Postbellum political advancements, though mitigated by the forces of factionalism, reactionary impulses, and occasional violence, seemed tangible and
perhaps inviolate. At his most politically active, Sauvinet had challenged the
white establishment in the courts and had successfully carried his point. In doing
so, however, he forever abandoned the racial ambiguity that had been his life's
constant companion. Physical appearance notwithstanding, because of his actions, Sauvinet and, by extension, his children now stood unmistakably as people
of color. One wonders whether, and if so at what point, Sauvinet realized that his
aspirations may simply have been a small piece of a larger political gambit run by
those whose objectives did not bear his own sense of justice. Was this understanding a factor in Sauvinet's suicide? We will never know for certain. His love for his
son and namesake is creditable, but Sauvinet also left behind a widow, two un-
married daughters, and another son. And he killed himself almost exactly ten
years after his first wife's death. Whatever the dark forces that drove Sauvinet's
despair, their depth was all too plain.[2]

The uncertainty that hovered over all aspects of life for New Orleans's mixed-
race elite must have weighed heavily upon Sauvinet's surviving children. His older
son, James Nelson, had already left home and was probably working as a traveling
musician at the time of Sauvinet's suicide. By the 1890s, he became a proprietor of
a traveling circus based in Texas. Perhaps in such an environment of noncon-
formists, James Sauvinet found a home where his own racial makeup and past
mattered little. His sisters, Clothilde and Angela, took a different path toward
securing a new identity. In 1886 Clothilde married a Creole man by the name of
Paul Perrault. Although Paul received a "colored" designation on his 1858 birth
certificate, by 1870, the very moment when Charles Sauvinet boldly stepped out
of line and declared himself a man of color, the entire Perrault family had passed
for white. So, too, did the children of Clothilde Sauvinet and Paul Perrault. Angela married a New Orleans man of Italian descent and, along with her offspring,
successfully crossed the color line without ever leaving the city. Their father's
exploits during Reconstruction were well known, even outside of the tightly knit
elite Afro-Creole community, so there could have been no question as to Angela
and Clothilde's origins. Their successful migration into white society reveals how

negotiable racial identity remained in New Orleans, even as late as the 1880s. Such permeability of the color line eventually animated the architects of a new order who hitched their dreams of white supremacy to implementing a Draconian "one-drop" standard for racial identification.[3]

Continued racial mobility was not the only aspect of the Republican era that endured into the so-called Redemption. Black political power, however diminished by the conservative ascendancy, also remained an important factor in New Orleans. Although they never mounted a credible challenge to take over the state government as part of a fusion campaign, as their counterparts had in Virginia and North Carolina, conservative and Democratic factionalists periodically offered Republicans exploitable opportunities. As it had since 1862, the U.S. Custom House in New Orleans stood as the bastion of Republicanism in Louisiana. Between 1877 and the beginning of Grover Cleveland's Democratic presidency in 1885, the power of federal patronage not only sustained the Republican Party's modest aspirations in Louisiana; it supplied a nurturing and protective environment where key members of New Orleans's Afro-Creole elite could continue their campaign for full citizenship. Although white supremacists had taken extraordinary, violent, and effective steps to crush black aspirations in some rural parts of Louisiana, the enduringly visible and viable presence of Afro-Creoles in the Custom House spoke to the depth of political reordering that had taken place after the war. Moreover, even as some reactionaries sought to foreclose the rights that had been gained by the Reconstruction amendments, others saw in the enfranchised black population the potential for political advantage. The notion that the Redemption was "the last battle of the Civil War" that signaled the final triumph of white supremacy has proved remarkably enduring in both the historical profession and the broader national historical consciousness. While the Redemption definitely redefined the battlefield, it did not produce clear-cut victors. Neither did it preclude other outcomes.[4]

Despite the self-congratulatory tone of those "Redeemers" who were either directly or indirectly responsible for the demise of Republican rule in Louisiana in 1877, it did not take long for most conservative whites in New Orleans to discover how limited the White League's triumph had been. Perhaps the most defining attribute of the Redemption in the city was just how little tangible change it brought about. The Republican Party was no longer in control of the state's executive branch, nor did the partisan Metropolitan Police continue to patrol the streets of New Orleans, but when it came down to fundamental issues of life in the Crescent City, little had changed. Crime, corruption, and the weak economy all remained and perhaps even worsened. Bourbon abuses in the rural parishes

sent a continual stream of black labor fleeing to both New Orleans and points
beyond, a factor that exacerbated preexisting racial and economic tensions. In
such an environment, the celebratory atmosphere that had accompanied the ascendancy of Francis Tillou Nicholls could not last long. Soon, the inherent contradictions in the White League coalition exerted their own centrifugal force
upon the organization, splitting it back into the elements that had only temporarily joined to defeat the Kellogg and Packard regimes. That the levers of power
were within reach only intensified the enmity between these former comrades.

The acrimony and factionalism that had been temporarily abated by the White
League resurfaced less than a year after Nicholls took office. By 1878 the Reformer
Democratic element in New Orleans began hurling the same kinds of accusations at Bourbon Democratic power brokers such as Louis Wiltz and Edmund A.
Burke as they had at Republicans Henry Clay Warmoth and William Pitt Kellogg. These self-styled reformers were largely a continuation of the Reform Party
begun by the city's business elites in 1872 with the help of similarly inclined
planters. Their grievances against the Bourbon Democracy—all too familiar—
included unchecked violence, corruption, and scandal and the assertion that the
men who controlled the reins of power did not represent "the people." Their
outrage would cause men like E. John Ellis, once devoted Democrats and now
Reformer Democrats, to make a bid to topple the very regime that they had
fought so ardently to put into power. As a group, the Redeemers themselves may
have declared the ascendancy their government to be the much-ballyhooed end
of Reconstruction, but their rhetoric bore the stamp of propagandistic wishful
thinking. In reality, there was no end in sight to the political or social divisions
that the Republican era had created among conservative whites in New Orleans
as well as greater Louisiana.

For these reasons, while the year 1877 represented a political milestone in
postbellum Louisiana, it was hardly an endpoint or the beginning of a new era in
and of itself. Historians studying the economic and social aspects of the postbellum South have accepted a more elastic notion of Reconstruction's timeline,
conceptualizing it as a process rather than an era and instead applying the term
postbellum to the period from 1865 until the turn of the century. Far fewer who
study the political consequences of the war have done the same. In accepting
1877 as the end of Reconstruction, however, we are in essence embracing a timeline supplied to us first by the Bourbon Redeemers and, by extension, later by the
Dunning School of Reconstruction historians. The bitterest critics of Republican
Reconstruction policy, the Dunningites, always charged that its purpose was to
force onto white Southerners the unnatural establishment of a Republican Party.

Following such logic, the defeat of this policy therefore signaled the end of Reconstruction, just as the Redeemers declared in 1877. Revisionist historians who came later offered a new interpretation of the Republicans' motives, but they did not fundamentally challenge the intellectual terrain or chronology staked out by the Dunning School.

Although there is a growing trend in the field to view the postbellum South in a broader geographical and chronological context, our collective notion of Reconstruction is still confined by the intellectually antiquated conceptual framework of 1862–77 and an obsession with the survival of Republican regimes in the South. Yet if we truly want to examine the postbellum era as a broader reconstruction of a society thrown into turmoil by the experience of war, defeat, and emancipation, then the presence of Republican governors and the date of 1877 both shrink in significance. They become even less significant when we acknowledge that white unity in Redemption was more mirage than anything else. The political and social discontent that raged in Louisiana after 1877 was in essence a continuation of the struggle that began with the Union army's conquest of the state in 1862. Moreover, while the Northern public may have retreated from its commitment to the "emancipationist legacy" of the war in 1877, black Southerners had not yet abandoned their own commitment to political relevance and social standing. And although many white "carpetbaggers" fled the state after 1877, key individuals such as Algernon Sydney Badger and Henry Clay Warmoth remained. Not until the U.S. Supreme Court declared the legality of "separate but equal" in 1896 and, perhaps even more importantly, paved the way for the regionwide disfranchisement of black Southerners in its 1898 ruling in *Williams v. Mississippi*, did white supremacy close the door on this age of upheaval. The intervening twenty years between 1878 and 1898 might constitute an era unto itself, as some have suggested, but they were in many ways merely a continuation of the essential struggles that began in New Orleans when Benjamin Butler's troops first stepped onto the Mississippi River levee.[5]

Commanding the White League during its dramatic victory on September 14, 1874, was a defining moment of Frederick Nash Ogden's eventful life. Even before the League returned to the city's streets in the early weeks of 1877, Ogden had appointed himself the guardian of the memory of comrades of his who had fallen in the 1874 battle on Canal Street. Ogden's papers at Tulane University contain very few pieces of correspondence either to or from himself. What documents remain reveal his efforts to attract notable New Orleanians and fellow White League veterans to annual ceremonies intended to both commemorate the dead and raise money for a more enduring memorial to their sacrifice. In the spring of 1878, these efforts had grown to include a series of comical mule races held at the fair-grounds. "Weather permitting," a newspaper ad promised, "the grand mule race for the benefit of a fund to erect a monument to the memory of our citizen soldiers who fell on the 14th of September, 1874, will come off at the fair grounds this af-ternoon." The reception committee included Ogden and notables who had played prominent roles in the battle, including William J. Behan and Reuben Pleasants. "How to bet on a running mule is something no fellow can find out with any de-gree of satisfaction to himself," mused the *Picayune*. Nevertheless, attendees en-gaged in spirited betting on animals named everything from Redemption and Whisky to Returning Board.[6]

Fred Ogden's labors to procure a monument to the White League dead were derailed by events that were out of his or anyone else's control. Not long after the conclusion of the mule races, rumors of a serious yellow fever outbreak began circulating in the city. The terror that such news produced in nineteenth-century New Orleans is difficult to translate into modern terms, but its portrayal in Wil-liam Wyler's classic 1938 production of *Jezebel*, however overly theatrical, was probably not far off the mark. Scientists had not identified the epidemiological origins of the disease, nor had they any accurate notion of the germ vector that spread it from one victim to another. Moreover, all known treatment and precau-tionary defenses seemed to have little impact upon the fever's lethality. On July 26, just two days after Charles Sauvinet's suicide, the patrons of a coffee house at the corner of Camp and St. Andrew Streets noticed that a customer who only an hour earlier had been complaining about fatigue suddenly dropped dead. It did not take long for the panic to spread. By the first of August, there were 46 recorded yellow fever fatalities in the city (including Charles Sauvinet Jr., whose death was later attributed to the epidemic). On the fifth, that number had mushroomed to 83, and by the thirteenth to 173. The impact of the disease was going to become far worse. Embargoes on all travel and shipping out of New Orleans cropped up all over the Mississippi River Valley: at Vicksburg, Cairo, Memphis, and else-where. Despite the dire public health crisis in their city, Crescent City merchants railed angrily against the growing quarantine. Meanwhile, the board of health, led by Dr. Samuel Choppin and heavily influenced by the chamber-of-commerce set, refused to declare the yellow fever outbreak an epidemic.[7]

The most prominent charitable organization that worked against the coming health crisis in New Orleans was the Howard Association, of which Fred Ogden was vice president. Founded in 1839, the Howards, as they were popularly known, were a particularly courageous and civic-minded group of men committed to mitigating the ill effects of the city's episodic bouts with yellow fever. Not only did they raise money for the treatment of the most indigent victims of the plague, but they volunteered tirelessly, operating makeshift hospital wards and providing in-home care to countless others, including those who had been so weakened by the fever that they could not feed themselves. In 1878 the association had a particularly difficult task before them. By the time the outbreak was declared finished at the start of November, at least forty-six hundred city residents had perished. Across the Mississippi Valley, more than twenty thousand died. Although his peers later saved their greatest praise for Ogden's dashing White League exploits, it was his service during the yellow fever epidemic of 1878 that was truly the soldier's finest hour. One woman later recalled Ogden's "going from house to house, ministering to the sick and dying, and never tiring of good works."[8]

Even as disease ravaged the Crescent City, a political storm brewed among its Democratic and conservative ranks that also drew Fred Ogden away from his plans to memorialize his White League comrades. Drawing an analogy that it probably later regretted, the *Picayune* observed, "The fever is among the politicians. It is steadily gaining ground, and will go on with increasing pulsation till October next, when a crisis will set in, and the patients must either die or pass the test with a small but assuring vitality left. In many years this city has not witnessed so much division in political circles; certainly not since the war." Referring to the collapse of the White League coalition, the editorial continued, "The Democratic Conservative party, which fought the campaign since 1872, has become dismembered. This is owing to the defeat of the ancient enemy and the impossibility of once more raising the old ghost, and the dissatisfaction, personal and official, which the last two years of Democratic and Conservative government have engendered."[9]

Although postbellum Louisiana contained many subsets of white conservative factionalism, the most meaningful ones in New Orleans were Reformer Democracy and the Ring/Lottery/Bourbon Democracy. The Reformers tended to be the more coherently defined faction. It built upon the foundation of the men who had gathered in 1872 to create the Reform Party, but its ranks in the city had since broadened outside of its Boston Club base and now attracted Democratic men in New Orleans who also belonged to the equally elite Pickwick Club. The Reformer Democrats also had a growing following in the countryside, claiming men William Ivy Hair termed the "patricians," who, at least in rhetoric, embodied the paternalistic noblesse oblige philosophy when dealing with groups whom they considered their social inferiors, whether black or white. It also attracted planters and merchants who believed investment in infrastructure and an amicable relationship with the North were desirable. The Reformer Democrats were almost universally opposed to the enormous influence of the corrupt Louisiana Lottery Company, which funneled profound amounts of cash to its protectors in the Bourbon Democracy. These and old-fashioned personal antagonisms divided the Reformers from their rivals the Bourbons.[10]

In New Orleans, the Bourbons were represented by the city's political machine, the Ring. The Ring had first emerged during the Republican era, and it focused upon patronage politics at the city level. It could be seen as the descendant of the Democratic machine that had thrived in the antebellum years, an organization whose power flowed from the ballots of white ethnic urban voters. If the Reformers were the men of the Boston Club, the Ring were the men of fraternal orders: the Hibernians, the Volunteer Firemen, and the Elks. Yet to characterize the Ring as entirely working-class would be inaccurate. Creole and Irish elites, along with a few Anglos, were prominent in the Ring's leadership. Although the Ring did not ally with the Bourbons in every political cause, it did so more often than not. The Bourbons, a group that held sway over a majority of the state's rural planters, had a reputation for hard-handedness with labor and fiduciary retrenchment. Several of their party leaders, like the Ring in New Orleans, were involved in lucrative and corrupt schemes that harnessed the power of the state for personal gain. The lottery was the most notable and remunerative, but the schemes also included everything from the convict-lease system to questionable real estate deals. While the Reformer Democrats had their share of ethical shortcomings, the abuses of the Bourbons have been well chronicled.[11]

Governor Nicholls had lent the anti-Republican/White League coalition an image of moderate respectability in its bid to wrest the reins of Louisiana's state government from Stephen B. Packard in the first months of 1877. As a chief executive, however, Nicholls's paternalistic stance toward blacks and Republicans and his overall conciliatory tone toward the members of the returning board who had tried to swing the election in favor of his opponent did not serve him well with Bourbon and Ring powerbrokers. Far more unacceptable was his ingratitude toward the Louisiana Lottery Company, particularly since its money had proved crucial to his victory. Nicholls often characterized the lottery as an undesirable, corrupting, and dangerously unaccountable force in state politics. Underestimating the monopoly's hold on the state, Nicholls actively worked toward the lottery's demise. Louis Wiltz, a machine politician from New Orleans and the lieutenant governor of the state, along with the deeply corrupt state treasurer, E. A. Burke, had sought every opportunity to rid themselves of Nicholls since the moment federal troops pulled out of the state. Political maneuverings and the yellow fever epidemic prevented that from happening in 1878, but by the start of 1879, these men, with the help of lottery money, had hatched a plan to place the state government firmly in lottery-friendly Bourbon hands.[12]

During the summer and fall of 1878, a movement had been afoot in Louisiana to authorize a convention to replace the Republican-era state constitution of 1868. Because so many different interest groups hoped to gain from a rewriting of the Pelican State's governing document, it was not surprising that voters overwhelmingly approved the measure when it was placed before them on the ballot that fall. The convention commenced in Baton Rouge the following April. For a variety of reasons, of which few were altruistic, conservative elements had rejected attempts to enact a poll tax as well as other measures intended to reduce electoral participation by blacks and poor whites. In 1879 most politicians in Louisiana still saw all voters, whether black or white, as people to be manipulated instead of disfranchised. For Wiltz and Burke, however, the constitution's renewal of the Louisiana Lottery's lucrative charter was of far greater import. Through parliamentary maneuvering and adept politicking, Burke was able to ensure the inclusion of language that guaranteed the lottery's future. With that task accomplished, the elimination of a governor who was hostile to its operation next became a priority. Governor Nicholls had actually signed a bill earlier in the spring of 1879 that would have led to the company's demise. The men who were beholden to the lottery needed little persuasion, then, to append a clause to the constitution in the waning days of the convention that called for the election of a new governor in the fall of 1879. With this ironic stroke of the pen, Nicholls, the multiple-amputee hero of Chancellorsville who had stood successfully as the Democratic Party's head in its quest for Redemption, was legislated out of office a year early by agents of the Louisiana Lottery—an economic force created by the Republican regime.[13]

One issue that did not divide white conservatives was the elimination of many of the previous state constitution's civil rights provisions. With the exception of the formation of Southern University—a college created expressly for black students— explicit segregationist language did not appear in the 1879 state constitution. Notably absent, however, was Article Thirteen, which had forbidden discrimination in public accommodations—the very law under which Charles Sauvinet and Peter Joseph had sued for damages. The new constitution closely followed the philosophy that governed the racial politics of the 1880s: the law stopped well short of codified segregation, but it eliminated any and all government-sponsored integration. When the U.S. Supreme Court ruled in the *Civil Rights Cases* (1883), it effectively dismantled the federal Civil Rights Act of 1875. From that moment forward, public accommodations in privately held businesses became a nonissue.

Not until the late 1880s did a renewed assault on integration in New Orleans emerge.[14]

Unlike Fred Ogden, who had enjoyed a brief moment in which to bask in his fame, E. John Ellis at the beginning of 1878 languished in a melancholy and self-pitying mood. His state of mind was due in part to financial problems that had caused an uncharacteristic rift with his brother Thomas, his closest friend and associate. With the vast majority of Ellis's time consumed with all things political, he had been largely unable to contribute to the law firm that he and Thomas had formed in 1874 with John McEnery. Characterizing himself as a "fifth wheel" in the enterprise, Ellis wrote his brother in late February that he planned to with-draw from the partnership and rescind any claim to fees from cases in which he did not labor. Despite his congressional salary, Ellis could barely support his fam-ily, had been constantly in debt, and was on the verge of losing his home. He was one of those rare Louisiana politicians, in his own era or ever since, who seemed unable to enrich himself through office-holding. Although he engaged in a vari-ety of commercial ventures while a member of the House and was not above using his status as a congressman to obtain perquisites, he was too honest, too unlucky, or simply not skilled enough to profit from any of them.[15]

Not only had politics caused Ellis financial strain; they had also hampered his ability to be a constant companion to his wife and a father to his children. He had earlier written to his mother that he "often [thought] of himself as the greatest ass and fool in the world, to let a little pride of place, a little ambitious dream, sepa-rate me this way from my heaven on earth." Nevertheless, he left his family be-hind once again for the 1878 legislative session, but by February, he began telling Thomas of his intentions not to run for reelection. Had his salary not been already pledged, John proclaimed, he would leave immediately. "My course is plain—I shall leave political life after the 4th of March, 1879, and devote myself to business." Making reference to the savage attacks that had been made upon him in the press by E. L. Jewell, the editor of the *New Orleans Bulletin* and some-thing of a professional blowhard, Ellis continued, "For me, I am sick of politics and public life." Seemingly resolved to leave politics behind, he declared, "My home, my noble faithful wife, my little children, have first claim on me."[16]

For all his expressions of remorse, however, Ellis could not help but throw himself into a variety of uphill political battles that in the end left him deeply disillusioned. Contrary to his melodramatic predictions at the beginning of the year, he won his third term to the House of Representatives in 1878, and the fol-lowing summer found him enmeshed in what proved to be the bitterest partisan contest of his long and embattled career. Like many of the planter elite and New Orleans mercantile reformers who had applauded Francis Nicholls's paternalistic efforts as governor, Ellis was outraged over the convention machinations that had resulted in the replacement of Nicholls with a slippery machine politician like Louis Wiltz. Ellis had worked tirelessly for the Democratic party since the days of the Knights of the White Camellia but always feared that its most corrupt and reactionary wing, dominated by the self-proclaimed Bourbons, would come to dominate the state through corruption. It was an outcome that his friend Charles Kennon had predicted long before Kellogg ever left office. Now that this fear had become a reality, Ellis looked for a solution just short of revolution that might rescue the cause of reform from the clutches of Bourbonism. Facing such a looming crisis, Ellis called upon his old friend Frederick Nash Ogden to once again take the field in defense of good government. The resulting movement marked the emergence of Reformer Democracy.

It had become clear to everyone that the constitutional convention of 1879 had positioned Louis Wiltz as the heir apparent for the Democratic gubernatorial nomination. Although he attributed his decision not to run to health concerns, Francis T. Nicholls had withdrawn from the race early, knowing full well that he would suffer a humiliating defeat if he attempted to secure reelection. And long before the convention met, there was significant grumbling in New Orleans about Burke's true objectives. Watching from the sidelines, P. B. S. Pinchback's *Weekly Louisianian* could only marvel at the deep rift that seemed to be growing among the Redeemers on account of Wiltz's emergence as the gubernatorial frontrunner. Mocking the pure intentions of the city's "reformer" element, the black newspaper noted, "The fight has opened in earnest between the conservative element and the bourbons. The industrial and business portion of our people have at last determined to go into the fight without gloves and purify at all Hazards the politics of our city by consigning to the shade of oblivion the professional politician, the trickster, adherents of a tyrannical system of oppression and corruption." At the beginning of September, E. John Ellis approached Fred Ogden in the hope that he might agree to challenge Wiltz's nomination. Whether Ogden was truly uninterested in running or merely did not want to appear to be profiting from his notoriety so close to the anniversary of the September 14, 1874, battle, the now forty-two-year-old soldier declined. His refusal to be a candidate threw a wrench into the plans of Ellis and those of other "anti-Ring" conservatives, but they did not give up hope. On the anniversary of the Canal Street battle, drawing broad parallels between Ogden's leadership of the White League and the need to rid the city and the state of corrupt politicians, both the *Times* and the *Picayune* resumed their effort to enlist the general as their candidate.[17]

The regular party press, under the aegis of E. A. Burke's *New Orleans Daily Democrat*, knew that any denunciation of Ogden's candidacy would have to carefully avoid the sort of direct character assassination that had long since become a regular staple of city political columns. Fred Ogden was simply too widely respected in Louisiana to engage in such tactics. In contrast, the supporters of the "Ogden Boom," as the general's supporters liked to call their movement, leveled savage criticism against Wiltz and the "Ring" supporters, whom they characterized as political parasites. This was a charge they had once laid at the feet of Republicans like Henry Clay Warmoth and William Pitt Kellogg. The Bourbon Democracy was not willing to passively endure the abuse of its opponents, actions that the *Daily Democrat* declared "unmanly." Burke's primary target for retaliation was not Fred Ogden, but instead Ogden's most outspoken promoter—the man who in 1879 emerged as the most prominent and credible critic of the Louisiana Democratic party, E. John Ellis.[18]

Ellis's criticisms of the corruption and jobbery that he claimed were rampant in the Democratic party were a staple of his political speeches that late summer, but he made far more serious accusations that resonated not only deep within the party but across the nation. He lashed out against the Bourbons who had been responsible for the bloody "bulldozing" in heavily black parishes during the fall 1878 elections. This increased level of violence against black agricultural workers, performed at the behest of the Louisiana Sugar Planter's Association, led to such great levels of despair among black farmers that many threatened to flee the state en masse. Their reaction, called "Kansas Fever," had gained the attention not only of the national press but also of the planter elite, who knew deep down that their prosperity hinged upon the availability of nominally content black labor. Ellis warned the Democrats that there was in Louisiana a "yet unorganized but strong party composed of the poorer class of people, who complain of the rapacity and exactions of Democratic officials, and who tell that Democratic success has brought no relief." He further charged that the state had done nothing to protect those Louisianians, whether black or white, who wished to vote for the candidate of their choosing. Ellis contrasted the situation with what he believed would occur under an Ogden administration: "He will enforce the law. This is all important. Louisiana suffers in the eyes of her sister states from the imputation that she is a lawless State; that life and liberty and property are not secure. This injures us by keeping away emigration, capital, enterprise, and it also injures the Democracy in the North." Ellis had never been afraid to candidly face the ugly truth, but he had never made so many enemies in doing so.[19]

The Democratic press in the city savagely and repeatedly abused Ellis for what it termed the "humiliating" and "untrue" accusations of "a Louisiana member of Congress, prominent as a Democrat and distinguished for his eloquence" who would dare make such charges for the purpose of "inflaming the Northern mind against us." In one particularly pointed editorial, the *Democrat* chided that Ellis's "intellect is so great, and the fervor of his fancy so hot, that his ideas and words, like the tropical luxuriance of a southern morass, often overcrop themselves and require, for any useful purpose, the pruning knife, or rather we should say, the ax of the woodsman." Yet the party was most outraged at Ellis's condemnation of the so-called Yazoo affair in Mississippi, where earlier in the year white gangs had murdered black political figures in an ambush. The newspaper claimed to not know whether these statements were to "gratify [Ohio Republican congressman] Mr. [Charles] Foster in Ohio, or the [African American weekly named the] *Inter-Ocean* in Chicago."[20]

Although they were far more circumspect in their direct attacks on Fred Ogden, among the more ironic of accusations made by the Bourbons was that his candidacy would fuel unrest among black Louisianians. These charges came even as Bourbon planters sought to suppress both labor unrest and political voice among Louisiana's black citizens. Referring to the White League's 1874 campaign, the *Democrat* observed, "the remembrance of that trial to establish an out-and-out white man's government is still today influencing the colored voter, and the nomination for Governor of the very man who is still considered the embodiment of the White League would be sufficient to create a panic among the masses of ignorant negroes." Similar statements ran in the French Creole *New Orleans Bee* and the German-language *Deutsche Zeitung*, both of which remained influential dailies in the ethnic neighborhoods of the city. The most damning statements, however, came from elite men whom Fred Ogden knew best. On September 24 the *Democrat* ran a series of chatty interviews about the state of political affairs with notable personalities in the city. While each of these men professed their firm belief in the purity of Ogden's motives and the strength of his character, they expressed doubts about his qualifications for the office. Among those endorsing Wiltz were Ogden's former White League comrade William J. Behan and the old Washington Artillery commander and White League aide James B. Walton, both of whom had ties to the Ring. Yet none expressed the criticism more succinctly than Paul Theard, who had once served with Aristée Tissot in the Tirailleurs d'Orleans back in 1861: "Ogden is known to the community as an honest

merchant, a good citizen and a brave soldier. That is much; but honesty and brav-
ery, priceless jewels though they be, do not suffice for the government of a great
people."[21]

By the time the convention took a floor vote, it was evident that Louis Wiltz
would emerge as the party's nominee for governor, and in 1879 that was tantamount to victory in the fall general election. Fearing that dissatisfied anti-Ring
reformers might not accept Wiltz as their own, the *Picayune* ran an editorial
aimed at cooling any ideas of that sort of third-party action by the Reformer
Democrats. "We do not even detect a subsidence of enthusiasm in favor of Democratic doctrine and measures—only this, that the whole Southern country living
freed from the sway of the Radicals and their wicked emissaries, there has been
a notable relaxation of effort on the part of Democrats, with an increasing tendency toward independent action on the part of numerous voters who have worn
Democratic colors more from a sense of present necessity than from any special
love of the party." Those men, noted the *Picayune*, showed their patriotism by
rallying around Wiltz. The Republican candidate that year was Judge Taylor
Beattie, a sugar planter and conservative scalawag who belonged to a circle of
men who believed that the GOP could survive best in Louisiana as a white man's
party. Beattie, ironically, was married to the sister of Fred Ogden's first cousin and
surrogate brother Robert Nash Ogden. As a female relative later recorded in her
memoirs, "Those were embarrassing days for the family, but the feeling was relieved by the election of a third man." That third man was Wiltz.[22]

As the past two years had shown, even though the Republican party no longer
enjoyed broad influence in Louisiana, no amount of Redeemer rhetoric could
fully convince the people of New Orleans that the return of Democratic rule had
brought any greater sense of amity to the city's streets. The government's inability
to confront dangerous crises in an effective manner had been made all too plain
by the yellow fever epidemic of 1878. While the city and state governments could
not be blamed for lacking the ability to cure the disease, their lack of coordination
and leadership undermined the public's confidence in their ability to set priorities
that reflected the common good. Self-interest had trumped civic duty both in the
failure to declare the disease an epidemic and in civil authorities' toleration of
unsanitary conditions that had allowed the pestilence to thrive in the first place.
At some level, the fever epidemic served as a metaphor for the consequences of
allowing widespread moral decay to take root in Louisiana's political landscape.
The leaders who engaged in petty squabbles or graft left the citizens of the Pelican State with little choice but to pay the tab.

The lack of energy invested in preventing a recurrence of the devastating 1878 yellow fever epidemic or in securing honest government also contrasted sharply with the city's preoccupation with Carnival the following February. Although the Mistick Krewe did not participate in 1879, the Pickwick Club having exhausted its coffers ministering to the fever's victims the previous summer, Rex made his annual appearance. To those who had endured the tragedy of the previous summer, such frivolity seemed grossly out of tune. No journal was more vocal in its denunciation than P. B. S. Pinchback's *Louisianian:* "Our commerce may go to decay, we may be girded around with a net-work of railways taking away our life-blood to animate other cities, while we are unable to break through the toils; thousands of our citizens may fall victims to a wasting pestilence from our poverty to keep clean gutters, streets, and lanes but when cruel destiny brings us the mighty Rex, our very rags, like Aladdin's lamp bring forth gold and ribbons and music and all the like to do homage to our omnipotent sovereign! Great is Mardi-Gras, but wondrously wise is New Orleans that can in her professed poverty maintain such a mighty monarch!"[23]

Although it struck some as frivolous, and although both Rex and Comus had increasingly become the exclusive province of the city's most elite citizens, Carnival remained a viable vehicle of popular expression in New Orleans. An important reason was the appearance of a host of new "krewes" in the 1880s, each adding a new voice to the street celebration of Mardi Gras. One particularly successful krewe that emerged in 1878 was called the Phunny Phorty Phellows. Customarily following the Rex procession, it had by 1880 become an eagerly anticipated feature of Mardi Gras Day. Satire had been the Phorties' stock-in-trade since the group's inception, and in 1880 it took direct aim at the shortcomings of city and state government. Included in its procession was a "pompously overdressed" artillery company (quite likely a play on the Washington Artillery); caricatures of "the City Fathers, who are always on hand for the occasion"; and the "Guest Dead Beats, who never miss the occasion," men whom Perry Young noted "found it a poor procession whose caricatures were recognized." The most pointed satire came at the expense of two particularly well-known city personages—General William J. Behan, who had been Fred Ogden's second-in-command in the White League, and Dr. Samuel Choppin, who had unsuccessfully and rather ineptly combated the yellow fever epidemic of 1878. A car titled "Our Guests, The Milish, our brave defenders of 8th January, 22nd February, 4th July, etc." depicted Behan with "his foot resting on a helpless Chinaman, his legend proclaiming, 'Sic Semper Tyrannis!'" The Phorties parodied Choppin as "Moses among the Bulrushes, looking for a Germ," which was "bottled and preserved, like his other theories, in his eye."

Although solemn ceremonies like those designed to commemorate the White League dead often found receptive audiences, the self-serving dimensions of such commemorative pageantry did not go unnoticed, as the Phunny Phorty Phellows revealed.[24]

Algernon Sydney Badger had just ascended the steps that connected a side entrance of the Custom House with a corridor that led to his office in the building when he noticed a shadowy figure lurking in a corner. The stranger rapidly approached and leveled a small five-shot revolver at the general's head, proclaiming "I've got you now!" Acting quickly, Badger grabbed the man by the collar with his right hand and the revolver with the left. At that instant, a shot rang out, the bullet narrowly missing Badger and flattening out against the granite wall behind him. A brief struggle ensued, and a blow from Badger sent the revolver clattering down the stairwell. By this time a crowd had gathered around the general, who, with the exception of burns to his hand from grasping the revolver at the very moment his assailant fired it, was unhurt. Onlookers could hardly have missed the fact that both men involved in the affray stood on prosthetic legs. The attacker, William Brown, had been a member of the Metropolitan Police under Badger's command during the September 14, 1874, battle on Canal Street. Like his commander, Brown had received wounds that required the amputation of a leg. More recently, he had worked for Badger when the stalwart Republican had received an appointment from Rutherford B. Hayes as the postmaster in New Orleans. Yet when Badger became collector of customs, he found himself unable to offer the down-on-his-luck Brown a job. Destitute and believing that his sacrifices as a veteran and a Metropolitan policeman entitled him to a place, Brown claimed that he did not to want to kill Badger but "to create a sensation. I knew the reporters would put my name in the papers, and then the authorities in Washington would understand how desperate I was." For his part, Badger did not care to press charges; once his hand was bandaged, he continued on with his day's work. In this bizarre episode, Badger once again demonstrated the courage that had earned him the admiration of his former White League enemies. Moreover, in an era noted for widespread abuse of federal patronage, he seemed like the model civil servant.[25]

When he took over the collectorship in March 1879, Badger replaced George L. Smith, who had been recently removed from office because his financial corruption and political chicanery had become too great to ignore. Onlookers of both parties were pleased with Badger's selection. Even the conservative *Picayune* found that it had to applaud his handling of the U.S. Post Office while in charge of that facility. Badger's appointment also portended well for black New Orleanians who had demonstrated their loyalty to the Republican party. Even though P. B. S. Pinchback had only two years earlier driven Badger away from his home with a Henry rifle, his *Louisianian* noted approvingly, "As Collector, the virtual head of the party, we see the brave, intelligent, quiet and amiable gentleman, the steadfast, true and fearless friend of our people, the practicable businessman, the skillful and sagacious party leader. Embodying within himself all of these great traits of character, we have every reason to feel proud of the President's selection, and at the same moment to congratulate him on his evident intention to please all classes in his new deal."[26]

The individuals who clearly gained the most from Badger's appointment as collector of customs, however, were the members of the city's Afro-Creole elite who had once belonged to the Metropolitan Police. Many of these men were also Union veterans who had served in the Native Guards alongside Charles Sauvinet. Among them was Rodolphe Desdunes, who, though too young to serve during the war, had been wounded while serving with the Metropolitans on September 14, 1874. So, too, was Badger's trusted subordinate Peter Joseph. Both joined the Custom House's ranks in 1879 and received numerous promotions thereafter. Others found work because of their political connections. Despite a November 1880 audit that placed him in a category of workers who were "competent but not required to perform full duty and overpaid," former lieutenant governor C. C. Antoine (who had opposed Badger's nomination as collector) collected a two-thousand-dollar annual salary as a clerk in the warehouse department.

Badger's loyalty to mixed-race subordinates allowed them to continue their political activism shielded from the threat of economic reprisal. Not only did tradesman-class men like Rodolphe Desdunes, Octave Rey, and Peter Joseph find work in the Custom House; so did elite activists such as Arnold Bertonneau. Along with Dr. Charles Roudanez, Bertonneau had met with Abraham Lincoln in 1864 to push the cause of universal male suffrage. More recently, he had sued the Orleans Parish school board so that his child could attend a white school instead of an inferior one reserved for black students. Bertonneau, a veteran of the Native Guards, had just lost this case in the state supreme court when Badger nominated him for employment in the Custom House. Paul Trévigne, the one-time editor of the radical *Tribune* and a longtime educator, and the lawyer Louis A. Martinet, who had served as a state legislator in the Republican era and later published the Afro-Creole activist newspaper the *Crusader*, also received jobs on Canal Street. Martinet, along with Desdunes, also later became one of the founding members of the Comité des Citoyens, the group that eventually mounted

Homer Plessy's challenge to Louisiana's separate-car law. Although much has (rightly) been made of the independent action of the city's Afro-Creole elite in challenging the onset of segregation, it is clear that Badger's decision to hire former comrades-in-arms from the Metropolitan Police and his willingness to recognize the important contributions made by men of color to the maintenance of Republicanism in Louisiana supplied this class with crucial organizational support. While some Northern Republicans may have abandoned the party in the South and, more specifically, abandoned their black electorate, Badger demonstrated that not all had lost their steadfast resolve after 1877.[27]

By the time Chester Arthur won the presidency in 1883, Badger had not only built a firm base of support among the Afro-Creole Republicans in New Orleans, but he also enjoyed the widespread support of the city's business community. George Nicholson, the proprietor of the *New Orleans Picayune*, sent a letter to President Arthur in February of that year noting that "Col. A.S. Badger . . . has given very general satisfaction in that position, and the citizens here would much prefer his reappointment rather than that the office should be filled by any other of the various applicants for the position." Another conservative Democrat wrote that "[Badger's] character, whether in public or in private life, has never, to my knowledge, been assailed." The clerk of the U.S. Circuit Court in New Orleans stated in a separate letter that Badger had "the respect and esteem of his late enemies and the confidence of the community." Adding weight to this assessment were the signatures of eighty-three members of the New Orleans Cotton Exchange, all supporting the Yankee's continuation as collector. Among the signatures from the Cotton Exchange's petition was that of E. John Ellis's father, Ezekiel Parke Ellis. It was a far cry from the abuse that conservatives heaped upon Badger during his tenure as the chief superintendent of the Metropolitan Police. Such amity did not last, but for a while the Reformer Democrats of New Orleans's business elite seemed to have more favorable things to say about its Republican collector of customs than it did about its Democratic governors.[28]

Some *Republicans*, however, were deeply unhappy with Badger. The party remained divided throughout the 1880s, and as a consequence its members rarely capitalized upon the fratricidal politics of the Redeemers. Some white Republicans believed that Badger had given far too much patronage to black New Orleanians. One such individual wrote a letter to President Chester Arthur in 1883 encouraging the appointment of another man as collector. "I think it becomes my duty as a white republican," he began, "to inform you as to the condition of things in this State. . . . During Mr. Casey's time there was [*sic*] but few negroes in the Custom House—today there is but few white men employed there." Like the author of this letter, conservative white Republicans believed that their party might have a future in Louisiana if they could only jettison its association with people of color. "There is considerable dissatisfaction in the Democratic ranks," the same letter-writer continued: "By appointing a man that will command the respect of the people I know the result will astonish you,"[29]

There is no question that Badger made effective political use of his Custom House employees. Although it caused a certain amount of consternation among various factions within the Republican party, Badger enlisted the aid of his federal employees to ensure political victory for William Pitt Kellogg in Louisiana's Third Congressional District, a territory that contained the state's sugar-growing region from Plaquemines Parish in the east to Iberia Parish in the west. Kellogg had managed to secure a seat in the Senate amid the turbulent political wrangling that took place in the early months of 1877. While he stood no chance of ever again serving as a senator from the now Democratically controlled state of Louisiana, he could run for the House in a district, tied as it was to protectionism, that had shown strong Republican tendencies. It was also the home of Henry Clay Warmoth's sprawling Magnolia Plantation as well as those of other influential planters who felt confident that they could obviate whatever negative political pressure the Democratic party might bring to bear upon the freedmen. When the 1882 fall canvass arrived, Badger deployed reliable Custom House employees to rally black turnout. Mindful of the political violence of the age, as a soldier he understood the necessity of guaranteeing the safety of his constituency. In the Third District, Badger demonstrated what resources and the determination to use them could accomplish. This all took place even as the Pendleton Bill, a piece of legislation designed to expressly forbid the use of federal employees for such purposes, moved through Congress. Victorious, Kellogg was the last Republican to represent the district for a century. When the Republicans lost control of the White House in 1884 and, as a consequence, control of the Custom House, it spelled trouble for the party in Louisiana.

E. John Ellis's foray into oppositional politics during the gubernatorial nomination campaign of 1879 created an enduring bitterness between himself and the Bourbon wing of the party. Although he spent the majority of the summer of 1880 campaigning for Winfield Scott Hancock's run for the presidency, it soon became clear that he would have to return to Louisiana to campaign in his own Orleans Parish–based district. Vacationing with his family in Blue Ridge Springs, Virginia, E. John Ellis wrote to his brother Thomas that he planned to return to New Orleans by August 10 to "organize my battle against the 'ringsters.'" Louis Wiltz and E. A. Burke, his two main antagonists, were unable to force the nomination of another Democrat, but neither had they forgotten Ellis's words from the previous year. That antagonism had only deepened by the time he once again sought reelection in 1882. "I want no political fellowship with the present regime in Louisiana. It must be and will be overthrown," he wrote to Thomas late that summer. Yet Ellis's apostasy did not necessarily strike a discordant tone with his constituents. He had prevailed over his Republican opponent in his overwhelmingly white district (something of an anomaly both in Louisiana and the Deep South) by a margin of only two thousand to three thousand votes in previous contests. This fact alone suggests the degree to which the Bourbon wing was fraudulently manipulating black ballots in other Louisiana districts with large numbers of freedmen. It also suggests that Orleans Parish whites, a majority of the city's electorate, were not wholly in step with the state's Democratic leadership and that Bourbon abuses clearly must have driven a significant number into the Republican fold—after 1877. Despite a last-minute underhanded attack by Burke's *Times-Democrat* in which the Bourbon kingmaker expressed doubts about Ellis's loyalty to the Democratic party, he won reelection in 1882. It was, however, the last time that Ellis ever ran for office.[30]

Ellis's disillusionment with the Louisiana Democracy was total by the time he ended his final term in Congress. In 1883 he again sought unsuccessfully to defeat the nomination of a Bourbon governor. As he had in 1879, he attracted the prestige of Fred Ogden to his cause. This time the Democrats nominated Samuel D. McEnery, the brother of John McEnery; Samuel had ascended to the governorship when Louis Wiltz died in office. In the brief time that he was governor, McEnery gained such a reputation for being a tool of the lottery that he earned the nickname McLottery. Later in 1883, E. A. Burke met with Ellis, hat in hand, offering to let bygones be bygones if Ellis could help secure federal funding for the International Exposition to be held in New Orleans in 1885—a feat Ellis successfully accomplished. Much of Ellis's efforts during his last term in office, however, centered upon trying to salvage his finances through a variety of schemes, none of which seemed to bring any relief. As an early biographer concluded, "the one consolation in his financial straits was the fact that even his enemies had to concede his honesty, otherwise, after ten years in Congress, his home would not be advertised for taxes." Reflecting on the condition of machine politics in Louisiana, Ellis came to the end of his political career believing that the only "safeguard of popular government" would be a competitive Republican party in the state. Coincidentally, Ellis was succeeded in office by Michael Hahn, a Republican and former wartime governor of Louisiana. Although the German-immigrant

Hahn attracted significant support among the city's ethnic wards, he could not have won without the support of Reformer Democrats who found Bourbonism to be an unpalatable option. After leaving office, Ellis periodically involved himself in political fights, most notably the effort to secure the nomination of Francis T. Nicholls as governor in 1888. Such conflict finally took its toll on Ellis, however. In the spring of 1889, at age forty-eight, he suffered a fatal heart attack at his home in Washington, DC.[31]

The election of Grover Cleveland in 1884, the first Democratic president in almost thirty years, should have been cause for celebration among Louisiana's conservative whites. Instead, it ended up being just one more indication of how deeply divided the state Democratic factions remained. Because of these divisions, and because the recently passed Pendleton Act theoretically placed some limits upon the shameless application of the spoils system, the Cleveland administration moved at a glacial pace in announcing its patronage appointments in New Orleans. Just as the prospect of landing a lucrative federal position had revealed the smallness of aspiring placeholders in the Republican camp during the Grant years, the same was now true of Louisiana Democrats who engaged in base squabbling over the fruit of partisan victory.

The first task at hand for Louisiana's Democrats was to urge Cleveland to remove Badger and his team of Republican employees from the Custom House. In a letter to the treasury department, former U.S. senator B. F. Jonas wondered why nobody had made "proper use" of the damning evidence he had offered for Badger's removal. "In it I made the statement which is known to every man, woman & child in this State, that the Custom House was the focus and head quarters of offensive Republican politics in this State, That every officer in it was an active partisan, and delegate to State & National Conventions, and a Member of the Active working political committees." Jonas went on to assert that instead of being retained because of the Pendleton Act, lower-level employees in the Custom House should be fired because of their partisan activities on behalf of Kellogg in the Third District. "The employees of the Custom House are with few exceptions most obnoxious and corrupt partisans. It would be most dangerous to entrench them in office," noted Jonas. A group letter from the Reform members of the Democratic Congressional delegation leveled the most specific allegations against Badger's men, accusing them of

> visiting the quarters and churches of the freedmen at night, attending political meetings, getting up political meetings, making speeches, influencing and

persuading negroes to vote the Republican ticket, brow-beating and intimidat-
ing colored men who desired to vote for the Democratic nominee for Congress, and the Democratic Presidential ticket, inspiring the colored women to
active exertions to prevent their husbands, fathers and brothers from voting the
Democratic ticket, breaking up meetings of colored men held in the interest of
the Democratic candidate for Congress, inciting turmoil and riot, and actually
assassination in cold blood [of] the Democratic colored leader of one meeting—
in short preaching a political crusade to the colored people against the Democratic party and its candidate telling them that the success of that party meant
the re-enslavement, &c, &c.

To President Cleveland, one member of the Boston Club put it more succinctly: "Our Democracy are anxious to be rid of the worthless negro politicians
who have been drawn into the Custom House from all parts of the State."[32]

Jonas, a Reformer Democrat and a member of the Boston Club, desired the
collectorship for himself. He, as well as his supporters, waged an equally strident
campaign to keep the Ring forces from placing their own man in the office. One
writer, who identified himself only as "A True Democrat," noted that if the treasury secretary wished to verify his claims of Badger's corruption, he could "just
inquire of any, or, all the Louisiana Representatives composing the Reform Democracy (excluding Senator Eustis & Congressman St. Martin who do not wish
any reform but 'Ring methods.') Keep all eyes on E.A. Burke, the so called Director General of the Cotton Exposition here, the Schemer has been in Washington
D.C. for the past sixty days trying to work a fine point on the administration,
which will develop itself very soon; (but so far he has failed.)." Another Jonas supporter writing to Cleveland bemoaned that J. B. Eustis, the Ring-supported choice
for the U.S. Senate, had prevailed in securing that office. "This is where Mr. Jonas
should be today but he was swindled by Hoodlum Ring Party who defeated him
with bribes and Promises from such men as Houston, Burke, and a great many
others who would like to see the custom house filled with the scum of this city."
Concluding, he noted angrily, "Should Mr. Jonas fail, then you might just as well
let Badger remain." The same Bostonian who wished for the expulsion of the
"worthless negro politicians" wrote to the president that "the Democratic party
of Louisiana is far from being united. Gibson, Eustis, Fitzpatrick, Houston,
McEnery, &c have not the confidence of the Democratic masses [and] are better
known as the Ring than as Democrats."[33]

Growing increasingly uncertain of its own ability to maintain political power in
Louisiana, E. A. Burke's Bourbon/Ring alliance began promoting an alternative

plan in which Fred Ogden might be given the collectorship of the New Orleans Custom House as a sign of compromise—a move that might lead to a healing between Reform and Bourbon Democratic political factions in the state. Fred Ogden himself must have known how remote the odds for success of such a scheme were, and unlike B. F. Jonas, he was not one to press his case. The only correspondence in Ogden's Treasury Department applicant folder crafted in his own hand was a rather plaintive note he penned in April 1885 to Louisiana senator J. B. Eustis: "On Dec. 11th [Senator Randall L.] Gibson wrote to me as follows; 'If I have the power I hope to show you that your friends and I look upon you as entitled to be one of the pillars of "Redeemed Louisiana."' These are his exact words." Ogden's pivotal role in bringing the Republican era in Louisiana to a close was undeniable, but spoils of victory were never his.[34]

Ogden did not receive the collectorship in New Orleans; moreover, the failure of Burke's scheme to secure his nomination revealed just how deeply divided white conservatives in Louisiana remained nearly a decade after the so-called Redemption. That same month, Leon Jastremski, an ally of Burke and McEnery and the chairman of Louisiana's state Democratic party, found himself aboard the same riverboat as a member of the state's congressional delegation, Newton C. Blanchard. When he floated the idea of Ogden's nomination to Blanchard, Jastremski found his overtures quickly and confidently rebuffed. He also felt that he had "reason to believe that the gentlemen of our Congressional delegation who style themselves 'Reformed Democrats' have determined to plunge the State into one of the bitterest political fights ever witnessed in Louisiana." Not only would the Reform Democrats who had once looked to Fred Ogden as a gubernatorial candidate not support a Bourbon scheme to make him collector, Jastremski noted, but Blanchard had indicated, "among other startling assertions . . . that General Nicholls would be nominated and elected Governor in 1888, and that they (the Reformed Democrats) would beat us with the negro." When relating this unsettling news to Senator Eustis, Jastremski assured him that he had conveyed to Blanchard that the Bourbons "had no desire to foster a war of factions, and would only engage in such a war when forced to do so. In that event, we would fight all along the line and through every Congressional District. I warned him that if this war was made his friends would under all probability suffer defeat."[35]

By the time of his own premature death from liver cancer in May 1886, Fred Ogden was in so much debt to Northern creditors that his widow renounced any claim to the estate. The large debt was undoubtedly due in no small part to Ogden's slavish devotion to the soldier's code of honor, an ethos that expressly

forbade the sort of grasping qualities that were essential survival skills in the postbellum world of politics and commerce. It was a trait that he seemed to share with
his friend E. John Ellis. While many other men who had compiled equally gallant records during the war adjusted with the times and thrived, Ogden always
shied away from profiting from his fame. Perhaps nothing was more emblematic
of this tendency than the results of an inventory of Ogden's defunct business, ordered by Judge Aristée Tissot. Among the bills and receipts, a clerk found a giant
pile of handwritten IOUs in the soldier's desk drawer. A couple of them represented large unpaid bills of customers, but the vast proportion were for small
amounts of money—from ten to two hundred dollars each—all from individuals
within the community, some from prominent men of means. The notaries inven-
torying Ogden's estate declared all of these debts "worthless."

Ten days after Ogden's funeral, some of the men who had served alongside
him in the White League gathered together to discuss erecting a monument to
a comrade who, though widely admired, had been treated rather shabbily by
those who had owed him the most. They offered Ogden's financially strapped
widow whatever site in Metairie Cemetery she desired—perhaps knowing that
while on his deathbed Fred Ogden had expressed the desire to be buried beneath
a great live oak that stood within its confines. Not until later that summer, however, did Laura Ogden find what she felt was an appropriate monument to the man
she knew best. While touring in the mountains of East Tennessee, she noticed a
massive red granite boulder lying deep in a ravine and knew in that instant that
there could be no more fitting marker for her late husband. Weighing more than
forty thousand pounds, it required seven days and a special permit from the mayor
to transport the massive stone from the St. Joseph Street wharf to Metairie Cemetery. Teamsters had to lay wide planks on the street under the wagon's wheels to
avoid damaging the roadbed. Once workmen finally positioned the marker amid
the city of ornate burial vaults, a sculptor came to the site and coarsely engraved
on its surface only "GEN. FRED N. OGDEN." "And the granite boulder stands in its
strength," noted the *Picayune*, "the simplest, yet perhaps the grandest monument
in New Orleans."[36]

Although it had been a decade since the Redeemers proclaimed their victory
over Reconstruction, the social and political turmoil fostered by the Republican
era continued unabated. What was so damning about the predicament that conservative whites found themselves in was that they could no longer blame their
problems on outside forces. Redemption forced them to finally confront the fundamental internal struggles that had always been present among their numbers
since the Civil War. With the struggle against Republican rule no longer serving

as a unifying force, the White League coalition split back into factions based in deeply rooted antagonisms. Ten years after the Redemption, it remained unclear which faction would emerge triumphant.

While the Democratic ascendancy in 1877 necessarily had a deleterious impact upon Republican and black political power, it failed to crush either. After the collapse of Stephen B. Packard's bid for the governorship, Republican and black political power converged within the Custom House's walls under the astute leadership of Algernon Sydney Badger. His experiences both as a politician and as a soldier taught him the importance of concentrating one's force in an engagement that was likely to result in success. These tactics resulted in the 1882 election of William P. Kellogg to the U.S. House of Representatives from Louisiana's Third District. So long as the Republicans held the White House, the party retained significance in Louisiana. By the start of 1886, however, not only did the Republicans lose control of Custom House patronage, but long-standing feuds within the state Republican party diminished its ability to capitalize on Redeemer factionalism.

CHAPTER NINE

A HARD-HANDED STABILITY

1886–1898

There are too many old men in control. The younger man claims
his place, and ought to have it. Aside from the governor and the
attorney general, most of us are old horses and will have to make
room for fresher blood.

— Aristée Louis Tissot, March 6, 1894

A t the stroke of midnight December 31, 1886, Louisiana's new "Sunday Law"
took effect. Widely unpopular in the "non-Sabbath revering city" of New Orleans, this new legislation made illegal the selling of a wide range of goods and
services, including groceries and alcohol, on the Christian Sabbath. The city's
most outspoken critic of the bill was the leader of the Anti-Sunday Law Society,
Joseph A. Walker—the same man who fifteen years earlier had asked Charles
Sauvinet to no longer drink at the Bank Coffeehouse. Unlike Sauvinet, Walker
had prospered in postbellum New Orleans. By 1886 he was the president of the
City Railway Company and the owner of the sprawling Crescent Billiard Hall, an
Italianate temple to urban hedonism located on the corner of Canal Street and
St. Charles Avenue. As both an economic force and an important figure in urban
ward politics, Walker's opinions mattered. He would soon discover, however, the
limits of his influence.[1]

Representing a group of five hundred city businessmen, Joseph Walker entered Aristée Tissot's Civil District Court on New Year's Day and promptly received
from Judge Tissot an injunction against the Sunday Law's enforcement. With
such legal protection in hand, Walker triumphantly strode out of the courtroom
and back to his saloon, where the party began in earnest; a large placard emblazoned with the word *open* was now prominently displayed on the Crescent's
door. Outside the urban core of New Orleans, however, editorial reaction to Tissot's order was both voluminous and overwhelmingly negative. A reporter for the

Picayune noted disdainfully that all the barrooms along St. Charles Avenue between Common and Canal were open in defiance of the law, "*one, adjoining the central station,* being in the same building as police headquarters." The Jackson, Mississippi, *Clarion* observed that the "opposition [to the law] has been so bold and outspoken that the experiment of enforcing the law has been watched with interest by all, and with concern by many." Indeed, Tissot's injunction, issued on shaky legal grounds, had caught the attention of a national audience. "The most remarkable feature of the proceeding is that the State of Louisiana could furnish a judge who would grant the injunction," continued the *Clarion's* disgusted editor. "Having ordered the writ he is now on record not only as being of the opinion that the citizens of Louisiana have the inalienable right to violate the Sabbath, but that he can enjoin the execution of a criminal statue." By February the State Supreme Court of Louisiana listened to Walker's application for Certiorari and Prohibition, and the outcome was a resounding quash of Tissot's defiant order. The high court ruled that the Sunday Law was a valid statute under the state's constitution and declared as well that Tissot had "no power of any kind to curtail, extend, suspend, or regulate" the action of the Orleans Parish criminal court.[2]

Given Tissot's broad training and impeccable reputation for legal probity, it is clear that his decision to issue an injunction against a criminal statute that so plainly fell outside the jurisdiction of his civil court stemmed from considerations beyond law. Although he had briefly dabbled with Henry Clay Warmoth's Republican militia in 1870, Tissot had been a more or less active member of the Democratic Party in New Orleans since his return from Paris in 1866. As a judge, he had administered the oath of office to both John McEnery in 1873 and Francis T. Nicholls in 1877. Like most other Democrats after the Redemption, however, Tissot had taken sides with one of the two opposing Democratic political factions in New Orleans, and by 1886 he stood squarely with the Ring. When the city's district courts underwent reorganization in the state constitution of 1879, Governor Louis Wiltz appointed Tissot, a loyal member of the Ring faction, to the same bench he had previously held as an elected official. Without question, many elite white New Orleanians like Tissot were allied with the urban political machine. Yet the city's ethnic ward patronage networks supplied the Ring's main electoral reservoir, and the Louisiana Lottery was its most powerful financial backer. In statewide contests, the Ring frequently cooperated with the Bourbon faction of the Democratic Party, which was managed by the corrupt state treasurer E. A. Burke, headed by Governor Samuel D. McEnery, and dominated by the planter oligarchy, who manipulated the ballots of the state's overwhelmingly black cotton-planting parishes. When Tissot enjoined the government against enforce-

ment of the Sunday law, he may well have believed that it represented an uncon-
stitutional infringement upon individual liberty. There could be no doubt, though,
that he recognized that the law was also a blatant attack upon those Sabbath-
violating urbanites who made up the backbone of the Ring's political coalition in
New Orleans. For a man widely respected for his gentlemanly manners and dedication to legal procedure, Tissot's extralegal injunction was a remarkable protest
indeed.[3]

Tissot's politics and social vision had always been local in focus; and without
question, his long tenure on the bench of Orleans Parish's Civil District Court
placed him into contact with a broad sweep of the city's residents. Among the
appellants who stood before him were Louise Drouet, the financially strapped
mixed-race woman who had sued her wealthy white Creole cousins for alimony
in 1873, and Jefferson Davis, the former president of the Confederacy. Guided by
a legal vision that placed all citizens on an equal footing in a court of law, Tissot
enjoyed a reputation for giving both prince and pauper equal consideration. As
one contemporary remembered him, "[Tissot's] friends were not restricted to sets
or classes, for he had hosts of them in every walk of life." At the same time, this
seemingly paternalistic man of laws ardently supported the political aspirations
of Samuel McEnery, a Bourbon reactionary whose trampling of both the state
and federal constitutions had caused the unjust sufferings of countless poor Louisianians of both races. Tissot's paradoxical social and political decisions, like those
of many other New Orleanians of the Civil War generation, defied easy ideological categorization. A lifetime of norm-shattering moments seemed to have forced
him to embrace the ambiguities of the age.[4]

Although much of Louisiana had always operated in a state of de facto segregation, even during the Republican era, startling examples of continued integration
and so-called social equality remained visible as late as the 1890s, particularly in
New Orleans. They could be found in saloons, at sporting events, on select railways, in brothels, and even among the faithful of the Roman Catholic Church. In
practical terms, such forms of integration scarcely affected the daily lives of middle-
class white men, let alone those middle- and upper-class white women whose purity the most ardent white supremacists claimed to be protecting. Moreover, such
interracial activity had not been legislated into existence by the carpetbaggers but
instead had emerged by either cultural or market forces. Yet from the standpoint
of symbolism, few could argue with the inflammatory power that periodic examples of black "social equality" wielded over political discourse, especially when
properly manipulated by those who hoped to gain from the issue. The *prospect* of

integration was just as potent as its actual presence. Although the White League coalition crumbled in the wake of its own successful bid to oust the Republicans from power, the memory of the techniques it employed to forge white political unity had not been forgotten. In the 1890s, Reformers and Bourbons alike summoned both the ghost of black ambition and the legend of the White League in a campaign of white supremacy whose objective was the final defeat of one of Reconstruction's remarkably enduring legacies.[5]

The most conspicuous remaining legacy of Republican rule, professional integration, and black political power in late nineteenth-century New Orleans was without question the Custom House on Canal Street. Although Collector Algernon Sydney Badger's coterie of Afro-Creole activists had lost their patronage jobs when Grover Cleveland's first term commenced in 1885, nearly all of them returned to their former positions when Benjamin Harrison appointed Henry Clay Warmoth to the post of collector of customs in 1889. In New Orleans, independent Afro-Creole professionals such as Dr. Charles Roudanez and Aristide Mary had always played a key role in those activist circles that led ultimately to the formation of the Comité des Citoyens, or Citizens' Committee. Yet it is also clear that the committee's gravitational center dwelt within the walls of the Custom House. Protected financially from economic reprisal, mixed-race federal employees such as Rodolphe Desdunes and Louis A. Martinet were to fight the last great postbellum battles of the segregation struggle. Of course, there was some irony here: Throughout his career as a Republican, Warmoth's latent conservatism had made him the frequent target of well-deserved black political criticism. Yet as collector of customs, Warmoth was responsible in an indirect but nonetheless crucial way for Homer Plessy's challenge to Louisiana's Separate Car Act of 1890.

The mixed-race activists who worked inside the Custom House on Canal Street found themselves by the late 1880s on a collision course with a new generation of white Louisiana lawmakers; these legislators sought to eliminate the state's remaining "social equality" laws that had been on the books since the days of Radical rule. In 1890 the legislature passed the Louisiana Separate Car Act, a bill first introduced by a twenty-nine-year-old representative from Ascension Parish named Joseph St. Amant. Four years later, Charles Gauthreaux, a thirty-one-year-old state senator from Orleans Parish, submitted a bill designed to outlaw interracial marriage. In 1896 the Supreme Court of the United States ruled in *Plessy v. Ferguson*, placing "separate but equal" into the nation's legal canon. Once this basis was established, the further codification of racial separation became a foregone conclusion.[6]

It did not require much deductive reasoning on the part of Louisiana's Democratic leaders during the late nineteenth century, however, to recognize that the Fifteenth Amendment to the U.S. Constitution, and not the perceived "social equality" of integration, was the more *tangible* of the two destabilizing legacies of the Republican era. Ratified in 1870, the amendment was the crowning achievement of the Radical ascendancy, granting the right of suffrage to all male citizens over the age of twenty-one regardless of race or prior condition of servitude. As the Custom House employees under Algernon Sydney Badger had demonstrated, even after 1877 the black franchise remained a threat when judiciously targeted at closely contested races. Moreover, in Louisiana's sugar-growing regions, otherwise deeply conservative planters would willfully harness the power of the black ballot by fielding Republican or independent candidates against Bourbon rivals who failed to respect their desire for protective measures against imported sugar. Even where violence and economic intimidation prevented its lawful use, the black franchise remained a potent and often ironic political weapon. When skillfully manipulated by Bourbon politicians, stolen black ballots effectively neutralized the electoral threats that periodically emanated from the piney-woods parishes dominated by poor whites or from discontented urban elites in the metropolis of New Orleans. Whether or not anyone appreciated the irony of the Bourbons' engaging in exactly the sort of fraud that they had once accused the Republicans of perpetrating, the effects of such skullduggery were undeniable. Both the actual exercise of the franchise by black citizens and the manipulation of the same by Bourbon oligarchs acted as political wildcards, upsetting traditional patterns of white political privilege. Until the black franchise could be eliminated, politics in Louisiana would always foster a palpable sense of uncertainty.

By the late 1880s, the realization had grown among a coalition of elite white Louisianians that stabilizing political life in the Pelican State hinged on their ability to concoct a mechanism capable of obliterating the intent of the suffrage amendment. Their crusade to accomplish this end took the form of a pseudo-Progressive campaign to enact "ballot reform." The movement probably originated more out of resentment against Bourbon manipulation of black ballots than from fears that black Louisianians would ever enjoy the ability to vote freely. Eventually, disfranchisement's proponents persuaded even the Bourbon cotton planters of Louisiana's river parishes to acknowledge that continued black voting opened a door to the threat of popular political insurgency. And the concerns of rural and urban powerbrokers were not confined to the destabilizing presence of black voters. The prospect that poor white farmers and laboring ethnic urbanites might vote together in a unified bloc always posed a hypothetical yet increasingly real

threat to elite rule. The solution to the problem of popular dissent and the instability it fostered was painfully obvious—the franchise would have to be severely
restricted. The result was the essential destruction of universal suffrage by Louisiana's 1898 "disfranchisement" constitution. In its wake emerged a new hard-
handed stability in which a select coterie of oligarchs ruled Louisiana unfettered
by the need to cultivate a meaningful popular following.

The campaign for segregation and disfranchisement in Louisiana was also
in large measure about the eclipsing of the Civil War generation by a younger
group of political leaders. While old war heroes such as Francis Tillou Nicholls
remained part of the political landscape, the individuals who drove the movement to crush Reconstruction's legacy were generally younger men who had been
born between 1855 and 1870. Aristée Louis Tissot observed this phenomenon
while serving in the Louisiana state senate in 1894. "There are too many old men
in control. The young men claim his place, and ought to have it," he noted. "Most
of us are old horses and will have to make room for fresher blood." As the 1890s
wore on, important civic figures such as Tissot gave way to a younger generation
of men. Unlike Tissot, whose life had been forged in the cataclysm of war and
defeat, this "fresher blood" had been raised in the powerful gospel of the Lost
Cause and did not harbor the same kinds of self-doubt about their own political
and social vision. Ironically, Tissot himself had been responsible in some measure
for the ideological indoctrination of this rising generation, having played a role
in forming the Broom Rangers, Jr., twenty-two years earlier. In the 1890s, these
younger men set about destroying the apparatuses that had so destabilized life for
their parents' generation.[7]

With the exception of the two-year term of Joseph Shakespeare as mayor between
1880 and 1882, the Ring had dominated city politics in New Orleans during the
1880s. This development was largely due to the 1882 rewriting of the city charter
that had placed municipal governance on the aldermanic system and, as a result,
empowered the ethnic ward politicking of the Ring. When the Sunday Law
passed the Louisiana legislature in the summer of 1886, it was only one symptom
of the greater resentment the Reformer Democrats harbored toward their political rivals—those Ring bosses who knew how to mobilize the vote of the "concert
saloon element." Of course, the level of vice and violence in New Orleans was
difficult to ignore, particularly when some of the most prominent offenders were
members of city government associated with the Ring. When Governor Samuel D.
McEnery tried to defend his political allies in the city, the editor of the *Picayune*

replied that "if he had said that the city had never been worse governed, and if he had added that its municipal elections had been so managed for many years as almost invariably to defeat the popular will, he would have come nearer to stating the extent of misrule in New Orleans." Despite their success in passing the Sunday Law, however, the Reformers failed in the same legislative session to enact a law designed to "purify the ballot-box" in New Orleans. This setback notwithstanding, the issue of ballot reform, as its proponents termed it, was not going to go away anytime soon. It was destined to become the one political goal that would eventually unite the Bourbons and the Reformers.[8]

The gubernatorial nomination fight between Samuel McEnery and Francis T. Nicholls in 1888 set the stage for an epic confrontation in New Orleans between the self-described "better element" Reformers and the ethnic ward bosses of the Ring. Nicholls had been one of the most vocal critics of Bourbon electoral fraud ever since his parliamentary removal from office by the Bourbon/Ring combination in 1879. The patrician general's objective of eliminating the manipulation of black votes matched well with the espoused goals of his Reformer Democratic allies in New Orleans who sought to limit the political influence of immigrants. Through a great deal of effort in the weeks leading up to the 1888 Democratic convention, Nicholls had been able to mitigate McEnery's edge by successfully challenging the credentials of a significant number of Bourbon delegates—men who had claimed their seats by virtue of stolen black ballots. Thus, with Nicholls and McEnery in relative political parity in Louisiana's countryside, observers soon realized that the metropolis held the key to the Democratic nomination. With so much at stake, and with six years of smoldering resentment fueling a strong Reformer voter turnout, the Nicholls camp managed to win a narrow victory over the Ring in the election of delegates. Their triumph was due in no small part to the emergence of the Young Men's Democratic Association, an oppositional organization led by a thirty-year-old lawyer by the name of William S. Parkerson. The YMDA was the youthful vanguard of the Reformer Democrats, as its members were drawn from the same class of urban elite that dominated professional circles in New Orleans. Moreover, the political rhetoric of the YMDA in 1888 clearly found its inspiration in the rhetoric that the White League's leadership had once employed against the Republican regime of William Pitt Kellogg.[9]

Using language reminiscent of editorials run after the White League's victory on September 14, 1874, the *Picayune's* giddy account of the day's voting revealed only partially how the city's underclass had been defeated. "Old citizens, whom ring rule disgusted into remaining away from the polls in years, rallied again in the cause of Nicholls and reform. . . . Without Mr. Patorno's imported Italians, Mayor Guillotte's police and the deluded 'Bund fur Freiheit und Recht' the McEneryites would not have obtained a corporal's guard of delegates in Orleans." Yet such rhetoric obscured the potential for violence found at the city's polling places. As Henry Clay Warmoth later recalled, it was not just a strong turnout that had fueled the Reformers' victory but the demand for "a free ballot and fair count," which had been assured "by 2,500 Winchester rifles in the hands of the Young Men's Democratic Association, who, with the aid of 1,200 Republican allies, swept the ring out of political existence." One area of the city that did not succumb to the YMDA's tactics was Aristée Tissot's Sixth Ward, where Tissot himself served as a delegate. The *Picayune* attributed the Ring victory there to "Alderman Patorno's services . . . because of the large army of recently arrived Italian emigrants who voted blindly at his dictation." The implications of the newspaper's observations were obvious. A threat to good government, such immigrants were not worthy of the franchise and should be kept away from the polls wherever possible. Noteworthy among the day's events was that, unlike the city's white ethnics, the Republican black elite of New Orleans voted in favor of the Nicholls faction.[10]

As early as 1885, members of the Reformer Democratic Party had vowed to return Francis Tillou Nicholls to the governorship and boasted that they would do so with the active assistance of black ballots. Whether they could make good on such a threat was debatable, but that they raised the issue at all revealed just how much conservative white politicians feared Louisiana's sizable black electorate. Moreover, in the closely contested nomination fight in New Orleans, black Republicans threw their small but important support behind Nicholls. This is not to say that the vast majority of black Louisianians enjoyed the ability to vote for the candidate of their choice, but rather that their presence on the registration rolls represented a substantial reservoir of ballots ready to be stolen. Ensuring political victory by such blatant disregard for the law had its risks, however. If black Louisianians ever managed to vote freely, it would spell doom for whoever opposed them. Without question, Nicholls would have been a far more palatable candidate to black voters in a straight-out contest against Samuel McEnery. Yet as it happened in 1888, Nicholls, not McEnery, had to worry about a fair count of black ballots.

Unhappy about his defeat in the nominating convention, McEnery announced afterward that he would ensure a "fair count" in the April 1888 general election between Nicholls and his Republican challenger, Henry Clay Warmoth. The warning could not have been more blatant—the Nicholls faction would take office, but it must recognize the needs of the Bourbons. At a lavish dinner on the third floor of Moreau's restaurant in New Orleans, Nicholls and his managers promised to appoint Samuel D. McEnery to the Louisiana Supreme Court in exchange for his continued manipulation of the black vote in favor of Nicholls—a move that would eliminate the growing Republican threat emanating from War-moth's campaign. Perhaps no other moment was more responsible for convincing Louisiana's white political titans of the need to eliminate the black franchise once and for all. Nicholls, who had pledged in 1877 to uphold the constitutional rights of black Louisianians, finally came to realize that no amount of paternalism could surmount the genuine desire of a long-oppressed people to vote as free men. And in the end, it was Nicholls who benefited from Bourbon fraud. The bargain also underscored that the self-styled Reformers were no more interested in true electoral integrity than the Bourbons had been. It is noteworthy that in making this deal with Nicholls, McEnery had bargained for his own position, but not those of his supporters. Aristée Louis Tissot, who had served as a McEnery delegate to the nominating convention, lost his position as a judge in the Orleans Parish Civil District Court when Governor Nicholls replaced him with a reliable political ally—E. John Ellis's older brother Thomas.[11]

There was one positive result that emerged from this rather dark political exchange. Treasurer E. A. Burke, who, along with many others in the McEnery faction, had lost his job quickly, then discovered that the new Nicholls administration was serious about reviewing for irregularities the books that he had kept while in office. The investigation ultimately revealed that he had swindled more than $1.2 million from the state treasury. Burke never returned to Louisiana to clear his name; instead he lived out his many remaining days in luxurious exile in Honduras. When he died in 1928, among his effects was the drawing wheel once used by the Louisiana Lottery. In a classic case of "waste not, want not," Burke sent for it when the Pelican State finally outlawed the official gambling racket in 1894. In Puerto Cortez, he reestablished an international gambling franchise and operated it successfully for many years.[12]

The election of Orleans Parish's Democratic delegates for the 1888 gubernatorial nomination was not the first time that Sicilian immigrants had faced the ire of the city's white elites and the disapprobation of its most influential newspapers—nor was it the last. Italians first came to New Orleans in significant numbers during the 1850s, but not until the postbellum era did a much larger contingent of poor newcomers begin turning up in the city. Although the vast majority of

Italians in New Orleans were among the laboring classes who worked along the city's docks, a few conspicuous individuals managed to become wealthy merchants and powerful political figures. Perhaps the best known among them was Joseph P. Macheca. He was born in the city during the antebellum era, was adopted by wealthy Maltese parents, and with his half siblings became a remarkably prosperous fruit importer. When Macheca returned from his Confederate service, he began building a "gang" of sorts, comprised of Sicilian dockworkers, and called them the Innocenti, or Innocents. These paradoxically named roughs had a political dimension and took part in the violence of 1868, hoping to carry the election for Seymour and Blair. Their ties to the Ring had roots in the Democratic Party's fight against Know-Nothingism during the antebellum era—bonds that only grew stronger in postbellum New Orleans. In 1874 Macheca formed his Innocenti into a company of White League volunteers and led them during the battle on Canal Street.[13]

By the 1880s, Italians had come to dominate not only the Esplanade Avenue side of the French Quarter but also the active imagination of the city's lawmen. Talk of an Italian "Mafia Society" was common in New Orleans by the 1880s, and although at times fanciful, such stories were not entirely without substance. The first widespread discussion of the Sicilian underworld came in 1881, when an aspiring young detective named David Hennessey nabbed a well-known Italian criminal who had been on the lam in the city. The arrest was so spectacular that it made international news—Hennessey supposedly declining a fifty-thousand-dollar bribe that the suspect had offered in return for setting him free. That same year, Algernon Sydney Badger wrote a note to an emerging young attorney, George Denegre, offering his candid assessment of testimony received from Sicilian witnesses: "Even when compelled or willing to testify, their evidence under oath or otherwise cannot be believed," observed Badger. Coincidentally, Badger knew both Hennessey and Macheca from his war and Reconstruction days. David Hennessey's father had served under Badger in the Unionist First Louisiana Cavalry and again in the Metropolitan Police until he was gunned down in a New Orleans barroom in 1867. Young Dave had also worked for Badger, serving as a messenger boy in the employ of the Metropolitan Police, and was likely present for the battle on September 14, 1874. For his part, Macheca boasted that he had been responsible for saving Badger's life during the White League battle—a claim that his fellow League veterans frequently contested. Fate once again linked the names of Badger, Macheca, and Hennessey in the winter of 1890–91.[14]

When the Reformer faction emerged victorious in returning Francis T. Nicholls to Louisiana's governorship in 1888, it also managed to return Joseph Shakespeare to the mayor's office in New Orleans. One of the mayor's new appointments was David Hennessey as chief of police. Hardly an innocent himself (he was widely believed to be a partner in a brothel), Hennessey nevertheless set about to clean up both the notoriously inefficient and corrupt police force and the crime-ridden city. Along the way he became deeply involved in an ongoing struggle between rival Sicilian families over controlling the unloading of fruit cargoes along the city's busy wharves. Hennessey suspected that the Matranga brothers, Charles and Tony, were using strong-arm Mafia-style tactics to take over the lucrative trade. It is also clear that he believed that Joseph Macheca, a powerful figure in the fruit importation business, was materially involved in their schemes. When Macheca returned to New Orleans from Puerto Cortez, Honduras, aboard the steamer *Breakwater* in early March 1890, either it was a case of profound coincidence or he was being trailed by none other than Robert Allan Pinkerton, the famous detective and a confidant of David Hennessey.[15]

Matters took a decided turn for the worse when on the foggy evening of October 15, 1890, a group of unknown assailants gunned down Chief Hennessey outside the door of his Girod Street home. City lore and numerous historians recount that before Hennessey died from his wounds the next day, he had fingered his assailants as "Dagoes." As his police chief lay dying in the next room, the outraged Mayor Shakespeare ordered the city police to round up anyone of Italian descent with even the remotest hint of a connection to the ongoing feud along the docks. Among the men that the police wanted to question about the Hennessey slaying were Charles Patorno, the brother of the alderman who had helped get out the vote for Samuel McEnery in 1888, and Joseph Macheca, the former White League captain and alleged crime boss. Learning that he was wanted by reading the front page of the *Picayune*, Macheca turned himself over to authorities the next day. It is likely that he could have easily fled on one of his steamers, and perhaps if he had sensed the magnitude of the personal disaster that was about to befall him and eight other suspects associated with the Hennessey murder, he would have done just that. What he did not know was that two working-class white women had identified him as the "well-dressed Italian" who had rented out a cottage adjacent to Hennessey's home from which the police chief's assassins reportedly stalked their victim. Others claimed that they had seen Macheca having dinner with the Matranga brothers at Fabacher's restaurant at the very moment when Hennessey was shot. These same unnamed accusers also reportedly heard

Macheca saying outside the restaurant, "Well, good night, boys, I did all I could. My only regret I have is that they did not do the —— up altogether." The implications of such evidence were clear to the editorial staff of the *Picayune*. "The reasonable inference," intoned the paper, "is that the party had already been advised of the shooting and that the chief was not killed outright, but was at that moment lying in the hospital."[16]

Aware that the rising tensions within the city might explode into mob violence if municipal authorities did not take forthright action to counter this perceived Mafia menace, Mayor Shakespeare assembled the special Committee of Fifty and empowered them to investigate the Hennessey homicide. On the group's executive committee sat respected older men like the now fifty-one-year-old Algernon Sydney Badger and the fifty-year-old Confederate veteran and former White League leader John Glynn, but the inclusion of other members revealed the emergence of the post–Civil War generation in civic affairs and the dominance of the Reformer Democrats and the YMDA. Walter Denegre, a thirty-two-year-old attorney and the youngest of twelve children born to a spectacularly wealthy New Orleans commission merchant, also served on the executive committee. Its chairman was Edgar H. Farrar, a forty-one-year-old lawyer who was a nephew of the recently deceased Jefferson Davis. Neither Denegre nor Farrar had served in the Confederacy—nor for that matter had they been in the White League. Recognizing Badger's broad experience in law enforcement, the mayor actively sought his advice as to what the city's course should be in dealing with future Italian immigrants. At Badger's urging, the next shipload of Italians to arrive after the Hennessey murder underwent a "rigid" inspection at the quarantine station by the crew of a Treasury Department revenue cutter to weed out "paupers, criminals," and "contract laborers." When it came to dealing with Italians, Badger was scarcely less hostile than the young Reformers who made up the majority of the committee's members.[17]

Just ten days after Hennessey's murder, the Committee of Fifty released a circular calling for a mass meeting to take place in Lafayette Square on Monday night, October 27. Considering the inflammatory editorial rhetoric that leapt off the pages of the city's dailies, the overall high feeling in the city toward Italians of all kinds, and the city's previous experience with "meetings of the people" in times of political and social crisis, it came as little surprise that a delegation of Italians made an urgent plea to the mayor asking that he call the thing off. Shakespeare himself began having doubts about the wisdom of this gathering by the time he and a delegation of city councilmen and Italian spokesmen met with the executive committee on the fourth floor of the Cotton Exchange the following day. The Committee of Fifty agreed to moderate its language significantly in its subsequent announcements, and the public meeting passed with little incident. Such peace did not last, though.[18]

In the months that passed between the October murder of Hennessey and the beginning of the trial for the first of the defendants the following March, the city's newspapers warned constantly about organized crime's ability to subvert justice. None of the important dailies were more vocal in their denunciations of Italians than the New Orleans *Daily States*, edited by the "redoubtable" race-baiter Henry J. Hearsey. Yet while historians have made much of Hearsey's inflammatory pronouncements leading up to and during the trial of the Sicilians accused of Hennessey's murder, he hardly held a monopoly on generating popular suspicion against all Italians. In general, the press kept up a constant drumbeat of mistrust, arguing that Sicilians would likely bribe or intimidate the jurors in the upcoming trial. The *Daily States* may have printed the names and addresses of the jury members, but so did the French-language *L'Abeille de la Nouvelle-Orléans*. The *Daily Picayune* took matters a step further by including illustrations of the jurors in its coverage of the trial. The message was clear: "respectable" citizens of New Orleans expected a guilty verdict, and the city's newspapermen were fully capable of engaging in intimidation of their own. Such tactics did not yield the desired effect, however. On March 13, 1891, the jury returned a mistrial for three of the defendants' cases and decided on acquittal in the other six, including that of Joseph Macheca. The shocking news had an electrifying effect on the youthful uptown elites who made up the backbone of the Committee of Fifty. The next day, the city's newspapers all ran editorials denouncing the ruling. They also included an ominous announcement by the committee inviting all law-abiding citizens to assemble at ten o'clock the following morning around the Clay Statue at the intersection of Canal/Royal/St. Charles.[19]

If editorial urging had failed to stir the crowd that converged on the Clay statue, the brief addresses given by three members of the Committee of Fifty surely did not. William S. Parkerson, who had played such a pivotal role in Shakespeare's 1888 election, led off with an inflammatory address. Next spoke Walter Denegre, whose words invoked the memory of the White League. "On September 14, 1874," noted Denegre, "such a crowd as I now see before me was assembled here, to assist the manhood of the Crescent City." John C. Wickliffe, the associate editor of an anti-Ring sheet called the *Daily Delta*, concluded the speeches by producing a list of eleven Sicilians worthy of death and beseeched the crowd to follow Parkerson, Denegre, and himself to a nearby gun shop, where they could buy the tools necessary for the day's work. The nine victims who died that day did not stand a chance. When Parkerson and the unruly mob arrived at the Orleans Parish prison at the corner of Orleans Avenue and Marais Street, they burst inside and set about their homicidal enterprise. Macheca, the "wealthiest Italian in New Orleans," met a swift death.[20]

"The scene at and about the Clay Statue this morning brought to mind very forcibly and vividly the popular and ominous uprising of that September nearly sixteen years ago," read an afternoon special of the *Daily States*. The allusion was hardly original and not altogether a surprise, but in many ways it made for a poor analogy. The 1874 clash was no riot—it was a well-planned insurrection against a government. And while white-supremacist in ideology, it did not target unarmed ethnic minorities. There were also problems with provenance. The 1891 mob ringleaders, Wickliffe, Parkerson, and Denegre, were all under age thirty-five. Denegre's older brother Henry had indeed fought for the White League in 1874, but these three had all still been in their teens during the battle. They were all contemporaries of the murdered David Hennessey. More-over, Macheca, whom they had killed, had been an actual White Leaguer in the 1874 battle. Further complicating the picture was the presence of individu-als of African descent among the lynch mob. Parkerson's intentions in reviving the victorious and united image of the White League were unmistakable: this new generation hoped to redefine the League's legacy for their own *exclusive* purposes, and they cloaked their objectives in remarkably similar rhetoric. Moreover, they hoped to forge the same sort of unity that the League once had. Only this time the enemy was not the hated carpetbagger but those Democratic rivals who continued to capitalize on the social and political instability that the Republican era had wrought.[21]

The scramble to define the legacy of the White League had begun immediately after the death of Frederick Nash Ogden in 1886. While he was still alive, no public figure, no matter how brazenly self-promoting, was willing to boast that he bore the League's mantle—any such claim simply would not have been credible. Although Ogden had been a reluctant gubernatorial candidate for the Reformer faction in 1879 and again in 1882, for the most part, he seemed disinclined to engage in the sort of partisanship that had persistently frayed the seams of the League coalition. The same was not true of the men who had served under him or, in some instances, *wished* they had served under him. With Ogden no longer able to speak for himself or the White League, others engaged in a concerted effort to equate their own Reformer-faction political aspirations with the League's storied exploits.

The erection of a monument to the White League dead had been a cause "near to the heart" of Ogden, and his many friends probably felt a tinge of guilt that it had not been brought to fruition within his lifetime. Although the group who gathered for this purpose after their commander's death immediately earmarked sufficient funds to procure an appropriate marker for Ogden's grave in Metairie Cemetery, they hoped to raise additional money to build a more elaborate and conspicuous marker to the White League's victory over the Metropolitan Police. Shortly after the battle on Canal Street, the city government had had the old Iron building at the foot of Canal Street sold for its scrap value. It had been the site of the heaviest fighting on September 14, 1874, and in 1882 the city council finally dedicated the parcel as "Liberty Place" in an ordinance that also called for the construction of a monument to the White Leaguers who had fallen during the battle. By 1887 the Liberty Monument Committee finally seemed ready to begin construction.[22]

Their proposal for such a monument did not go unnoticed or unopposed, however, by those who had suffered the most from the White League's victory. John L. Minor of the *Weekly Pelican* made a prescient observation about the White League not long after the announcement of the fund-raising drive: "And now we are to have another monument; this time to commemorate the 'White Leaguers' who lost their lives on the 14th of September, 1874. Before the monument fever stops, we will have one to Jeff. Davis. It is meet and proper that such should be the case. Treason must be honored, so say some people." It also took the memorial committee a lot longer to raise enough funds for the White League monument than they had anticipated. Perhaps it was a case of coincidence, but the pot finally grew to a sufficient size the summer following the lynching of the Italians at the parish prison. Now in a hurry to set the monument in place by the battle's anniversary, the committee purchased a second-hand obelisk for the event.[23]

On September 14, 1891, under a sweltering late summer sun, crowds finally gathered for a ceremony commemorating the laying of the new monument's cornerstone. Aging White League veterans assembled for one last time to march with their companies in the dedication ceremony. Hoping to get a peek at their heroes, spectators crowded Canal Street at the wharves by the river and stretched many blocks in either direction; others watched from the galleries and balconies of adjacent buildings. As a pulley lowered the monument's cornerstone in place, a band struck up a stirring rendition of "America," an audible link between commemoration and sectional reconciliation. Unlike the dedication of Lost Cause monuments to Confederate heroes, the League's memorial actually celebrated a

victory, albeit one whose incompleteness very few seemed willing to acknowledge. Much of the rhetoric during the festivities carried a theme of American
instead of just Southern patriotism. It also reiterated phrases remarkably similar
to the ones used by the Young Men's Democratic Association to promote their
agenda of "ballot reform." The press reminded those assembled that they paid
tribute to the men who "fell in defense of God-given rights, solemnly recognized
in the wisest laws and constitutions, the right to self-government and the right to
bear arms for the protection of those rights." In another ominous editorial, the
Daily States congratulated the White League for promoting peace by destroying
"the alarming growth of the military spirit among the negroes."[24]

By November 1891, a turbulent generation after Redemption, the Liberty
Monument finally stood complete—a thirty-foot-high granite obelisk sitting atop
a stout rectangular block of stone flanked by four decorative columns. Sturdy,
though somewhat generic in style, this new addition to the landscape stood
prominently at the foot of the expansive "neutral ground" of Canal Street. It was
but one monument of many placed during a spasm of commemorative mania. In
the same year the city's veterans dedicated Memorial Hall, a forty-thousand-
dollar neo-Gothic and vaguely ecclesiastical-looking museum honoring the heroic exploits of New Orleans sons who had served the Lost Cause. The new
generation scrupulously paid homage to the Civil War generation even as they
assumed power from their elders, consumed by a vision of setting right what they
clearly saw as the failures of the previous thirty years.[25]

On December 4, 1886, the first issue of the *Weekly Pelican* came off the presses
in New Orleans. Its editor, John L. Minor, declared the paper "the only live progressive paper managed by a colored man in New Orleans." It was, of course, not
the only black paper currently being printed in the city—the Protestant *Southwest
Christian Advocate* also hailed from the Crescent City—but that paper's editorial
focus was on religion and its distribution was regionwide. Minor's paper definitely
filled a void among the city's numerous publications. The *New Orleans Republican*, once owned by Henry Clay Warmoth, ceased publication in 1878. P. B. S.
Pinchback's *Weekly Louisianian* succumbed in 1882. Born in 1859 in Kentucky,
Minor had come to Louisiana sometime after the war and was living in East Carroll Parish by 1880. As a mixed-race clerk living in a neighborhood almost exclusively made up of black laborers, he surely stood out. Two important characteris-
tics distinguished East Carroll Parish: blacks outnumbered whites in a nearly
seven-to-one ratio, and it was the most productive cotton-producing county in the
entire South. It hardly comes as a surprise, therefore, that by the time Minor came

to New Orleans, he was fully aware of both the plight of Louisiana's poor blacks and the relative impotence of the Republican Party in the state's cotton belt. As a consequence, the *Weekly Pelican* exhibited a distinct radical flavor and was deeply sympathetic to the cause of the Knights of Labor. It was also critical of what it termed the "conservative" Badger faction of the Republican Party. Conspicuously absent from the *Pelican's* pages were stories that chronicled the achievements of the city's traditional black elite. Instead, its editor found space for the occasional dig at his Custom House rivals. When Louis A. Martinet announced in 1887 his plans to begin the publication of a newspaper, Minor mused sarcastically that "its politics will be Democratic, supposedly of the Nicholls stripe, as Mr. Martinet is a reformer."[26]

Factional divisions had always dogged Republicans in Louisiana, and they were often just as damaging to the party's prospects as Democratic antagonism was. After 1877, in the face of even greater obstacles, the party faced further atomization. This discord and the reasons that fueled it were not unique to the Pelican State, but the acrimony there was particularly acute. Rural blacks like the ones whom John L. Minor claimed to represent felt justifiably abandoned by the party's white leadership in New Orleans. So, too, did a large number of black Louisianians who had come to the city since the end of the war. Cultural divisions between these newcomers and the better-established black elite in New Orleans created further tensions. The majority of the rural blacks who had flocked to the Crescent City were poor, darker-skinned, Anglo, and Protestant. They were also grossly underrepresented in the Warmoth-Badger faction of the party and held comparatively few of the important federal patronage jobs that Louisiana's Republicans controlled. At the same time, the conspicuous presence of Afro-Creoles in the Custom House increasingly alienated a cadre of "lily-white" Republicans who had concluded by the late 1880s that the party's only hope for survival in the state was to become a strictly white man's party. Further complicating matters, Republicans were also divided over the future of the Louisiana Lottery. Rent by no fewer than three distinct factions, they had a difficult time after 1877. By the late 1880s, holding together the party's disparate fragments seemed to occupy most of its leadership's energy.

Black Republicans' resentment toward white Republicans emerged from many quarters, but one issue that proved particularly contentious in the late 1880s was the status of black veterans who hoped to participate in the pageantry of the Grand Army of the Republic. The feud over the GAR had obvious political dimensions, and it was clear that the discontented hoped to employ the issue to gain leverage with the party leadership. In rhetoric that he clearly aimed at Algernon

Sydney Badger, John L. Minor began to question the wisdom of his fellow men of color who continued to defend the deeds of their white erstwhile political allies. "The declarations made long ago by our Southern fellow-citizens that our so-called white leaders cared naught for us, only so far as they could use us for the elevation of themselves, either socially or otherwise" rang true, he argued. Particularly after "the cold shoulder has been given to us by our late comrades in arms," which would "go far to confirm the warnings given against the element as a class." The Department of the Gulf's commander rejected repeated requests from black GAR encampments to participate in the region's Decoration Day ceremonies, deeming them "inexpedient." The *Weekly Pelican* was circumspect as to the party responsible for offering the "cold shoulder" but by way of implication noted that the outgoing departmental commander, Algernon Sydney Badger, had only recently been replaced by "a soldier entirely unknown to us."[27]

Although historians have most often identified Henry Clay Warmoth as the most powerful Republican in late-nineteenth-century Louisiana, one could make an equally strong argument that Badger was the man who held the keys to the party as the century came to a close. Surely that is how John L. Minor saw things when he urged a meeting that would "unite" his insurgent faction of the party with the "conservative Badger" Republicans in the fall of 1887. The two men chosen to lead the outsiders' delegation, however, were a decidedly odd couple—particularly given the black editor's antagonistic comments about opportunism of the party's white leadership. They included General "Baldy" Smith, a former Union commander who had once led black troops during the war, and H. C. Minor (no relation to John L. Minor), a wealthy white sugar planter who hoped that Republican rule would mean increased tariff protectionism. Perhaps what made H. C. Minor an even more incomprehensible spokesman for the black franchise and labor rights was that he had been a power behind the recent "Thibodeaux Massacre" in which the state's sugar planters hired armed henchmen to violently disperse striking black cane workers. Indeed, the *Weekly Pelican's* plan was just another occasion when a disgruntled black Republican faction made a short-sighted and morally incomprehensible alliance in an ill-fated effort to secure limited near-term gains. The only result of the exchange was that the wealthy sugar-planting interests managed to get H. C. Minor nominated as the party's candidate for a special congressional election.[28]

John L. Minor's *Weekly Pelican* ceased regular publication in 1889, silencing one vocal critic of Badger's leadership of the party, but the divisions that diminished whatever hope the Republicans might have had for effectiveness remained. Early that same year, a group of influential sugar planters met in New Iberia, where they concocted a blueprint for transforming the state's Republican Party into an organization run strictly by white men. That they hoped to preserve the black ballot at all flowed not from any egalitarian impulse but instead from the belief that they, like the Bourbons, could rely on it for an ample reservoir of easily manipulated votes. These planters also desired to seize control of the numerous federal patronage appointments in Louisiana. When news of the "New Iberia Plan" reached Badger, he was not enthusiastic. "The party could not afford to be controlled by a small coterie whose purpose it was to ostracize so large a part of the members of the party," he told reporters. Yet Badger's words failed to stop the "lily-white" movement in its tracks. The same sugar-planting clique bombarded Benjamin Harrison with familiar objections when the president nominated Warmoth as collector of customs later that summer. "His name is odious to all the white people of Louisiana who feel inclined to support the Republican ticket," warned one such individual. "We have a great many Sugar Planters who are willing to support H.C. Minor . . . but if such appointments as Warmoth is [sic] to be forced upon them, they will go back to the Democratic fold." Minor himself telegraphed the president threatening to withdraw his name from the congressional race if Warmoth's name was not withdrawn. Even Louisiana's sole Republican member of Congress, Dudley Coleman, threw his weight against Warmoth's nomination, although it was admittedly not a great deal of weight—Coleman not only was a Confederate veteran; he had formed an artillery company of the White League that fought during the 1874 battle on Canal Street. When such entreaties from white Republicans failed, these same individuals funded a delegation of disgruntled black protestant ministers, including the editor of the *Southwestern Christian Advocate*, to travel to Washington and plead for Warmoth's removal, but to no greater avail. The self-serving and conditional nature of the sugar planters' support of Republicanism and the equally self-serving accusations of their sometimes black and white allies fooled nobody in Washington, DC, and the Senate proceeded to confirm Warmoth in the spring of 1890. Among his supporters, curiously enough, were the business elite of New Orleans, many of whom had found common cause with the Reformer Democrats of the YMDA. Warmoth also owed his Senate confirmation, ironically, to J. B. Eustis, a Louisiana Bourbon Democrat who "eulogized the nominee highly" in his endorsement.[29]

Warmoth's first appointment in the New Orleans Custom House was Algernon Sydney Badger as special deputy collector, a move that had positive implications for those Afro-Creoles who had been political allies and veterans of the Metropolitan Police. Badger, in turn, likely played a key role in their reappointment to the Custom House, a vantage point from which they engaged in further activism. Among the individuals reinstated to their former jobs were activists and former Metropolitans Rodolphe Desdunes, Octave Rey, and J. O. Lainez. Another was Antoine, who was William Pitt Kellogg's former lieutenant governor and by 1889 a member of the Citizens' Committee. Paul Trévigne, the renowned educator and frequent contributor to the Comité des Citoyens's newspaper, the *Crusader*, also regained employment. And Warmoth appointed Francis E. Dumas, a former Afro-Creole slaveholder, army major, political opponent, and financial supporter of the radical *L'Union*. Both highly educated men, Dumas and Trévigne received an eight-hundred-dollar annual salary as "unclassified clerks." Warmoth's appointments, likely influenced by Badger, had gathered the intelligentsia of Afro-Creole New Orleans into the employment of the federal government.[30]

Badger also remained steadfastly loyal to his black former comrades-in-arms from the army. John L. Minor had once hinted in 1887 that the former cavalryman might have been responsible for the rejection of black GAR posts by the regional department. By 1891 Badger felt it necessary to set the record straight. In an interview with a *Picayune* reporter, he shared his strong views about the rights of black veterans to belong to the venerable organization: "I am frank in saying that I was the first man in the encampment to cast a vote for the admission of the colored ex-soldier. My name was the first on the roll and I set the example for those who chose to follow it, but the majority vote was against admitting the colored delegates, and so the encampment went on record as excluding or failing to recognize the negro. . . . I do not see any great difference between sitting with colored delegates in the national encampment and the departmental encampment, and we have frequently sat with them at the national encampment." In the wake of the row at the regional encampment, however, Badger concluded that, for the time being, separate encampments might be in everyone's best interests. A year later, he changed his mind and confronted the matter head-on.[31]

In the summer of 1892, The National Encampment of the GAR ordered the Department of the Gulf to admit black posts, a move that threatened to split the organization in two. In ordering the change, the national commander-in-chief of the GAR removed Frederic Speed, a Mississippi judge, from his post as Department of the Gulf commander and replaced him with Badger. Speed's comments regarding his removal revealed much about both Badger's character and the way in which white Union men in the South viewed the aspirations of black veterans. "The colored people have an unfortunate tendency to mix up their politics with everything else in which they engage. The Grand Army will be no exception," predicted Speed. But the deposed commander deeply lamented that Badger had seen fit to cast his lot with black soldiers. "I can't understand what should induce a man of gentlemanly instincts and associations such as General Badger to go into this black organization and subject himself to the ill-will of so many of his comrades and former friends, unless it be politics." Yet Speed had to concede that Badger was "an enemy not to be despised; a man of courage and ability." Concluding that the general was "to-day the strongest man in Louisiana in a political point of view," Speed observed that "Warmoth is a dolt next to Badger." When the *Picayune's* reporter suggested that Badger could be scared out of leading a black Grand Army by a renewed White League, Speed scoffed, "Scare him out of it! Great Scott, Badger don't know what scare is. He wasn't made upon that plan."[32]

Even though some of Louisiana's black Republicans periodically expressed dissatisfaction with Badger's leadership of the party, the record of his efforts to maintain their inclusion suggests that he was probably their most able and diligent advocate. The *Picayune* observed of Badger, "He has not lost an iota of that old Massachusetts spirit and liberality and justice to all citizens without regard to race, creed, and condition." At the same time, Badger managed to achieve the unthinkable in New Orleans: with the exception of a handful of bitterly partisan enemies, he had won over the same people who once derided him as the foolhardy tool of black Republicanism. That he did so without abandoning his Republicanism or his black allies is particularly remarkable. Badger accomplished this feat not by making back-room deals or cloaking himself in the amnesiac glow of Lost Cause rhetoric. His success came instead from an unfailing constancy of purpose and loyalty. New Orleanians, both black and white, admired such abstract principles in men, probably because in the late nineteenth century they were all too rare. Yet Badger did not necessarily ascribe to broad racial egalitarianism, nor was he a true revolutionary. As his role in the Hennessey controversy revealed, when it came to Italians, he was capable of hard-fisted rule. Badger also shared similarities with Warmoth, attributes he exhibited in his dealings with John L. Minor, Afro-Creole elites, and the Grand Army. He was willing to recognize what he considered the earned rights of black comrades but stopped well short of advocating the sort of ardent racially egalitarian advocacy that Minor had sought. Badger's conservatism probably had much to do with his reputation among the city's white elite. Reflecting on his accomplishments in 1890, the *Picayune* observed that "no men in the city of New Orleans are more thoroughly known than General Badger; his tall, commanding figure makes him a conspicuous character on our streets. He is respected by everybody who knows him, and though his political views differ from the majority, yet he is looked upon by those who differ from him in politics as a straightforward, honorable gentleman."[33]

When the incoming Democratic administration of Francis Tillou Nicholls dismantled the Metropolitan Police in 1877, Captain Peter Joseph found himself out of a job. Like many other mixed-race members of the force, however, it did not take long for him to find employment in the U.S. Custom House, now under the control of his old commander, Algernon Sydney Badger. There he eventually rose to the rank of captain of night inspectors. More than simply a way to put food on the table, Joseph's employment also allowed him to continue being an active member of the Republican Party. By 1877 he had already established himself as an important figure in the city's black political circles. On numerous occasions, Joseph had served as an elector and delegate to both state and national Republican conventions and was a conspicuous member in the party's nominating process for state offices. As an on-again, off-again employee of the Customs Service, between 1877 and 1892 Joseph fought a rear-guard action against those who hoped to foreclose the power that mixed-race men such as himself had managed to amass during the postbellum era.[34]

Peter Joseph's Civil War and immediate postbellum experience had shaped both who he was as a person and the nature of his political activism in New Orleans. In 1884 he renewed his affinity for martial regimen by forming a militia company called the Orleans Light Guard. This in itself might be just a footnote of black life in New Orleans after 1877, except when one considers the fate that black militias suffered both in rural Louisiana and elsewhere in the South during the era of Redemption. Joseph's company of armed black men not only operated in post–White League New Orleans; in 1889 it traveled to Washington, DC, on the Queen and Crescent Railroad to take part in the inaugural parade of Benjamin Harrison. Accompanying the Orleans Guard to the inauguration were two other black militia companies from the city, including one called the Larendon Rifles.[35]

Unfortunately, while the presence of Joseph's Orleans Guard spoke to the continued agency of black New Orleanians as a body, this militia had little influence on the tightening grip of white reaction outside of the city. Faced with declining profits and increased labor militancy, elite white planters from the state's sugar and cotton regions systematically forced unwilling black workers into abusive labor contracts. Unable to offer physical protection, Peter Joseph instead joined a large crowd of fellow black activists at Geddes Hall to lodge a "dignified

protest against the recent slaughter of innocent negroes in the country parishes."
The Orleans Guard had no ability whatsoever to protect black voters in the hinterland. Leading New Orleans black activists had been reduced to offering verbal
resistance against those who forced black labor into "a condition of abject serf-
dom and peonage . . . executed by armed bodies of men, styling themselves as
regulators." The solutions offered by the Geddes Hall assembly were equally de-
featist, suggesting that these victims of the planter elite repeat the black exodus
to Kansas of a decade earlier. Perhaps during that warm summer evening, Joseph
came to the realization that for himself, as for the state's black sugar workers,
flight from Louisiana might offer the only viable path toward full citizenship.
Both the street parading of the Orleans Guard and the public assembly at Geddes
Hall represented the backbone of urban political culture for the Civil War generation of black activists—forms that they bequeathed to a new generation at the
dawn of Jim Crow. Yet while remarkable in their ability to sustain black political
consciousness, lacking a supportive party structure or meaningful white allies,
neither was enough to protect the rights of blacks against encroachment by the
forces of white supremacy in the 1890s. By 1888 Peter Joseph had to be fully aware
of this trend.[36]

Joseph's accomplishments in the following two years as a black man and as a
Republican were bittersweet. In June 1891 the Orleans Light Guard celebrated its
seventh anniversary. After its parade through the streets of the city, its members
presented Joseph with a gold medal in recognition of his leadership. The following month, Governor Francis Tillou Nicholls appointed Joseph a trustee of
Southern University, an institution where two of his daughters now taught. Politically, he was a staunch ally of Henry Clay Warmoth and Algernon Sydney Badger
and was an important figure in the Custom House's ranks. From such a vantage
point, however, he watched the party atomize into utter insignificance. In April
1892, with competing factions unable to reconcile their differences, the Republicans nominated rival tickets for everything ranging from mayor to governor,
thereby ensuring defeat at all points. A key objective of both factions had been
control over the state's federal patronage. When Democrat Grover Cleveland won
his second term in office in November 1892, Louisiana's Republicans lost even
this. Cleveland's first term had dealt a disruptive blow to Republican aspirations in
the state. His second term proved even more disastrous.[37]

Peter Joseph's ultimate exodus from New Orleans may have been more dignified than that made by poor black sugar laborers who fled to Kansas, but it was
really just another outcome of the same root cause. On October 17, 1892, just four
days after Homer Plessy's trial began in the Orleans Parish Criminal Courtroom

of Judge John Ferguson, and less than two weeks after the birth of his youngest child, Peter Joseph announced his resignation from the Custom House. He had unquestionably exhibited courage in postbellum New Orleans, but Joseph was also a practical man. By late 1892 he probably saw the pending disaster that the city's black activists soon faced. According to his friends, Joseph had recently made a trip to the West "and was so well pleased with the country that he made up his mind to take up his residence there." His destination was Denver, Colorado, where his youngest son, Sumner Geddes Joseph, was attending a college—the only "colored boy" in his school. In a scene reminiscent of Ralph Ellison's *Invisible Man*, Sumner Joseph had shown such "ability" that "his classmates selected him to deliver the oration on Columbus Day." Peter Joseph also had a daughter living in Denver who was married to one of the more famous black doctors of the era, Paul E. Spratlin.[38] Forty-eight years old and with a family for which he must provide, Joseph made an understandable decision. He had been remarkably successful for a man who had born a slave and had been "nothing but a young fellow working at odd jobs" when the Civil War ended. If his children were to realize any benefit from his effort, they would need to leave the city of their birth.[39]

In 1905, nearly forty years to the day after he received a draft notice from the U.S. Army, the aging Peter Joseph made his first application to receive a veteran's pension. On the questionnaire, he indicated a variety of ailments that kept him from continuing his occupation as a brick mason. To another question asking for the applicant's skin color, Joseph replied, "like a white man." It was a truthful statement. A business card that he had printed in 1893 featured a photograph of a fair-skinned, bearded man with light eyes. It is unclear whether Joseph ever collected any pension money, because he died only two months after his initial application. His widow, however, received benefits until her death in 1912. Not long after her death, Sumner Geddes Joseph, the promising son who had been named for the great abolitionist, moved to Kenosha, Wisconsin. There he and his wife began a new life—crossing the color line and living as white people.[40]

Six weeks after the laying of the White League monument's cornerstone, and only seven months after the lynching of the Italians who had been acquitted of the Hennessey assassination, the Democratic Ring finally had its turn to express its political views on the streets of New Orleans. On October 27, 1891, twelve thousand Democratic ward clubmen staged a grand torchlight parade and rally for their perennial Bourbon/Ring candidate for executive office, Samuel D. McEnery. Seated in a carriage at the head of the procession was the event's grand marshal, Aristée Louis Tissot. The parade that fall evening was notable for several things, not the least of which was the participation of an Italian Democratic club that featured Charles Matranga as one of its senior officers. After the lynching death of Joseph Macheca, Matranga had emerged as perhaps the most powerful Sicilian crime boss in New Orleans. Banners held aloft by the parading ward clubs distilled the McEnery/Ring campaign into a series of pithy if sometimes misleading slogans. Among the more shameless of these was one that lauded McEnery, a man who had reduced state expenditures on schools to a minuscule appropriation, as the "Education Governor." The improbable claim rested on McEnery's promise to renew the charter of the Louisiana Lottery for an annual $1.25 million, the money presumably to go into education. But the majority of the banners, like the one that declared "White Supremacy—True Democracy—The Majority Rules" reflected a hybrid of the city's growing racial caste-consciousness and the Ring's vaguely Jacksonian urban political philosophy. Others made thinly veiled references to the mob action of the Young Men's Democratic Association against the Hennessey defendants by proclaiming, "Where there is no law, there is no freedom" and "The Press, The Educator—Not Shotguns."[41]

Victory in 1892 did not belong to Samuel McEnery or the lottery forces that fueled his campaign, however. With his own poor record and his opponent's ceaseless hammering away at the former governor's ties with the corrupt lottery, McEnery was soundly defeated by the Reformer candidate, Murphy J. Foster. Just forty-three years old when he took office, Foster, like his allies in the Young Men's Democratic Association, represented the emergence of a new generation of political leadership. Foster's only real distinction during the Republican era had come in 1873, when at age twenty-three he became one of the handful of Fusionist legislators unwise enough to be arrested by Algernon Sydney Badger and the Metropolitan Police when they stormed the Odd Fellows' Hall after Fred Ogden's failed raid on the Cabildo. It was not until the late 1880s that Foster became influential in the statehouse, but by 1890 his floor leadership had proved crucial to the passage of Louisiana's Separate Car Law.

There was no mistaking that something important had changed in the state with the elevation of Foster. The Louisiana Senate that had met in 1880 represented the Civil War generation in several key aspects. The average birth year of its thirty-six members was 1839, and more than 60 percent of the body had served in the Confederate army from the state of Louisiana (see appendix C). The men who assembled in the state senate chamber in 1892, however, were clearly the "fresher blood" of whom Tissot spoke. Although still nearly half claimed some veteran status, their average birth year was 1847. Like the leaders of the Hennessey lynch mob, they were on average slightly younger than the men who had joined the White League in New Orleans in 1874. Among them was a senator from East Baton Rouge Parish named John D. Fisher. In the waning months of the war, at just eighteen years of age, Fisher had joined Fred Ogden's band of cavalrymen. Also serving in 1892 was Orleans Parish senator Charles Gauthreaux, born in 1861, who in the coming session introduced a bill outlawing interracial marriage. Not all of the Civil War generation had relinquished their claim on power, however. When the new legislative session began the following spring, Aristée Louis Tissot was among the new members of the state senate.

Despite being an important political figure in New Orleans since the Seymour and Blair campaign of 1868, Tissot's only elective office had been as judge of the Orleans Parish Civil District Court. As a legislator, he revealed both a complexity of character and an ambiguous sensibility about race that, along with the Civil War generation, seemed to be quickly retreating into obscurity. We will probably never know where, when, or under what context Tissot first established his working relationship with the Afro-Creole elites who made up the members of the Comité des Citoyens. What is clear, however, is that he had developed a keen appreciation for their plight, particularly as it related to the increasingly Draconian legislation that made its way through the Louisiana statehouse during the first term of Murphy J. Foster.

One of the chief political goals of the Reformer political faction was the authoring of a new state constitution that would replace the one crafted in 1879. The objectives of this process were fairly clear. The Reformers hoped not only to destroy the Louisiana Lottery, their rivals' greatest financial backer, but to also rewrite the state's election laws so as to severely restrict the franchise. The Reformers aimed these tough voting qualifications at ethnic urbanites in New Orleans and Populist insurgents in the hinterland as well as black Louisianians. When a reporter for the *Picayune* caught up with Tissot in the days leading up to the 1894 session, he pressed the senator for his opinions about the proposal for a new governing document. "The existing order of things will be in many respects changed," acknowledged Tissot. "It has existed long enough. We are twenty years behind any other large city in the union, and the incubus of played-out laws must be removed." Yet when asked about a recent proposal for "ballot reform," Tissot remained unwavering in his position. "I can say without having studied the issues championed by Mr. Farrar that I am not in favor of restricting in any way the right of suffrage. A man does not learn anything from books. He is competent to judge even if he cannot read or write, if he has mixed with men and used his faculties. A flannel shirt is as good as a white one." The "Mr. Farrar" to whom Tissot referred was, of course, Edgar H. Farrar, the chairman of the Committee of Fifty appointed by Mayor Shakespeare to investigate the Hennessey assassination—the same committee that had empowered the individuals who lynched the Sicilian defendants.[42]

The legislative session of 1894 was not given over exclusively to rigging Louisiana's political apparatus. A series of new bills aimed at tightening segregation's grip on the state also occupied the floor, including a proposal to "provide separate street cars for the races" in the city of New Orleans. In response to the bill, Aristée Louis Tissot took the podium and read a petition of protest written by the Comité des Citoyens. Tissot's open defiance of his own party's stance on segregation was notable, particularly with the *Plessy* case already working its way through the federal court system. Yet this deed was hardly an isolated incident. When Charles Gauthreaux introduced his bill to criminalize interracial marriage, Tissot again spoke up and read the committee's petition of protest. "With the race prejudice in this community," said the document, "persons suspected or accused of mixed blood, will have either to leave the State or resign themselves to a life of persecution without end and without limit." Few people understood the nature of interracial marriage better than Tissot. As a judge, he had ruled on cases that dealt with this very issue, including one as late as 1887 whose outcome led the *Weekly Pelican* to make the sarcastic rejoinder, "Judge Tissot has decided that the marriage of whites and blacks in this State is legal. Under this decree a white woman received a colored man's money and property." The *Pelican*'s grossly inaccurate characterization notwithstanding, Tissot had consistently endorsed the validity of interracial unions.[43]

Both time and circumstances eventually caught up with both Tissot and the Comité des Citoyens. Despite Tissot's ardent protests against the "arbitrary measure," in 1894 Governor Foster signed into law an amendment that essentially reversed the 1870 statute that had legalized interracial marriage. A "ballot reform" measure introduced that same year failed, but after Foster's narrow 1896 victory against a bizarre Populist–sugar planter insurgency in 1896, the then-supreme Reformers rewrote the state constitution, essentially eliminating the vote of most black Louisianians. Aristée Louis Tissot succumbed to kidney failure while recuperating at his summer home in Biloxi, Mississippi, on January 2, 1896. Ever uncharitable in its editorial stance, the *Daily States*, the foremost organ of white supremacy in New Orleans, ran a terse obituary of Tissot on page three. On the same issue's cover appeared a political cartoon depicting the white maidenhood of Louisiana being protected from the dogs of hell (communism, bounty, negro domination, and carpetbaggery) by the shield of white supremacy. In his memoir of Afro-Creole New Orleans, Rodolphe Lucien Desdunes noted that with the passing of Tissot, "the people remained abandoned to their miseries, to such an extent that they could look upon Christian charity as a novel paradox." Five months after Tissot's death, the U.S. Supreme Court delivered its opinion in the *Plessy* case, effectively destroying whatever morale the committee had once sustained. With the Fifteenth Amendment thrown into shadow and a great deal of the Fourteenth Amendment greatly diminished, the war's turbulent legacy in Louisiana had finally been thrown into abeyance.[44]

CONCLUSION

RECONSIDERING THE LESSONS OF RECONSTRUCTION

> Young men and women with ambition and political aspirations
> may well take in cognizance of one fact: Gratitude is practically
> unknown among politicians.
> —Henry Clay Warmoth, *War, Politics, and Reconstruction*

Laboring under the civil rights and cold war paradigms, twentieth-century revisionist historians found in the struggles of Southern reconstruction an inspirational precedent for their own generation's quest for both freedom and racial equality. In the process, they placed the Republicans, a complex interracial and intersectional coalition, into a broader lexicon of heroes who, through an "unfinished revolution," advanced the cause of American liberty as defined by political and social egalitarianism. Conversely, the revisionists depicted conservative white Southerners as unflinching agents of reaction and proto-totalitarianism. Informed as they were by the geopolitical realities of their era, it is not surprising that they placed ideology at the center of their narrative of Reconstruction. Even when the postrevisionists showed how some Republicans fell short of their egalitarian rhetoric, they still based their historical judgments in the belief that Reconstruction's goal was a conscious social revolution. Indeed, whether interpreted through the lens of race, or that of class, or that of gender, the deeds of historical actors almost always had some purpose in a broader political and ideological context.

Yet with the teleological inevitability of the cold war now shattered and the question of civil rights and personal freedoms entering its own era of ambiguity, perhaps now is the time for a new generation of historians to reconsider the motivations of both the Republicans and their conservative rivals in the postbellum South. This study has been informed in no small measure by such a philosophy. Those New Orleanians who lived through the difficult Civil War and postbellum decades knew that they had been party to a revolution. As I have suggested, however, the animus for change they witnessed was often ambiguous. While an ideologically driven campaign to foster radical social and political progress in New Orleans may have been the objective of some members of the city's Civil War generation, it was just one of many impulses that caused postbellum instability. Perhaps in our own ambiguous twenty-first-century social paradigm and geopolitical reality, we can accept that many late-nineteenth-century Americans merely sought to find a foothold in a society rendered unfamiliar and unstable by the consequences of a brutal civil war. At its most basic level, what defined life in the postbellum South was not just the Civil War generation's quest for abstractions such as free-dom and equality but their desire for postbellum stability—in their society, in their politics, and in their private lives.

For such reasons, we should be wary of making comparisons between postbel-lum Southern Republicans and the idealistic civil rights volunteers who worked for racial progress in the South during the 1960s. While numerous nineteenth-century Republicans, particularly among the emergent black political leadership, harbored deep convictions about racial equality, and although the party's rhetoric often inspired a desire for social progress among those whom they led, Republi-cans did not necessarily envision fostering a *social* revolution at an institutional level. Like Americans everywhere in the nascent Gilded Age, the men of the Republican Party sought first to carve out a stable financial and political future of their own. Nor were such impulses confined to white Republicans. Often their black counterparts succumbed to the allure of place-holding, even to the point of sacrificing racial solidarity for their own political survival. It seems unreasonable to expect otherwise. Such conclusions should not be interpreted as a moral ver-dict on Louisiana's Republicans but instead a reflection on a historiography that has for nearly the last half century expected, and perhaps even needed, too much from these individuals. One can certainly find ample evidence of the war's "emancipationist legacy" and that it fomented an "unfinished revolution" in the region, but many of these men did not necessarily see themselves as the agents of such a program. Their ambitions were more personal in nature.[1]

Perhaps the greatest irony of the postbellum era, then, is that whereas many Republicans did not seek revolution, their actions ended up fostering one. Henry Clay Warmoth may not even have believed racial egalitarianism desirable, yet his ambitious politicking had so undermined conservative opposition that he proba-bly came the closest of any Louisiana Republican to forging a durable biracial polity. Most revisionist and postrevisionist historians have judged Warmoth harshly because he rejected civil rights legislation aimed at securing equal accom-modations in places of public resort. Although the governor's stance on equality

fell short of the late-twentieth-century political mainstream, h
Republicanism's foes in Louisiana was probably the single most i
in Louisiana's being among the last states redeemed. As a con
moth's actions were responsible for increased social mobility an
agency in the state. Likewise, though Algernon Sydney Badger may not have ex
hibited the character flaws that clouded Warmoth's reputation, and though he
proved more loyal to the party standard, his sense of egalitarianism was equally
qualified. Badger was successful not only because he shared many of the values
held by conservative white elites in New Orleans but also because of his reputation for moral probity. Yet he extended his trust and support only to those individuals he believed had demonstrated their fitness for preferment. Radical black
rivals, whether Oscar J. Dunn in 1871 or John L. Minor in 1888, could expect no
quarter from Badger. Thus, while he held a position of authority in the Custom
House, Badger employed only those Afro-Creole Radicals who had shown loyalty
to Republicanism and had demonstrated their worthiness as comrades-in-arms.
In the end, neither Badger nor Warmoth played a direct role in the actions of the
Comité des Citoyens, but their loyalties and political maneuvering had made the
committee's struggle against segregation possible.

In dramatic contrast with the intense scrutiny that Southern Republicanism
has received in the last forty years, critical analyses of their white conservative
rivals have been limited. Their role as two-dimensional villains remains a conve-
nient staple of Reconstruction's historical narrative, when in reality their motivations and relationships with Republicanism and one another were complex and
often ambiguous. When defeated Confederates returned to New Orleans after
the war, they brought along a vast range of ideas about what the future should
hold. These divisions among white Southerners not only proved particularly enduring, lasting well into the late nineteenth century; they were responsible for
much, and perhaps most, of the postbellum era's political and social acrimony. It
is clear that few former Confederates expected the sort of sweeping changes that
took place as a result of the Radical ascendancy, yet to characterize these men as
harboring a monolithic set of political or social values would be inaccurate in the
extreme. The rise of Henry Clay Warmoth in 1868 exposed in a dramatic fashion
the numerous fault lines that had developed among white Louisianians of all
classes during the war and the immediate postbellum period. So, too, did the
variety of relationships that conservative white New Orleanians held with their
mixed-race fellow citizens. The least appreciated aspect of postbellum politics in
New Orleans is that conservatives were every bit as much at war with one another
as they were with the so-called carpetbaggers, scalawags, or black Republicans.[2]

If ambiguity clouded Republicans' ideological vision in the postbellum era, the same could be said for their conservative rivals in New Orleans, both before and after 1877. Conservative divisions, like Republican divisions, often stemmed less from ideological matters than from practical, partisan, or personal consider-ations. Such rifts grew into a deep-seated factionalism during the Republican era and were mitigated only temporarily during the White League insurrection of 1874–77. Once the reins of power were back in white conservative hands, this fac-tionalism resumed with even greater fervor. Despite employing the rhetoric of "hon-est government" and "fair elections" when attacking their Bourbon Democratic rivals, the conservatives ultimately proved that they sought neither. Instead of eliminating the Bourbon electoral abuses, the Reformer coalition in New Orleans eventually became complicit in the very type of fraud they had so loudly decried. Their solutions probably had more to do with preserving the rule of elite oligarchy than with their espoused concern for honest elections or even white supremacy. The Redeemers also did as much to crush the aspirations of their most idealistic mem-bers as to undermine the public's faith in the electoral process. Some of the city's Reformers, like E. John Ellis, probably believed that the goal of their peers was to "purify the ballot box." Had he lived to see the Reform movement through to its conclusion, Ellis probably would have seen how wrong he had been.

If any conscious social revolution took place during the postbellum era, whether "unfinished" or merely "unwitting," it was brought about not by politi-cians but by individuals who, in acting out roles that defied the antebellum status quo, aspired to construct a new definition of individual liberty. They did not move in particularly powerful political circles, as had Warmoth, Pinchback, and Bad-ger. In New Orleans, these agents of change came predominantly from the city's antebellum free black population. No matter how destabilizing the unmistakably black freedmen may have been in terms of labor and large-scale political ques-tions, the vast majority of them never presented any serious challenge to the un-derpinnings of white supremacy. Although dark-complexioned former slaves might, on occasion, have reached a political office or attained some social standing within the community, their distinct racial identity within nineteenth-century American society always stood as a barrier to true mobility. The racial ambiguity of the city's substantial mixed-race population, however, placed them at the center of the era's most fundamental questions of race and place. Some members of this caste used their unique position to take an active role in challenging the hypocrisy of race-based laws, particularly once they discovered that statues aimed at the freedmen applied equally to all men of color. Educated, frequently persons of means, and in some cases bearing only a trace of African ancestry, these individuals used the

courts to lay a powerful claim to privileges that white Southerners had for generations set aside for themselves. By securing victories in court, mixed-race appellants opened the door to social mobility, in law if not practice, to all people of
color.

Emancipation forced the elite mixed-race community in New Orleans to
make a difficult choice about their own racial self-identification. They could attempt to pass for white, and if successful, they might put the question of social
equality behind them forever. Conversely, they could attempt to secure their status by championing legislation or legal action that guaranteed political and civil
rights. Doing neither meant passively accepting whatever fate awaited all people
of color. A complex equation of familial, personal, and ideological impulses,
often conflicting, influenced the choices mixed-race New Orleanians made in
this crucial period. Charles Sauvinet had clear moments of egalitarian vision—
serving in the army, testifying before Congress in the wake of the 1866 riot, and
serving as civil sheriff of Orleans Parish. But he was vague about his racial identity, clearly had an eye toward professional advancement, and seemed to sue the
Bank Coffeehouse out of personal indignation as much as anything else. Guided
by the heart, Marie Louise Drouet sought to claim her familial position and possibly establish a new identity; perhaps she was unaware of the broader implications of her suit. Peter Joseph was an active Republican but hedged his ideological
purity in favor of the welfare of his family. Sauvinet, Drouet, and Joseph all played
important roles in shaping the dialogue over social equality in New Orleans, but
it would be difficult to characterize any of them as ideological crusaders.

The racial ambiguity exhibited by mixed-race New Orleanians also undermined efforts by a new generation of white political figures to establish a modernized system of racial categorization in the late 1880s. As a consequence, those of
mixed race became the chief target of a carefully orchestrated campaign of white
reaction. It is not surprising that the greatest villain in D. W. Griffith's celluloid
adaptation of Thomas Dixon's racist turn-of-the-century novels is the mixed-race
Silas Lynch, a man whose "unnatural" combination of white and black blood
endowed him with the most pernicious qualities of both. White-supremacist crusaders of Dixon's generation relied heavily on such melodramatic cultural props
as a way to erode the kind of sympathy that elite whites of an earlier age had shown
to mixed-race New Orleanians. The postbellum generation's ambition for social
control was not unique to the South; it was part of a broader impulse in the Western world. In 1899, one year after the state legislature disfranchised the vast majority of black Louisianians on the pretext that they lacked the requisite ability to
participate in representative democracy, Rudyard Kipling's *White Man's Burden*

appeared in the pages of *McClure's* magazine. While Kipling packaged this poem as an endorsement of Progressive imperialism, it fairly dripped with the ideology of black racial inferiority. Arguably, Thomas Dixon found inspiration in Kipling, for in 1902 he titled the first book of his Reconstruction trilogy *The Leopard's Spots: A Romance of the White Man's Burden*. While New Orleans had a tangible legacy of racial separation, pseudoscientific ideas about race, emerging from a growing army of phrenologists at Northern and European universities, lent justification for the creation of the Jim Crow apparatus. One must look no further than George Washington Cable's *Grandissimes* for evidence of such intellectual trends in late-nineteenth-century New Orleans. Speaking "of those whose scientific hunger drives them to dig for *crania Americana*," Cable demurs that they will never find a skull with a "shapelier contour" than that of the Natchez princess Lufka-Humma. Disfranchisement and imperialism, both trends Cable found odious, were symptoms of the same disorder. With so much working against mixed-race people in New Orleans at the century's end, it is little wonder that so many elected to cross the color line.[3]

As these themes suggest, any study of Reconstruction that ends in 1877 is necessarily incomplete. The emergence of the so-called Redeemers in 1877 may have brought a regime change to Louisiana, but it did not make a meaningful difference in the lives of many who were the movement's most active participants. Perhaps the most remarkable fact of Redemption is how little it actually accomplished both politically and socially. When the conservatives under Francis Tillou Nicholls, aided by the White League and abetted by the federal government, finally overthrew Republican rule in Louisiana, they not only failed to destroy the party of Lincoln; they failed to bring about the kind of white supremacy for which the more counterrevolutionary among them had hoped. If anything, the removal of the Republican regime only intensified the factionalism that had always divided the Civil War generation.

Federal patronage in the hands of the Republican Party also underscored the chimerical quality of the Redemption. In New Orleans the Custom House on Canal Street quickly emerged as the most conspicuous bastion of black political power and professional integration. While the Louisiana Constitution of 1879 may have eliminated civil rights legislation that guaranteed public accommodations in places of public resort, it neither imposed segregation nor disfranchised black voters. Fear that the federal government would intervene if such laws were passed played a role in the document's crafting, but so did Bourbon greed. It did not take long for the Bourbons to realize that they might benefit from black ballots and manipulate them in favor of their own faction, much as they had once accused the Republicans of doing. Self-styled Reformers in New Orleans soon realized that the Bourbons' newfound appreciation for the black franchise meant that their struggle against the revolutionary political changes of Reconstruction had really only begun.

Not until a new group of young men overtook the Civil War generation did a new coordinated strategy of white supremacy emerge in New Orleans. The struggles of war and postbellum life had shaped the outlook of this new generation of men, most of whom were born too late to have participated in the war. The Fusion campaign of 1872 and, more importantly, the White League rebellion of 1874 served as the defining moments of their young adulthood. These experiences also bound them to their immediate elders, the generation of junior Confederate officers who had emerged as the conservative leadership after the war. Yet by the late 1880s, nonveterans began their ascent to power both in New Orleans and across the state, culminating in the 1896 gubernatorial victory of one of their own, Murphy J. Foster. By the turn of the twentieth century, these youthful architects of white supremacy had finally concocted a system of governance that could mitigate the threat that postbellum chaos had once posed to their rule. Their goal had been to reestablish something as close as possible to the social stability of the antebellum era, a condition that they had never experienced firsthand but instead learned about from the Lost Cause rhetoric employed by the Civil War generation. Their solution was thoroughly modern in outlook, though, couched in the pseudoscience of Progressive reform. "Ballot reform" became the rally cry for what resulted in the disfranchisement of many blacks but also targeted, however ineffectively, the ethnic urban poor. By performing a variety of legal and philosophical contortions over the definition of "whiteness," these same individuals crafted a modern system of apartheid that codified white personal space and enacted into law a system of social deference and stability that had once been maintained largely by custom in the slaveholding era. Without question, factionalism remained a staple of New Orleans and Louisiana politics, but not until the 1950s did the question of race and place reemerge as a central issue.

The city that emerged reincarnated in the wake of the 1898 disfranchisement constitution was in fundamental ways different from the New Orleans of 1861, but the systematic separation of races and the obsessive zeal with which the state and local government sought to preserve it mirrored closely the social control of the old slave system. Yet nobody could argue that stability had not been achieved. It was a stability that exacted an enormous toll and had taken a generation and a half to bring about.

Doane, Harmon	H. Doane	52	w	500		Life insurance	VT	2	
Duhart, A. H.	Adolph Duhart	37	m			Teacher	LA	5	
Dumont, Andrew	exact	26	m			Recorder	LA	14	
Dunn, F. McK.	M. F. Dunn	25	w			Retail clerk	LA	2	Living in a boarding house
Fourchy, Paul	exact	36	w	10,000		Insurance company president	LA	5	
Gardner, L. H.	Levingston Gardner	33	w	500		Retail dry goods	LA	6	
Gaschen, F.	Frederick Garchen	37	w	1,000	15,000	Flour dealer	Switzerland	7	
Geddis, Benj	not found								
Grunewald, Louis	exact	24	w			Cotton factor	Germany		Related to piano family
Hemard, Chas	exact	40	w	1,000	8,000	Commission merchant	France	2	2 younger brothers born in LA work as clerks for him, live in house
Hennessey, Jno	Jno. R. Hennessey	37	w	1,500	9,000	Sheet iron broker	Ireland	10	The one other plausible Jno. Hennessey was born in Ireland, was age 35, and worked at a cotton press.

(continued)

Name	Alternate name in census	Age	Race	Real estate ($)	Property ($)	Occupation	Birthplace	Ward	Notes
Ingraham, J. M.	Jos. M. Ingraham	31	m		100	(illegible)	LA	7	Dry goods store (possibly)
Jamison, D.	David Jamison	48	w			Drygoods merchant	Ireland	2	
Kenner, R. M. J.	Richard Kenner	29	m		500	Custom-house officer	LA	4	
Krost, C.	not found								
Leeds, Charles J.	exact	47	w	50,000	1,000	Foundry	LA	2	President of Leeds Foundry
Letcheford, W. H.	W. H. Letcheford	59	w				England	4	
Leverich, W. E.	exact	71	w			Cotton commission merchant	NY	3	1 grandchild, 4 domestic servants
McCloskey	Hugh		w						White League; poster of Walker bond
Merrick, Judge E. T.	A. T. Merrick	50	w	100,000	13,000	Attorney at law	MA	13	
Mitchell, Archibald	exact	51	w	20,000	1,200	Superintendent in foundry	Scotland	2	
Morphy, D. E.	exact	50	w			Auctioneer	LA	2	

Name	Match	Age	Race	Value 1	Value 2	Occupation	Origin	No.	Notes
Musgrove, R. G.	not found								
Newman, S. B.	exact	56	w	50,000		Cotton factor	MS	11	Son, S. B. Newman Jr., killed Sept. 14, 1874.
Oehmichen, Valsin	exact	42	w		10,000	Retail & wholesale hardware	LA	5	
Peale, Andrew	exact	29	w			Cotton broker	LA		Son in father's firm
Pohlhana, J. H.	not found								
Poursine, P.	exact	30	w			Coffee dealer	LA	2	Boston Club
Randolph, W. M.	W. A. Randolph	35	w			Cotton weigher	NC	11	Lives next door to John Randolph, cotton broker (father?)
Robinson, W. C.	not found								
Schneider, Christian	exact	64	w		25,000	Art broker	France	10	
Seig, Rudolph	exact	42	w		4,500	Commission merchant	Prussia	10	
Shaery, E.	not found								
Southmayd, C. G.	Charles Southmayd	34	w			Clerk, commission merchant	LA	12	Boston Club; lives with mother, 10,000/2,000 property

(continued)

Name	Alternate name in census	Age	Race	Real estate ($)	Property ($)	Occupation	Birthplace	Ward	Notes
Tuyes, John	exact	18	w			Clerk in store	LA	6	In home of father Jules, president of insurance co.
Tyler, E. A.	Edward Tyler	56	w	40,000	100,000	Jeweler	MA	10	
Wagner, J. M.	J. A. Wagner	36	w			Retail grocer	Bavaria	8	Younger brother (A. J. Wagner, born in LA) also a retail grocer; Boston Club
Warren, J. J.	James Warren	54	w		1,200	Commission merchant	MS	10	Boston Club
Weiss, J.	J. Weis	45	W	3,000		Carpenter	Württemburg (Germany)	8	
West, B. J.	exact	37	w	40,000	6,500	Merchant	England	13	
West, Douglass	Douglas West	43	w			Cotton factor	MS	10	
Wilson, C. A.	Wilson, John	37	w	2,500	2,500	Wholesale merchant	LA	1	Closest possible match

Wintz, F.	Fred Wintz	52	w	25,000	2,000	President of city railroad	France	12	Second-youngest son born 1861 and named Jeff Davis.
Woods, J. B.	not found								
Totals				**459,500**	**293,000**				

Statistics

Average age:	41.6	Foreign-born:	16
Total number:	54	White:	38
Not identified:	11	Mixed-race:	5

Sources: Daily Picayune, 19 Feb. 1872; *1870 U.S. Federal Census.*

B. White League Roster Sample

This sample of 133 names represents approximately 10 percent of the names listed in the appendix of Stuart Omer Landry's *The Battle of Liberty Place: The Overthrow of Carpet-Bag Misrule in New Orleans, September 14, 1874* (New Orleans: Pelican, 1955). The White League roster in Landry was culled to participants in the 1874 battle (as opposed to later action in 1877). Programs in the White League Papers in the Special Collections at the Hill Memorial Library at Tulane University identify individuals who fought on Canal Street. In order to ascertain accurate ages for participants, the online subscription service Ancestry.com was used to locate names in the censuses. Most of the names listed here appeared in more than one census, suggesting a high degree of reliability. The censuses also revealed connections between these individuals and siblings, particularly older brothers, or fathers who fought in the war, as well as the occupational status of individuals and households. The same patterns emerged when the data were cross-referenced with Andrew B. Booth's *Records of Louisiana Confederate Soldiers and Confederate Commands* (New Orleans, 1920), but that source also indicated the sort of war record accrued by the veterans who served in the White League. It became clear that the White League overwhelmingly attracted the youngest of veterans as well as men who had been too young to fight in the Civil War.

Name	W.L. Rank	W.L. Group	Birth Year	Birthplace	Census	Veteran	C.W. Unit	Notes
Babcock, C. E.	pvt.	Co. B, 6th D WL	1846	LA	1880	N		City clerk in 1880
Babcock, O. E.	pvt.	Btn. A, LFA	1834	NY	1870	Y	WA	Enlisted in same unit, same day, as F. N. Ogden.
Bachelot, E.	pvt.	Sec. A, 5th wd WL						
Bachemin, John	pvt.	Co. C, CCWL	1848	LA	1870	Y	20th La. Inf.	
Bailey, N. E.	pvt.	Co. A, 1st La. Inf.						
Bailey, N. E., Jr.	pvt.	Co. D, 1st La. Inf.						Pvt. dropped by 1862—too young?

Name	Rank	Unit	Birth Year	Birthplace	Census Year	Y/N	Regiment	Notes
Bailey, R. A.	pvt.	Co. C, CCWL	1847	LA	1870	N		Clerk in grocery; father is major grocery wholesaler.
Bailey, Dr. Walter, Jr.	pvt.	Co. C, CCWL	1818	MA	1870	N		
Baker, Alf. T	2d lt.	Btn. A, LFA	1850	England	1880	N		Clerk in hardware store in 1870
Baker, John P.	pvt.	Co. A, 1st La. Inf.	1844	LA		Y	WA	Age computed from parole.
Baker, H. H. (Henry)	2d cpl.	Co. E, CCWL						
Baker, Harry	pvt.	Btn. A, LFA	1857	LA	1870	N		Younger brother of Alfred T. Baker
Balfour, C. C.	pvt.	Sec. A, CCWL	1838	MS	1880	Y	8th CS Cav.	Grocery clerk in 1880 Prob. born 1838—Mississippi—C. C. is likely his brother. Per 1850 census
Balfour, James R.	1st lt.	Sec. A, CCWL						
Banister, M.	pvt.	Btn. A, LFA						M. Banister only appears on 1866 tax register. Many Banisters from Jackson, LA, in war, etc.
Bardon, E. N.	1st lt.	Washington WL				Y	Watson Bty	Sgt. in same reg't. as Toledano. Was paroled at Port Hudson because he was enlisted man.

(continued)

Name	W.L. Rank	W.L. Group	Birth Year	Birthplace	Census	Veteran	C.W. Unit	Notes
Barnett, Alfred R.	pvt.	Co. H, 6th wd WL	1853	LA	1870	N		
Barnett, C.	pvt.	Sec. C, 5th wd WL						
Barnett, W. H.	pvt.	Co. C, 1st La. Inf.						
Barre, J.	pvt.	Sec. A, 5th wd WL	1811	France	1870	Y	European Brig. (militia)	
Barrett, D. (David)	cpl.	Co. G, CCWL	1845	Ireland	1880	Y	20th La. Inf.	Captured at Corinth 1862, exchanged, deserted 1863.
Barrett, James	pvt.	Co. G, CCWL						
Barrett, John	pvt.	Co. C, CCWL	1842	Ireland	1870	Y		Likely a veteran. Several possible John Barretts
Barringer, J. H. (James)	pvt.	Btn. A, LFA	1854	LA	1870	N		
Barringer, L. G.	pvt.	Btn. A, LFA						
Barry, John	pvt.	Sec. C, 5th wd WL	1845	MD	1870	Y		Several likely candidates in Booth
Bartlett, J. T.	pvt.	Co. C, 1st La. Inf.						
Bartlette, O.	pvt.	Co. C, 1st La. Inf.						All Louisiana Bartlette listed in 1870 Census are mixed-race.
Barton, ? (James?)	1st lt.	Washington WL	1832	LA				None probable listed as LA veteran.

Name	Rank	Unit	Birth	Birthplace	Census		Notes
Barton, T. S. (prb. T. H.)	pvt.	Co. C, CCWL	1848	LA	1880	N	Mechanic in 1880, brother to James Barton
Bateson, C. E.	pvt.	Co. C, CCWL	1850	England	1880	N	Living in St. Louis, commission merchant
Bath, T. J. (Thomas)	pvt.	Co. B, CCWL	1850	Ireland	1880	N	Laborer
Baxter, Thomas		Sec. E, CCWL					
Bayhi, J. R. (James)	pvt.	Washington WL	1847	LA	1870	N	Lives in Plaquemines.
Bayle, A.	pvt.	Sec. A, 5th wd WL					
Bayon, Dr. Henri	pvt.	Sec. A, 5th wd WL	1830	LA	1870	N	Not listed in Booth.
Beanham	sgt.	Co. G, CCWL	1847	LA	1870	N	Could be William H, b. 1847, clerk in cotton office, or John, b. 1851, lottery clerk—both children of Irish immigrants. No La. Conf. listed for either.
Beattie, G. W.	pvt.	Co. D, 1st La. Inf.					
Beattie, W. A.	pvt.	Co. D, 1st La. Inf.					
Beaulieu, Ned	pvt.	St. John WL					
Beauregard, James	pvt.	Sec. C, 5th wd WL	1855	LA	1880	N	Clerk. Living with uncle Emile Gamet, a sugar broker

(continued)

Name	W.L. Rank	W.L. Group	Birth Year	Birthplace	Census	Veteran	C.W. Unit	Notes
Bedford, W. D. (William)	pvt.	Co. G, CCWL	1826	PA	1870			No way of determining veteran status
Beers, George M.	pvt.	Co. A, 1st La. Inf.	1856	MA	1870	N		At 14, he was clerking in law office. Father cotton broker
Beggs, James	pvt.	Co. B, 6th D WL						
Behan, W. J.	col.	CCWL	1841	KY	1870	Y	Wash. Art.	
Bein, C. W.	pvt.	Co. C, CCWL	1853	LA	1880	N		Merchant in 1880
Bell, Hezekiah S.	2d sgt.	Co. C, CCWL	1830	PA	1870			Employee of William S. Pike, printer with 400,000 in real estate—book keeper
Bell, P. B. (Patrick)	pvt.	Co. A, 1st La. Inf.	1854	LA	1870	N		Son of bank night watchman
Bell, Wm. A.	aide to Ogden		1837	KY	1870	Y		Son-in-law of Michel Musson, business partner of Fred Ogden
Bellanger, A.	pvt.	Sec. A, 5th wd WL	1830	LA	1880	Y	Orleans Guard	Never went beyond militia duty according to Booth.
Bender, Frank	pvt.	Co. F, CCWL	1854	LA	1870	N		Older brother a clerk in 1870
Bercegeay, C (Cezaire)	pvt.	Sec. C, 5th wd WL	1858	LA	1880 & 1870	N		From Ascension Parish—perhaps in school in 1874

Name	Rank	Unit	Birth	Birthplace	Census	Y/N	Regiment	Notes
Bercegeay, Emanuel	pvt.	Bty. C, LFA	1853	LA	1880			Merchant from St. Mary Parish
Berg, Fred	pvt.	Co. C, 1st La. Inf.	1850	Denmark	1880	N		House painter
Berry, W. A.	pvt.	Co. F, CCWL	1851	LA	1870	N		Clerk
Berwin, George	2d lt.	Washington WL				Y	21st La. Inf.	Not on rolls after 1861
Betz, J. W.	pvt.	Co. C, 1st La. Inf.	1828	Denmark	1880	N		Not listed in Booth.
Betz, Mike	pvt.	Washington WL						
Bezou, Dr. H. (Henry)	pvt.	Sec. A, 5th wd WL	1850	LA	1880	N		
Bienvenu, F. A.	pvt.	Sec. A, 5th wd WL						
Bienvenu, Nemours	1st lt.	Co. H, 6th wd WL	1840	LA	1860	Y		The Bienvenu family from St. Bernard Parish
Bienvenu, R. H.	pvt.	Co. H, 6th wd WL	1846	LA	1880	N		
Bienville, Neuville	pvt.	Co. H, 6th wd WL	1843	LA	1860	Y		
Biers, J. S.	pvt.	Co. B, 6th D WL	1836	NY	1880	Y	15th La. Inf.	
Biggar, J. R.	pvt.	Sec. D, CCWL	1828	Ireland	1870	Y	Lafayette Art.	
Birmingham, P. (Bermingham, Peter)	pvt.	Co. K, 10th wd WL						

(continued)

Name	W.L. Rank	W.L. Group	Birth Year	Birthplace	Census	Veteran	C.W. Unit	Notes
Black, D. C. (David)	pvt.	Co. C, CCWL	1848	LA	1870	N		Father is cotton merchant, David works as clerk in house. Possible conscript/deserter in 22d La. Inf.
Blaffer, J. A.	pvt.	Co. B, CCWL	1838	KY	1880	Y	Wash. Art.	Listed as "Merchant."
Blanchard, Dawson A.	capt.	Co. C, 1st La. Inf.	1844	LA	1870	Y	Staff	Seems to have bounced around a lot in war. Clerk in store
Bloch, S. (Simon)	pvt.	Co. H, 6th wd WL	1833	France	1870	Y	22d & 23d La. Inf.	Enlisted in Dec. 61—with Tissot's company.
Block, John T.	pvt.	Co. C, CCWL	1836	MO	1880	Y	La. Guard Bty.	Served entire war.
Bloodgood, C. B.	pvt.	Co. C, CCWL						
Boarman, Charles B.	3d lt.	Co. B, 1st La. Inf.						
Boarman, J. R.	pvt.	Co. A, 1st La. Inf.						
Bobb, Leslie	pvt.	Sec. E, CCWL	1853	New Orleans	1880	N		Stenographer in 1880
Boisblanc, Chris	pvt.	Bty. C, LFA	1849	LA	1870	N		
Bolton, A.	pvt.	Washington WL						

Name	Rank	Unit	Birth	Place	Census	Vet	Regiment	Notes
Bond, R. C.	3d lt.	Sec. A, CCWL	1834	MD	1880	Y	1st La. Hvy. Art.	Volunteered 1861, surrendered both at Ft. St. Philip & Vicksburg, Meridian—1880 Tax Collector. Ascension Parish at end of war
Booth, George	pvt.	Co. A, 1st La. Inf.	1852	LA	1880	N		Father owns hat shop. Parents immigrants. In 1880 C. W. a clerk in hat store. Younger brother a lawyer
Borge, James	en. man.	7th wd WL	1829	FL	1880	Y	Capt. Borge's Co.	Militia. Of Maltese/ Gibraltar parents
Borland, Euclid, Jr.	capt.B117	Co. A, 1st La. Inf.	1843	MS	1880	Y	6th Va. Inf.	Enlisted as pvt. in 1861, promoted to capt.
Bosworth, M. (Millard)	pvt.	Sec. E, CCWL	1853	LA	1870	N		Father is wealthy ice dealer.
Bosworth, Wm (William, Sr.)	pvt.	Co. C, 1st La. Inf.		CT	1870	N		
Bosworth, Wm.	pvt.	Sec. E, CCWL	1855	LA	1880	N		Clerk in 1880
Boulet, Wm.	pvt.	9th wd WL	1847	LA	1870	N		Works in furniture store 1870.
Bouligny, Ed (Edgar)	pvt.	Sec. A, CCWL	1853	LA	1870	N		Father a cotton & sugar broker
Bolliemet, R. H. (Roland)	pvt.	Co. C, CCWL	1846	AL	1880	Y	2nd Ala. Militia Regt.	Clerk in store
Boulware, A., Jr.	pvt.	Co. F, CCWL						

(continued)

Name	W.L. Rank	W.L. Group	Birth Year	Birthplace	Census	Veteran	C.W. Unit	Notes
Bouny, P. L.	1st lt.	Sec. A, 5th wd WL						Broker in 1880
Bowman, M. M. (Maurice)	pvt.	Sec. E, CCWL	1846	LA	1880	N		
Boylan, T. N.	pvt.	Sec. A, CCWL	1834	New Orleans	1880	Y	2d La. Inf.	Chief of police in 1880
Boyle, C. H. (Cornelius)	sgt.	Co. K, 10th wd WL	1840	Ireland	1870	Y	Capt. Brennan's Co.	Assuming C. Boyle is Cornelius. Eliminated three other possibilities through death records, all nonveterans, all born in 1846. Working as blacksmith in 1870
Bozant, John	1st lt.	Co. B, 6th D WL	1836	LA	1880	Y	Crescent Reg't. La. Inf.	Laborer in 1880
Bozonier, A. (Antoine)	pvt.	Bat. C, L.F.A.	1841	LA	1870	Y	La. Lt. Aty.	Bank clerk in 1870—killed in battle.
Brandenb(u)rg, Thos.	pvt.	Sec. D, CCWL	1847	LA	1870	N		Tinsmith in 1870—son of tinsmith. Older brother John, b. 1842, d. Feb. 9, 1865, in Elmira Prison (Booth 1.91).

Name	Rank	Unit	Birth	Place	Census	Slave	Other service	Notes
Braud, E. (Emile)	2d lt.	Co. H, 6th wd WL	1826	LA	1880	Y	St. James Militia	Shown in Ascension Parish, 1880. Could also be Edouard, veteran, not shown in census.
Breedon, Monk	pvt.	Co. D, 1st La. Inf.	1858	LA	1870	N		Father is house painter.
Breen, Chas. H.	pvt.	Co. B, 6th D WL	1854	LA	1870	N		Grocery clerk in 1870
Brewer, E. M.	pvt.	Co. A, 1st La. Inf.						
Brewster, John	pvt.	Co. H, 6th wd WL	1835	Ireland	1870	Y	21st La. Inf.	Boardinghouse keeper in 1870. Was 2d lt. in infantry. Surrendered at Vicksburg. Deserted in late 1863.
Bringier, M. S. (Marius)	pvt.	Sec. A, CCWL	1850	LA	1880	N		Clerk in 1880
Brower, E. M.	pvt.	Co. A, 1st La. Inf.						Most Browers listed in both censuses are mixed-race. The only E. Brower is Ensley Brower (in birth records and census). He is mixed-race.
Brown, And. K. (Andrew)	3d cpl.	Co. C, CCWL	1830	NY	1870			Cotton clerk
Brown, D. F.	1st cpl.	Sec. D, CCWL						Too many Browns to identify with accuracy.
Brown, D. W.	pvt.	Washington WL						
Brown, H. W.	pvt.	Co. C, CCWL						

(continued)

Name	W.L. Rank	W.L. Group	Birth Year	Birthplace	Census	Veteran	C.W. Unit	Notes
Brown, M. M.	5th sgt.	Sec. E, CCWL						
Brown, W. H.	3d sgt.	Co. B, CCWL						
Brown, W. L.	1st cpl.	Sec. E, CCWL						
Brugier, August(e)	en. man.	7th wd WL	1830	New Orleans	Birth	Y	Chasseurs a pied militia	In militia unit during war. Not in census but positive ID in birth records
Brulard, Charles		Bat. C, L.F.A.						
Brunnard, Aug. (Bernhard, Auguste)	pvt.	Bat. C, L.F.A.	1841	LA	1870	N		Baker
Brur s, D. J., Dr.	surgeon		1836	SC	1880	Y	Staff	White League pamphleteer
Bryan, Henry H.	pvt.	Co. A, 1st La. Inf.	1845	TN	1870	Y	14th La. Inf.	Lawyer in 1870
Buck, S. H.	1st lt.	Co. C, CCWL	1842	Prussia	1870			
Buckley, Thomas	pvt.	Co. H, 6th wd WL						
Buckner, James	pvt.	Sec. A, CCWL	1853	Alabama	1880	N		On Ogden's staff
Buddecke, Chas. B.	sgt.	Co. D, 1st La. Inf.	1845	LA	1880	N		Commission merchant
Budge, Ben	pvt.	Co. F, CCWL	1847	LA	1870	N		
Buhler, J. R.	pvt.	Sec. A, CCWL		LA	1880	N		
Buisson, Theodule	2d lt.	Sec. C, 5th wd WL	1839	LA	1880	Y	Dreaux's Cav.	Officer in C.W.—judge in 1880
Bunce, Wm. F.	pvt.	Sec. E, CCWL	1848	LA	1880	N		Living in Lake Charles, 1880
Burckel, Jacob	pvt.	Washington WL						

Name	Rank	Company	Birth	State	Source	Veteran	Regiment	Notes
Burns, Dan	pvt.	Sec. D, CCWL						
Burns, Ed	pvt.	Co. B, CCWL	1835	LA	Booth	Y	6th La. Inf.	
Burvant, Pascal (Borvant)	pvt.	Co. H, 6th wd WL	1852	LA	1870	N		
Butterfield, J.	pvt.	Co. F, CCWL						
Butts, Wm.	pvt.	Sec. A, 5th wd WL						
Byrd, John G.	1st cpl.	Co. C, CCWL	1845	LA	1870	Y	Greenleaf's Cav.	Clerk in 1870—enlisted in 1863 at Mobile. Spent much of time in service sick.
Byrnes, J.	pvt.	Sec. D, CCWL	1856	LA	1870	N		Father was a clerk in coal yard, 1870.
Byrnes, Nat	pvt.	Co. C, 1st La. Inf.						
Byrnes, Richard	cpl.	Bat. C, L.F.A.						

Statistics
  133 names searched   37 of 83 veterans
  87 identified by birth year = 65%   26 born on or after 1850 = 29.9%
  83 identified by veteran status = 62%   % of those identified as veterans = 44.5%
  Birth year: average = 1843.42, median = 1845.5

Sources: U.S. federal censuses for 1850, 1860, 1870, and 1880, from www.ancestry.com; Booth, Records of Louisiana Confederate Soldiers; Landry, Battle of Liberty Place, appendix.

C. Louisiana Senate, 1880 versus 1892

On the face of things, the data between the 1880 and 1892 Louisiana Senate is not particularly revealing. A closer look, however, indicates that while the average age remained fairly constant through those twelve years, a generational shift in power took place. The state senate of 1880 clearly reflected the Civil War generation, whereas the body that legislated in 1892 contained a significant proportion of the postbellum generation. Only three members of the 1892 senate had been officers in the Confederate army. Another interesting note is that there was very little incumbency in the state senate (also true for the state House), which may have lent instability to Louisiana's legislative basis.

| | | | 1880 | | | | |
| | | | Veteran | | Years in Legislature | | |
Parish	Name	Birth Year	Rank	Unit	Begin	End	Party
Acadia, St. Landry	Fontenot, Theodore S.	1846	pvt.	2nd La. Res	1880	1885	D
	Robertson, William A.	1838	surgeon	6th La. Inf.	1880	1884	D
Ascension, St. James	Simms, Richard (Sims)	1841	pvt.		1880	1892	D
Assumption, Lafourche, Point	Cahan, Mayer	1845	pvt.	European Brig. La. Mil.	1880	1888	R
Coupee, Terrebonne	Stewart, Jordan	—	—	—	1880	1888	R
Avoyelles	Parlange, Charles	1852	—	—	1880	1885	D
Bienville, Bossier, Claiborne, Webster	Vance, John C.	1840	probable		1880	1885	D
	Watkins, J. D.	1829	maj.	1st La. Res. Btn.	1880	1884	D
Caddo	Nutt, L. M.	1835	capt.	Red River Rangers	1880	1882	D
	Foster, Murphy J.	1849	—	—	1880	1892	D
	Nunez, Adrien	1827	—	—	1880	1884	D
Caldwell, Franklin, Jackson, Ouichita, Richland	Aby, Thomas Y.	1839	surgeon	Wash. Art.	1880	1885	D
	Kidd, E. E.	1837	pvt.	28th La. Inf.	1880	1884	D
Catahoula, Grant, Winn	Brian, Benjamin F.	1834	pvt.	Wash. Art.	1880	1884	I

(continued)

		1892				
		Veteran		Years in Legislature		
Name	Birth Year	Rank	Unit	Begin	End	Party
Hayes, D. B.	1846	—	—	1892	1894	D
Ward, C. W.	1864	—	—	1892	1896	D
McCall, Henry	1847	—	—	1892	1896	D
Shaffer, John D.	1858	—	—	1892	1896	D
Perkins, J. S.	1844	pvt.	8th La. Inf.	1892	1894	D
Heard, T. J.	1850	—	—	1892	1896	D
Wren, G. L. P.	1866	—	—	1892	1896	D
Stroud, W. A.	1838	sgt.	9th La. Inf.	1892	1896	D
Currie, Andrew	1843	pvt.	Red River Rangers	1892	1896	D
Caffery, Don	1836	—	—	1892	1894	D
Henry, S. P.	1857	—	—	1892	1894	D
Womack, W. R.	1842	pvt.	28th La. Inf.	1892	1896	D
Brumby, G. B.	1848	—	—	1892	1896	D
Brian, Benjamin F.	1834	pvt.	Wash. Art.	1892	1896	P

(*continued*)

Parish	Name	Birth Year	Veteran		Years in Legislature		Party
			Rank	Unit	Begin	End	
Concordia, Tensas	Walton, George L.	1830	capt.	25th La. Inf.	1880	1884	D
DeSoto, Nachitoches,	Cunningham, M. J.	1842	pvt.	1st La. Hvy. Art.	1880	1884	D
Red River, Sabine	Marston, B. W.	1841	pvt.	Wash. Art.	1880	1884	D
E. Baton Rouge	Buffington, Thomas J., Dr.	1822	capt.	9th La. Inf.	1880	1884	D
E. Carroll, Madison	Lucas, Hugh R.	1828	maj.	11th Tenn. Inf.	1880	1884	D
E. Feliciana, W. Feliciana	Leake, William W.	1833	capt.	1st La. Cav.	1880	1884	D
Iberia, Lafayette, St. Martin	Perry, Robert S.	1836	adj.	8th La. Inf.	1880	1884	D
Iberville, W. Baton Rouge	Montan, D. C.	1834	—	—	1880	1884	D
Jefferson, St. Charles, SJB	Demas, Henry	1848	—	—	1880	1892	R
Lincoln, Morehouse, Union, W. Carroll	Newton, C.	—	—	—	1880	1892	D
	Steele, O. B.	1849	—	—	1880	1884	D
Livingston, St. Helena, St. Tammany, Tangipahoa, Washington	Settoon, John	1840	pvt.	7th La. Inf.	1880	1884	D
	Augustin, J. Numa	1851	—	—	1880	1884	D
	Campbell, Thomas	1814	—	—	1880	1884	D
Orleans, Plaquemines, St. Bernard	Davey, Robert C.	1854	—	—	1880	1884	D
	Estopinal, Albert	1845	sgt.	22d La. Inf.	1880	1900	D
	Hagan, James	1830	pvt.	7th La. Inf.	1880	1884	D
	Harris, Edwin	—	—	—	1880	1884	D
	Pollock, John F.	1837	capt.	Greenleaf's Cav.	1880	1884	D
	Rogers, Wynne	1846	—	—	1880	1884	D

(continued)

Name	Birth Year	Veteran		Years in Legislature		Party
		Rank	Unit	Begin	End	
Cordill, Charles C.	1846	pvt.	Woods La. Cav.	1884	1912	D
Pugh, J. C.	1852	—	—	1892	1896	D
Fike, J. J.	1843	pvt.	11th La. Inf.	1892	1896	D
Fisher, John D.	1847	pvt.	Ogden's La. Cav.	1892	1900	D
Montgomery, George W.	1842	cpl.	Wash. Art.	1884	1896	D
Pipes, D. W.	1845	pvt.	Wash. Art.	1892	1896	D
Avery, Dudley	1843	lt. col.	18th La. Inf.	1892	1896	D
Lefebre, Victor	1857	—	—	1892	1896	D
Marrero, L. H.	1852	—	—	1892	1896	D
VanHook, W. A.	—	—	—	1892	1896	D
Lott, Hiram R.	—	—	—	1888	1896	D
Newsom, H. C.	1852	—	—	1892	1896	D
Estinopal, Albert	1845	sgt.	22d La. Inf.	1880	1900	D
Guillote, J. Vaslin	—	—	—	1892	1894	D
Tissot, A. L.	1840	lt. col.	23d La. Inf.	1892	1896	D
Gauthreaux, Charles	1861	—	—	1892	1896	D
Flynn, John Q.	1853	—	—	1892	1896	D
Davey, Robert C.	1854	—	—	1892	1894	D
McCarthy, Dennis	1842	pvt.	15th La. Inf.	1892	1896	D
Downing, R. H.	1839	—	—	1892	1896	D

(*continued*)

| Parish | Name | Birth Year | 1880 Veteran | | Years in Legislature | | Party |
			Rank	Unit	Begin	End	
Orleans, Plaquemines, St. Bernard	Story, Hampton	1853	—	—	1880	1884	D
Rapides, Vernon	Luckett, R. L.	1838	asst. surg.	Crescent Reg't.	1880	1884	D

Statistics
 Average birth year = 1839
 33 of 36 (91%) identified by age
 22 of 36 (61%) identified as in Confederate service
 Average age at time of taking office = 41

Sources: 1870, 1880, 1900 U.S. federal censuses, from www.ancestry.com; Andrew B. Booth, *Records of Louisiana Confederate Soldiers and Confederate Commands* (New Orleans, 1920); Arthur E. McEnany, ed., *Membership in the Louisiana Senate, 1880–2008* (Baton Rouge: Secretary of State, 2004).

| Name | Birth Year | Veteran | | Years in Legislature | | Party |
		Rank	Unit	Begin	End	
Levert, J. B.	1837	pvt.	1st La. Cav.	1892	1896	D
Seip, Frederick	1841	2nd lt.	Crescent Reg't.	1888	1896	D

Statistics
 Average birth year = 1847
 33 of 36 (91%) identified by age
 16 of 36 (44.4%) identified as in Confederate service
 Average age at time of taking office = 45

NOTES

INTRODUCTION

1. Henry Clay Warmoth, *War, Politics, and Reconstruction: Stormy Days in Louisiana* (Columbia: Univ. of South Carolina Press, 2006), xlix.

2. William Archibald Dunning, *Reconstruction: Political and Economic, 1865–1877* (New York: Harper Bros., 1907). The last major Dunning-school history of Reconstruction is Ellis Merton Coulter, *The South during Reconstruction, 1865–1877* (Baton Rouge: Louisiana State Univ. Press, 1947).

3. Key revisionist works include John Hope Franklin, *Reconstruction after the Civil War* (Chicago: Univ. of Chicago Press, 1961); Kenneth M. Stampp, *The Era of Reconstruction, 1865–1877* (New York: Knopf, 1965); and Kenneth M. Stampp and Leon F. Litwack, eds., *Reconstruction: An Anthology of Revisionist Writings* (Baton Rouge: Louisiana State Univ. Press, 1968). Key "postrevisionist" works include Michael Les Benedict, *A Compromise of Principle: Congressional Republicans and Reconstruction, 1863–1869* (New York: Norton, 1974); William S. McFeeley, *Yankee Stepfather: General O. O. Howard and the Freedmen* (New Haven, CT: Yale Univ. Press, 1968); and Eric Foner, *Reconstruction: America's Unfinished Revolution, 1863–1877* (New York: Harper & Row, 1988). For a single-volume treatment of the many directions in contemporary Reconstruction historiography, see Thomas J. Brown, ed., *Reconstructions: New Perspectives on the Postbellum United States* (New York: Oxford Univ. Press, 2007).

CHAPTER 1: POOR NEW ORLEANS!

Epigraph. Samuel Wilson Jr. and Patricia Brady, eds., *Queen of the South: New Orleans, 1853–1862: The Journal of Thomas K. Wharton* (New Orleans: Historic New Orleans Collections, 1999), 60.

1. Ellis prison diary, E. P. Ellis Family Papers, Louisiana and Lower Mississippi Valley Collections, Hill Memorial Library, Louisiana State Univ., Baton Rouge; *Baltimore Sun*, 28 Jan. 1861; *Macon Daily Telegraph*, 28 Jan. 1861.

2. Ellis prison diary.

3. *Statistical Abstract of the United States*, vol. 1 (Washington, DC: Government Printing Office, 1878); *Seventh Census*, vol. 1, *Statistics of the Population of the United*

States, (Washington, DC: Government Printing Office, 1862). For a visual portrayal of New Orleans's busy port scene, see the landscape by Marie Adrien Persac in Wilson and Brady, *Queen of the South*, 181.

4. John M. Sacher, *A Perfect War of Politics: Parties, Politicians, and Democracy in Louisiana, 1824–1861* (Baton Rouge: Louisiana State Univ. Press, 2003), 287–95; John D. Winters, *The Civil War in Louisiana* (Baton Rouge: Louisiana State Univ. Press, 1963), 14–15.

5. Winters, *The Civil War in Louisiana*, 428–29; Peter S. Carmichael, *The Last Generation: Young Virginians in Peace, War, and Reunion* (Chapel Hill: Univ. of North Carolina Press, 2005).

6. Bertram Wyatt-Brown, *The Shaping of Southern Culture: Honor, Grace, and War, 1760s–1880s* (Chapel Hill: Univ. of North Carolina Press, 2001), 154–202. Influential in helping historians understand the personal motivations of Civil War–era men is Stephen W. Berry II, *All That Makes a Man: Love and Ambition in the Civil War South* (Oxford: Oxford Univ. Press, 2003), 3–16. For views on what motivated soldiers to fight, see James M. McPherson, *For Cause and Comrades: Why Men Fought in the Civil War* (New York: Oxford Univ. Press, 1997).

7. Robert Cinnamond Tucker, "The Life and Public Service of E. John Ellis," *Louisiana Historical Quarterly* 29, no. 3 (July 1946): 679–84. According to slave schedules, Ellis's father owned ten slaves in 1860. *1860 U.S. Federal Census—Slave Schedules*, M653, National Archives. All census records were drawn from www.ancestry.com.

8. Quotes in Tucker, "Life of Ellis," 685–86; Sacher, *A Perfect War of Politics*, 232–40, 267.

9. Quotes in Ellis prison diary; Tucker, "Life of Ellis," 687.

10. Ellis prison diary; quotes in Tucker, "Life of Ellis," 689.

11. *Diocese of Baton Rouge: Catholic Church Records*, vol. 5, 1830–39 (Baton Rouge: Diocese of Baton Rouge, Dept. of Archives, 1984), 469; Edith Ogden Harrison, "*Strange to Say—*": *Recollections of Persons and Events in New Orleans and Chicago* (Chicago: A. Kroch & Son, 1949), 3–4; Stuart Omer Landry, *The Battle of Liberty Place: The Overthrow of Carpet-Bag Rule in New Orleans, September 14, 1874* (Gretna: Pelican, 1955), 201–2; *1850 US Federal Census, Slave Schedules*, Rapides Parish, La.; there were many Ogdens in New Orleans in 1860, as there are today. For the Democratic activity of Frederick Nash Ogden Jr.'s uncle Judge Octavius Nash Ogden, see *The American Almanac and Repository of Useful Knowledge* (Boston, 1859), 4; his uncle Abner Nash Ogden was a prominent New Orleans judge and attorney who in 1860 had an estate worth forty thousand dollars. *1860 US Federal Census*, roll M653_412, p. 0, image 130. For a novelistic though quite accurate account of Robert Nash Ogden's role in mediating the 1858 Know-Nothing conflict, see Herbert Asbury, *The French Quarter: An Informal History of the New Orleans Underworld* (New York: Alfred A. Knopf, 1936), 294–314; Lawrence V. Alstyne and Charles B. Ogden, eds., *The Ogden Family in America: The Elizabethtown Branch and their English Ancestors* (Philadelphia: J. B. Lippincott, 1907), 362; according to the Louisiana Marriage Database, Louisiana State Archives, Baton Rouge (available also through www.ancestry.com), Frederick Nash Ogden married Carmelite Lopez in West Baton Rouge in 1836.

12. Harrison, *"Strange to Say,"* 41. In 1860 Ogden lived in a boardinghouse with Emile Bozonier, another clerk. *1860 US Federal Census,* roll M653_421, p. o, image 64; James K. Hogue speculates that a resignation certificate for C. L. Jackson signed by filibusterer William Walker found in the Frederick Nash Ogden Papers at Tulane University is evidence that F. N. Ogden served with Walker in Nicaragua. It almost certainly belonged to Ogden's future brother-in-law, Columbus Jackson, of Mississippi, who would have been nineteen years old in 1857. *1850 US Federal Census,* M432_372, p. 131, image 263. James K Hogue, *Uncivil War: Five New Orleans Street Battles and the Rise and Fall of Radical Reconstruction* (Baton Rouge: Louisiana State Univ. Press, 2006), 129; *1880 U.S. Federal Census,* roll T9_464, p. 259.400; *New Orleans Times,* 28 Sept. 1879.

13. Andrew B. Booth, ed., *Records of Louisiana Confederate Soldiers and Confederate Commands* (New Orleans, 1920), 2:19; United States War Department, *The War of the Rebellion: A Compilation of the Official Records of the Union and Confederate Armies* (Washington, DC: Government Printing Office, 1880–1901) (hereafter O.R.), ser. 1, 2:188–89.

14. Glenn Conrad, ed., *Dictionary of Louisiana Biography* (New Orleans: Louisiana Historical Association, 1988), 1:97; O.R., ser. 1, 6:575.

15. O.R., ser. 1, 6:622–23.

16. Winters, *The Civil War in Louisiana,* 74–93; O.R., ser. 1, 6:594, 624, 825, quote on 825.

17. Kate Mason Rowland and Mrs. Morris L. Croxall, eds., *The Journal of Julia LeGrand, New Orleans: 1862–1863* (Richmond, VA: Everett Waddey, 1911), 81; Devereux quotes in O.R., ser. 1, 6:595.

18. Aristée L. Tissot, Compiled Service Record, RG 109, War Department of Confederate Records, Compiled Service Records, NA; Samuel Wilson Jr., *The Pitot House on Bayou St. John* (New Orleans: Louisiana Landmarks Society, 1992), 5–6, 39–42.

19. Tissot, service record; *L'Abielle de la Nouvelle-Orléans (New Orleans Bee),* 27, 28 April 1861.

20. Napier Bartlett, *Military Record of Louisiana: Including Biographical and Historical Papers Relating to the Military Organizations of the State* (Baton Rouge: Louisiana State Univ. Press, 1964), 252.

21. Ibid. It has become pro forma in scholarship on Creole New Orleans to stake out a definition of the potentially contentious term *Creole.* I defer to the judgment of Joseph Tregle, who applies the term to all individuals of Latin ancestry, of any race, born in Louisiana. See Joseph G. Tregle Jr., "Creoles and Americans," in *Creole New Orleans: Race and Americanization,* ed. Arnold R. Hirsch and Joseph Logsdon (Baton Rouge: Louisiana State Univ. Press, 1992), 140. For a discussion of the variant definitions of *Creole,* particularly in Afro-Creole terms, see Sybil Kein, ed., *Creole: The History and Legacy of Louisiana's Free People of Color* (Baton Rouge: Louisiana State Univ. Press, 2000), xiii–xvii; Gwendolyn Midlo Hall, "The Formation of Afro-Creole Culture," in Hirsch and Logsdon, *Creole New Orleans,* 60–61; Edward Larocque Tinker, *Les écrits de langue française en Louisiane au XIXème siècle: Essais biographique et bibliographique* (Paris: H. Champion, 1932); Placide Canonge Jr.'s

grandmother and great-grandmother were born on St. Domingue in the eighteenth century. *1850 U.S. Federal Census*, M432_238, p. 153, image 307. The Tissots also have the amazing distinction of having been counted twice, five months apart, in the 1850 census. *1850 U.S. Federal Census*, M432_232, p. 93, image 187; Paul F. Lachance, "The Foreign French," in Hirsch and Logsdon, *Creole New Orleans*, 101–30.

22. *Dallas Weekly Herald*, 26 Sept. 1874; Stanley Arthur, ed., *Old Families of Louisiana* (New Orleans, 1931), 277; *New Orleans Daily Picayune*, 18 Dec. 1848; physical features of Toledano from a photograph montage, Louisiana State Museum, New Orleans; *Louise Marie Drouet v. the Succession of L. F. Drouet*, No. 4800, 26 La. Ann. 323 (1874).

23. In 1860 Toledano lived in Jefferson City, part of the present-day Twelfth Ward. *1860 US Federal Census*, roll M653_412, p. 0, image 131; *Drouet v. Succession of Drouet*; *New Orleans Directory for 1842* (New Orleans: Pitts & Clarke, 1842). In 1820 L. F. Drouet's father, Jean Louis Drouet, owned thirty-five slaves. *1820 United States Federal Census*, roll M_33, p. 121. In 1850, L. F. Drouet lived alone and listed his real estate value at twenty-six thousand dollars. *1850 U.S. Federal Census*, roll M432_237, p. 192; property transfer, 22 Aug. 1847, Onesiphore Drouet, notary, New Orleans Notarial Archives; *New Orleans Bee*, 13 April 1847; Earl C. Woods and Charles E. Nolan, eds, *Sacramental Records of the Archdiocese of New Orleans* (New Orleans: Archives of the Archdiocese of New Orleans, 1988).

24. By 1857, Toledano had established himself as an independent cotton weigher. He first appears in the profession in *Mygatt & Company's Directory* (New Orleans: L. Pessou & B. Simon, 1857); *Gardner's New Orleans Directory* (New Orleans: Charles Gardner, 1861); Winters, *The Civil War in Louisiana*, 45.

25. E. A. Toledano, Compiled Service Record, RG 109, War Department of Confederate Records, Compiled Service Records, NA; Frank A. Montgomery, *Reminiscences of a Mississippian in Peace and War* (Cincinnati: Robert Clarke, 1901) 63–65; John Miller, "From Professor to Civil War Hero: Confederate Lt. Colonel Daniel Beltzhoover," Emmitsburg Area Historical Society, Emmitsburg, MD.

26. O.R., ser. 1, 3:328, 359–60; Toledano service record; *Fayetteville (N.C.) Observer*, 11 Nov. 1861.

27. Caryn Cossé Bell, *Revolution, Romanticism, and the Afro-Creole Protest Tradition in Louisiana, 1718–1868* (Baton Rouge: Louisiana State Univ. Press, 1997), 229. For a discussion of antebellum New Orleans's three-tiered racial caste system, see Kimberly S. Hangar, "Origins of New Orleans's Free Creoles of Color," in *Creoles of Color of the Gulf South*, ed. James H. Dormon (Knoxville: Univ. of Tennessee Press, 1996), 22–23; see also Jerah Johnson, "Colonial New Orleans," in Hirsch and Logsdon, *Creole New Orleans*, 53–55; Rodolphe Lucien Desdunes, *Our People and Our History: Fifty Creole Portraits*, trans. Dorothea Olga McCants (Baton Rouge: Louisiana State Univ. Press, 1973), 3–9, 111, 134–35; Joseph Logsdon and Caryn Cossé Bell, "The Americanization of Black New Orleans," in Hirsch and Logsdon, *Creole New Orleans*, 207–11; Judith Kelleher Schafer, *Becoming Free, Remaining Free: Manumission and Enslavement in New Orleans, 1846–1862* (Baton Rouge: Louisiana State Univ. Press, 2003), xiv–xvi, 1.

28. Michael P. Johnson and James L. Roark, *Black Masters: A Free Family of Color in the Old South* (New York: Norton, 1986); Jean Joseph Veaudechamp, *Joseph Sauvinet*, oil on canvas, 1832, Louisiana State Museum, New Orleans; Roulhac Toledano, *The National Trust Guide to New Orleans* (New York: John Wiley, 1996), 58; Samuel Wilson Jr., "Early History," in *New Orleans Architecture*, vol. 4, *The Creole Faubourgs*, ed. Roulhac Toledano, Mary Louise Christovich, and Sallie Evans (Gretna, LA: Pelican, 1974), 3–11; *Sauvinet v. Walker*, No. 3513, 27 La. Ann. 14, (1875). Joseph Sauvinet lived on Barracks (now Governor Nicholls) Street, nine doors down from E. A. Toledano's uncle Raphael. *1840 US Federal Census*, roll M704_402, p. 153.

29. James G. Hollandsworth, *The Louisiana Native Guards: The Black Military Experience during the Civil War* (Baton Rouge: Louisiana State Univ. Press, 1995), 1–3, quote on 3; Rosemarie Fay Loomis, *Negro Soldiers: Free Men of Color in the Battle of New Orleans—War of 1812* (New Orleans: Aux Quartres Vents, 1991), appendix.

30. Arthur W. Bergeron Jr., "Louisiana's Free Men of Color in Gray," in *Louisianians in the Civil War*, ed. Lawrence Lee Hewitt and Arthur Bergeron Jr. (Columbia, MO: Univ. of Missouri Press, 2002), 105.

31. Hollandsworth, *Native Guards*, 3–8. For the primary advocate of free Afro-Creole antagonism and fear toward the Confederate cause, see Bell, *Revolution, Romanticism, and Afro-Creole Protest*, 231–32; for an opposite view, see David C. Rankin, "The Impact of the Civil War on the Free Colored Community of New Orleans," in *Perspectives in American History*, ed. Donald Fleming (Cambridge, MA: Harvard Univ. Press, 1978), xi, 381; see also Justin Nystrom, "Racial Identity and Reconstruction: New Orleans's Free People of Color and the Dilemma of Emancipation," in *The Great Task Remaining Before Us. Reconstruction as America's Continuing Civil War*, ed. Paul Cimbala and Randal Miller (New York: Fordham Univ. Press, 2010).

32. Ellis prison diary.

33. Ibid.

34. Ibid.

35. *O.R.*, ser. 1, 6:510–20; Winters, *The Civil War in Louisiana*, 90–93.

36. *O.R.*, ser. 1, 6:553; Landry, *Battle of Liberty Place*, 202; Winters, *The Civil War in Louisiana*, 95–96.

37. *O.R.*, ser. 1, 6:586–87; only four of the twelve companies of the Twenty-third remained by the time it transferred to Vicksburg. Company K retained its designation until reconsolidated in 1863.

38. Hollandsworth, *Native Guards*, 8–11.

39. Rowland and Croxall, *Journal of Julia LeGrand*, 40–41, emphasis in original; *O.R.*, ser. 1, 6:576–77.

40. Winters, *The Civil War in Louisiana*, 95–102.

CHAPTER 2: THE DAWNING OF NEW REALITIES

Epigraph. Kate Mason Rowland and Mrs. Morris L. Croxall, eds., *The Journal of Julia LeGrand, New Orleans: 1862–1863* (Richmond: Everett Waddey, 1911), 80.

1. Sauvinet later testified that he was "an officer in the United States army at the time General Butler first arrived," a statement so obviously untrue as to suggest a purposeful misrepresentation. Other scholars have assumed that Sauvinet always presented himself as a man of color, but the evidence for such conclusions is always circumstantial, at least when it pertains to the period before 1870. House Report 16, *The New Orleans Riots*, 39th Cong., 2nd sess., no. 1304, 2:44–46.

2. George Fredrickson, *The Inner Civil War: Northern Intellectuals and the Crisis of the Union* (New York: Harper & Row, 1965); Louis Menand, *The Metaphysical Club: A Story of Ideas in America* (New York: Farrar, Straus & Giroux, 2001); "hearts of fire" is the famous nugget from Oliver Wendell Holmes's 1884 Memorial Day speech. Max Lerner, ed., *The Mind and Faith of Justice Holmes: His Speeches, Essays, Letters, and Judicial Opinions* (Boston: Little, Brown, 1943), 5; Reid Mitchell, *Civil War Soldiers* (New York: Viking Penguin Group, 1988), 88.

3. As Reid Mitchell notes, soldiers lost their prewar identities and created new ones. Mitchell, *Civil War Soldiers*, 56; Oliver Wendell Holmes Jr., "The Soldier's Faith," delivered May 30, 1895 at the invitation of Harvard University's graduating class and printed in Sheldon M. Novick, ed., *The Collected Works of Justice Holmes: Complete Public Writings and Selected Judicial Opinions of Oliver Wendell Holmes* (Chicago: University of Chicago Press, 1995), 486–91; quotes on 486 and 487. See also note 45 below.

4. Joy J. Jackson, "Keeping Law and Order in New Orleans under General Butler, 1862," in *Louisianans in the Civil War*, ed. Lawrence Lee Hewitt and Arthur W. Bergeron (Columbia: Univ. of Missouri Press, 2002), 22–24; John D. Winters, *The Civil War in Louisiana* (Baton Rouge: Louisiana State Univ. Press, 1963), 45–46.

5. Joe Gray Taylor, *Louisiana Reconstructed, 1862–1877* (Baton Rouge: Louisiana State Univ. Press, 1974), 4. The *Macon Daily Telegraph*, 29 May 1862, carried the report about Martha Walton; Butler's edict is found in Jackson, "Keeping Law and Order," 23–24; Rowland and Croxall, *Journal of Julia LeGrand*, 159; Abby Day Slocumb to Col. J. B. Walton, 17 July 1862, Walton-Glenny Papers, Williams Research Center, Historic New Orleans Collection, New Orleans.

6. Edward Larocque Tinker, *Creole City: Its Past and Its People* (New York: Longmans, 1953), 87; Taylor, *Louisiana Reconstructed*, 2–3; Joseph G. Dawson III, *Army Generals and Reconstruction: Louisiana, 1862–1877* (Baton Rouge: Louisiana State Univ. Press, 1982), 5–47.

7. Dawson, *Army Generals*, 10–11.

8. Rodolphe Lucien Desdunes, *Our People and Our History: Fifty Creole Portraits*, trans. Dorothea Olga McCants (Baton Rouge: Louisiana State Univ. Press, 1973), 118–20; James G. Hollandsworth, *The Louisiana Native Guards: The Black Military Experience during the Civil War* (Baton Rouge: Louisiana State Univ. Press, 1995).

9. Desdunes, *Our People and Our History*, 119–20.

10. Hollandsworth, *Native Guards*, 14–22; Abby Day Slocomb to Col. J. B. Walton, n.d., Walton-Glenny Papers.

11. C. S. Sauvinet, Compiled Service Record, RG 94, Records of the Adjutant General's Office, Compiled Service Records, National Archives.

12. Edwin C. Bearss, *Historic Resource Study: Ship Island, Harrison County, Mississippi* (Denver: National Park Service, 1984), 205–10.

13. Dawson, *Army Generals*, 12–14; Hollandsworth, *Native Guards*, 44–75.

14. Bearss, *Historic Resource Study*, 210–13; Sauvinet service record; Orleans Parish Birth Records, James Nelson Sauvinet, Charles Silas Sauvinet, and Marie Clothilde Sauvinet, all 34:442–43.

15. Hollandsworth places Sauvinet not only at this raid but in command of it. None of the sources cited by Hollandsworth that I have consulted suggest this, however. Sauvinet was a quartermaster, and as such he was not part of combat arms. Other prominent Afro-Creole officers, such as William B. Barrett, were involved in the raid, however. Hollandsworth, *Native Guards*, 71–74; House Rep., Misc. Docs., 39th Cong., 2nd sess., vol. 1304 16, 45.

16. Hollandsworth, *Native Guards*, 21–22, 71–74; quotes in Sauvinet service record.

17. Winters, *The Civil War in Louisiana*, 149–50.

18. Algernon Sydney Badger, Compiled Service Record, RG 94, Records of the Adjutant General's Office, Compiled Service Records, NA; Jane B. Hewett et al., eds., *Supplement to the Official Records of the Union and Confederate Armies* (Wilmington, NC: Broadfoot, 1994–2000), part 2, vol. 23, pp. 433–53.

19. Badger service record; Hewett et al., *Supplement to the Official Records*, part 2, vol. 23, pp. 433–53.

20. United States War Department, *The War of the Rebellion: A Compilation of the Official Records of the Union and Confederate Armies* (Washington, DC: Government Printing Office, 1880–1901) (hereafter O.R.), ser. 1, vol. 49, pt. 1, pp. 280, quotes on 308. The most influential work to cast honor in regional terms is Bertram Wyatt-Brown, *Honor and Violence in the Old South* (New York: Oxford Univ. Press, 1986).

21. A. L. Tissot, Compiled Service Record; F. N. Ogden, Compiled Service Record, both RG 109, War Department of Confederate Records, Compiled Service Records, NA; Winters, *The Civil War in Louisiana*, 111–12.

22. Ogden service record; William L. Shea and Terrence J. Winschel, *Vicksburg Is the Key: The Struggle for the Mississippi River* (Lincoln: Univ. of Nebraska Press, 2003), 18; Warren E. Grabau, *Ninety-Eight Days: A Geographer's View of the Vicksburg Campaign* (Knoxville: Univ. of Tennessee Press, 2000), 41–42, 8.

23. Hewett et al., *Supplement to the Official Records*, vol. 24, ser. 36, pp. 497–508; Tissot service record.

24. Shea and Wischell, *Vicksburg Is the Key*, 18–26; Hewett, *Supplement to the Official Records*, vol. 24, ser. 36, pp. 503–4; O.R., ser. 1, 15:10.

25. Tissot service record.

26. Rowland and Croxall, *Journal of Julia LeGrand*, 238; *1860 U.S. Federal Census*, roll m653_592, image 499 (all census records were drawn from www.ancestry.com); Ogden Papers, Howard-Tilton Memorial Library, Tulane Univ.; *New Orleans Daily Picayune*, 14 Sept. 1893.

27. Tissot and Ogden service records; *O.R.*, ser. 1, pt. 1, 24:319–20; *Daily Picayune*, 15 May 1887.

28. Arthur W. Bergeron Jr., *Guide to Louisiana Confederate Military Units* (Baton Rouge: Louisiana State Univ. Press, 1989), 53, 59, 67, 161; Howell Carter, *A Cavalryman's Reminiscences of the Civil War* (New Orleans: American Printing, 1900), 107–8, 187–88, "Ogden comes in front" on 188; "had just emerged" in *O.R.*, ser. 1, vol. 39, pt. 3, p. 622. The returning officer was Daniel Gober, who had once commanded E. John Ellis's unit, the Sixteenth Louisiana.

29. Rankin County, Mississippi, Database of Marriages (online at www.ancestry.com), 22 July 1864; *O.R.*, ser. 1, vol. 41, pt. 3, p. 357. Thomas C. W. Ellis, Compiled Service Record, RG 109, War Department of Confederate Records, Compiled Service Records, NA.

30. *O.R.*, vol. 17, pt. 1, ser. 1, pp. 314–15, 375, 411–13, 421–26; Peter Cozzens, *The Darkest Days of the War: The Battles of Iuka & Corinth* (Chapel Hill: Univ. of North Carolina Press, 1997), 272–73, 295.

31. Andrew B. Booth, ed., *Records of Louisiana Confederate Soldiers and Confederate Commands* (New Orleans, 1920), 843; Bergeron, *Guide to Louisiana Units*, 36–37; Edward Cunningham, *The Port Hudson Campaign, 1862–1863* (Baton Rouge: Louisiana State Univ. Press, 1963); Lawrence Lee Hewitt, *Port Hudson: Confederate Bastion on the Mississippi* (Baton Rouge: Louisiana State Univ. Press, 1987); Desdunes, *Our People and Our History*, 121, 124–25, Cailloux quote on 121.

32. Emma Walton to James B. Walton, 11 July 1863, Walton-Glenny Papers; E. A. Toledano, Compiled Service Record, RG 109, War Department of Confederate Records, Compiled Service Records, NA.

33. Emma Walton to James B. Walton, 4 Oct. 1863, Walton-Glenny Papers; E. A. Toledano service record.

34. E. John Ellis to Mary Ellis, 22 Feb. 1864, E. P. Ellis Family Papers, Louisiana and Lower Mississippi Valley Collections, Hill Memorial Library, Louisiana State Univ., Baton Rouge.

35. Robert Cinnamond Tucker, "The Life and Public Service of E. John Ellis," *Louisiana Historical Quarterly* 29, no. 3 (July 1946): 686; quotes in Ellis prison diary, Ellis Family Papers.

36. Ellis prison diary.

37. E. John Ellis to "My Dear Friend," 31 May 1864, Ellis Family Papers.

38. E. John Ellis to Mary Ellis, 16 Sept. 1864; to "My Dear Mother," 27 Dec. 1864; Ellis prison diary, all in Ellis Family Papers.

39. For the most thorough and perhaps the most flattering treatment of Henry Clay Warmoth, see Richard Nelson Current, *Those Terrible Carpetbaggers: A Reinterpretation* (New York: Oxford Univ. Press, 1988).

40. Warmoth Diary, 22, 26 May; 2, 3, 4, 15, 17, 18 June; 7, 24 July; 4–19 Aug. 1863, Henry Clay Warmoth Papers, Southern Historical Collection, Manuscripts Division, Collection No. 752, Univ. of North Carolina, Chapel Hill.

41. Warmoth Diary, 30, 31 Aug.; 14 Sept. 1863; Henry Clay Warmoth, *War, Politics, and Reconstruction: Stormy Days in Louisiana* (New York: Macmillan, 1930), 20.

42. Warmoth Diary, 13 Oct.–9 Dec. 1863; Warmoth, *War, Politics, and Reconstruction*, 22–23.

43. Warmoth Diary, 9 Feb.–7 May 1864; Warmoth, *War, Politics, and Reconstruction*, 24–25.

44. Warmoth Diary, 24 May–31 Oct. 1864.

45. Holmes, "The Soldier's Faith." The literature on the importance of ideology and its role in sustaining victory in the Civil War is vast. For examples, see David N. Donald, ed., *Why the North Won the Civil War* (Baton Rouge: Louisiana State Univ. Press, 1960); Paul Escott, *After Secession: Jefferson Davis and the Failure of Confederate Nationalism* (Baton Rouge: Louisiana State Univ. Press, 1978); James McPherson, *For Cause and Comrades: Why Men Fought in the Civil War* (New York: Oxford Univ. Press, 1997).

CHAPTER 3: HOMECOMINGS AND PERSONAL RECONSTRUCTIONS

Epigraph. Testimony of C. S. Souvinet [*sic*], House Report 16, *The New Orleans Riots*, 39th Cong., 2nd sess., no. 1304, 2:44–46.

1. Ellis prison diary, E. P. Ellis Family Papers, Louisiana and Lower Mississippi Valley Collections, Hill Memorial Library, Louisiana State Univ., Baton Rouge.

2. Robert Cinnamond Tucker, "The Life and Public Service of E. John Ellis," *Louisiana Historical Quarterly* 29, no. 3 (July 1946): 712.

3. For literature that examines the gendered and psychological dimensions of postbellum life, see Bertram Wyatt-Brown, *The Shaping of Southern Culture: Honor, Grace, and War, 1760s–1880s* (Chapel Hill: Univ. of North Carolina Press, 2001); Laura F. Edwards, *Gendered Strife and Confusion: The Political Culture of Reconstruction* (Urbana: Univ. of Illinois Press, 1997).

4. Lawrence Powell, *New Masters: Northern Planters during the Civil War and Reconstruction* (New Haven, CT: Yale Univ. Press, 1980), 10–23.

5. James K. Hogue, *Uncivil War: Five New Orleans Street Battles and the Rise and Fall of Radical Reconstruction* (Baton Rouge: Louisiana State Univ. Press, 2006), 9; John Hope Franklin, *The Militant South, 1800–1861* (Cambridge, MA: Harvard Univ. Press, 1956); Bertram Wyatt-Brown, *Southern Honor: Ethics and Behavior in the Old South* (New York: Oxford Univ. Press, 1982). The original Clausewitz maxim, "War is simply a continuation of political intercourse, with the addition of other means," was first published in German in 1852. It appears in English in Carl von Clausewitz, *On War*, trans. Michael Eliot Howard and Peter Paret (Princeton, NJ: Princeton Univ. Press, 1989), 605.

6. Whitelaw Reid, *After the War: A Southern Tour: May 1, 1865, to May 1, 1866.* (Cincinnati: Moore, Wilstach & Baldwin, 1866), 227–39, quotes on 228, 239.

7. Although she went by the name Louise Drouet, this narrative uses her full name, Louise Marie Drouet, to more clearly distinguish her from her father, Louis Drouet. Quotes reflect direct testimony of Henry Schwartz in *Louise Marie Drouet v. the Succession of L. F. Drouet*, No. 4800, 26 La. Ann. 323 (1874). This case originated

as No. 36201, Second District Court for the Parish of Orleans. Pagination given for an individual's testimony comes from the fair copy of the lower court's proceedings as found in the state supreme court archives at the University of New Orleans.

8. One thing is certain, that Louis F. Drouet was a wealthy man. *New Orleans Directory for 1842* (New Orleans: Pitts and Clarke, 1842). In 1820 L. F. Drouet's father, Jean Louis Drouet, owned thirty-five slaves. *1820 United States Federal Census*, roll M_33, p. 121 (all census records were drawn from www.ancestry.com). In 1850 L. F. Drouet lived alone and listed his real estate value at twenty-six thousand dollars. *1850 U.S. Federal Census*, roll M432_237, p. 192. Property transfer, 22 Aug. 1847, Onesiphore Drouet, notary, New Orleans Notarial Archives. Gwendolyn Midlo Hall, "The Formation of Afro-Creole Culture," in *Creole New Orleans: Race and Americanization*, ed. Arnold R. Hirsch and Joseph Logsdon (Baton Rouge: Louisiana State Univ. Press, 1992), 60–61. Testimony from Eugenie Bazile described their relationship specifically as "placée." *Drouet v. Succession of Drouet*, 16–17. Drouet rented the home, located between Felicity and Richards, from Mary Postille, f.w.c. Testimony of Mrs. Frederichs, ibid., 7–8; *1870 U.S. Federal Census*, roll M593_524, p. 560. For a discussion of the custom of *plaçage*, see Violet Harrington Bryan, "Marcus Christian's Treatment of *Les Gens de Coleur Libre*," in *Creole: The History and Legacy of Louisiana's Free People of Color*, ed. Sybil Kein (Baton Rouge: Louisiana State Univ. Press, 2000), 50–53; Joan M. Martin, "*Plaçage* and the Louisiana *Gens de Coleur Libre*: How Race and Sex Defined the Lifestyles of Free Women of Color," ibid., 65–68.

9. For the relationship between Morgan and Bresson, see testimony of Mrs. Frederichs, 11; of Porée, 13, *Drouet v. Succession of Drouet*.

10. Testimony of Eugenie Bazile, *Drouet v. Succession of Drouet*, 16; birth certificate, Louise Marie Drouet, Louisiana Birth Records, Orleans Parish, State Archives, Baton Rouge, LA, 60:809; testimony of William Bresson, *Drouet v. Succession of Drouet*, 25–26. Sometime around 1854, Elizabeth Bresson began a relationship with a "quarteroon" by the name of John Bull. This union lasted no longer than any of Elizabeth's previous liaisons, perhaps a year to a year and a half. Ibid. Louise Marie Drouet later spoke of the visits to her father, and neighbors of L. F. Drouet made note of them as well. See testimony of Mr. Schwartz, 32–33; Mrs. Schwartz, 35; P. Ryan, 38; Louise Marie Drouet, 21, ibid.

11. Testimony of Mr. Schwartz, 27–30, of Mrs. Schwartz, 35–38, *Drouet v. Succession of Drouet*.

12. Testimony of E. A. Toledano, 46–47, ibid. Neither Louise Marie Drouet nor Arthur Toledano claimed any knowledge of each other before 1865.

13. Ibid.; M. Boniface Adams, "The Gift of Religious Leadership: Henriette Delille and the Foundation of the Holy Family Sisters," in *Cross, Crozier, and Crucible: A Volume Celebrating the Bicentennial of a Catholic Diocese in Louisiana*, ed. Glen R. Conrad (New Orleans: Archdiocese of New Orleans, 1993), 370–73. For a firsthand history of the order, see Mary Bernard Deggs, *No Cross, No Crown: Black Nuns in Nineteenth-Century New Orleans*, (Bloomington: Indiana Univ. Press, 2002). Bayou Road is now called Governor Nicholls Street.

14. *Drouet v. Succession of Drouet*; *1870 U.S. Federal Census*, roll 593_519, p. 350; "Succession of E. A. Toledano" (1874), Orleans Parish Second District Succession Records, 1846–1880, no. 37465.

15. For a general discussion of racial passing in the postbellum South, see Joel Williamson, *New People: Miscegenation and Mulattoes in the United States* (Baton Rouge: Louisiana State Univ. Press, 1995). On increased white Creole anxiety about racial identity, see Virginia Dominguez, *White by Definition: Social Classification in Creole Louisiana* (New Brunswick, NJ: Rutgers Univ. Press, 1994), 133–42. For the collapse of the three-tiered racial caste system, see Joseph Logsdon and Caryn Cossé Bell, "The Americanization of Black New Orleans," in Hirsch and Logsdon, *Creole New Orleans*.

16. The subject of racial passing has been generally handled in a more complete fashion in the arena of popular culture and literary criticism. For the best of this line see Gayle Wald, *Crossing the Line: Racial Passing in Twentieth-Century U.S. Literature and Culture* (Durham, NC: Duke Univ. Press, 2000); Shirley Thompson, "'Ah Toucoutou, ye conin vous': History and Memory in Creole New Orleans," *American Quarterly* 53, no. 2. (2001): 232–66.

17. Arthur W. Bergeron, *Guide to Louisiana Confederate Military Units* (Baton Rouge: Louisiana State Univ. Press, 1989), 53; quotes are from *New Orleans Daily Picayune*, 15 Oct. 1865.

18. Joe Gray Taylor, *Louisiana Reconstructed, 1862–1877* (Baton Rouge: Louisiana State Univ. Press, 1974), 50–53.

19. Ibid., 60–61; Wolfgang Schivelbusch, *The Culture of Defeat: On National Trauma, Mourning, and Recovery*, trans. Jefferson Chase (New York: Metropolitan Books, 2003), 8–10.

20. E. J. Ellis to T. C. W. Ellis, 3 Feb. 1866; T. C. W. Ellis to E. P. Ellis, 6 Feb. 1866, both in Ellis Family Papers.

21. Reid Mitchell, *All on Mardi Gras Day: Episodes in the History of New Orleans Carnival* (Cambridge, MA: Harvard Univ. Press, 1995), 11–16; Augusto P. Miceli, *The Pickwick Club of New Orleans* (New Orleans: Pickwick Press, 1964), 10–30.

22. B. W. Wrenn, *Mardi Gras, New Orleans: Its Ancient and Modern Observance: History of the Mystick Krewe of Comus and Knights of Momus with Scenes, Sketches, and Incidents of the Reign of His Magesty, the King of Carnival*, presented to the patrons of "The Great Kennesaw Route and Its Connections," Atlanta, GA, 1874, a pamphlet in Hargrett Library, Univ. of Georgia, Athens, 18–19.

23. *New York Times*, 4 Nov. 1865. The salvage of the *Republic's* valuable cargo in 2002 served as the subject for a National Geographic documentary, "Civil War Gold" (DVD), National Geographic, Washington, DC, 2004.

24. House Report 16, 2:45–46.

25. Ibid., 2:45.

26. Taylor, *Louisiana Reconstructed*, 81; James G. Hollandsworth Jr., *An Absolute Massacre: The New Orleans Race Riot of July 30, 1866* (Baton Rouge: Louisiana State Univ. Press, 2001), 70–75; quote in Joseph G. Dawson III, *Army Generals and Reconstruction: Louisiana, 1862–1877* (Baton Rouge: Louisiana State Univ. Press, 1982), 32–37.

27. Hollandsworth, *Absolute Massacre*; Taylor, *Louisiana Reconstructed*, 110; Dan Carter, *When the War Was Over: The Failure of Self-Reconstruction in the South* (Baton Rouge: Louisiana State Univ. Press, 1985), 231, 248–53.

28. House Report 16, 2:45. Other witnesses of color are identified as "(colored)" in the testimony. Sauvinet is not.

29. Ibid.

30. Richard Nelson Current, *Those Terrible Carpetbaggers: A Reinterpretation* (New York: Oxford Univ. Press, 1988), 22–23; Warmoth Diary, Feb. 18, 1865, Henry Clay Warmoth Papers, Southern Historical Collection, Manuscripts Division, Collection No. 752, Univ. of North Carolina, Chapel Hill.

31. Warmoth Diary, Feb. 21, 1865; Current, *Those Terrible Carpetbaggers*, 11–17, quote on 17.

32. Warmoth Diary, May 25, 1864.

33. Caryn Cossé Bell, *Revolution, Romanticism, and the Afro-Creole Protest Tradition in Louisiana, 1718–1868* (Baton Rouge: Louisiana State Univ. Press, 1997), 270–74.

34. Current, *Those Terrible Carpetbaggers*, 14–20.

35. Taylor, *Louisiana Reconstructed*, 141–42; Dawson, *Army Generals*, 56–57; *New Orleans Bee*, 1, 3 Aug. 1867.

36. Peter Joseph, Civil War Pension Record, Compiled Service Record, both in RG 94, National Archives; Freedmen's Bank Account Records, New Orleans Branch, RG 105, NA.

37. E. J. Ellis to E. P. Ellis, 5 Feb. 1867; to "Dear Mother," 29 May 1867, both in Ellis Family Papers.

38. E. John Ellis to T. C. W. Ellis, 10 Aug. 1867, Ellis Family Papers.

39. George C. Rable, *But There Was No Peace: The Role of Violence in the Politics of Reconstruction* (Athens: Univ. of Georgia Press, 1984), 74–75, 106, 110; quote in House Misc. Doc. 154, 41st Cong., 2nd sess., ser. set no. 1435, vol. 1, 296. Although James K. Hogue claims that there is little information about the Knights of the White Camellia, one may find extensive testimony from its members, such as Ellis, in House Misc. Doc. 154. Hogue, *Uncivil War*, 66.

40. House Misc. Doc. 154, 297–98, 300–305.

41. Ibid., 225, 303.

42. Frank L. Richardson, "My Recollections of the Battle of the Fourteenth of September, 1874, in New Orleans, Louisiana," *Louisiana Historical Quarterly* 3 (October 1920): 498–501; Walter Prichard, ed., "The Origin and Activities of the 'White League' in New Orleans (Reminiscences of a Participant in the Movement)," *Louisiana Historical Quarterly* (Spring 1940): 530; Dennis Charles Rousey, *Policing the Southern City: New Orleans, 1805–1889* (Baton Rouge: Louisiana State Univ. Press, 1996), 126–58. In addition to Rousey's data, information about members of the Metropolitan Police was obtained by using the U.S. Federal Census for 1870 to cross-reference the names printed in the *New Orleans Republican*, 15–18 Sept. 1874, of Metropolitans injured in the September 14, 1874, battle.

43. *Biographical and Historical Memoirs of Louisiana* (Chicago: Goodspeed, 1892), 2:257–58.

44. For the activities of the Ogdens in 1868, see House Misc. Doc, 154, part 2, 176–77, 246, 469, 559–61, 752.

45. Ibid., 719–25.

46. Ibid.

47. David W. Blight, *Race and Reunion: The Civil War in American Memory* (Cambridge, MA: Harvard Univ. Press, 2001).

CHAPTER 4: CARPETBAGGER PRINCE

Epigraph. Oscar J. Dunn to Horace Greeley, as reprinted in W. E. B. Du Bois, *Black Reconstruction in America, 1860–1880* (New York: Harcourt & Brace, 1935), 479.

1. Affidavit of John F. Claiborne, House Misc. Doc. 211, 179, House Reports, 42nd Cong., 2nd sess., ser. set. no. 1527, vol. 4.

2. Henry Clay Warmoth, *War, Politics, and Reconstruction: Stormy Days in Louisiana.* (New York: Macmillan, 1930). For early Dunningite histories of Warmoth, see Alcée Fortier, *A History of Louisiana* (New York: Goupil, 1905); Ella Lonn, *Reconstruction in Louisiana after 1868* (New York: G. P. Putnam's, 1918); James J. A. Fortier, ed., *Carpet-Bag Misrule in Louisiana: The Tragedy of the Reconstruction Era following the War between the States* (New Orleans: Louisiana State Museum, 1933). Perhaps the earliest "revisionist" interpretation of Louisiana's Reconstruction experience was expressed in Rodolphe Desdunes's *Our People, Our History: Fifty Creole Portraits*, trans. Dorothea Olga McCants (Baton Rouge: Louisiana State Univ. Press, 1973), 135, where he describes Warmoth's administration as an "era of knaves and adventurers." Du Bois, *Black Reconstruction in America*, 461; Eric Foner, *Reconstruction: America's Unfinished Revolution, 1863–1877* (New York: Harper & Row, 1988), 331–32. The most generous portrayal of Warmoth is found in Richard Nelson Current, *Those Terrible Carpetbaggers: A Reinterpretation* (New York: Oxford Univ. Press, 1988).

3. Charles Louis Roudanez and John Baptiste Roudanez were the founders of *L'Union.*

4. In some respects, this position revisits much earlier scholarship by T. Harry Williams, who also noticed within New Orleans a subtext of political ambiguity. T. Harry Williams, "An Analysis of Some Reconstruction Attitudes," *Journal of Southern History* 12, no. 4 (November 1946): 469–86. Arguably, William Jefferson Clinton used this same strategy, albeit far more successfully, to secure victory in 1992 and reelection in 1996. John Rodrigue's foreword in the reprint of Warmoth's memoir poses similar questions about the importance of his career. Henry Clay Warmoth, *War, Politics, and Reconstruction: Stormy Days in Louisiana* (Columbia: Univ. of South Carolina Press, 2006), ix–xv.

5. Claude Gernade Bowers, *The Tragic Era: The Revolution after Lincoln* (Cambridge: Houghton Mifflin, 1929); Kenneth M. Stampp, *The Era of Reconstruction,*

1865–1877 (New York: Knopf, 1965); Kenneth M. Stampp and Leon F. Litwack, eds., *Reconstruction: An Anthology of Revisionist Writings* (Baton Rouge: Louisiana State Univ. Press, 1969); Hans L. Trefousse, *The Radical Republicans: Lincoln's Vanguard for Racial Justice* (New York: Knopf, 1969).

6. Du Bois, *Black Reconstruction in America*, 183–87, quote on 472.

7. Joe Gray Taylor, *Louisiana Reconstructed, 1862–1877* (Baton Rouge: Louisiana State Univ. Press, 1974), 174–77.

8. Dennis C. Rousey, *Policing the Southern City: New Orleans, 1805–1889* (Baton Rouge: Louisiana State Univ. Press, 1996), 130–33; New Orleans Metropolitan Police, Arrest Records, 1870–1873, New Orleans City Archives, New Orleans; *New Orleans Daily Picayune*, 9 Feb. 1872.

9. Taylor, *Louisiana Reconstructed*, 177; Warmoth, *War, Politics, and Reconstruction* (2006), 165; "Report of the Adjutant General's Office," Louisiana State Militia, Dec. 31, 1870, Military Archives, Jackson Barracks, LA.

10. David W. Blight, *Race and Reunion: The Civil War in American Memory* (Cambridge, MA: Harvard Univ. Press, 2001); Andrew B. Booth, ed., *Records of Louisiana Confederate Soldiers and Confederate Commands* (New Orleans, 1920), 1:156, 3:988; James Keith Hogue, "Bayonet Rule: Five Street Battles in New Orleans and the Rise and Fall of Radical Reconstruction" (Ph.D. diss., Princeton Univ., 1998), 133–42; William Miller Owen, *In Camp and Battle with the Washington Artillery: A Narrative of Events during the Late Civil War from Bull Run to Appomattox and Spanish Fort* (Boston: Ticknor, 1885); 1870 U.S. Federal Census, roll 593_524, p. 310 (all census records were drawn from www.ancestry.com); Walton-Glenny Papers, Williams Research Center, Historic New Orleans Collection, New Orleans.

11. *Daily Picayune*, 15 May 1887.

12. *Report of the Adjutant General; New Orleans Times-Democrat*, 8 Jan. 1896, *Daily Picayune*, 28 Oct. 1868; *New Orleans Times*, 24 Oct. 1872; Desdunes, *Our People and Our History*, 90–91; 1870 U.S. Federal Census, roll M593_521, pp. 224, 112; Booth, *Records of Louisiana Confederate Soldiers*, 3:839, 3:282, 2:939.

13. *Gardner's New Orleans Directory for 1866* (New Orleans: Charles Gardner, 1866); William Garrett Piston, *Lee's Tarnished Lieutenant: James Longstreet and His Place in Southern History* (Athens: Univ. of Georgia Press, 1987), 104–38. Ironically, Longstreet's greatest critic, Jubal Early, turned up in New Orleans frequently during this time, his celebrity being used by the carpetbagger-run Louisiana Lottery Company to lend "credibility" to the drawing of lottery numbers for an immodest annual salary of thirty thousand dollars. See Arlin Turner, *George W. Cable: A Biography* (Durham, NC: Duke Univ. Press, 1956), 48.

14. Robert Cinnamond Tucker, "The Life and Public Service of E. John Ellis," *Louisiana Historical Quarterly* 29, no. 3 (July 1946): 713; E. John Ellis to T. C. W. Ellis, 27 Jan. 1869, 6 Mar. 1869, both in E. P. Ellis Family Papers, Louisiana and Lower Mississippi Valley Collections, Hill Memorial Library, Louisiana State Univ., Baton Rouge; House Misc. Doc. 154, 41st Cong., 2nd sess., ser. set no. 1435, vol. 1, no. 5, 294–306.

15. House Misc. Doc. 154, 299, 304–5; *Biographical Directory of the United States Congress*, http://bioguide.congress.gov.

16. Booth, *Records of Louisiana Confederate Soldiers*, 2:544; *1870 U.S. Federal Census*, roll 593_532, p. 94; Charles E. Kennon to Thomas C. W. Ellis, 27 June 1870, Ellis Family Papers.

17. Charles E. Kennon to "Friend Tom," 11 Nov. 1870, Ellis Family Papers.

18. *New Orleans Times Picayune*, 8 Feb. 1871. By all accounts, Carter emerges as an unsavory figure. For more information on George Carter, see Taylor, *Louisiana Reconstructed*, 213–14.

19. *Times Picayune*, 16 Feb. 1871.

20. *Daily Picayune*, 22 Feb. 1871; Elizabeth Heale, *The Faerie Queen: A Reader's Guide* (Cambridge: Cambridge Univ. Press, 1999), 1–11.

21. *Sauvinet v. Walker*, No. 3513, 27 La. Ann. 14, (1875).

22. Ibid.

23. Ibid.

24. Ibid.

25. *New Orleans Weekly Louisianian*, 2 Mar. 1871.

26. The five men who posted Walker's bond were Charles Cavaroc, William B. Schmidt, William Solomon, Hugh McCloskey, and John H. Rareshide. *Sauvinet v. Walker*. Cavaroc and Rareshide belonged to the Pickwick Club.

27. Taylor, *Louisiana Reconstructed*, 141, 151–55, 211; Jane Dailey, "Deference and Violence in the Postbellum Urban South: Manners and Massacres in Danville, Virginia," *Journal of Southern History* 63, no. 3 (August 1997): 553–90.

28. *State v. Arthur Toledano* (1871), Sixth District Recorder's Court, Orleans Parish, Louisiana; *1870 U.S. Federal Census*, roll M593_519, p. 336. The Carrollton Railroad operates today as the St. Charles Avenue streetcar.

29. *State v. Arthur Toledano*.

30. Ibid.

31. Although Pinchback was such an important figure of the Reconstruction period, there is no serious scholarly book-length biography of him. The best source remains Agnes Smith Grosz, "The Political Career of P. B. S. Pinchback," *Louisiana Historical Quarterly* 27 (1944): 527–612; James Haskins, *Pinkney Benton Stewart Pinchback* (New York: Macmillan, 1973), 3–18, 21–25; Hollandsworth, *Native Guards*, 28, quote on 75.

32. Haskins, *Pinchback*, 38–47, quote on 52.

33. Grosz, "Political Career of Pinchback," 534–40.

34. Ibid. For biographical data on Antoine, see David C. Rankin, "The Origins of Black Leadership in New Orleans during Reconstruction," *Journal of Southern History* 40, no. 3 (August 1974): 436.

35. Charles Vincent, *Black Legislators in Louisiana during Reconstruction* (Baton Rouge: Louisiana State Univ. Press, 1976), 33, 134–35; A. E. Perkins, "James Henri Burch and Oscar James Dunn in Louisiana," *Journal of Negro History* 22, no. 3 (July 1937): 326–27; Rankin, "Black Leadership in New Orleans," 437.

36. Joseph G. Dawson III, *Army Generals and Reconstruction: Louisiana 1862–1877* (Baton Rouge: Louisiana State Univ. Press, 1982), 227; Taylor, *Louisiana Reconstructed*, 210–16; Current, *Those Terrible Carpetbaggers*, 124.

37. For an account of the supposed friction between Warmoth and the Afro-Creole elite, see Caryn Cossé Bell, *Revolution, Romanticism, and the Afro-Creole Protest Tradition in Louisiana, 1718–1868* (Baton Rouge: Louisiana State Univ. Press, 1997), 256–75. For the involvement of Rey and Rápp in the Metropolitan Police's campaign against the Custom House faction, see House Misc. Doc. 211, 183–84, 404. Others supporting Warmoth included Joseph A. Raynal and the long-serving secretary of the Louisiana House of Representatives William Vigers, both elite Afro-Creoles.

38. None of the secondary works consulted for this book refer to House Misc. Doc. 211, which chronicles in detail the infighting between Republican factions in 1871–72.

39. House Misc. Doc. 211, 184; Wynne and Riley quotes on 177–79; remaining quotes on 186–87.

40. Ibid., 195–97.

41. *New Orleans Times*, 4 Aug. 1871.

42. Current, *Those Terrible Carpetbaggers*, 251–52.

43. House Misc. Doc. 211, 176, quotes on 184–87.

44. *Weekly Louisianan*, 11 Jan. 1872; Perkins, "Burch and Dunn in Louisiana," 328–30; Taylor, *Louisiana Reconstructed*, 218–21, quote on 218.

45. House Misc. Doc. 211, 26, 105.

46. Ibid., 20–25, 71, 101–7; Taylor, *Louisiana Reconstructed*, 223–27.

47. *Daily Picayune*, 9 Jan. 1872.

48. E. John Ellis to Thomas C. W. Ellis, 12 Jan. 1872, Ellis Family Papers.

49. Taylor, *Louisiana Reconstructed*, 227; quote in *Daily Picayune*, 20 Feb. 1872.

CHAPTER 5: LESSONS OF THE STREET

Epigraph. *New Orleans Morning Star and Catholic Messenger*, 23 June 1872.

1. *New Orleans Daily Picayune*, 9 Feb. 1872.

2. Robert Tallant, *Mardi Gras* (New York: Doubleday, 1948), 137; first two quotes in Reid Mitchell, *All on Mardi Gras Day: Episodes in the History of New Orleans Carnival* (Cambridge, MA: Harvard Univ. Press, 1995), 59–60; remaining quotes in *Daily Picayune*, 14 Feb. 1872.

3. *Daily Picayune*, 13 Feb. 1872.

4. Tallant, *Mardi Gras*, 137; Henri Schindler, *Mardi Gras, New Orleans* (Paris: Flammarion, 1997), 48; Mitchell, *All on Mardi Gras Day*, 57–64.

5. Mary P. Ryan, *Civic Wars: Life in the American City during the Nineteenth Century* (Berkeley: Univ. of California Press, 1997), 17; see also Simon P. Newman, *Parades and the Politics of the Street: Festive Culture in the Early American Republic* (Philadelphia: Univ. of Pennsylvania Press, 1997).

6. *Daily Picayune*, 18 Feb. 1872. A list of vice presidents appears in this column. To determine the backgrounds of these men, I cross-referenced a sample of the list with the 1870 *U.S. Federal Census* (see appendix A); Stuart Omer Landry, *History of*

the Boston Club (New Orleans: Pelican, 1938), 106–9; *Jewell's Crescent City Illustrated* (New Orleans, 1873).

7. *Daily Picayune*, 18 Feb. 1872; Joe Gray Taylor, *Louisiana Reconstructed, 1862–1877* (Baton Rouge: Louisiana State Univ. Press, 1974), 228; all quotes in "Address of the Provisional State Central Committee of the Reform Party to the People of Louisiana," New Orleans, 12 Mar. 1872, Dr. D. W. Brickell Papers, Louisiana and Lower Mississippi Valley Collections, Hill Memorial Library, Louisiana State Univ.

8. *Weekly Louisianian*, 29 Feb. 1872.

9. Michael Perman, *The Road to Redemption: Southern Politics, 1869–1879* (Chapel Hill: Univ. of North Carolina Press, 1984), 57–86; Richard Zuczek, *State of Rebellion: Reconstruction in South Carolina* (Columbia: Univ. of South Carolina Press, 1996), 75–77.

10. For a good discussion of the national forces behind the Liberal Republican movement of 1872 and its intersection with H. C. Warmoth, see Richard Nelson Current, *Those Terrible Carpetbaggers: A Reinterpretation* (New York: Oxford Univ. Press, 1988), 261–81; Robert Burg, "Amnesty, Civil Rights, and the Meaning of Liberal Republicanism," *American Nineteenth Century History* 4, no. 3 (Autumn 2003): 29–60; Matthew T. Downey, "Horace Greeley and the Politicians: The Liberal Republican Convention in 1872," *Journal of American History* 53, no. 4 (March 1967): 727–50; Andrew L. Slap, *The Doom of Reconstruction: The Liberal Republicans in the Civil War Era* (New York: Fordham Univ. Press, 2006); Charles J. C. Puckette to Henry Clay Warmoth, 19 June 1872, H. C. Warmoth Papers, Louisiana and Lower Mississippi Valley Collections, Hill Memorial Library, Louisiana State Univ., Baton Rouge.

11. Andrew B. Booth, ed., *Records of Louisiana Confederate Soldiers and Confederate Commands* (New Orleans, 1920), 3:102; *1870 U.S. Federal Census*, roll M593_520, p. 712 (all census records were drawn from www.ancestry.com); Stuart Omer Landry, *The Battle of Liberty Place: The Overthrow of Carpet-Bag Misrule in New Orleans, September 14, 1874* (New Orleans: Pelican, 1955), 198–200; *Daily Picayune*, 20 Jan. 1871; Henry Clay Warmoth, *War, Politics, and Reconstruction: Stormy Days in Louisiana* (New York: Macmillan, 1930), 195.

12. Ironically, in Landry's *Battle of Liberty Place*, the author goes through great gyrations to correct an error in Ella Lonn's *Reconstruction in Louisiana after 1868* (New York: G. P. Putnam's, 1918) that misidentified Penn as a mulatto. I have found no evidence to suggest that Penn was anything but white. Electronic genealogical tools, though far from perfect, were essential to establishing the paper trail that led to the discovery of Penn's illegitimate daughter. Emily Josephine Keating birth certificate, Orleans Parish Birth Records, 6:383; Blanche Penn birth certificate, Orleans Parish Birth Records, 23:309; Josephine Keating death certificate, Orleans Parish Death Records, 43:18; *1860 U.S. Federal Census*, roll M653_417, p. 290; *1870 U.S. Federal Census*, roll M593_520, p. 667. In the 1870 census, Blanche Penn declared herself as "white" despite being the only such child in a household of mixed-race relatives who were classified as "mulatto."

13. Warmoth, *War, Politics, and Reconstruction*, 166–75.

14. Ibid.

15. Charlie Kennon to Thomas Ellis, Ellis prison diary, 22 May 1872, in E. P. Ellis Family Papers, Louisiana and Lower Mississippi Valley Collections, Hill Memorial Library, Louisiana State Univ., Baton Rouge.

16. Ibid.; E. John Ellis to My Dear Brother, 22 June 1872, both in Ellis Family Papers.

17. Quotes in *Gardner's New Orleans Directory for 1868* (New Orleans: Charles Gardner, 1868), n.p.; Warmoth, *War, Politics, and Reconstruction*, 189–96; Taylor, *Louisiana Reconstructed*, 232.

18. Democratic Central Committee quoted in *Daily Picayune*, 8 Sept. 1872; Taylor, *Louisiana Reconstructed*, 232; Landry, *Battle of Liberty Place*, 198; *Jewell's Crescent City Illustrated*, n.p.

19. Taylor, *Louisiana Reconstructed*, 232–35.

20. *New Orleans Times*, 12 Sept. 1872.

21. Quotes ibid.; Taylor, *Louisiana Reconstructed*, 235–36.

22. *New Orleans Bee*, 7, 9 Sept. 1872; *New Orleans Times-Democrat*, 8 Jan. 1896.

23. Quote in *Daily Picayune*, 8 Sept. 1872. For a description of the flag presentation ritual in Civil War America, see Reid Mitchell, *Civil War Soldiers* (New York: Viking, 1988), 18–20.

24. *Daily Picayune*, 8 Sept. 1872.

25. Ibid., 22 Sept. 1872.

26. Agnes Smith Grosz, "The Political Career of P. B. S. Pinchback," *Louisiana Historical Quarterly* 27 (1944): 551–54.

27. Taylor, *Louisiana Reconstructed*, 235.

28. The complicated machinations and legal battle between the Fusion and Republican tickets has been well covered in a variety of other sources. The clearest presentation still is found in Taylor, *Louisiana Reconstructed*, 245–49.

29. James B. Walton to Brig. Gen. A. S. Badger, 13 Dec. 1872, James B. Walton Papers, Williams Research Center, Historic New Orleans Collection, New Orleans.

30. Quotes in Perry Young, *The Mistik Krewe: Chronicles of Comus and His Kin* (New Orleans, 1931), 107–10; *Daily Picayune*, 6 Jan. 1872.

31. *Daily Picayune*, 6, 13, 25 Jan. 1873; Taylor, *Louisiana Reconstructed*, 241; E. John Ellis to T. C. W. Ellis, 13 Jan. 1873, Ellis Family Papers.

32. Mitchell, *All on Mardi Gras Day*, 71; Young, *Mistik Krewe*, 112. The *Republican* tried to put a positive spin on the episode by suggesting that it was merely a symbol of Rex's divine rule. *Republican*, 26 Feb. 1873.

33. *Republican*, 25 Feb. 1873; "portrayed as" in Young, *Mistik Krewe*, 118; Mitchell, *All on Mardi Gras Day*, 65–66; Augusto P. Miceli. *The Pickwick Club of New Orleans* (New Orleans: Pickwick Press, 1964), 66–67. It is probable that the "Missing Link" with pink collar was intended as a representation of Caesar C. Antoine.

34. *Republican*, 27 Feb. 1873; Joseph G. Dawson III, *Army Generals and Reconstruction: Louisiana, 1862–1877* (Baton Rouge: Louisiana State Univ. Press, 1982), 141–43; V. Voigt, New Orleans, to John McEnery, 19 Mar. 1873, private collection of John McEnery Robertson.

35. Dawson, *Army Generals*, 143; *Republican*, 6, 7 Mar. 1873; *Picayune*, 6–7 Mar. 1873.

36. Dawson, *Army Generals*, 141–43; *Morning Star and Catholic Messenger*, 9 Mar. 1873.

37. Quote in *Republican*, 7 Mar. 1873; *Daily Picayune*, 7 Mar. 1873.

CHAPTER 6: CASTE AND CONFLICT

Epigraph. *Le Carillion*, 13 July 1873, trans. in *White by Definition: Social Classification in Creole Louisiana*, by Virginia R. Domínguez (New Brunswick, NJ: Rutgers Univ. Press, 1986), 139–40, 292.

1. *Louise Marie Drouet v. the Succession of L. F. Drouet*, No. 4800, 26 La. Ann. 323 (1874); *1870 U.S. Federal Census*, roll M593_524, p. 327. (All census records were drawn from www.ancestry.com.)

2. *Drouet v. Succession of Drouet*.

3. On the emergence of polygenistic thought in scientific circles and its relationship with Darwinism in the late antebellum and early postbellum eras, see Louis Menand, *The Metaphysical Club: A Story of Ideas in America* (New York: Farrar, Strauss & Giroux, 2001), 109–12, 143–44; George M. Frederickson, *The Black Image in the White Mind: The Debate on Afro-American Character and Destiny, 1817–1914* (New York: Harper and Row, 1971); Darwin quoted in Christopher Benfey, *Degas in New Orleans: Encounters in the Creole World of Kate Chopin and George Washington Cable* (Berkeley: Univ. of California Press, 1999), 179.

4. Justin Nystrom, "Racial Identity and Reconstruction: New Orleans's Free People of Color and the Dilemma of Emancipation," in *The Great Task Remaining Before Us: Reconstruction as America's Continuing Civil War*, ed. Paul Cimbala and Randal Miller (New York: Fordham Univ. Press, 2010). Whereas literary critics have written much about racial passing in popular fiction, the historical literature on the topic is relatively thin. The principal synthesis in this regard is Joel Williamson, *New People: Miscegenation and Mulattos in the United States* (New York: Free Press, 1995); see also Stephan Talty, *Mulatto America: At the Crossroads of Black and White Culture; A Social History* (New York: HarperCollins, 2003); Shirley Elizabeth Thompson, "'Ah Toucoutou, ye conin vous': History and Memory in Creole New Orleans," *American Quarterly* 53 (June 2001); Frances Jerome Woods, *Marginality and Identity: A Colored Creole Family through Ten Generations* (Baton Rouge: Louisiana State Univ. Press, 1972); Gary B. Mills, *The Forgotten People: Cane River's Creoles of Color* (Baton Rouge: Louisiana State Univ. Press, 1977).

5. *Drouet v. Succession of Drouet*.

6. Ibid. Sylvanie Morgan married Eugene Duvernay, a cigar maker. Duvernay's father was a free man of color and his mother, Amenaide Meunier, had been manumitted as a young woman for "the good behavior and the great and important services that she rendered the family" in 1834. Meunier was about nineteen at the time of her emancipation. Orleans Parish Police Jury, Emancipation Records, 18A (1834), New

Orleans City Archives; 1870 *U.S. Federal Census*, roll M593_524, p. 327; birth certificate, Elizabeth Duvernay, Louisiana Birth Records, Orleans Parish, State Archives, Baton Rouge, 47:283.

7. *Drouet v. Succession of Drouet.*

8. Ibid.; Glenn Conrad, ed., *Dictionary of Louisiana Biography*, vol. 1 (New Orleans: Louisiana Historical Association, 1988); Charles Conrad Jr. was not only Davidson B. Penn's brother-in-law; they had lived under the same roof in 1870. Conrad was married to Penn's sister, and all lived in the home of the Penn patriarch, Alfred Penn, one of the city's wealthiest men. 1870 *U.S. Federal Census*, roll M593_520, p. 712; quotes in attorney brief, *Drouet v. Succession of Drouet.*

9. Louise Marie's attorneys did not know that her mother, Elizabeth Bresson, had had her daughter's birth certified by Orleans Parish. Birth certificate, Louise Marie Drouet, 13 July 1847, 60:809, Orleans Parish Birth Records; Dominguez, *White by Definition*, 27–29.

10. *New Orleans Daily Picayune*, 15 May 1887.

11. Toledano testimony, *Drouet v. Succession of Drouet.*

12. Dominguez, *White by Definition*, 27–29; Charles Waddell Chesnutt, *The House behind the Cedars* (New York: Houghton Mifflin, 1900; reprint, Athens: Univ. of Georgia Press, 2000), 3, quote on 34 (page numbers are from the reprint edition).

13. Dominguez, *White by Definition*, 134–42.

14. Edgar Degas to Desire Dihau, 11 Nov. 1872, in *Edgar Germain Hilaire Degas Letters*, ed. Marcel Guerin (Oxford: Bruno Cassirer, 1947), 15; Benfey, *Degas in New Orleans*, 79–80.

15. Marilyn Brown, "The DeGas-Musson Papers: An Annotated Inventory," 1991, Howard-Tilton Memorial Library, Tulane University, 19–22, 49–51.

16. Christopher Benfey was the first to posit that the man in the duster was Ogden. Benfey, *Degas in New Orleans*, 282. For a likeness of Ogden, see James J. A. Fortier, ed., *Carpet-Bag Misrule in Louisiana: The Tragedy of the Reconstruction Era following the War between the States* (New Orleans: Louisiana State Museum, 1933); Edgar Degas, *A Cotton Office in New Orleans*, Municipal Museum, Pau, France. For other analyses of this painting, see Marilyn Brown, *Degas and the Business of Art: A Cotton Office in New Orleans* (University Park: Pennsylvania State Univ. Press, 1994), 1–14.

17. Brown, *Degas and the Business of Art*, 29–31; Augusto P. Miceli, *The Pickwick Club of New Orleans* (New Orleans: Pickwick Press, 1964), appendix H.

18. Walter Prichard, ed., "The Origin and Activities of the 'White League' in New Orleans (Reminiscences of a Participant in the Movement)," *Louisiana Historical Quarterly* (Spring 1940): 532.

19. *Daily Picayune*, 17 July 1873; T. Harry Williams, *Romance and Realism in Southern Politics* (Athens: Univ. of Georgia Press, 1961), 22–30; T. Harry Williams, "The Louisiana Unification Movement of 1873," *Journal of Southern History* 11, no. 3 (August 1945): 349–69; Christopher Benfey discovered through genealogical research that Edmund Rillieux was the son of Musson's uncle Vincent Rillieux—Musson's mother's brother. Thus, Rillieux was also a cousin of Edgar Degas. See Benfey, *Degas in New Orleans*, 26–29, 182.

20. *Daily Picayune*, 18 June 1873.

21. Ibid., 1 July 1873.

22. *New Orleans Morning Star and Catholic Messenger*, 6 July 1873; for a figure as important to Lost Cause mythology as Father Ryan, there is an incredible paucity of material on the man. See Louis Joseph Maloof, "Abram J. Ryan, the Editor" (M.A. thesis, Univ. of Georgia, 1950); and I. Dillard, "Father Ryan, Poet-Priest of the Confederacy," *Missouri Historical Review* 36 (October 1941): 61–66.

23. *Daily Picayune*, 16 July 1873; Williams, "Louisiana Unification Movement," 364–66.

24. *Morning Star and Catholic Messenger*, 27 July 1873; Rodolphe Lucien Desdunes, *Our People and Our History: Fifty Creole Portraits*, trans. Dorothea Olga McCants (Baton Rouge: Louisiana State Univ. Press, 1973), 139.

25. T. Harry Williams came to some of these same conclusions in 1946. Williams, "Louisiana Unification Movement."

26. Joseph G. Tregle Jr., "Creoles and Americans," in *Creole New Orleans: Race and Americanization*, ed. Arnold R. Hirsch and Joseph Logsdon (Baton Rouge: Louisiana State Univ. Press, 1992), 170–74; Domínguez, *White by Definition*, 136–42, quote on 291.

27. Tregle, "Creoles and Americans," 171; Thompson, "Ah Toucoutou," 232–67; Shirley Elizabeth Thompson, "The Passing of a People: Creoles of Color in Mid-Nineteenth Century New Orleans" (Ph.D. diss, Harvard Univ., 2001).

28. Menand, *The Metaphysical Club*, 141–45, note 144; Josiah C. Nott, *Two Lectures on the Connection between the Biblical and Physical History of Man, Delivered by Invitation by the Chair of Political Economy, etc., of the Louisiana University, December, 1848* (New York: Bartlett and Welford, 1849).

29. Benfey, *Degas in New Orleans*, 118; George Washington Cable, "Belles Demoiselles Plantation," in his *Creoles and Cajuns, Stories of Old Louisiana* (Garden City, NY: Doubleday, 1959), 62–79; Tregle, "Creoles and Americans," 175–80; Rouquette quoted in Dominguez, *White by Definition*, 142. "Bastard sprout" was also undoubtedly a slam at Cable's diminutive physical stature.

30. Arlin Turner, *George W. Cable: A Biography* (Durham. NC: Duke Univ. Press, 1956), 35–69; Benfey, *Degas in New Orleans*, 185, 197–99.

31. Joe Gray Taylor, *Louisiana Reconstructed, 1862–1877* (Baton Rouge: Louisiana State Univ. Press, 1974), 259.

32. *Peter Joseph v. David Bidwell*, No. 5419, 28 La. Ann. 382 (1876).

33. Ibid.

34. For examples of integration attempts at saloons, see *Daily Picayune*, 10, 17, 21 May 1874, quote in 21 May issue; *New Orleans Republican*, 25 June 1874. The customer who forcibly removed Smith was E. L. Jewell, the publisher of the *New Orleans Bulletin* and the *New Orleans Crescent City Illustrated*.

35. Ted Tunnell, *Crucible of Reconstruction: War, Radicalism, and Race in Louisiana, 1862–1877* (Baton Rouge: Louisiana State Univ. Press, 1984), 189–93; Taylor, *Louisiana Reconstructed*, 267–71. The Colfax Massacre is the subject of two recent works that argue that it was the event upon which Reconstruction hinged. See Charles

Lane, *The Day Freedom Died: The Colfax Massacre, the Supreme Court, and the Betrayal of Reconstruction* (New York: Henry Holt, 2008); and LeeAnna Keith, *The Colfax Massacre: The Untold Story of Black Power, White Terror, and the Death of Reconstruction* (New York: Oxford Univ. Press, 2008).

36. Stuart Omer Landry, *History of the Boston Club* (New Orleans: Pelican, 1938), 115.

37. Thomas Dixon Jr., *The Clansman: An Historical Romance of the Ku Klux Klan* (New York: Doubleday, 1905).

CHAPTER 7: THE REDEEMER'S CARNIVAL

Epigraph. J. C. Murphy, New Orleans, to Flora Murphy, Napoleonville, LA, 17 Sept. 1874, Murphy Family Papers, Williams Research Center, Historic New Orleans Collection, New Orleans.

1. Perry Young, *The Mistik Krewe: Chronicles of Comus and His Kin* (New Orleans, 1931), 130–31; The "others" with "united plans" were the Fusionists.

2. H. Oscar Lesage Jr., "The White League in Louisiana and Its Participation in Reconstruction Riots," *Louisiana Historical Quarterly* 28 (Spring 1935): 640–42; Committee White League, Opelousas, LA, to Hon. Alexandre DeClouet, St. Martinville, 19 June 1874; Address to White League Rally, 20 June 1874, St. Martinville, both in Alexandre DeClouet Papers, Louisiana and Lower Mississippi Valley Collections, Hill Memorial Library, Louisiana State Univ., Baton Rouge.

3. George C. Rable, *But There Was No Peace: The Role of Violence in the Politics of Reconstruction* (Athens: Univ. of Georgia Press, 1984), 74–75, 106, 110; Joe Gray Taylor, *Louisiana Reconstructed, 1862–1877* (Baton Rouge: Louisiana State Univ. Press, 1974), 272–73; Address to White League Rally; Richard Slotkin, *Gunfighter Nation: The Myth of the Frontier in Twentieth-Century America* (New York: Harper-Collins, 1992), 133–35.

4. *New Orleans Daily Picayune*, 24 June 1874; Walter Prichard, ed., "The Origin and Activities of the 'White League' in New Orleans (Reminiscences of a Participant in the Movement)," *Louisiana Historical Quarterly* (Spring 1940): 532.

5. *Daily Picayune*, 30 June 1874, emphasis in original.

6. *New Orleans Republican*, 1 July 1874; *New Orleans Weekly Louisianian*, 4 July 1874; *Daily Picayune*, 4 July 1874.

7. *Daily Picayune*, 1, 2 July 1874; see appendix B. Using a smaller sample in an unpublished thesis on the men of the Crescent City White League, Jennifer Lawrence concludes that only 7 percent of the Crescent City White League were laborers, whereas more than 50 percent worked in the commodities-related businesses along Factor's Row. Jennifer Lawrence, "The Crescent City White League, 1874" (honors thesis, Tulane Univ., 1992), 23, table 1; Nathaniel Chearas Hughes, *The Pride of the Confederate Artillery: The Washington Artillery in the Army of the Tennessee* (Baton Rouge: Louisiana State Univ. Press, 1997), 1–3. For political parades, see *Daily Picayune*, 8, 12, 19, 22 Sept. 1872.

8. Eric Foner, *Reconstruction: America's Unfinished Revolution, 1863–1877* (New York: Harper & Row, 1988), 551; Taylor, *Louisiana Reconstructed*, 291. For the computation of the average age of the White League, see appendix B. Scholars are really only beginning to examine the youthful experiences of the generation that came of age in the wake of the war. See Edmund L. Drago, *Confederate Phoenix: Rebel Children and Their Families in South Carolina* (New York: Fordham Univ. Press, 2008).

9. James M. McPherson, *For Cause and Comrades: Why Men Fought in the Civil War* (New York: Oxford Univ. Press, 1997), 61, 168; Bertram Wyatt-Brown. *Southern Honor: Ethics and Behavior in the Old South* (New York: Oxford Univ. Press, 1982); "I hope" quote in Philip S. Armitage, Unity Plantation, to JCM, New Orleans, 4 Sept. 1874, Murphy Family Papers; Mortimer Norton Wisdom to Mother, 28 Jan. 1873; Adelaide Wisdom Benjamin to Justin Nystrom, 20 Sept. 1999, both in Adelaide Wisdom Benjamin private papers; Augusto P. Miceli, *The Pickwick Club of New Orleans* (New Orleans: Pickwick Press, 1964), appendix J.

10. Oliver Wendell Holmes Jr., "The Soldier's Faith," delivered May 30, 1895, at the invitation of Harvard University's graduating class and printed in Sheldon M. Novick, ed., *The Collected Works of Justice Holmes: Complete Public Writings and Selected Judicial Opinions of Oliver Wendell Holmes* (Chicago: University of Chicago Press, 1995), 486.

11. E. John Ellis to T. C. W. Ellis, 12 Nov. 1873, E. P Ellis Family Papers, Louisiana and Lower Mississippi Valley Collections, Hill Memorial Library, Louisiana State Univ., Baton Rouge.

12. E. John Ellis to T. C. W. Ellis, 24 June 1874, Ellis Family Papers.

13. Marshall Harvey Twitchell, *Carpetbagger from Vermont: The Autobiography of Marshall Harvey Twitchell*, ed. Ted Tunnell (Baton Rouge: Louisiana State Univ. Press, 1989), 140–48; Taylor, *Louisiana Reconstructed*, 287–91; Ted Tunnell, *Crucible of Reconstruction: War, Radicalism, and Race in Louisiana, 1862–1877* (Baton Rouge: Louisiana State Univ. Press, 1984), 96–202; Ted Tunnell, *Edge of the Sword: The Ordeal of Carpetbagger Marshall H. Twitchell in the Civil War and Reconstruction* (Baton Rouge: Louisiana State Univ. Press, 2001), 145.

14. *New Orleans Morning Star and Catholic Messenger*, 16 Aug. 1874. Ogden was a Catholic.

15. David Rabb Cargill, "Reconstruction and the White League in Lincoln Parish, Louisiana" (master's thesis, Louisiana Tech Univ., 1993), 120.

16. *Daily Picayune*, 2 Sept. 1874.

17. Rable, *But There Was No Peace*, 111–12, 145–47; Joseph G. Dawson III, *Army Generals and Reconstruction: Louisiana, 1862–1877* (Baton Rouge: Louisiana State Univ. Press, 1982), 161, 165.

18. "Large shipment" in House Reports, 43rd Cong., 2nd sess., no. 101, p. 198; *Daily Picayune*, 9, 11, 12 Sept. 1874, quote in 11 Sept. issue; *New York Times*, 9 Sept. 1874.

19. Stuart Omer Landry, *The Battle of Liberty Place: The Overthrow of Carpet-Bag Misrule in New Orleans, September 14, 1874* (New Orleans: Pelican, 1955), 83, 89; quote in Robert Cinnamond Tucker, "The Life and Public Service of E. John Ellis," *Louisiana Historical Quarterly* 29, no. 3 (July 1946): 722; W. O. Hart, "History of the

Events Leading up to the Battle of Liberty Place," *Louisiana Historical Quarterly* 7 (1924): 578.

20. Landry, *Battle of Liberty Place*, 84–85; *Daily Picayune*, 13 Sept. 1874; Hart, "History of Events," 579–80.

21. Landry, *Battle of Liberty Place*, 158.

22. Ibid., 88–91.

23. Hart, "History of Events," 580–81; D. B. Penn to Fred Ogden, 14 Sept. 1874, Ogden Papers, Howard-Tilton Memorial Library, Tulane Univ., New Orleans.

24. Unless otherwise noted, the narrative of the battle is a composite of the following sources, employing the most corroborative evidence: *Daily Picayune*, 15, 16, 17 Sept. 1874; Frank L. Richardson, "My Recollections of the Battle of the Fourteenth of September, 1874, in New Orleans, Louisiana," *Louisiana Historical Quarterly* 3 (October 1920), 498–501; Prichard, "Origin and Activities of 'White League,'" 533–38; *Republican*, 15, 16 Sept. 1874; Badger testimony, House Reports, 43rd Cong., 2nd sess., no. 261, part 2, pp. 400–401; Ogden testimony, House Reports, 43rd Cong., 2nd sess., no. 101, pp. 213–14; Landry, *Battle of Liberty Place*, 96–132; Hart, "History of Events," 582–600; Andrew B. Booth, ed., *Records of Louisiana Confederate Soldiers and Confederate Commands* (New Orleans, 1920), 2:562. The total number of White League participants given in different sources varies greatly. The number fifteen hundred appears to agree the most with the evidence.

25. Eagle Hall stands today on a wedge-shaped piece of ground bounded by Urania, Felicity, and Prytania streets.

26. Charity Hospital Admissions Book, 1874–76, New Orleans Public Library.

27. Landry, *Battle of Liberty Place*, 204–20; Record of Inquests and Views, Orleans Parish Coroner's Office, vol. 23 (1872–74), Medical dist. 2, 3; vol. 24 (1872–74), Medical dist. 1, 4, 5, 6, NOPL.

28. *Daily Picayune*, 15 Sept. 1874; Braxton Bragg, Galveston, to Fred Ogden, New Orleans, 14 Sept. 1874; J. R. Bayler, San Antonio, to Fred Ogden, 15 Sept. 1874; T. A. Baylor, Louisville, to Fred Ogden, 15 Sept. 1874, Ogden Papers.

29. *Daily Picayune*, 16 Sept. 1874; House Reports, 43rd Cong., 2nd sess., no. 101, pp. 199–200; Anon. W. L. member to "My darling wife," 15 Sept. 1874, RG 262, no. 6760, Archives, Louisiana State Museum Historical Center, New Orleans.

30. Landry, *Battle of Liberty Place*, 143–44.

31. *Frank Leslie's Illustrated*, 3 Oct. 1874; Dawson, *Army Generals*, 175–76.

32. Dawson, *Army Generals*, 177; E. John Ellis, New Orleans, to Thomas C. W. Ellis, 21 Sept. 1874, Ellis Family Papers.

33. Taylor, *Louisiana Reconstructed*, 306; *Daily Picayune*, 4 Jan. 1875; William Gillette, *Retreat from Reconstruction, 1869–1879* (Baton Rouge: Louisiana State Univ. Press, 1979), 44–45; Reid Mitchell, *All on Mardi Gras Day: Episodes in the History of New Orleans Carnival* (Cambridge, MA: Harvard Univ. Press, 1995), 72–73; *Morning Star and Catholic Messenger*, 20 Sept. 1874.

34. It served in a fashion similar to that of the Western mythology of violence that associated the victor with merit. Richard Slotkin writes, "In this regression to savagery, a new sort of democracy is forged as the conditions of warfare bring humbly

born men of merit to the fore." Of course, however, the men of the White League were not "humbly born." Slotkin, *Gunfighter Nation*, 135.

35. *Succession of Drouet* (1872).

36. *1900 United States Federal Census*, roll T623_574, p. 3A (all census records were drawn from www.ancestry.com); Louisiana Marriage Records Index, Louisiana State Archives, Baton Rouge, 6:590; Louise Drouet Ducloslange death certificate, Louisiana Death Records Index, 161:188.

37. *1910 U.S. Federal Census*, roll T624_27, part 2; *1920 U.S. Federal Census*, roll T625_35, p. 27A; *1930 U.S. Federal Census*, roll 1775, p. 16B.

38. Taylor, *Louisiana Reconstructed*, 482–93; Eric Foner, *Reconstruction*, 569; Michael Perman, *The Road to Redemption: Southern Politics, 1869–1879* (Chapel Hill: Univ. of North Carolina Press, 1984), 160.

39. Prichard, "Origin and Activities of 'White League,'" 539–41; Taylor, *Louisiana Reconstructed*, 496–540.

40. *Centenary of Louisiana Supreme Court* (New Orleans, 1913), 31.

41. *Daily Picayune*, 9, 10 Jan. 1877; *New Orleans Times*, 9, 10 Jan. 1877; quote in *New York Times*, 5 Dec. 1879.

42. *New York Times*, 5 Dec. 1879.

43. Taylor, *Louisiana Reconstructed*, 495–96; C. Vann Woodward, *Reunion and Reaction: The Compromise of 1877 and the End of Reconstruction* (Boston: Little, Brown, 1951), 192–95; Michael Les Benedict, "Southern Democrats in the Crisis of 1876–1877: A Reconsideration of *Reunion and Reaction*," *Journal of Southern History* 46, no. 4 (November 1980): 489–524. E. A. Burke went on to swindle Louisiana taxpayers of hundreds of thousands of dollars and eventually fled to Honduras to avoid prosecution. He became the poster child for Bourbon political abuses. Edward F. Haas, *Political Leadership in a Southern City: New Orleans in the Progressive Era, 1896–1902* (Ruston, LA: McGinty, 1988), 17; E. J. Ellis to Father, 22 Feb. 1877, Ellis Family Papers.

44. *Daily Picayune*, 8, 9, 10, 13 Feb. 1877; Young, *Mistick Krewe*, 141–50; James Gill, *Lords of Misrule: Mardi Gras and the Politics of Race in New Orleans* (Jackson: Univ. of Mississippi Press, 1997), 125–28.

CHAPTER 8: THE SEASON OF REDEEMER DISCONTENT

Epigraph. Notation appended to letter, Charles Kennon to Tom Ellis, 2 April 1878. E. P. Ellis Family Papers, Louisiana and Lower Mississippi Valley Collections, Hill Memorial Library, Louisiana State Univ., Baton Rouge.

1. *New Orleans Times*, 24 July 1878.

2. New Orleans, Louisiana, Death Records Index, 1804–1949, 71:573.

3. *Houston Directory, 1889–1890* (Houston, TX: Morrison & Fourmy, 1889); *1910 U.S. Federal Census*, roll T624_1519, p. 317B (all census records were drawn from www.ancestry.com); *1920 U.S. Federal Census*, roll T625_1763, p. 8B (James N. Sauvinet); birth certificate, Paul Perrault, 11 Dec. 1858, Orleans Parish Birth Certificate

Index, 23:68; *1870 U.S. Federal Census*, roll M593_523, p. 749, image 260; *1900 U.S. Federal Census*, roll T623_572, p. 22A. A wealth of genealogical data on the Sauvinets descended from Angela C. Sauvinet D'Arpa was placed on the Web by Rosemary DeFiglio, a great-granddaughter of C. S. Sauvinet. Formerly posted at http://rand .pratt.edu/~defiglio/tree.html, the site is no longer active. A hard copy of the site's contents is in Nystrom's possession.

4. The material here revisits the influential, much-debated, and frequently de-bunked thesis presented by C. Vann Woodward more than a half century ago in *The Strange Career of Jim Crow* (New York: Oxford Univ. Press, 1955) and countered by Howard Rabinowitz, *Race Relations in the Urban South, 1865–1890* (New York: Oxford Univ. Press, 1978). Later scholars have also revisited the theme of enduring racial flexibility with regard to politics. See Jane Dailey, *Before Jim Crow: The Politics of Race in Postemancipation Virginia* (Chapel Hill: Univ. of North Carolina Press, 2000); and Glenda Gilmore, *Gender and Jim Crow: Women and the Politics of White Supremacy in North Carolina* (Chapel Hill: Univ. of North Carolina Press, 1996). Several new works come to the tidy conclusion that Redemption put an end to Reconstruction's struggles—in Louisiana and in the South at large. See Nicholas Leman, *Redemption: The Last Battle of the Civil War* (New York: FS&G, 2006); LeeAnna Keith, *The Untold Story of Black Power, White Terror, and the Death of Reconstruction* (New York: Oxford Univ. Press, 2008); Charles Lane, *The Day Freedom Died: The Colfax Massacre, the Supreme Court, and the Betrayal of Reconstruction* (New York: Henry Holt, 2008).

5. For an essay that takes a broad view of Reconstruction's economic effects, see Stephen A. West, "'A General Remodeling of Every Thing': Economy and Race in the Post-Emancipation South," in *Reconstructions: New Perspectives on the Postbellum United States*, ed. Thomas J. Brown (New York: Oxford Univ. Press, 2007). The scholarship of Heather Cox Richardson has effectively challenged the 1862–77 time line for the Reconstruction-era North. For the most recent of her works, see *West from Appomattox: The Reconstruction of America after the Civil War* (New Haven, CT: Yale Univ. Press, 2007). Other works have hinted at a more elastic conceptualization of the postbellum timeframe. See Dailey, *Before Jim Crow*; Kathleen Clark, *Defining Moments: African American Commemoration and Political Culture in the South, 1863–1913* (Chapel Hill: Univ. of North Carolina Press, 2005); Michael Perman, *Struggle for Mastery: Disfranchisement in the South, 1888–1908* (Chapel Hill: Univ. of North Carolina Press, 2001).

6. Frederick Nash Ogden Papers, Howard-Tilton Memorial Library, Tulane Univ., New Orleans; *New Orleans Daily Picayune*, 18 May, 1 June 1878.

7. *Daily Picayune*, 24 July 1878–30 Aug. 1878.

8. Ibid., 17 Aug. 1878; William L. Robinson, *Diary of a Samaritan by a Member of the Howard Association of New Orleans* (New York: Harper Brothers, 1860); Khaled J. Bloom, *The Mississippi Valley's Great Yellow Fever Epidemic of 1878* (Baton Rouge: Louisiana State Univ. Press, 1993); JoAnn Carrigan, *Saffron Scourge: A History of Yellow Fever in Louisiana* (Lafayette: Center for Louisiana Studies, Univ. of South West Louisiana, 1994); quote in *New Orleans Times*, 20 Sept. 1879.

9. *Daily Picayune*, 5 June 1878.

10. William Ivy Hair, *Bourbonism and Agrarian Protest: Louisiana Politics, 1877–1900* (Baton Rouge: Louisiana State Univ. Press, 1969), 21, 24.

11. Joy L. Jackson, *New Orleans in the Gilded Age: Politics and Urban Progress, 1880–1896* (Baton Rouge: Louisiana State Univ. Press, 1969), 28–54; Hair, *Bourbonism and Agrarian Protest*, 108–12, 129–31.

12. Hair, *Bourbonism and Agrarian Protest*, 25–33.

13. Ibid., 99–106.

14. Roger A Fischer, *The Segregation Struggle in Louisiana, 1862–77* (Urbana: Univ. of Illinois Press, 1974), 143–47.

15. Robert Cinnamond Tucker, "The Life and Public Service of E. John Ellis," *Louisiana Historical Quarterly* 29, no. 3 (July 1946): 739–41.

16. E. J. Ellis to his mother, 31 Jan. 1871; to T. C. W. Ellis, 28 Feb., 4 Mar. 1878, all in Ellis Family Papers.

17. *New Orleans Weekly Louisianian*, 8 Feb. 1879. Ogden had more than once refused to appear in public ceremonies on September 14, a day he believed was for the honoring of the White League dead instead of its living participants. To one group that had volunteered to serve as his honor guard at a public ceremony, Ogden replied, "I shall on that memorable day, in a private way only, pay my humble tribute of respect to the heroic dead who have glorified it." *New Orleans Times*, 6, 10, 14 Sept. 1879; *Daily Picayune*, 14 Sept. 1879.

18. *New Orleans Daily Democrat*, 31 Sept. 1879.

19. Ibid., 23 Sept. 1879.

20. Ibid.

21. Ibid., 24, 28 Sept. 1879.

22. *Daily Picayune*, 10 Oct. 1879; Edith H. Harrison, *"Strange to Say—": Recollections of Persons and Events in New Orleans and Chicago* (Chicago: A Kroch, 1949), 41.

23. *Weekly Louisianian*, 1 Mar. 1879.

24. Perry Young, *The Mistick Krewe: Chronicles of Comus and his Kin* (New Orleans, 1931), 156–57.

25. *New Orleans Times*, 5 Aug. 1879.

26. A detailed account of the charges and defenses of George L. Smith, General Anderson, and James Madison Wells can be found in Department of the Treasury: Records Relating to Custom House Nominations, 1849–1910, RG 56-246, box 116, National Archives; *Daily Picayune*, 2 Aug. 1878; *Weekly Louisianian*, 8 Feb. 1879.

27. Applications for Appointments as Customs Service Officers, RG 56-246, box 17, NA; Appointment Registers of Customs Service Employees, RG 56-241, 11:365, 421, NA; Eric Foner, *Freedom's Lawmakers: A Directory of Black Officeholders during Reconstruction* (New York: Oxford Univ. Press, 1993), 18; *Bertonneau v. Board of Directors of City Schools*, 3 Woods 117, 1878 U.S. App. LEXIS 1614, 3 F. Cas. 294, F. Cas. No. 1361 (C.C.D. La. 1878).

28. George M. Nicholson to Chester Arthur, 17 Feb. 1883; F. A. Woolfley to Chester Arthur, 5 Feb. 1883; Albert C. Janin to the president, 5 Feb. 1883; New Orleans Cotton Exchange President, Officers, and Members Recommend A. S. Badger for

reappointment as Collector of Customs, Feb. 1883, all in Department of the Treasury: Records Relating to Custom House Nominations, RG 56-247, box 58, NA.

29. John G. Smith to Chester A. Arthur, 10 Feb. 1883, Department of the Treasury: Records Relating to Custom House Nominations, RG 56-247, box 58, NA.

30. E. J. Ellis to T. C. W. Ellis, 27 July 1880, Ellis Family Papers; Tucker, "Life of Ellis," 747–48.

31. Tucker, "Life of Ellis," 748–53, quote on 751.

32. B. F. Jonas to Daniel Manning, 18 June 1885; Newton C. Blanchard, John Floyd King, Alfred B. Irion, and Edward J. Gay to Grover Cleveland, n.d.; James Jeffries to Grover Cleveland, 18 April 1885, all in Department of the Treasury: Records Relating to Custom House Nominations, RG 56-247, box 58, NA.

33. "A True Democrat" to Col. Daniel Lamont, 14 April 1885; P.A.L. to Grover Cleveland, 6 April 1885; H. F. Lawler to Grover Cleveland, 30 Mar. 1885, ibid.

34. F. N. Ogden to J. B. Eustis, 4 April 1885, ibid., box 60.

35. Leon Jastremski to Jas. B. Eustis, 10 April 1885, ibid.

36. Glenn Conrad, ed., *Dictionary of Louisiana Biography* (New Orleans: Louisiana Historical Association, 1988), 2:614–15; "Succession of Frederick Nash Ogden" (1886), Orleans Parish Succession Records, no. 18074, New Orleans Public Library; *Daily Picayune*, 14 Sept. 1893. Ironically, one of the prominent guests at Odgen's funeral was his former nemesis Algernon Sydney Badger. *Daily Picayune*, 26 May 1886.

CHAPTER 9: A HARD-HANDED STABILITY

Epigraph. *New Orleans Daily Picayune*, 7 Mar. 1894.

1. For editorial material regarding the bill's passage, see *Daily Picayune*, 12, 26, 27, 29 May 1886; 1, 11, 22 June 1886; *New York Times*, 12 June 1886, 5 Jan. 1887. An 1880 Carnival season ad for the Crescent Billiard Hall announced a matinee billiards exhibition by the "Knights of the Cue" for an admission price of 50 cents. The galleries of the Crescent were reserved for ladies. *New Orleans Times-Democrat*, 8 Feb. 1880. The Crescent moved to its new location in 1875. The second floor has been home to the Pickwick Club since 1950.

2. *Daily Picayune*, 3 Jan. 1887; *New York Times*, 1, 5 Jan. 1887; *Jackson (Miss.) Clarion*, 12 Jan. 1887; *State ex rel. Joseph A. Walker and Valentine Mertz v. The Judge of Section "A," Criminal District Court for the Parish of Orleans et al*, No. 9684, 39 La. Ann. 132; 1 So. 437; 1887. Although "Blue laws" are such a prominent feature on the American landscape, the literature on them is remarkably thin. See Peter Wallenstein, *Blue Laws and Black Codes: Conflict, Courts, and Change in Twentieth-Century Virginia* (Charlottesville: Univ. of Virginia Press, 2004).

3. Joy J. Jackson, *New Orleans in the Gilded Age: Politics and Urban Progress, 1880–1896* (Baton Rouge: Louisiana State Univ. Press, 1969), 49–50.

4. *Chicago Daily Tribune*, 21 July 1879. Sarah A. Dorsey, an eccentric and wealthy widow, bequeathed her vast fortune—including the Mississippi Gulf Coast property of Beauvoir—to Jefferson Davis, causing some to suspect that her fondness for the

former Confederate president sprang more from amorous attachment than patriotic zeal. Tissot found no fault with her will, despite the vocal objections of Dorsey's relatives; *Daily Picayune*, 3 Jan. 1896.

5. Roger A. Fischer, *The Segregation Struggle in Louisiana, 1862–77* (Urbana: Univ. of Illinois Press, 1974), 149–51; James B. Bennett, *Religion and the Rise of Jim Crow in New Orleans* (Princeton, NJ: Princeton Univ. Press, 2005).

6. Keith Weldon Medley, *We as Freemen: Plessy v. Fergusson* (New Orleans: Pelican, 2003), 93–95; 1860 *U.S. Federal Census*, roll T9_456, image 0316 (all census records were drawn from www.ancestry.com); 1870 *U.S. Federal Census*, roll M593_505, p. 143, image 287. Coincidentally, Joseph St. Amant's oldest brother had served under Frederick Nash Ogden during the war and was paroled with Ogden at Gainesville, Alabama, in May 1865. See Andrew B. Booth, ed., *Records of Louisiana Confederate Soldiers and Confederate Commands* (New Orleans, 1920), 3:669; Rodolphe Lucien Desdunes, *Our People and Our History: Fifty Creole Portraits*, trans. Dorothea Olga McCants (Baton Rouge: Louisiana State Univ. Press, 1973), 146–47.

7. *Daily Picayune*, 7 Mar. 1894.

8. Jackson, *New Orleans in the Gilded Age*, 45–47; *Daily Picayune*, 18 May ("concert saloon" quote), 10 June (remaining quotes) 1886.

9. Nicholls made specific accusations against McEnery's manipulation of black ballots in Tensas Parish, creating broad journalistic sensation in the North. Henry Clay Warmoth, *War, Politics, and Reconstruction: Stormy Days in Louisiana* (New York: Macmillan, 1930), 249–50.

10. Jackson, *New Orleans in the Gilded Age*, 33, 96; William Ivy Hair, *Bourbonism and Agrarian Protest: Louisiana Politics, 1877–1900* (Baton Rouge: Louisiana State Univ. Press, 1969), 138; *Daily Picayune*, 6 Jan. 1888; *Washington Post*, 1 Nov. 1890; Warmoth, *War, Politics, and Reconstruction*, 252–54. It should be noted that in 1888 the Sixth Ward constituted a narrow strip of land between St. Philip Street and Esplanade Avenue running from the Mississippi River to the head of Bayou St. John. While Tissot lived at the elegant Pitot House on the bayou, the portion of the Sixth that lay inside the French Quarter was dominated by Italian immigrants.

11. Hair, *Bourbonism and Agrarian Protest*, 139–40; *Daily Picayune*, 3 Jan. 1896.

12. James F. Vivian, "Major E. A. Burke: The Honduras Exile, 1889–1928," *Louisiana History* 15 (Spring 1974): 175–81; Robert Glenk, *Louisiana State Museum, New Orleans: Handbook of Information concerning Its Historic Buildings and the Treasures They Contain* (New Orleans, 1934), 262–63.

13. Thomas Hunt and Martha Sheldon, *Deep Water: Joseph P. Macheca and the Birth of the American Mafia* (Lincoln, NE: iUniverse, 2007), 72–92; Richard Gambino, *Vendetta: A True Story of the Worst Lynching in America, the Mass Murder of Italian-Americans in New Orleans in 1891, the Vicious Motivations behind It, and the Tragic Repercussions That Linger to This Day* (New York: Doubleday, 1977), 44–48.

14. A. S. Badger to George Denegre, 21 April 1881, Williams Research Center, Historic New Orleans Collection, New Orleans; also in Clive Webb, "The Lynching of Sicilian Immigrants in the American South, 1886–1910," *American Nineteenth*

Century History 3, no. 1 (March 2002): 45–76, cited on 51; Gambino, *Vendetta*, 26–35; Jackson, *New Orleans in the Gilded Age*, 246–47.

15. Jackson, *New Orleans in the Gilded Age*, 244–48. The Pinkertons and Hennessey had worked with one another, and it was on William Pinkerton's advice that Shakespeare appointed Hennessey as chief of police; Herbert Asbury, *The French Quarter: An Informal History of the New Orleans Underworld* (New York: Alfred A. Knopf, 1936), 409–11; New Orleans Passenger Lists, 1820–1945, roll M259_73.

16. *Daily Picayune*, 19 Oct. 1890. For another narrative of the Hennessey murder, see James Gill, *Lords of Misrule: Mardi Gras and the Politics of Race in New Orleans* (Jackson: Univ. of Mississippi Press, 1997), 145–54.

17. *Daily Picayune*, 19, 26 Oct. 1890, quotes in 26 Oct. issue. John Glynn Jr. (1841–1913) was, ironically enough, himself an Irish immigrant who had come to New Orleans as a boy during the great potato famine. He served for the duration of the war as a lieutenant in the Orleans Guard Battery and was a captain of artillery in the White League battle of September 14, 1874. 1850 *United States Census*, roll M432_238, p. 44, image 89; Stuart Omer Landry, *The Battle of Liberty Place: The Overthrow of Carpet-Bag Rule in New Orleans, September 14, 1874* (New Orleans: Pelican, 1951), 236; Andrew B. Booth, ed., *Records of Louisiana Confederate Soldiers and Confederate Commands* (New Orleans, 1920), 2:41; 1860 *United States Census*, roll M653_417, image 291; 1910 *United States Census*, roll T624_523, p. 5A; Donald E. Collins, *The Death and Resurrection of Jefferson Davis* (New York: Rowman & Littlefield, 2005), 87.

18. *Daily Picayune*, 26 Oct. 1890.

19. Gill, *Lords of Misrule*, 143–50. A survey of the *Daily Picayune*, the *Times-Democrat*, the *New Orleans Daily States*, and *L'Abeille de la Nouvelle-Orléans* from mid-February through mid-March 1891 reveal a strong bias against the defendants.

20. *Daily States*, 14 Mar. 1891; Jackson, *New Orleans in the Gilded Age*, 249; Gill, *Lords of Misrule*, 150–52.

21. *Daily States*, 14 Mar. 1891. Lawrence Powell infers a commonality between the White League and the mob that lynched the Italian prisoners. See "A Concrete Symbol," *Southern Exposure* (Spring 1990): 40–43; Webb, "Lynching of Sicilian Immigrants," 62–63.

22. Jackson, *New Orleans in the Gilded Age*, 75; New Orleans City Ordinance 8151, 15 Nov. 15, 1882, copy in Dorothy Mae Taylor Papers, City Archives, New Orleans Public Library; *Daily Picayune*, 5 June 1886; *Daily States*, 15 Sept. 1891.

23. *New Orleans Weekly Pelican*, 30 April 1887.

24. *Daily States*, 14, 15 Sept. 1891; David Blight, *Race and Reunion: The Civil War in American Memory* (Cambridge, MA: Harvard Univ. Press, 2001), 65–97.

25. The museum is located at 929 Camp Street.

26. *Weekly Pelican*, 4 Dec. 1886, 8 Oct. 1887; 1880 *United States Census*, roll T9_453, p. 610.4; Hair, *Bourbonism and Agrarian Protest*, 40–41.

27. *Weekly Pelican*, 16 July (Minor quotes), 25 June (remaining quotes) 1887.

28. *Daily Picayune*, 26 Oct. 1887, 24 Jan. 1888; Rebecca Jarvis Scott, *Degrees of Freedom: Louisiana and Cuba after Slavery* (Cambridge, MA: Belknap Press of Harvard Univ. Press, 2005), 86. Born in 1848, H. C. Minor belonged essentially to the

post–Civil War generation. He grew up in Ascension Parish and likely knew Louisiana political titan Duncan F. Kenner. *1860 United States Census*, roll M653_407, image 45. For the best overall treatment of the postbellum period in Louisiana's sugar-growing regions, see John C. Rodrigue, *Reconstruction in the Cane Fields: From Slavery to Free Labor in Louisiana's Sugar Parishes, 1862–1880* (Baton Rouge: Louisiana State Univ. Press, 1996).

29. Badger quoted in *Daily Picayune*, 30 April 1889; *New York Times*, 10 Aug. 1889, 4 Mar. 1890; *Washington Post*, 26 Jan., 4 Feb. 1890; "his name" in John K. Atkins to Benjamin Harrison, 20 Aug. 1889; "We have" in A. H. Leonard to "the President," 3 Jan. 1890; A. E. P. Albert et al. to Benjamin Harrison, 11 Jan. 1890, all in Department of the Treasury: Records Relating to Custom House Nominations, 1849–1910, RG 56-247, box 64, National Archives; Stuart Omer Landry, *The Battle of Liberty Place: The Overthrow of Carpet-Bag Misrule in New Orleans, September 14, 1874* (New Orleans: Pelican, 1955), 123–24. H. Dudley Coleman was a fixture at later nineteenth- and early-twentieth-century commemoration ceremonies at the Liberty Monument; "eulogized" in *Washington Post*, 4 Mar. 1891.

30. Department of the Treasury: Records Relating to Custom House Nominations, 1849–1910, RG 56-246, boxes 122, 123, NA; Caryn Cossé Bell, *Revolution, Romanticism, and the Afro-Creole Protest Tradition in Louisiana, 1718–1868* (Baton Rouge: Louisiana State Univ. Press, 1997), 227–28, 233.

31. *Daily Picayune*, 16 Aug. 1891; Fischer, *The Segregation Struggle in Louisiana*, 148.

32. *Daily Picayune*, 20 June 1892.

33. Ibid., 27 April 1890, 16 Aug. 1891.

34. *Southwest Christian Advocate*, 20 July 1876; *Chicago Inter-Ocean*, 17 Feb. 1877; Department of the Treasury: Records Relating to Custom House Nominations, 1849–1910, RG 56-246, boxes 117, 118, NA.

35. *Daily Picayune*, 28 Dec. 1888, 17 Feb. 1889, 2 Jun. 1891.

36. *Chicago Inter-Ocean*, 30 Aug. 1888.

37. *Daily Picayune*, 16 Mar., 2 June, 3 July 1891, 13 April 1892.

38. Ibid., 18 Oct., 2 Nov. 1892, quotes in 2 Nov. issue; Medley, *We as Freemen*, 159.

39. Peter Joseph, Civil War Pension Record, NA.

40. Peter Joseph, Pension Record; *1900 U.S. Federal Census*, roll T623_118, page 9A; World War I Draft Registration Cards, M1509 (online database accessible via www.ancestry.com), NA. Sumner Geddes Joseph passed as white the rest of his life. See *1930 U.S. Federal Census*, roll 2578, page 9A.

41. Quotes in *Daily Picayune*, 28 Oct. 1891; Hair, *Bourbonism and Agrarian Protest*, 221.

42. *Daily Picayune*, 7 Mar. 1894.

43. *Official Journal of the Proceedings of the Senate of the State of Louisiana at the Regular Session* (Baton Rouge, 1894), "provide separate street cars" on 125, "With the race prejudice" on 305–7; *Weekly Pelican*, 25 June 1887; *Succession of Pierre Dejean* (*Jules, Victor J, and Arthur Dejean v. Mrs. Josephine Schaeffer, Widow of Pierre Dejean*), No. 19588, 24 June 1887, Division A Orleans Parish Civil District Court.

44. Hair, *Agrarianism and Bourbon Protest*, 234–67; *Daily Picayune*, 3 Jan. 1896; Desdunes, *Our People and Our History*, 145–46.

CONCLUSION

Epigraph. Henry Clay Warmoth, *War, Politics, and Reconstruction: Stormy Days in Louisiana* (New York: Macmillan, 1930), 265.

1. For the most prominent contemporary critic of average Republican officeholders in the postbellum South, see Mark W. Summers, *The Era of Good Stealings* (New York: Oxford Univ. Press, 1993) and *Party Games: Getting, Keeping, and Using Power in Gilded Age Politics* (Chapel Hill: Univ. of North Carolina Press, 2004). Eric Foner, *Reconstruction: America's Unfinished Revolution, 1863–1877* (New York: Harper & Row, 1988). The key work suggesting the centrality of the Civil War's "emancipationist legacy" and that the collapse of Reconstruction came as a retreat from that legacy is David W. Blight, *Race and Reunion: The Civil War in American Memory* (Cambridge, MA: Harvard Univ. Press, 2001).

2. The two most current and in-depth studies of conservative politics during Reconstruction remain William Gillette, *Retreat from Reconstruction, 1869–1879* (Baton Rouge: Louisiana State Univ. Press, 1979); and Michael Perman, *The Road to Redemption: Southern Politics, 1869–1879* (Chapel Hill: Univ. of North Carolina Press, 1984).

3. Thomas Dixon, *The Leopard's Spots: A Romance of the White Man's Burden, 1865–1900* (New York: Doubleday, 1902); George Washington Cable, *The Grandissimes* (New York: Scribner's Sons, 1880), 22–24.

BIOGRAPHICAL SKETCHES OF KEY FIGURES

ALGERNON SYDNEY BADGER (1839–1905). A shop clerk in Boston when the Civil War began, Badger was among the first volunteers from his state to enlist in the Union cause. He accompanied the invasion force of General Benjamin Butler to New Orleans in 1862, and later that year he accepted a captain's commission in the First Louisiana Cavalry (U.S.). Badger saw extensive action during the war and rose to the brevetted rank of lieutenant colonel. He settled in New Orleans after the war, and in 1867 he became a precinct captain in the Metropolitan Police. By 1870 Badger had taken command of the Metropolitans as general superintendent. In this capacity he led his men against the White League during the 1874 Battle of Liberty Place, where he received life-threatening wounds that required the amputation of his leg. Despite the collapse of Republican rule in Louisiana, Badger remained active in the party and served frequently as state chairman. He also held numerous federal patronage posts, including postmaster and collector of customs in New Orleans. Badger also served as the commander of the Department of the Gulf encampment of the Grand Army of the Republic. Despite being perhaps the most prominent Republican in Louisiana by the end of the nineteenth century, Badger enjoyed broad respect among the conservative business elite of New Orleans.

EZEKIEL JOHN ELLIS (1840–1889). Witness to the secession crisis of 1860–61 while finishing his legal studies at the University of Louisiana in New Orleans, Ellis went on to volunteer for service in the Sixteenth Louisiana, a regiment raised in his home town of Tangipahoa. He rose to the rank of captain and became a prisoner of war at Missionary Ridge outside of Chattanooga in November 1863. He spent the remainder of the war at the Johnson's Island prison near Sandusky, Ohio. Upon returning home, Ellis, though a prewar Whig, became actively involved with the Democratic party, and in 1867 he served as "chief of circle" of his local chapter of the Knights of the White Camellia. With the Radical ascendancy, Ellis moved to New Orleans and formed a law partnership with his

older brother Thomas Cargill Warner Ellis. A close confidant of leading Demo-
cratic figures, Ellis was an architect of the Fusionism campaign of 1872 and was
privy to the 1874 White League plan to overthrow the Republican government of
William Pitt Kellogg. In the fall 1874 midterm elections, he won a seat in the U.S.
House of Representatives from Louisiana's Second District. From this vantage
point, Ellis played a key role as one of the negotiators in the Compromise of 1877.
Despite his devotion to the cause, Ellis fell afoul of the Bourbon wing of the
Democratic party after Redemption and twice tried unsuccessfully to nominate
Frederick Nash Ogden as a Reformer gubernatorial candidate. He served five
terms in the U.S. House and died in Washington, DC, in 1889.

PETER JOSEPH (1843–1905). Although he was born into slavery (by his own
admission), Joseph lived the life of a free person of color until he was drafted into
the U.S. Army in May of 1865. He forged friendships with key Republicans during
his service and became a sergeant in the Metropolitan Police afterward, in 1868.
A trusted subordinate of Algernon Sydney Badger, Joseph played a key role in
maintaining Henry Clay Warmoth's rule during the 1870–71 putsch attempt
mounted by the governor's Custom House rivals. For his loyalty, Joseph received a
promotion to captain. As a fervent Republican activist, he gained notoriety by suing
the popular Academy of Music theater for racial discrimination in 1874. Later that
year, Joseph took part in the Battle of Liberty Place. After 1877 he found employment under Badger as a captain of night inspectors in the U.S. Custom House. A
regular delegate to the state Republican convention, Joseph remained in politics
until he moved from the city in 1892. He died in Denver, Colorado, in 1905.

FREDERICK NASH OGDEN (1837–1886). Raised in New Orleans by his politically powerful uncle, Fred Ogden was working in the mercantile trades by the
time he was fifteen years old. He volunteered for the war on the day after the firing on Fort Sumter and was his company's color bearer at the First Battle of Bull
Run. He went on to fight during the defense of New Orleans, surrender at the
siege of Vicksburg, and end the war commanding a skeleton battalion of cavalry
in the Trans-Mississippi. Ogden returned to New Orleans after the war to engage
in commerce and politics. As president of the Crescent City Democratic Club,
he organized street violence against Republicans during the election of 1868, and
in 1873 he led a Fusionist "militia" in an unsuccessful bid to overthrow the Republican government of William Pitt Kellogg. Eighteen months later, he led the
successful White League in the September 14, 1874, Battle of Liberty Place, a
moment that made him a bona fide Lost Cause hero. Yet after 1877, Odgen's life
was full of disappointment. He worked tirelessly as vice president of the Howard

Association during the 1878 yellow fever epidemic but could not stem its enormous death toll. Both in 1879 and in 1883, Ogden failed to secure the gubernatorial nomination of the Democratic party. He died in 1886 of liver cancer, with his business in a state of insolvency.

CHARLES ST. ALBIN SAUVINET (1830–1878). The son of a Frenchman and a free woman of color from St. Domingue, Sauvinet belonged to the Afro-Creole elite of New Orleans. With secession, he formed a company of Native Guards for the state of Louisiana and served as its captain. After the city's fall, however, Sauvinet quickly tendered his services to conquering Union authorities. As a translator to the provost court, Sauvinet played a key role in the negotiations that led to the formation of three companies of black troops by General Benjamin Butler. Sauvinet ultimately served as regimental quartermaster of one of these companies, and he ended the war as a captain and the longest-serving black officer in the Union army. Following the war, Sauvinet worked as the chief cashier of the Freedmen's Bank and served on the city council as well. He was also quartermaster of the state militia. In 1872 he won the office of Orleans Parish civil sheriff. Not long afterward, Sauvinet sued the Bank Coffeehouse for racial discrimination and won damages of one thousand dollars. He died in 1878 by committing suicide at his home on Kelerec Street.

ARISTÉE LOUIS TISSOT (1839–1896). A native of New Orleans, Tissot had recently passed the bar and was practicing law in his father's office when Louisiana seceded from the Union. By April 1861, he had raised a volunteer company of riflemen, which eventually became part of the Twenty-third Louisiana. Frequently at odds with his superiors, Tissot accepted his parole after the surrender at Vicksburg and spent the rest of the war furthering his studies in France. After he returned in 1866, he was involved in a variety of civic and political causes, including the Democratic Broom Rangers and Governor H. C. Warmoth's Republican militia. In 1872 he won a seat as a judge in the Orleans Parish Second District Court, a post he held for nearly twenty years. Although a dedicated Democrat and a loyal follower of the party's Bourbon/Ring faction, Tissot became an ardent defender of Afro-Creole rights. Serving in the state senate in 1894, he read several petitions on behalf of the Citizens' Committee. Tissot died in 1896 at his home on Bayou St. John.

EDMUND ARTHUR TOLEDANO (1830–1874). A member of one of the city's old Creole families, Toledano was a prosperous cotton merchant at the start of the Civil War. He joined the Watson Battery early in the conflict and fought at battles from Frankfurt, Kentucky, to Shiloh and Corinth. Toledano was taken prisoner after the surrender at Port Hudson and spent the remainder of the war with other Louisiana Confederate officers at the Johnson's Island prison. Upon returning to New Orleans in 1865, Toledano found that his uncle Louis Drouet had taken Drouet's mixed-race daughter (previously unknown to Toledano) to live with him. Although the three had related to one another as an interracial family for nearly seven years, Toledano moved to disinherit Marie Louise Drouet after her father's death in 1872. He later joined the White League and died at the head of Canal Street during the Battle of Liberty Place on September, 14, 1874.

HENRY CLAY WARMOTH (1842–1931). A native of Missouri, Warmoth first set foot in New Orleans in 1864 as a boy colonel in the Union army. He flourished in the city's unstable postwar political atmosphere and by adeptly using connections managed to win the symbolic post of territorial delegate. In 1868, at age twenty-six, Warmoth became governor of Louisiana. His shrewdness in politics was matched only by the intense envy and hatred of his rivals; by 1871 internal feuds had undermined his hold on the Republican party. A member of the party's more conservative wing, Warmoth briefly endorsed the politics of Fusionism in 1872 and was later impeached for it. Yet he remained active in state and national Republican politics in Louisiana much longer than most of his more "radical" rivals. In 1888 Warmoth challenged Francis T. Nicholls for the governorship of Louisiana and may well have won had it not been for extensive voter fraud. He was appointed collector of customs in New Orleans in 1890, where he hired many of the Creole activists who later challenged Louisiana's Separate Car Law. Warmoth's classic memoir *War, Politics, and Reconstruction* appeared in print a year before his death in 1931.

SOURCES AND METHODOLOGY

A key objective of this work has been to move beyond the "postrevisionist" school of Reconstruction historiography and reexamine postbellum life, seeing it less as an ideological struggle leading toward an "unfinished [political and social] revolution" and more as a portrait of individuals who, in trying to come to grips with a cataclysmic reordering of their lives, shaped broader social and political outcomes. The subtitle of Eric Foner's landmark work *Reconstruction: America's Unfinished Revolution, 1863–1877* (New York: Harper & Row, 1988) implies in the word *unfinished* that there was a conscious "beginning" to this reordering of Southern society—a revolution promulgated by the federal government and other entities that made an important yet incomplete contribution to the greater narrative of American progress. This volume, in contrast, argues that, in the process of quelling the chaos they confronted in their personal lives, individuals fostered, organically and often unwittingly, the revolutions *and* counterrevolutions that New Orleans witnessed between 1861 and 1898. While most of the scholarship produced since the publication of Foner's synthesis continues to adopt its conceptual framework, several important works have approached postbellum tension from a fresh, if not mutually exclusive, vantage point. Laura Edwards's focus on gendered relationships in *Gendered Strife and Confusion: The Political Culture of Reconstruction* (Urbana: University of Illinois Press, 1997) and, even more so, Heather Cox Richardson's focus on the politics of Reconstruction in the context of the West in *West from Appomattox: The Reconstruction of America after the Civil War* (New Haven, CT: Yale University Press, 2007) suggest new avenues for transcending old questions of revisionism. Students desiring an efficient survey of current trends in Reconstruction historiography should consult Thomas J. Brown's excellent edited volume *Reconstructions: New Perspectives on the Postbellum United States* (New York: Oxford University Press, 2007).

Recent scholarship on honor and intellectual culture in nineteenth-century America was essential to this book's conceptualization, particularly with regard to establishing the importance of the individual postbellum society. Bertram Wyatt-Brown's *The Shaping of Southern Culture: Honor, Grace, and War, 1760s–1880s* (Chapel Hill: University of North Carolina Press, 2001), a work that is arguably both deeper and more useful than his influential earlier studies on honor, as well as Stephen Berry's *All That Makes a Man: Love and Ambition in the Civil War South* (New York: Oxford University Press, 2003), offers useful insight into the inner thoughts of the Civil War generation, particularly men. Reid Mitchell's *Civil War Soldiers* (New York: Viking, 1988) and, even more so, James McPherson's *For Cause and Comrades: Why Men Fought in the Civil War* (New York: Oxford University Press, 1997) navigate, if in a somewhat indirect fashion, the tension between personal and ideological impulses during the war itself. Louis Menand's Pulitzer-winning *The Metaphysical Club: A Story of Ideas in America* (New York: Farrar, Straus & Giroux, 2001) and George Fredrickson's much earlier *The Inner Civil War: Northern Intellectuals and the Crisis of the Union* (New York: Harper & Row, 1965) both explore pragmatism, the most influential philosophy to come out of postbellum America. They also compellingly argue that the writings of the nation's intellectuals did not occur in academic or legalistic isolation but reflected trends broadly visible in American society.

Although numerous works have analyzed the relationship between the generation who fought and won the American Revolution and the one that came immediately after it, there are few generational studies examining Civil War and postbellum America. Ironically, it has been the many authors of popular Civil War history who have picked up on this trend, often unwittingly in the process of penning comparative or group biography. Some recent examples include Jack Hurst, *Men of Fire: Grant, Forrest, and the Campaign That Decided the Civil War* (New York: Basic Books, 2007) and Ralph Kirshner, *The Class of 1861: Custer, Ames, and Their Classmates after West Point* (Carbondale: Southern Illinois University Press, 1999), yet few of these efforts at prosopography qualify as systematic analyses of common experience. The most notable example of scholarly generational study of the Civil War era is Peter S. Carmichael's recent work *The Last Generation: Young Virginians in Peace, War, and Reunion* (Chapel Hill: University of North Carolina Press, 2005), which makes insightful comparisons between the Civil War and antebellum generations. Stephen Kantrowitz's *Ben Tillman and the Reconstruction of White Supremacy* (Chapel Hill: University of North Carolina Press, 2000) touches on the tension between the Civil War and postbellum generations. For a thought-provoking look at the formation of the postbellum generation, see Edmund L. Drago, *Confederate Phoenix: Rebel Children and Their Families in South Carolina* (New York: Fordham University Press, 2008).

The literature on the Redeemers, conservative reaction, and white violence is not as vast as one might suspect. Two works that were influential in shaping this project when it was in its dissertation phase and that remain relevant to the field are William Gillette's *Retreat from Reconstruction, 1868–1879* (Baton Rouge: Louisiana State University Press, 1979) and Michael Perman's *Road to Redemption: Southern Politics, 1869–1879* (Chapel Hill: University of North Carolina Press, 1984). Though focusing on Republicans, Richard Nelson Current's *Those Terrible Carpetbaggers: A Reinterpretation* (New York: Oxford University Press, 1988) was influential not only in the structural approach of this book, but also for his well-balanced interpretation of the motivations of postbellum political figures. The scholarship on Reconstruction-era organized violence has been relatively stagnant. Although several works have appeared on this topic since Alan Trelease's *White Terror: The Ku-Klux Klan Conspiracy and Southern Reconstruction* (New York, Harper & Row, 1971), few offer any meaningful new analysis of those who participated in such violence. One exception is George Rable, *But There Was No Peace: The Role of Violence in the Politics of Reconstruction* (Athens: University of Georgia Press, 1984). James K. Hogue's *Uncivil War: Five New Orleans Street Battles and the Rise and Fall of Radical Reconstruction* (Baton Rouge: Louisiana State University Press, 2006) looks at postbellum violence in New Orleans as an extension of military history, but it differs significantly from the political and cultural analysis presented here—and even more in terms of interpretation. The work of Western cultural historian Richard Slotkin, particularly *Gunfighter Nation: The Myth of the Frontier in Twentieth-Century America* (New York: HarperCollins, 1992), was more influential than any work on Reconstruction in helping reevaluate the role violence played in postbellum New Orleans.

Increasingly, historians seem willing to dispense with the 1862–77 chronology of Reconstruction and to embrace a more elastic "Civil War era" or "postbellum" paradigm. It should be easy to read C. Van Woodward's classic *Origins of the New South, 1877–1913* (Baton Rouge: Louisiana State University Press, 1951) and see that the problems faced by the Redeemers were essentially the same postwar dilemmas that had dogged earlier Republican efforts. One early successful effort at constructing an inclusive Civil War era is Paul Escott, *Many Excellent People: Power and Privilege in North Carolina, 1850–1900* (Chapel Hill: University of North Carolina Press, 1985). Jane Dailey's analysis of Virginia in *Before Jim Crow: The Politics of Race in Postemancipation Virginia* (Chapel Hill: University of North Carolina Press, 2000) was very influential in forming the ideas presented in this study about the limited nature of the Redeemers' victory as well as the need to transcend the 1877 paradigm. Kathleen Clark's *Defining Moments: African Amer-*

ican Commemoration and Political Culture in the South, 1863–1913 (Chapel Hill: University of North Carolina Press, 2005), a work that fuses political and cultural analysis with the study of memory, also effectively demonstrates the long shadow cast by the Civil War.

All works produced today that deal with Louisiana in the second half of the nineteenth century stand, to one degree or another, on the shoulders of several key historians. Joe Gray Taylor's *Louisiana Reconstructed, 1862–1877* (Baton Rouge: Louisiana State University Press, 1974) and William Ivy Hair's *Bourbonism and Agrarian Protest: Louisiana Politics, 1877–1900* (Baton Rouge: Louisiana State University Press, 1969) remain essential reference works. Likewise, no single volume has superseded *The Civil War in Louisiana* (Baton Rouge: Louisiana State University Press, 1963), by John D. Winters. At some important level, urban history hinges upon the completeness of local knowledge. In this vein, Joy Jackson's *New Orleans in the Gilded Age: Politics and Urban Progress, 1880–1896* (Baton Rouge: Louisiana State University Press, 1969) and Dennis Rousey's *Policing the Southern City: New Orleans, 1805–1889* (Baton Rouge: Louisiana State University Press, 1996) supply important background on the social and political composition of late-nineteenth-century New Orleans.

New Orleans is a city with a proud literary heritage, and works written about it during the nineteenth and early twentieth centuries can be extremely helpful for ferreting out elusive cultural echoes—if used with care. Some examples include George Washington Cable, *Old Creole Days* (1879), *The Grandissimes* (1880), and *Madame Delphine* (1881); Grace Elizabeth King, *New Orleans: The Place and the People* (New York: Macmillan, 1895); Henry C. Castellanos, *New Orleans as It Was: Episodes of Louisiana Life* (New Orleans: Graham & Son, 1895); and Edward Larocque Tinker, *Pen, Pills, and Pistols: A Louisiana Chronicle* (New York: 1934).

The culture and politics of Afro-Creole New Orleans has been written about extensively, but never more authoritatively than in the work edited by Joseph Logsdon and Arnold Hirsch, *Creole New Orleans: Race and Americanization* (Baton Rouge: Louisiana State University Press, 1992). Caryn Cossé Bell's *Revolution, Romanticism, and the Afro-Creole Protest Tradition in Louisiana, 1718–1868* (Baton Rouge: Louisiana State University Press,1997), while emphasizing a sort of pan-Afro-Creole unity, makes a good starting point for scholars interested in free black New Orleans. Older scholarship such as John Blassingame's *Black New Orleans, 1860–1880* (Chicago: University of Chicago Press, 1973), Roger Fischer's *The Segregation Struggle in Louisiana, 1862–77* (Urbana: University of Illinois Press, 1974), and David Rankin's "The Origins of Black Leadership in New Orleans during Reconstruction," *Journal of Southern History* (August 1974), remain important to our understanding of black life in the Crescent City, particularly among elites. All of these scholars were, in turn, influenced by Rodolphe Lucien Desdunes's *Our People and Our History: Fifty Creole Portraits*, trans. Dorothea Olga McCants (Baton Rouge: Louisiana State University Press, 1973), which appeared in French in 1911, and Charles Barthelemy Roussève's *The Negro in Louisiana: Aspects of His History and His Literature* (New Orleans: Xavier University Press, 1937). Judith K. Schafer's *Becoming Free, Remaining Free: Manumission and Enslavement in New Orleans, 1846–1862* (Baton Rouge: Louisiana University Press, 2003) not only supplies useful background on the interplay between white, free black, and enslaved worlds in antebellum New Orleans, but its methodological approach reveals the enormous research potential of the Orleans Parish court records housed at the city library.

The primary materials consulted for this study are diverse, and their selection reflects the research philosophy employed by its author. The most useful personal papers were those of E. John and Thomas C. W. in the E. P. Ellis Family Papers, Louisiana and Lower Mississippi Valley Collections, Hill Memorial Library, Louisiana State University, Baton Rouge (Mss. 136), and the Henry Clay Warmoth papers in the Southern Historical Collection, Manuscripts Division, Collection No. 752, University of North Carolina, Chapel Hill. Warmoth's memoir, *War, Politics, and Reconstruction: Stormy Days in Louisiana* (New York: Macmillan Co., 1930), is perhaps one of the most remarkable of its kind, not only because of its subject's prominence but also because it serves as one of the last great firsthand accounts written by the Civil War generation.

The subjects found in this volume, however, were selected not because of the availability of conventional papers, but because their lives revealed much about life in postbellum New Orleans. Documenting the lives of most of the individuals that appear in these pages required the assembly of many fragments, the most compelling of which the author had no reasonable expectation to find. Frederick Nash Ogden and Algernon Sydney Badger are important figures who appear in most works that have dealt with Reconstruction in Louisiana, yet despite their obvious importance, a century's-worth of scholarship has yielded little insight into their lives. Aristee Louis Tissot became part of the narrative simply because his name kept turning up as the lives of others were being researched. In short, he demanded his own inclusion. The fact that none of these men left behind anything approaching meaningful personal papers has largely relegated them to bit-player status in the historical record, yet they played pivotal roles in the postbellum struggle. This fact alone should serve as an exhortation to others to stray from the easy path and dig deeply and creatively in order to document nineteenth-century

Americans, the vast majority of whose personal papers have *not* survived in the archives.

The archives of the Louisiana State Supreme Court at the University of New Orleans, as well as those of the Orleans Parish first and second district courts at the Main Branch of the New Orleans Public Library, offered a detailed glimpse into everyday life in nineteenth-century New Orleans and proved invaluable in telling the story of individuals who did not leave behind volumes of correspondence. Successions, criminal cases, and civil suits were essential in revealing the private lives of Louise Marie Drouet, Arthur Toledano, Charles Sauvinet, and Peter Joseph. State Supreme Court cases are searchable in LEXIS/NEXIS. Online indexes for the vast wealth of legal documents at the New Orleans Public Library remain a resource of the future. Treasury Department records that detailed the workings of the U.S. Custom House on Canal Street revealed a great deal about the political and social activities of Afro-Creole activists and the Republican party after 1877 (RG 56-246, 56-247, National Archives). Modern genealogical tools that have become available in the past decade were essential for establishing personal ties between individuals and made the charting of shifting racial identities possible (for instance, census records searched through a subscription service such as Ancestry.com offer great data-mining potential). A variety of other governmental and published primary sources, such as veterans' pension records (RG 15, National Archives), birth and death records (Orleans Parish Birth Index and Louisiana Death Records Index, both available online at the Louisiana Secretary of State site), wills, and compiled military service records (RG 94, RG 109, National Archives) allowed for the piecing together of lives that might otherwise have gone undocumented. Contemporary newspapers on microfilm supplied much information; they included the *Daily Picayune*, the *New Orleans Times*, the *New Orleans Republican*, the *Weekly Louisianian*, the *Morning Star and Catholic Messenger*, the *New Orleans Bee*, the *Daily Pelican* and the *Weekly Pelican*, the *New Orleans Democrat*, and the *New Orleans Daily States*. Several important New Orleans papers from the nineteenth century became available online as research on this book was near its end, including the *Picayune* and the *Times*. Moreover, the full-text online version of the *U.S. Congressional Serial Set* available through the Readex Corporation yielded numerous heretofore uncited documents. Despite the frequent shortcomings of searching capability encountered with such resources, the prospect of these and the ever-increasing volume and quality of digital information in general should hearten future fragment gatherers.

INDEX

Warmoth, Henry Clay. Afro Creole elite and, 69–70, 80, 90–91, 152, 288n37; background, 47; civil rights and, 87, 96–97, 100–102, 240–41; Civil War service, 47–50, 54; conservatives and, 117, 120, 123–26, 128, 132; Fusionism and, 126–28, 131–32, 134, 137; interpretations of Reconstruction and, 1–3, 5, 83–85, 113–14, 280n39, 285n2; Liberal Republicanism and, 121–23, 289n10; political career 1865–1868, 68–70, 74; political career after 1877, 181, 190, 214, 218–19, 226–31, 233; political strategy of, 74–77, 79, 83–91, 94–95, 100–101, 120, 122, 131, 167, 185, 241, 285n4; Republican factionalism and, 82, 87, 94–95, 103–12, 117–18, 121, 131–32; mentioned, 92, 94, 115–16, 121, 137, 139, 156, 161, 163, 189, 197, 204, 212, 231, 239, 242
Washington Artillery, 30, 33, 89, 91, 95, 110–11, 115, 165, 173, 198, 200
Washington Parish, 73
Watson, Augustus C., 18
Watson's Battery, 18, 22, 42–43, 59
Weekly Louisianian, 98, 103, 108, 121, 164, 196, 200, 202, 226
Weekly Pelican, 225–28, 237
Wells, James Madison, 62, 66–68, 70, 299n26
Whig Party, 10, 13, 73, 94, 120

White, Edward Douglas, 119, 248
White League: creation of, 161–62, founding in New Orleans, 163–67; memory of, 224–25; monument to, 225–26
white supremacy: barriers to establishing, 142, 148, 153, 159, 188, 242–43; conservatives and, 85–86, 114, 213, 242; cultural expressions of, 135, 183; interpretations of Reconstruction and, 1, 53, 83–85, 188, 190, 244; triumph of, 214, 233, 235, 237–38, 245; White League and, 161, 224
Wickliffe, John C., 223–24
Wilder, Douglas, 132
Williamson, George, 125
Williamson, Joel, 291n4
Williams v. Mississippi, 190
Wiltz, Louis, 130, 189, 193–94, 196–99, 204–5, 212
Wisdom, Mortimer Norton, 165
Wyatt-Brown, Bertram, 9, 56
Wyler, William, 191
Wyly, William Gillespie, 97–98

Yazoo Affair, 198
yellow fever, 169; epidemic of 1878, 186, 191–93, 199–200
Young, Perry, 200
Young Men's Democratic Association, 217–18, 222, 229